Chris Marker
Staring Back

CHRIS MARKER
STARING BACK

Wexner Center for the Arts
The Ohio State University
Columbus, Ohio

The MIT Press
Cambridge, Massachusetts
London, England

THIS PUBLICATION ACCOMPANIES THE EXHIBITION

Chris Marker
Staring Back

Wexner Center for the Arts
The Ohio State University

May 12–August 12, 2007

CURATOR
Bill Horrigan

PROJECT STAFF

CURATORIAL ASSISTANT
Molly Reinhoudt

LEAD PREPARATOR
Will Fugman

REGISTRAR
Megan Cavanaugh

GRAPHIC DESIGNER
M. Christopher Jones

EDITOR
Ann Bremner

Staring Back was organized by the Wexner Center for the Arts.

It was presented with support from the Corporate Annual Fund of the Wexner Center Foundation and Wexner Center members.

Accommodations were provided by The Blackwell Inn.

PUBLISHED BY
Wexner Center for the Arts
The Ohio State University
1871 North High Street
Columbus, Ohio 43210-1393
USA
Tel: +(614) 292-0330
Fax: +(614) 292-3369
http://www.wexarts.org

Printed in Spain.

Printed on Scheufelen PhoeniXmotion (Xenon) paper with endpapers of Permalin Products Multicolor Antique (Coal).

DISTRIBUTED BY
The MIT Press
55 Hayward Street
Cambridge, MA 02142-1493
USA
Tel: +(617) 253-5646
Fax: +(617) 258-6779
http://mitpress.mit.edu

MIT Press books may be purchased at special quantity discounts for business or sales promotional use. For information, please e-mail *special_sales@mitpress.mit.edu* or write to Special Sales Department, The MIT Press, 55 Hayward Street, Cambridge, MA 02142.

ISBN: 978-0-262-08365-2

Library of Congress Control Number: 2007924387

10 9 8 7 6 5 4 3 2

It's six a.m. all over the world.
Six a.m. over the Saint-Martin canal.
Six a.m. over the Göta canal in Sweden.
Six a.m. over Havana.
Six a.m. over the forbidden city of Peking.
The day is dawning…

—Chris Marker, *If I Had Four Camels*

Contents

I Stare 1 1
The Case of the Grinning Cat 44
They Stare 52
I Stare 2 80
Beast of... 126

Director's Foreword 135
Sherri Geldin

Some Other Time 137
Bill Horrigan

In Hindsight 151
Molly Nesbit

Filmography and Bibliography 154

Acknowledgments 157

Since he passed a law
that triggered the demos
that lured me to film them
and from which I made stills
that attracted the attention
of Bill Horrigan
and thus led to this,

this exhibition
is humbly dedicated
to Mr. Dominique Galouzeau de Villepin,
then France's Prime Minister.

—C. M.

I Stare 1

Watch the tree.

Tense faces, on that afternoon of February 13, 1962. One week ago, a strong demonstration about the war in Algeria ended up with eight dead. A trifle for Mogadishu, a tragedy for Paris. Now they bury the dead. Maurice Thorez, the Communist leader, stands like the statue of the ghost he soon will be, just like his party.

Straight in the middle of the frame, on the balcony, among those tense faces, a young tree recently planted. Forget the faces for a moment, just watch the tree.

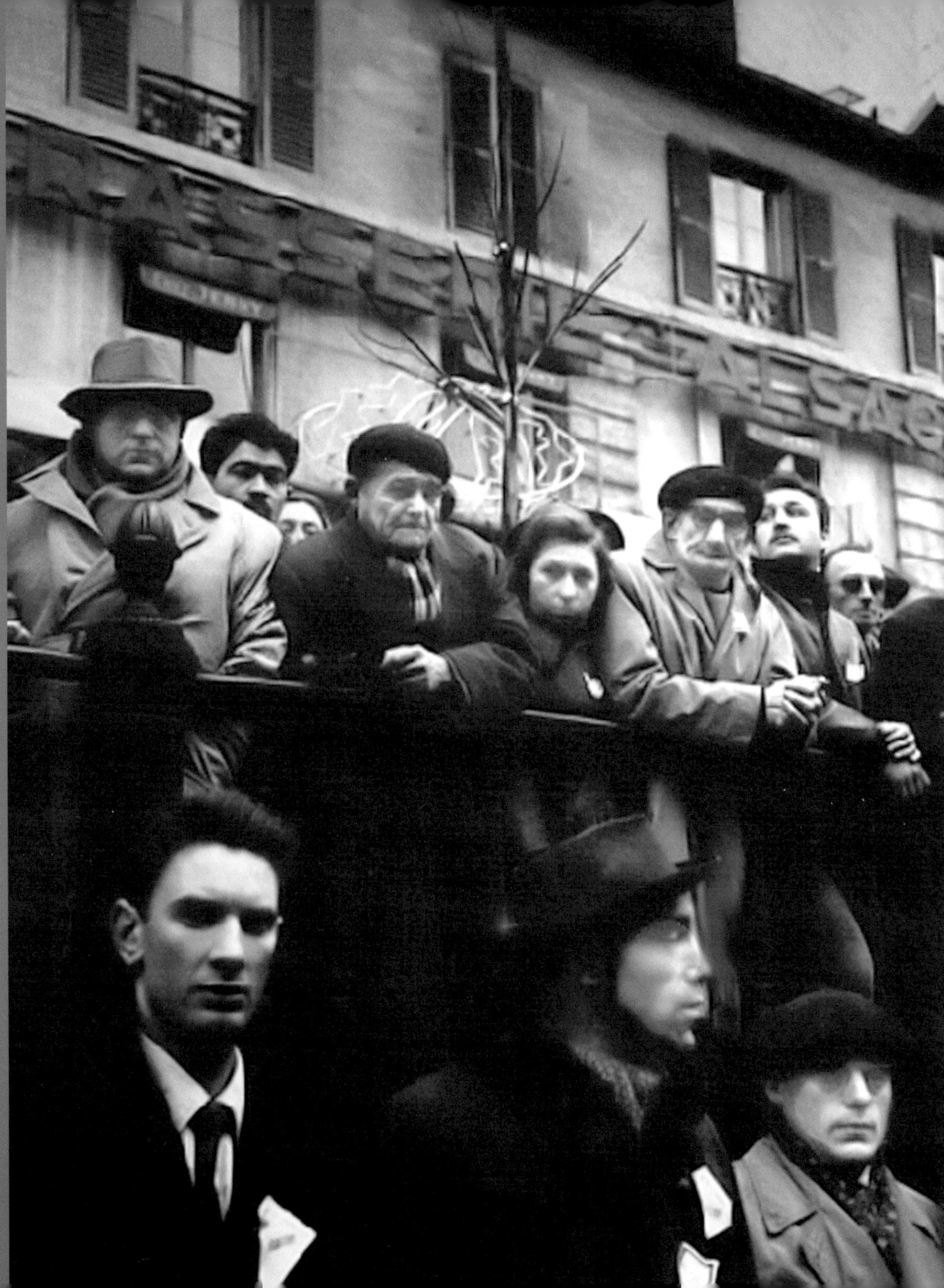

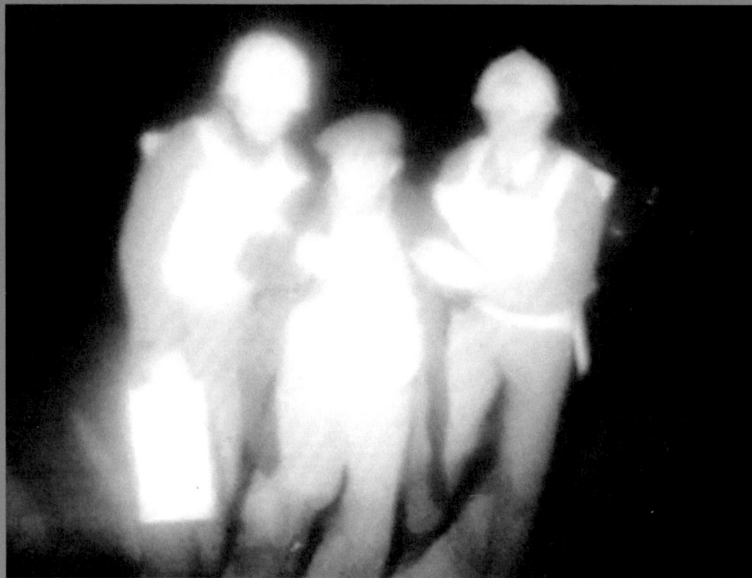
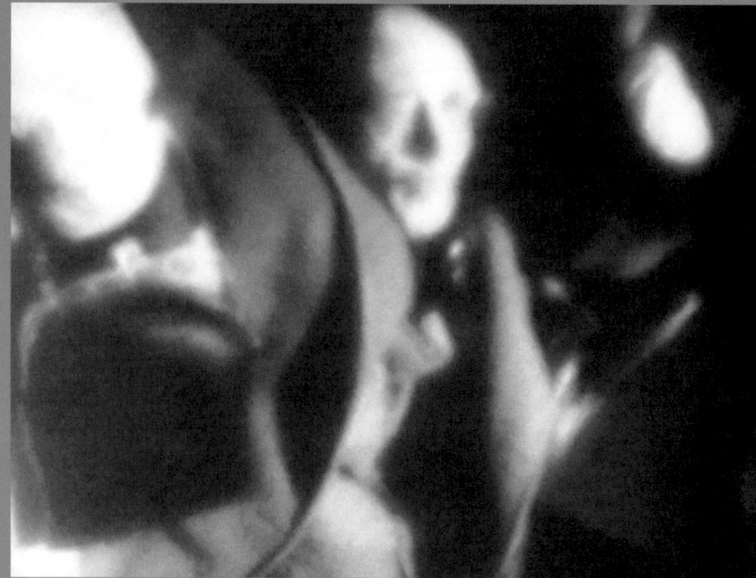
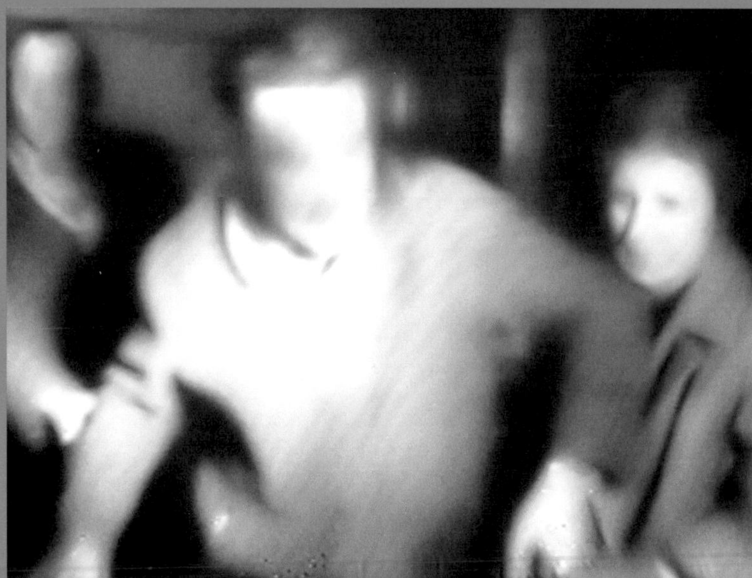
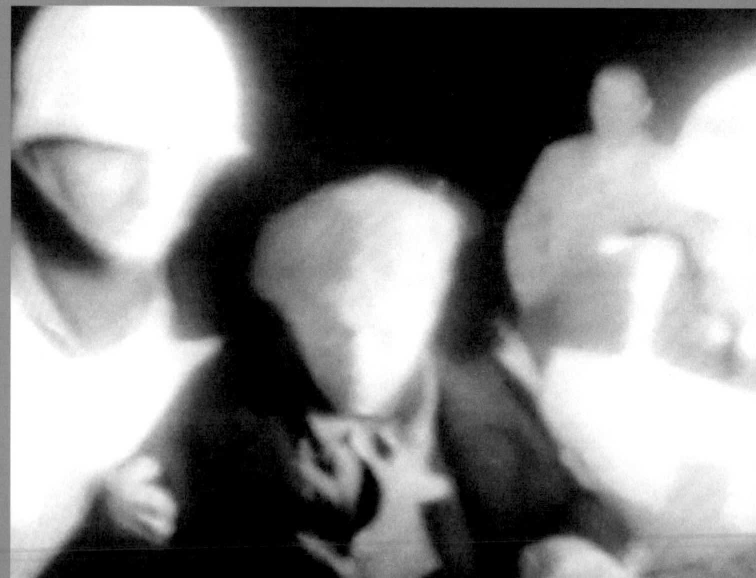

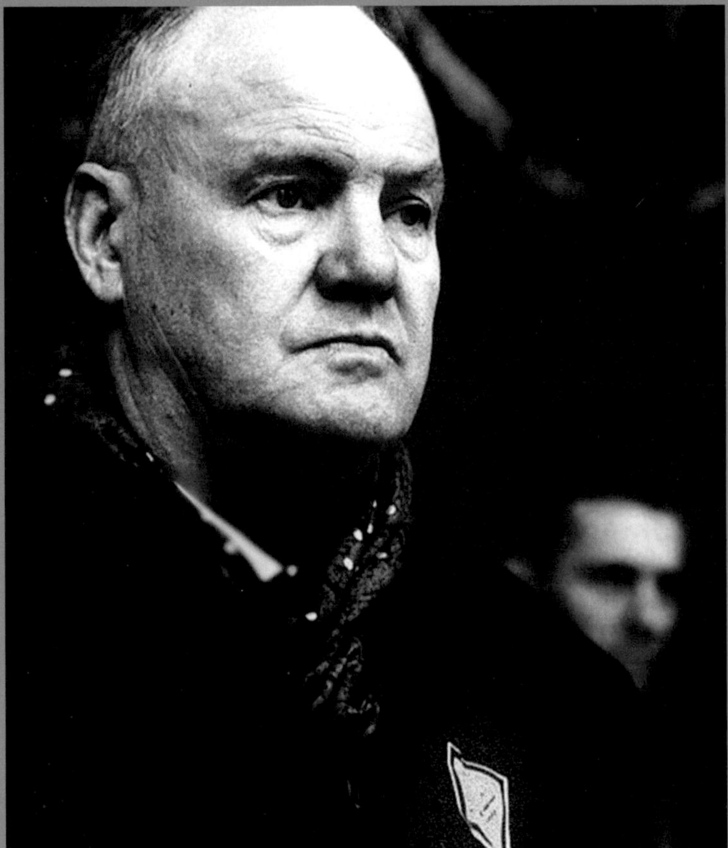

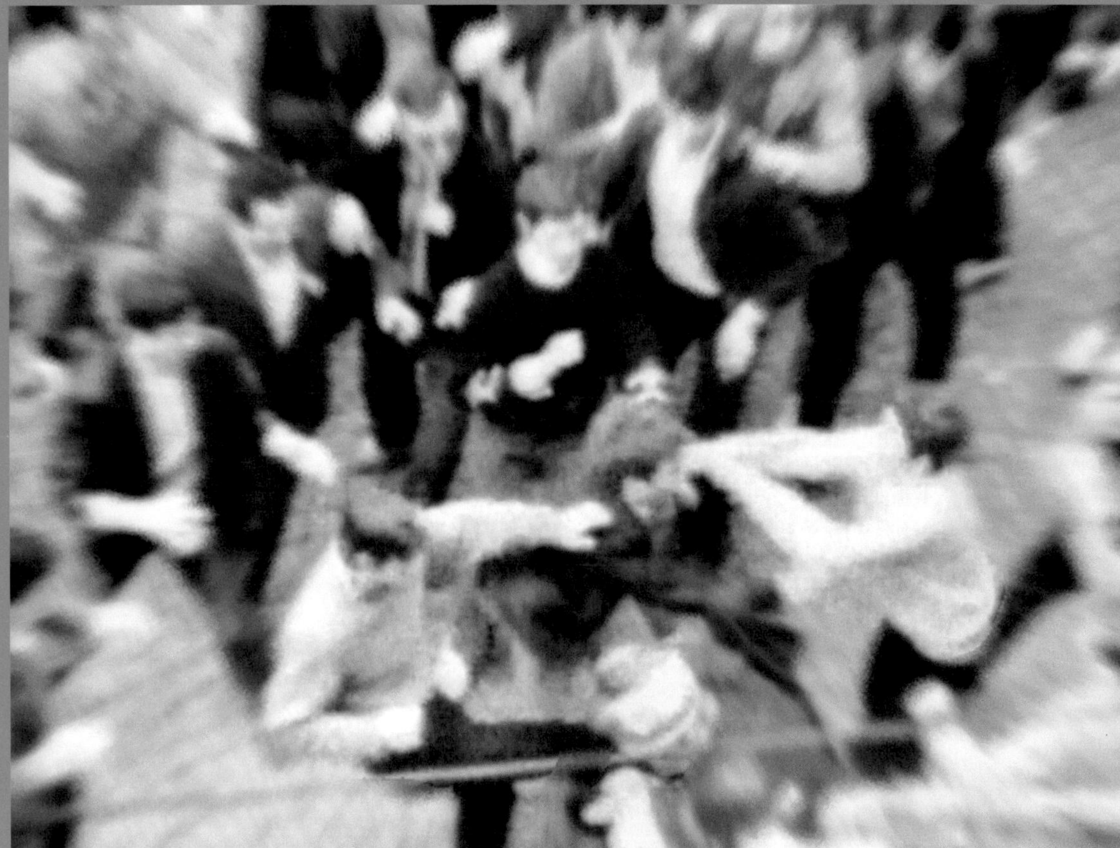

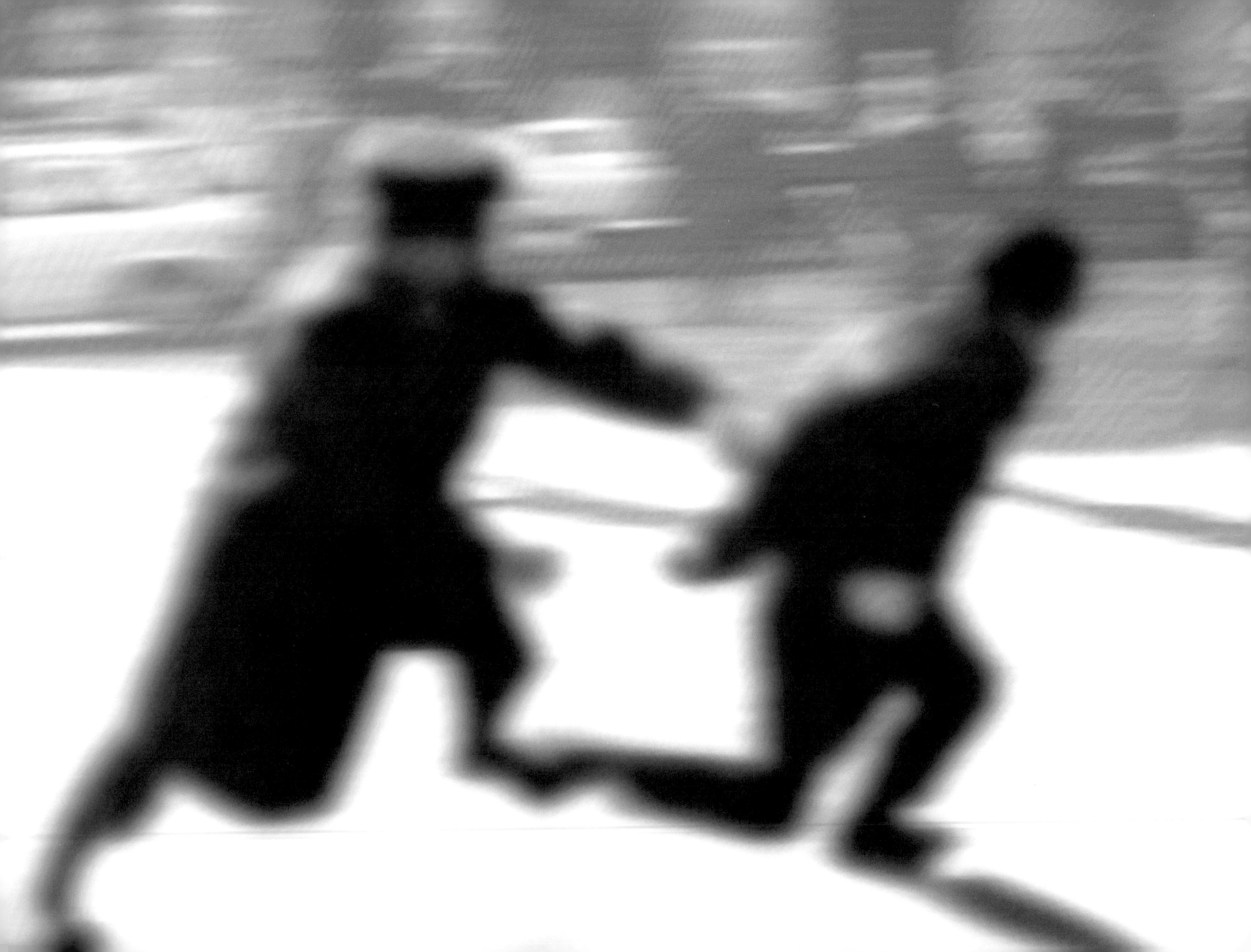

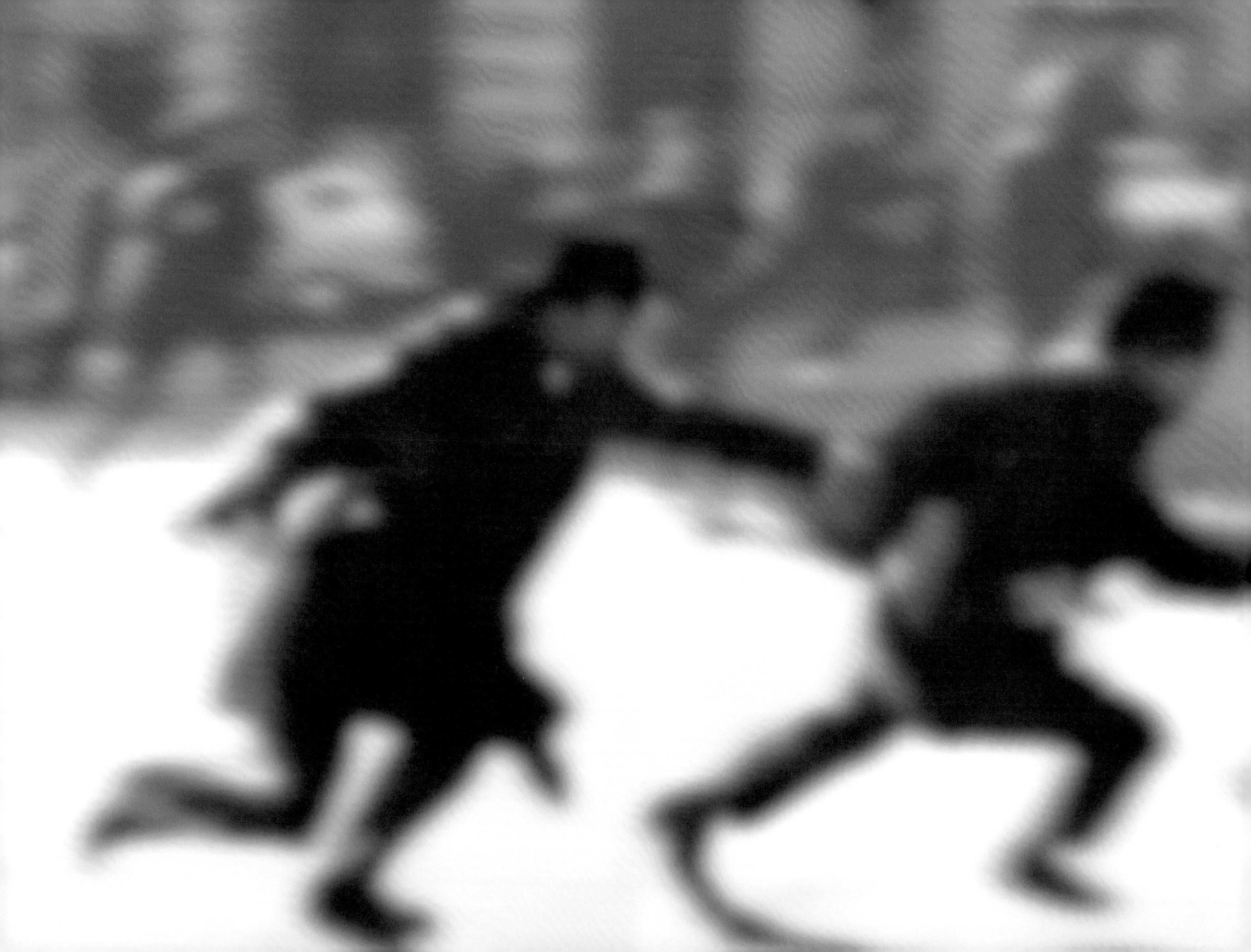

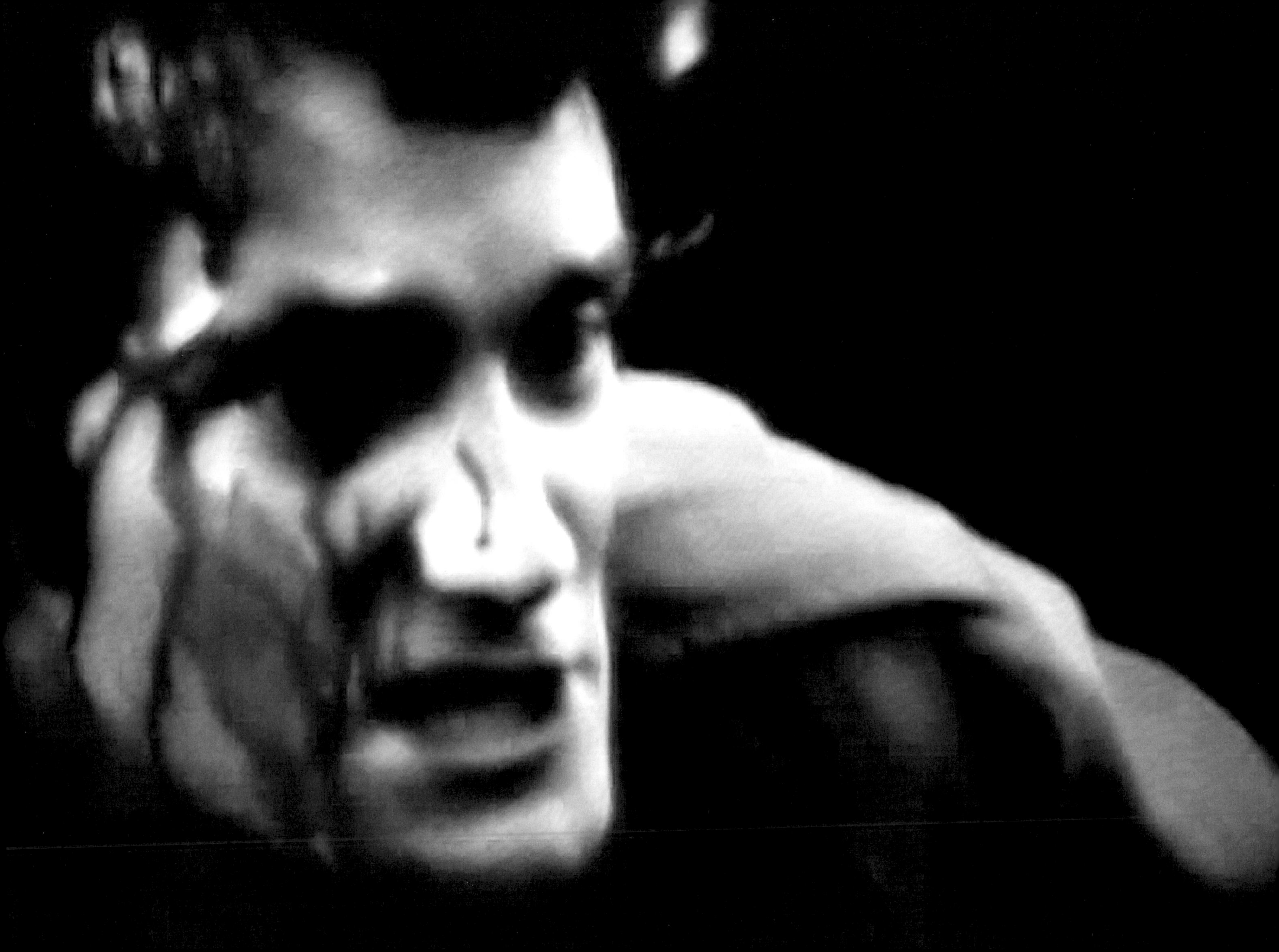

During those years, I came to the conclusion that the only sensible weapon against the cops could be a film camera. Not that glorious but, at times, efficient. With a small 16mm contraption, stolen from an UNESCO drawer, I caught my first demo footage, rather fuzzy, stealing light from the television people. And that was a turning point in my film "career" (that despicable word). In another time I guess I would have been content with filming girls and cats. But you don't choose your time.

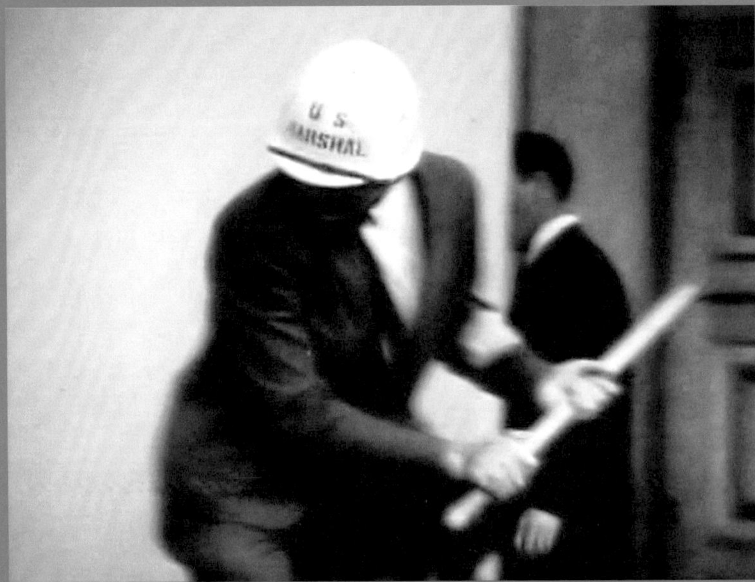

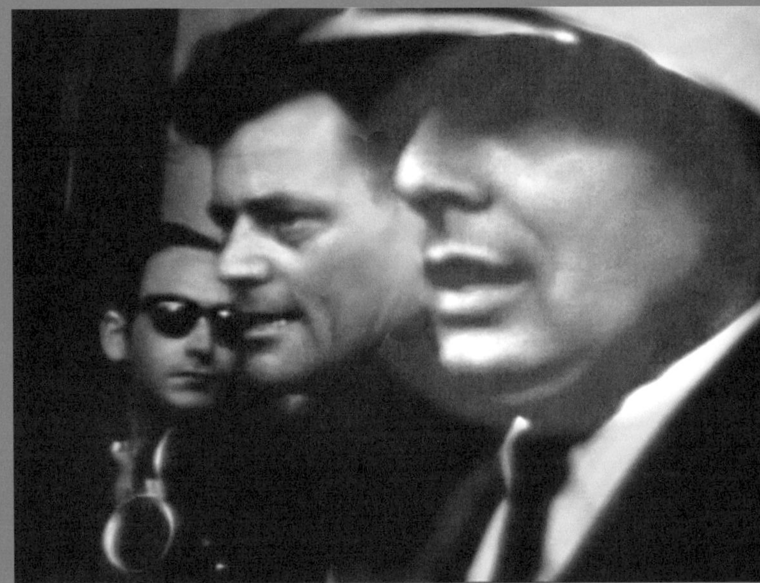

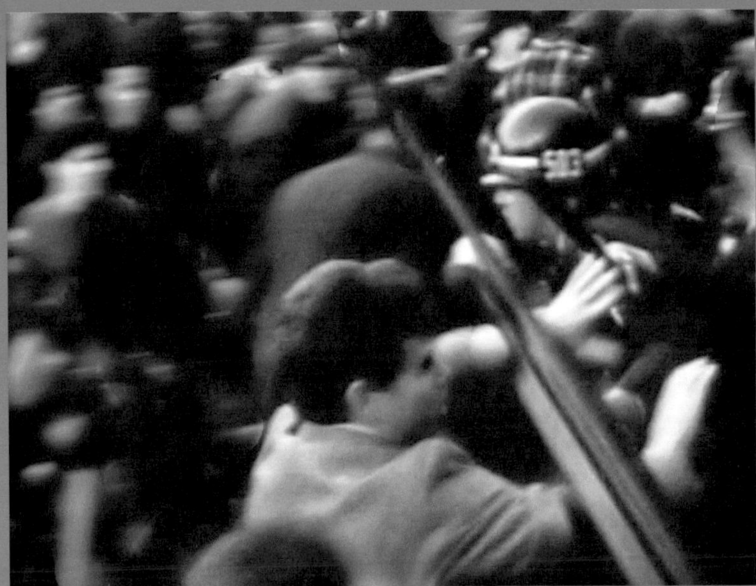

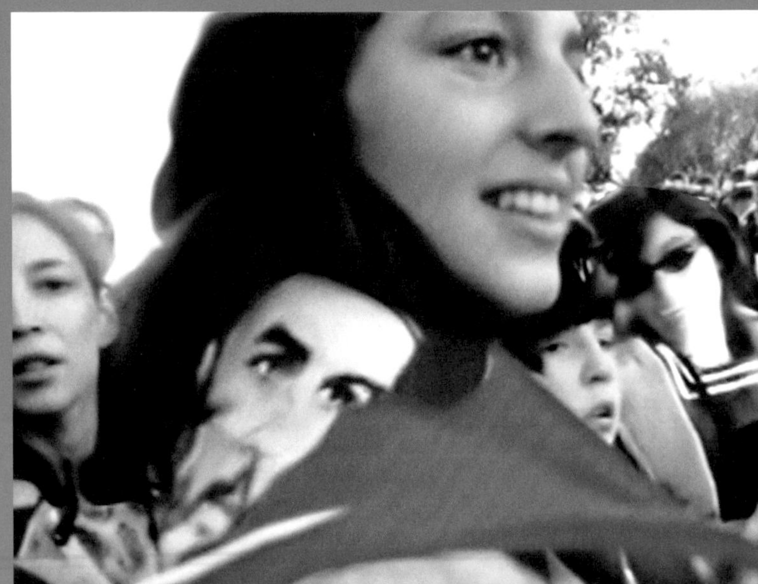

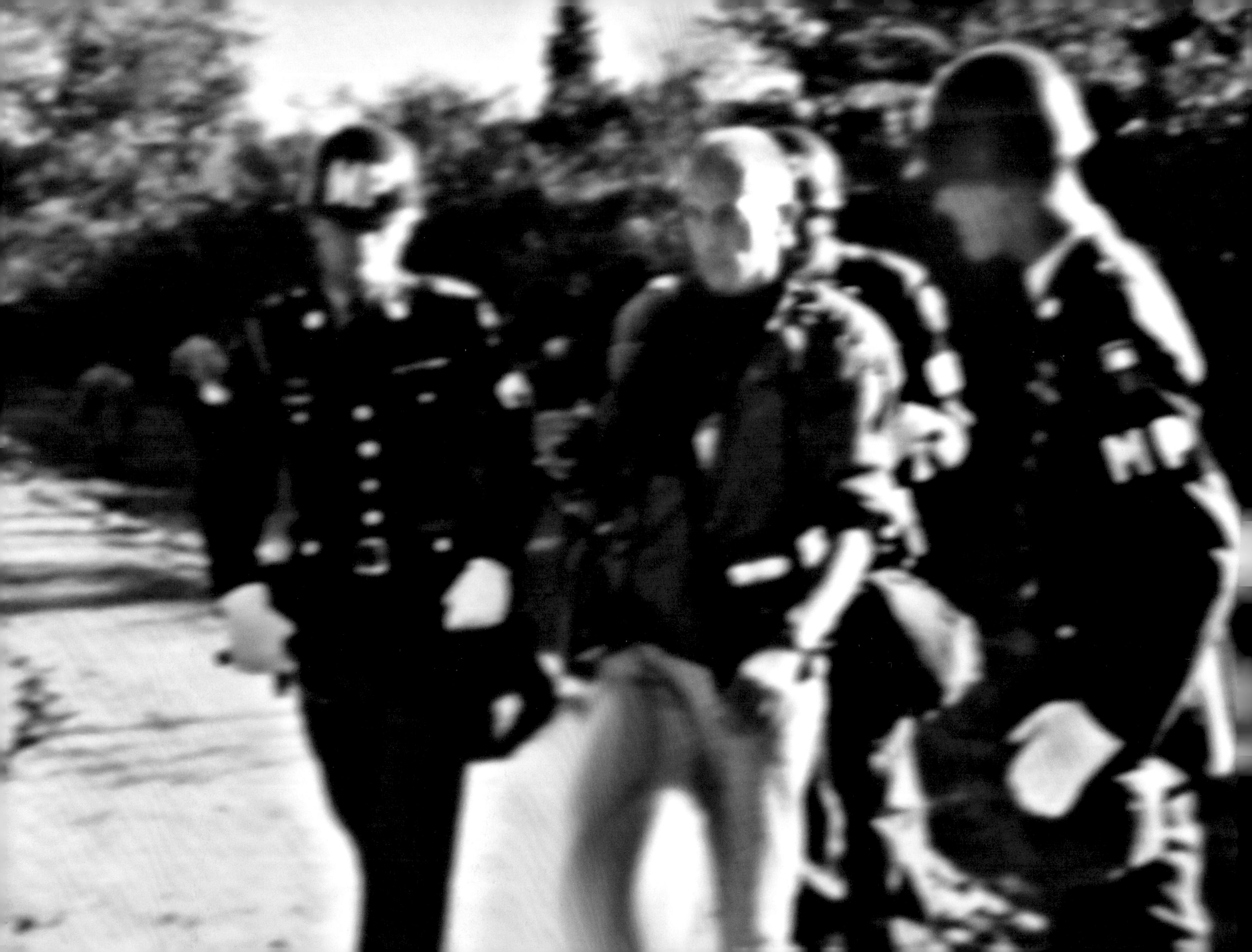
MP

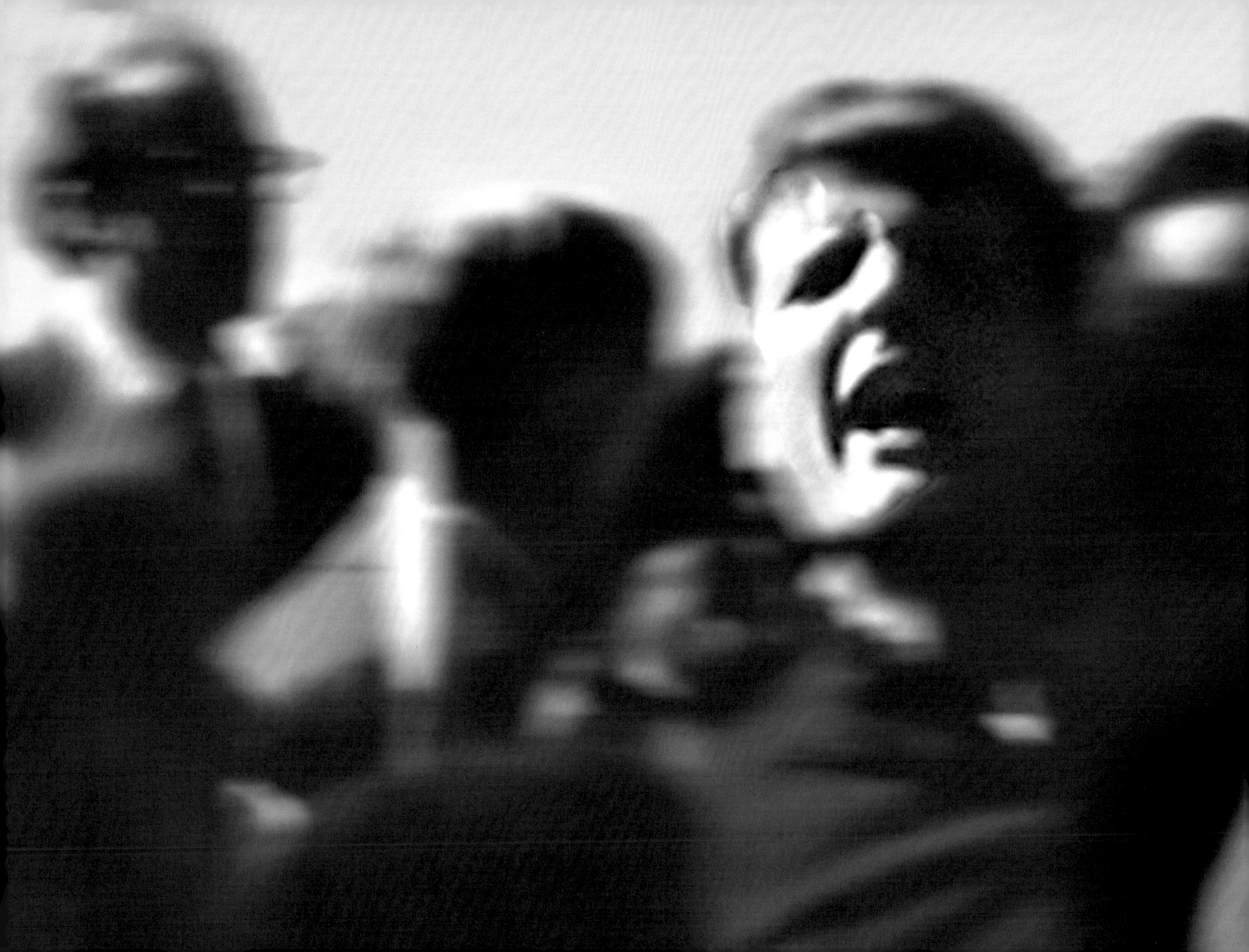

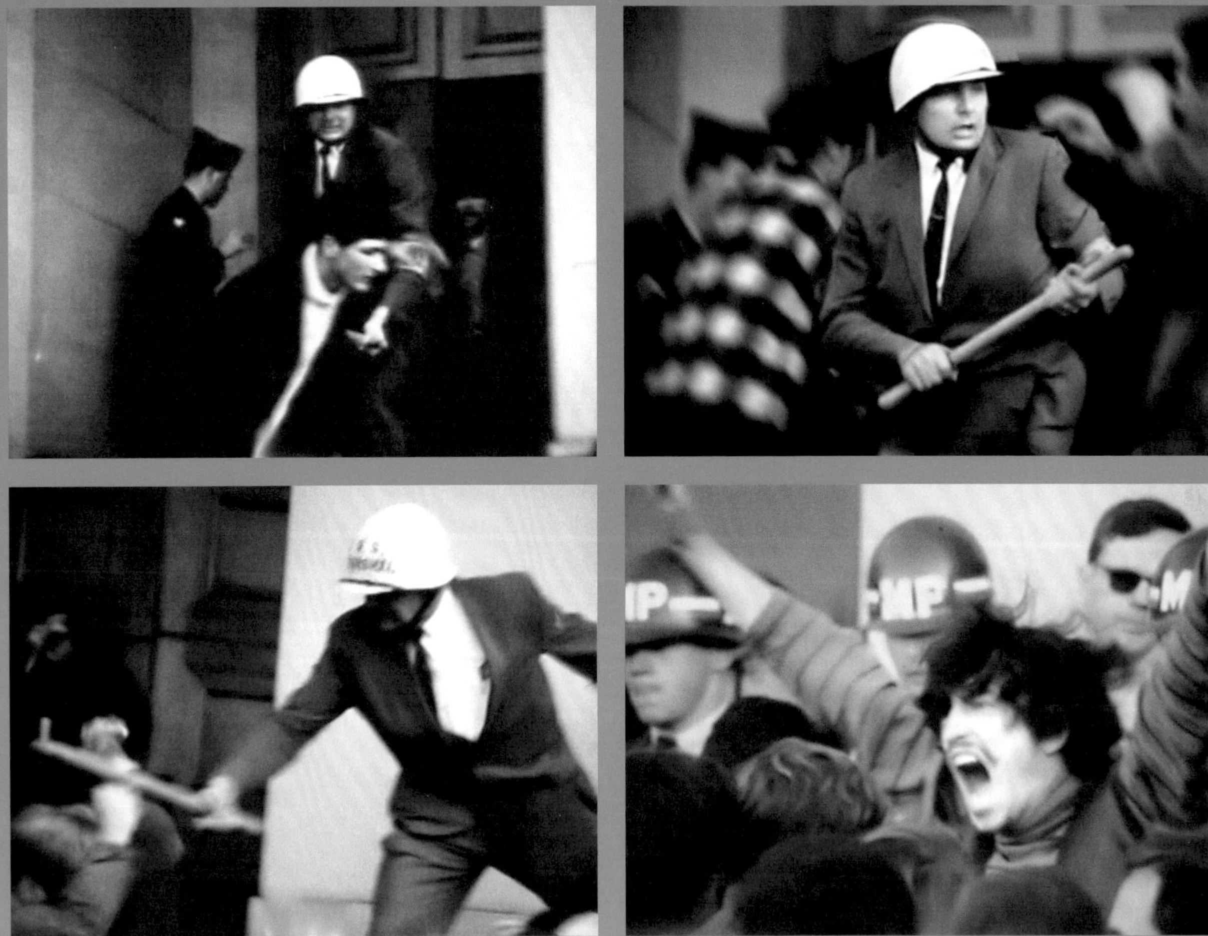

The Pentagon, October 1967. Rumor has it that they brought U.S. marshals from the South. Something fishy in the whole thing. How come we crossed the line so easily, at the right place, when the whole Pentagon lawn was held by military in full regalia? Dr. Spock tried to be arrested: no policeman would dare, for fear of retaliation by the memsahib. Norman Mailer was arrested on the spot, so he didn't see anything, and he wrote a 300-page book about the event. I spent the whole day and the following night covering the demo, and I made a 20-minute film. Guess who's the pro.

Then came May 1968. The *"utopia of uniting in a common struggle those who revolt against poverty and those who revolt against wealth."* I wrote that in *Sans Soleil*, and I'm conscious that it is extremely bad manners to quote oneself, but I'm at a loss to summarize it better. In exchange I offer another quotation, from the other side of the ocean. Later on, Abbie Hoffman wrote: *"We were young, we were reckless, arrogant, silly, headstrong—and we were right."*

Yet he also said: *"We ended the idea that you can send a million soldiers ten thousand miles away to fight a war that people do not support."* How could he figure that one day those very people could support, at least for a while, the wrong war?

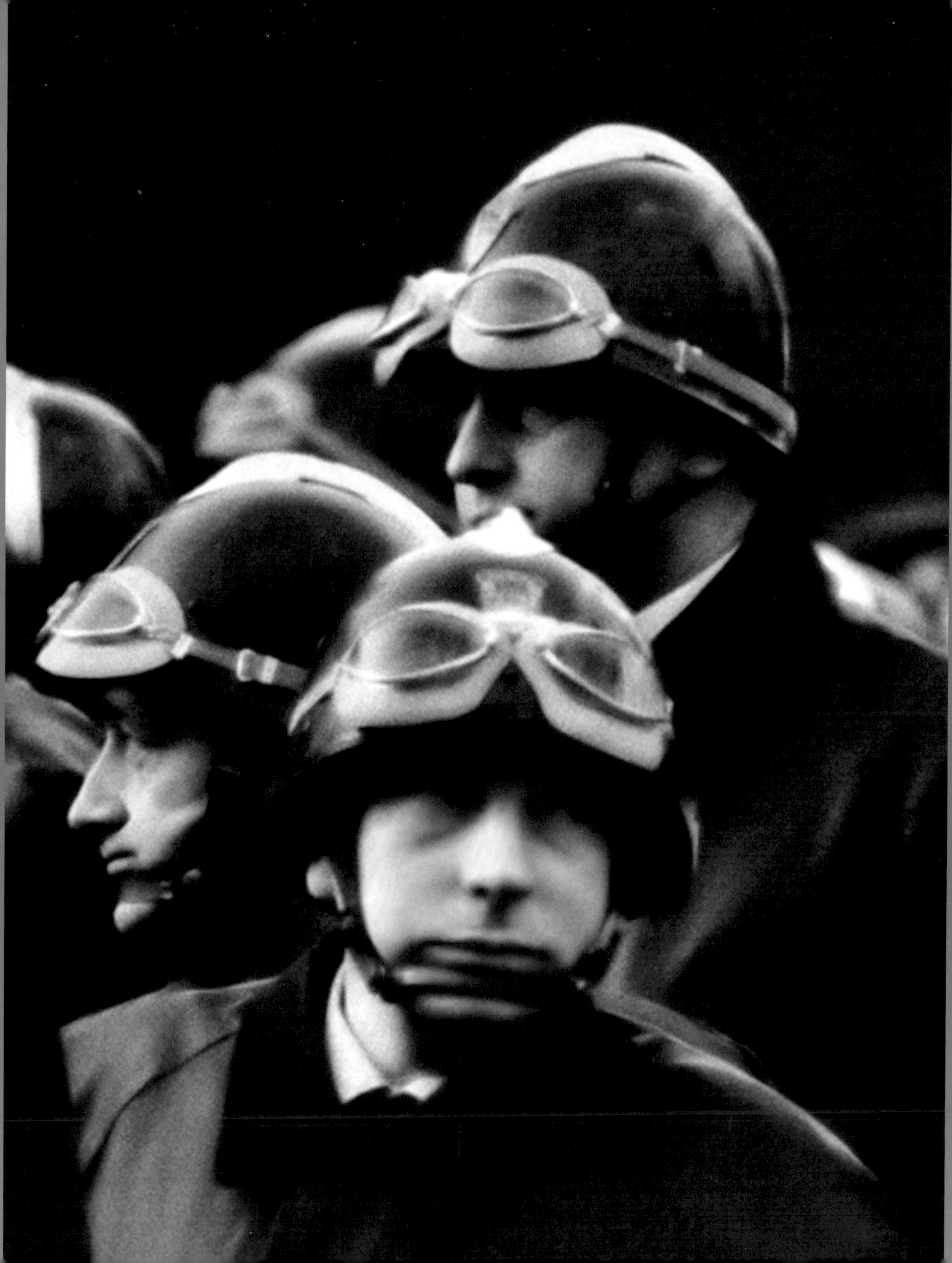

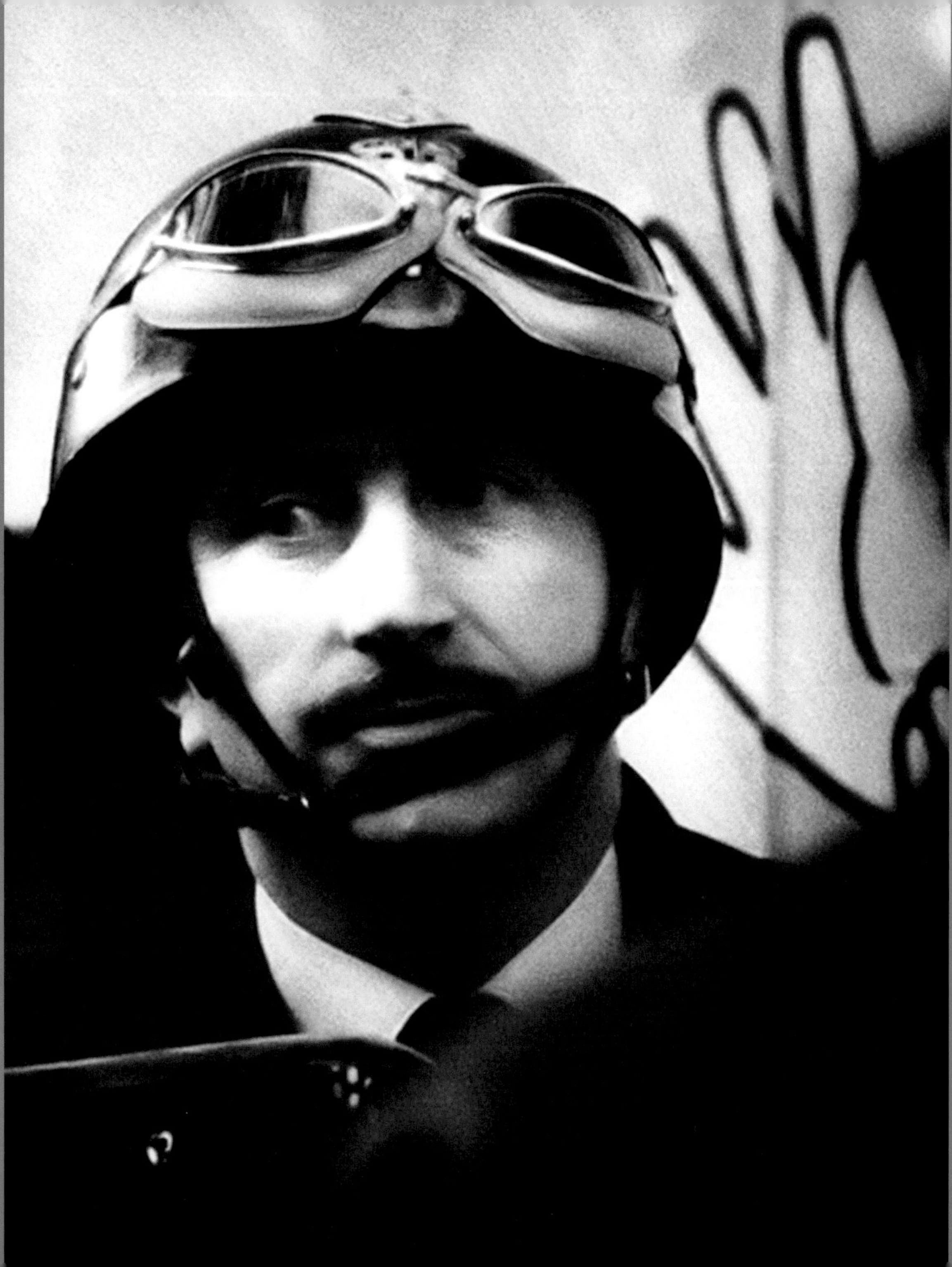

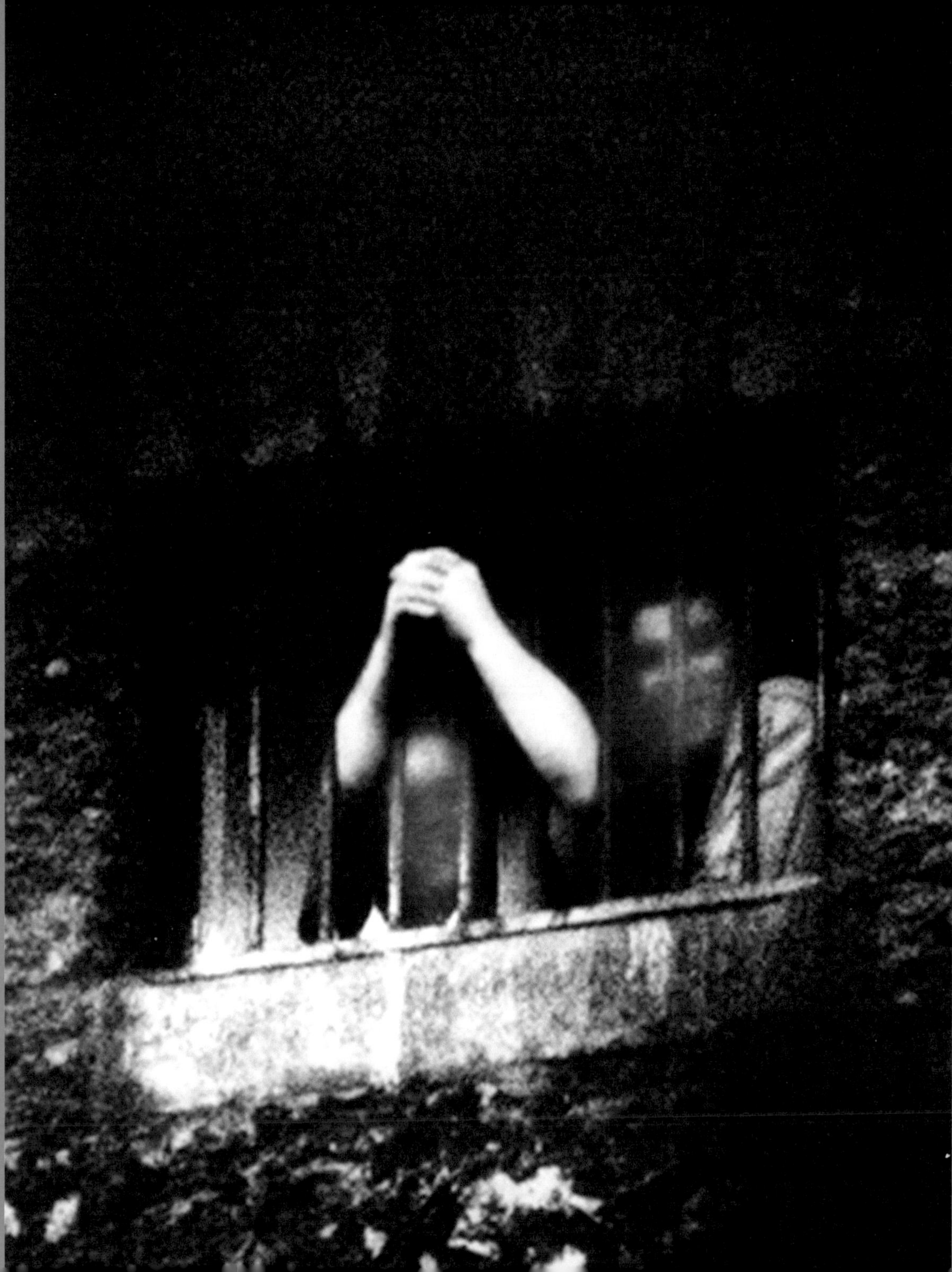

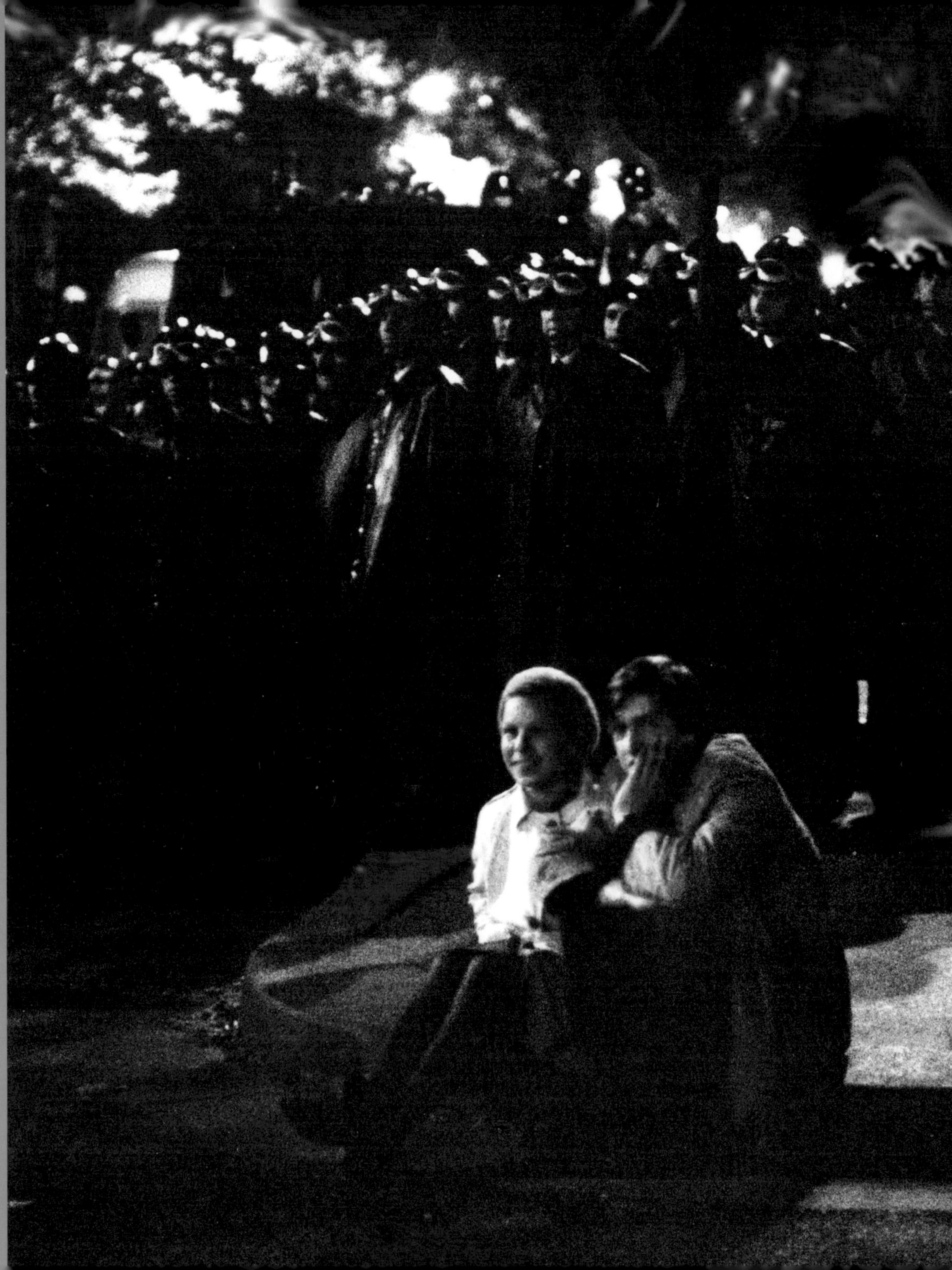

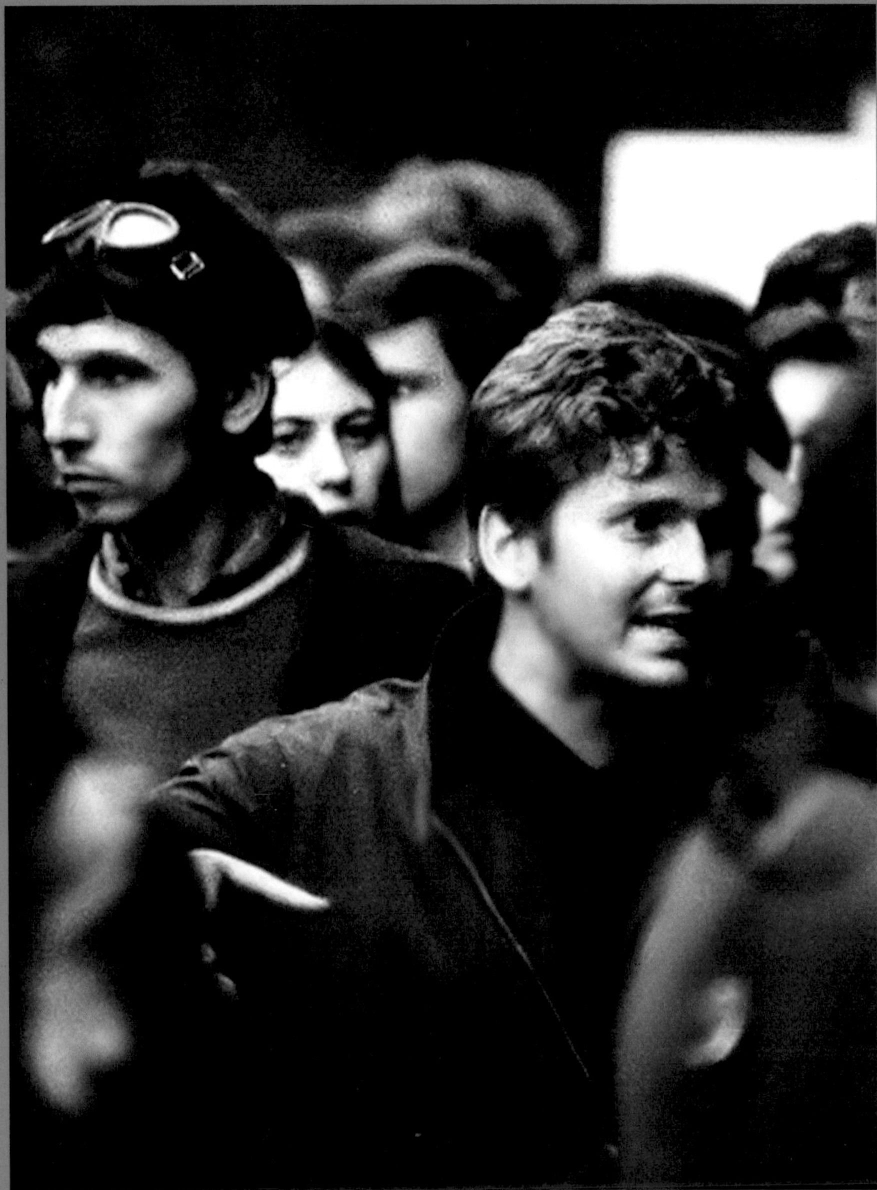

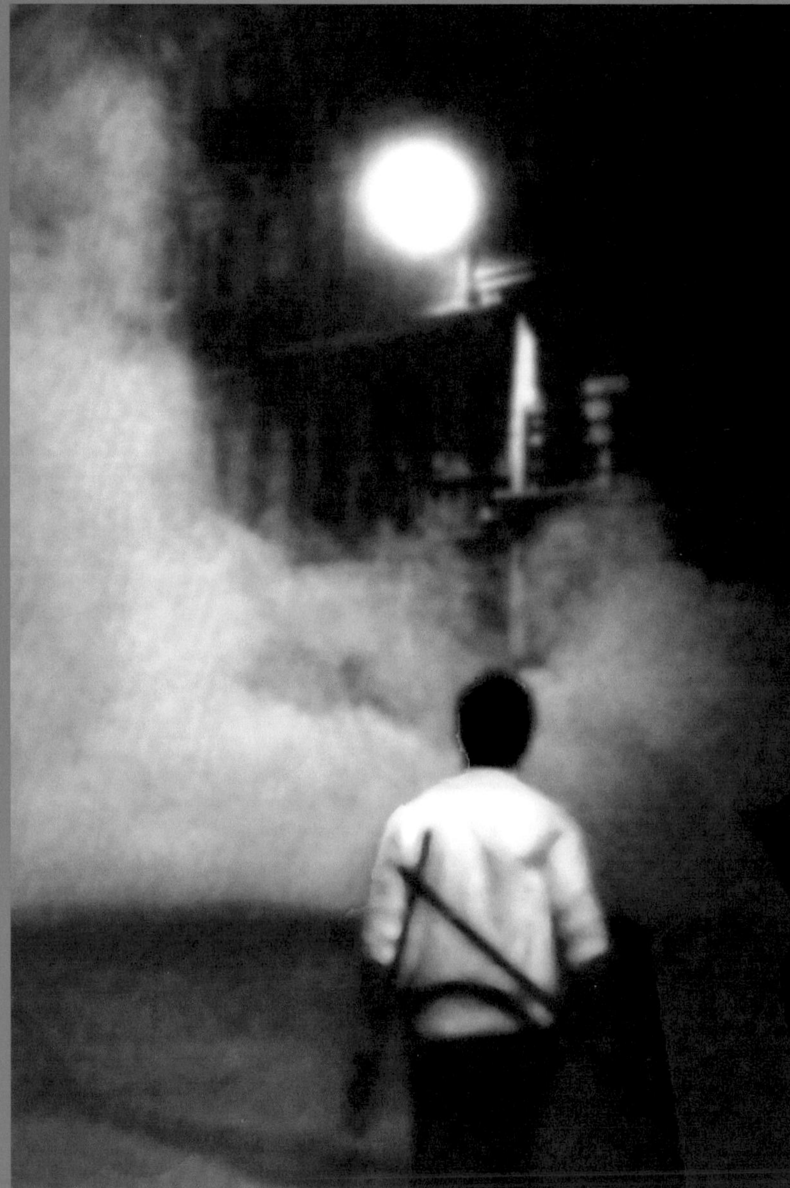

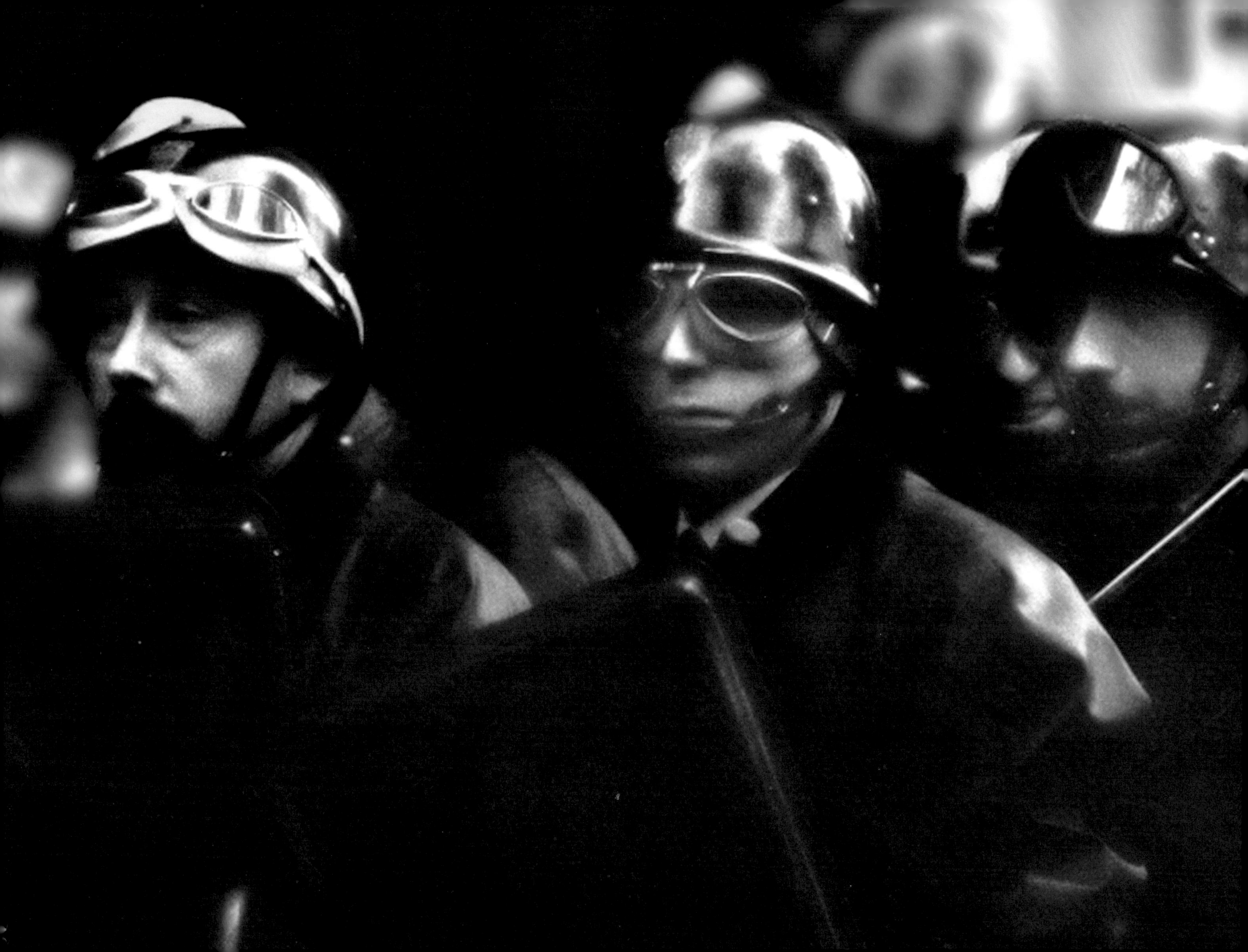

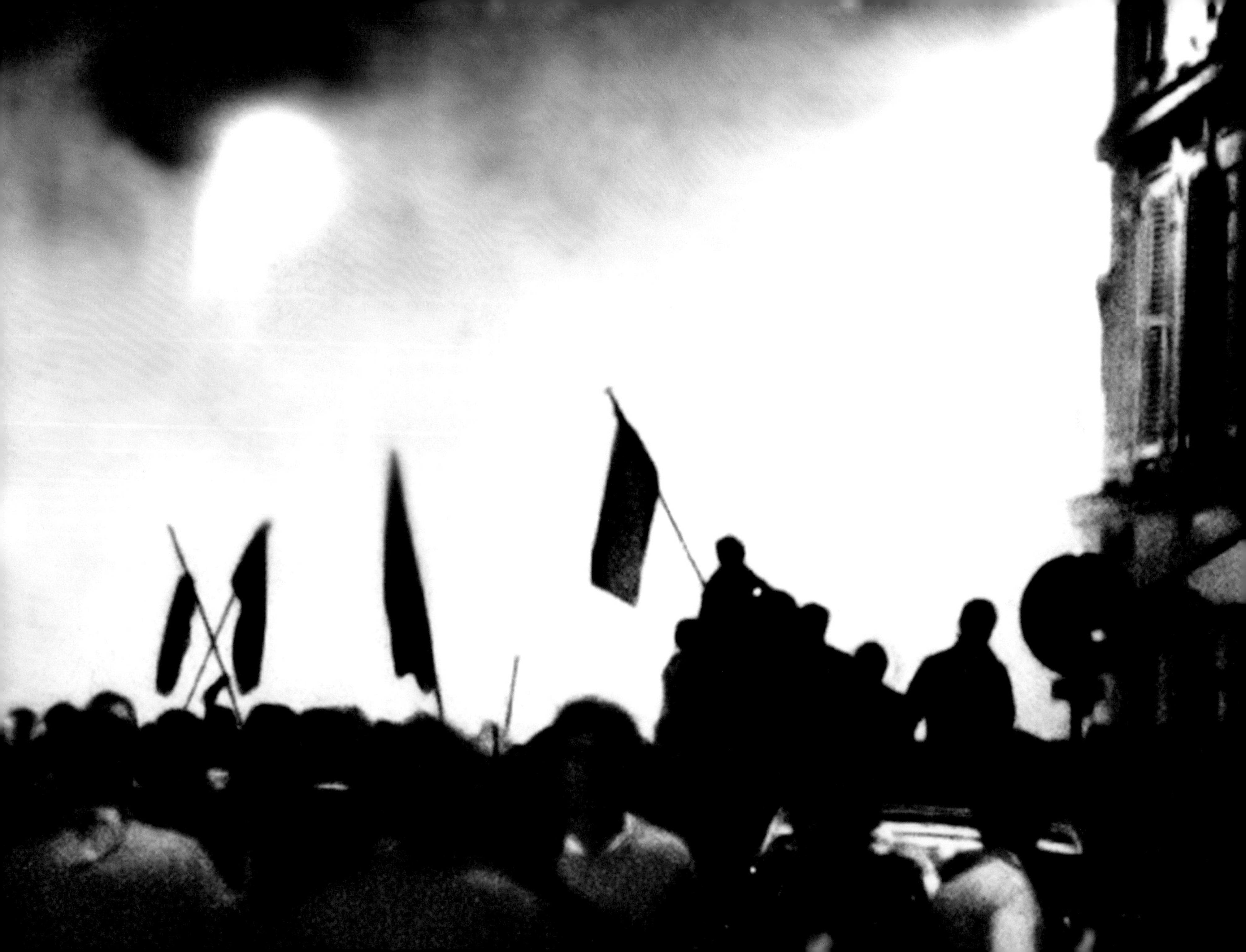

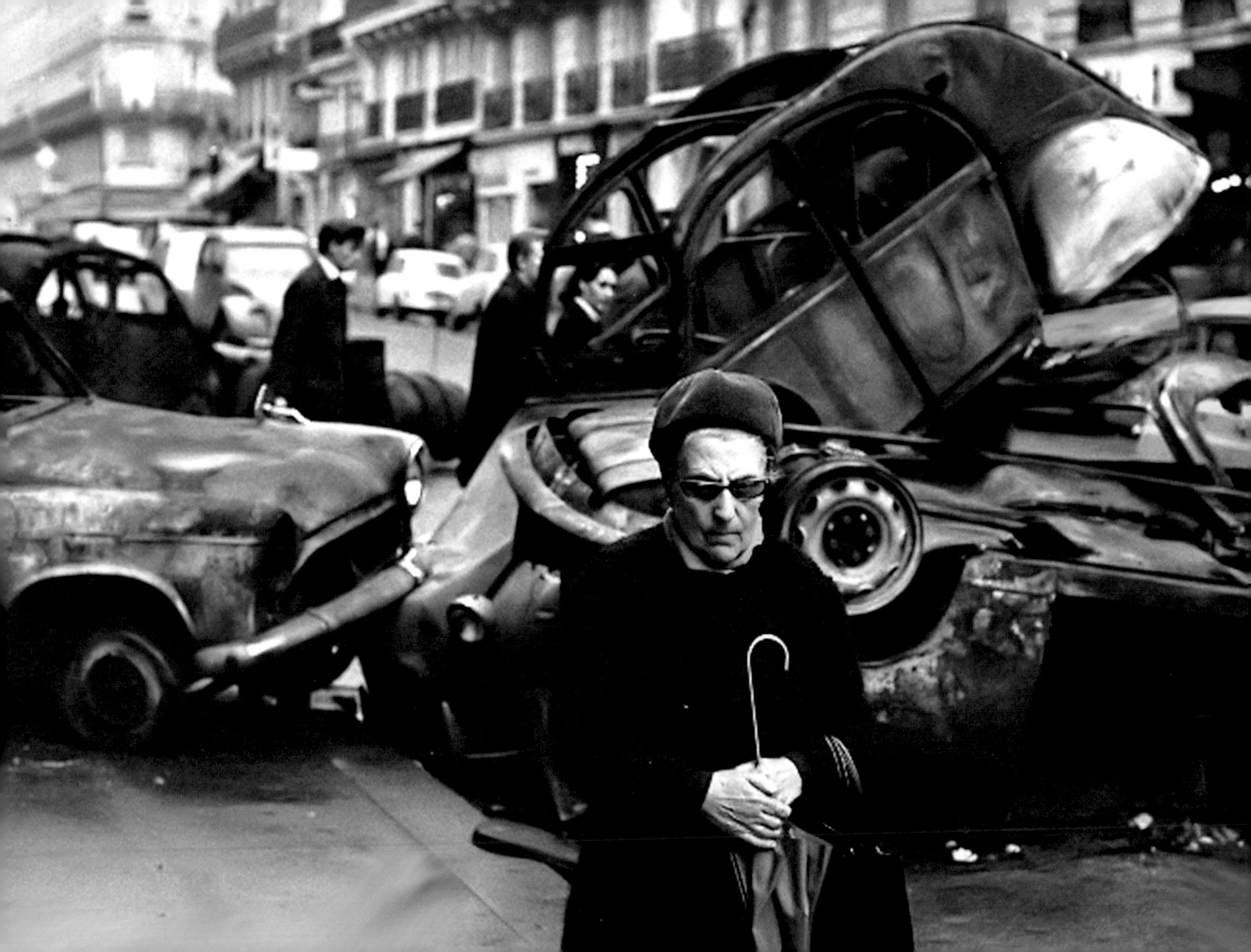

The "Spirit of May" still hangs over the demos. Nostalgia, contempt, ritual slander ("those belated *soixante-huitards*"), sometimes incentive: we'll do as good. But at the beginning of 2002, the consensus is that the French youth are fed up with politics. Then comes the shock of the presidential election. For the first time in a democratic country, the extreme Right contender appears in the final round (not out of his debatable merits, but from the insane dispersal—seven candidates—of the Left). At once the youngsters invade the street. Many for the first time. Thanks to Mr. Le Pen, a new generation takes the baton.

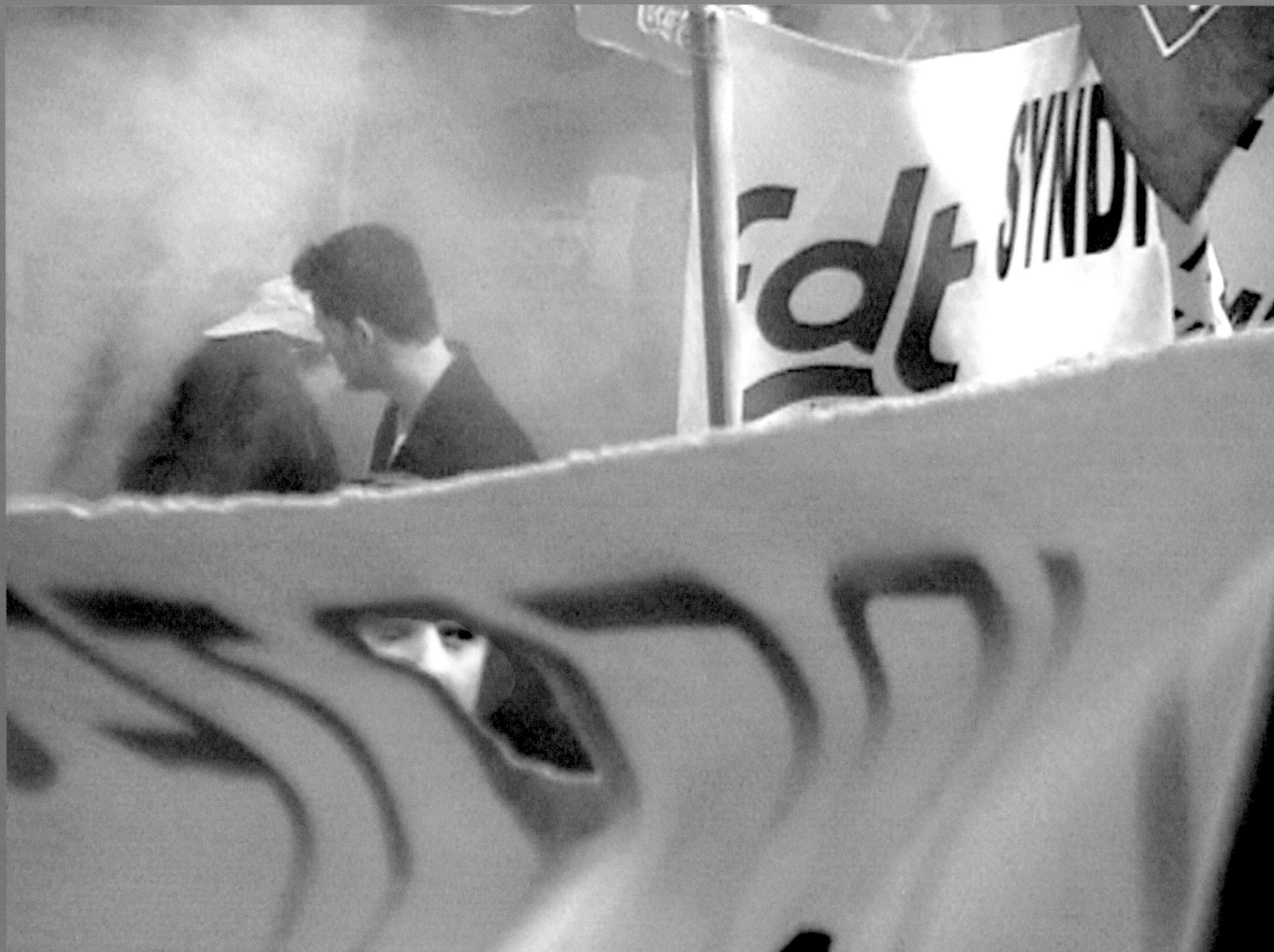

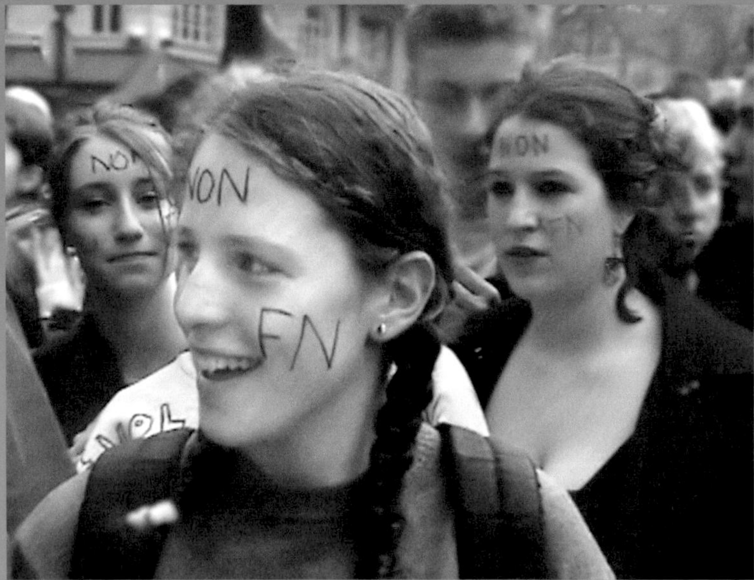
NON
NON
FN
NON
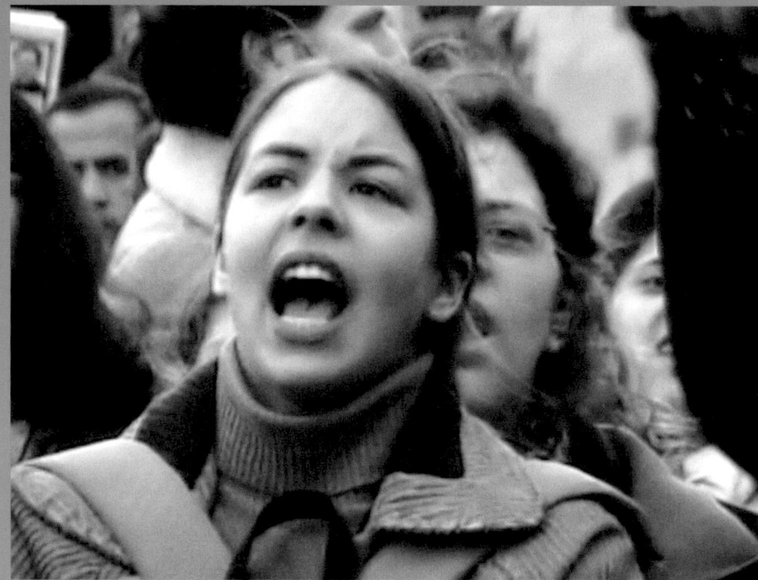
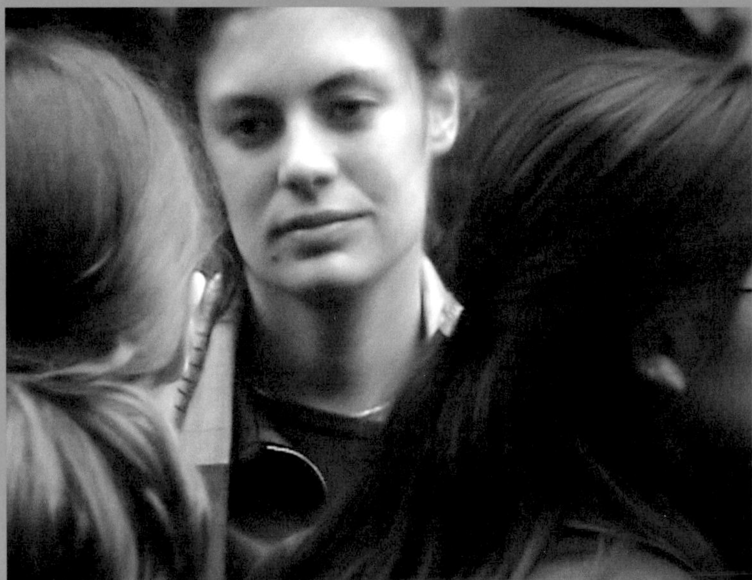
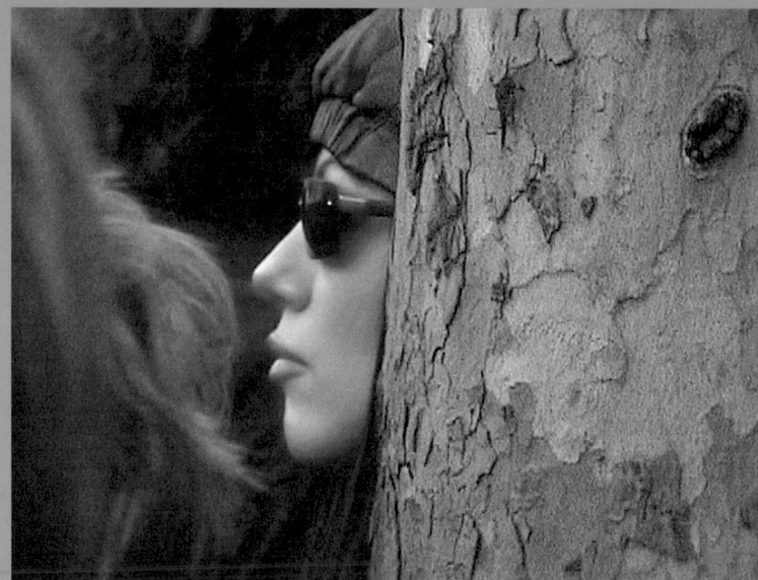

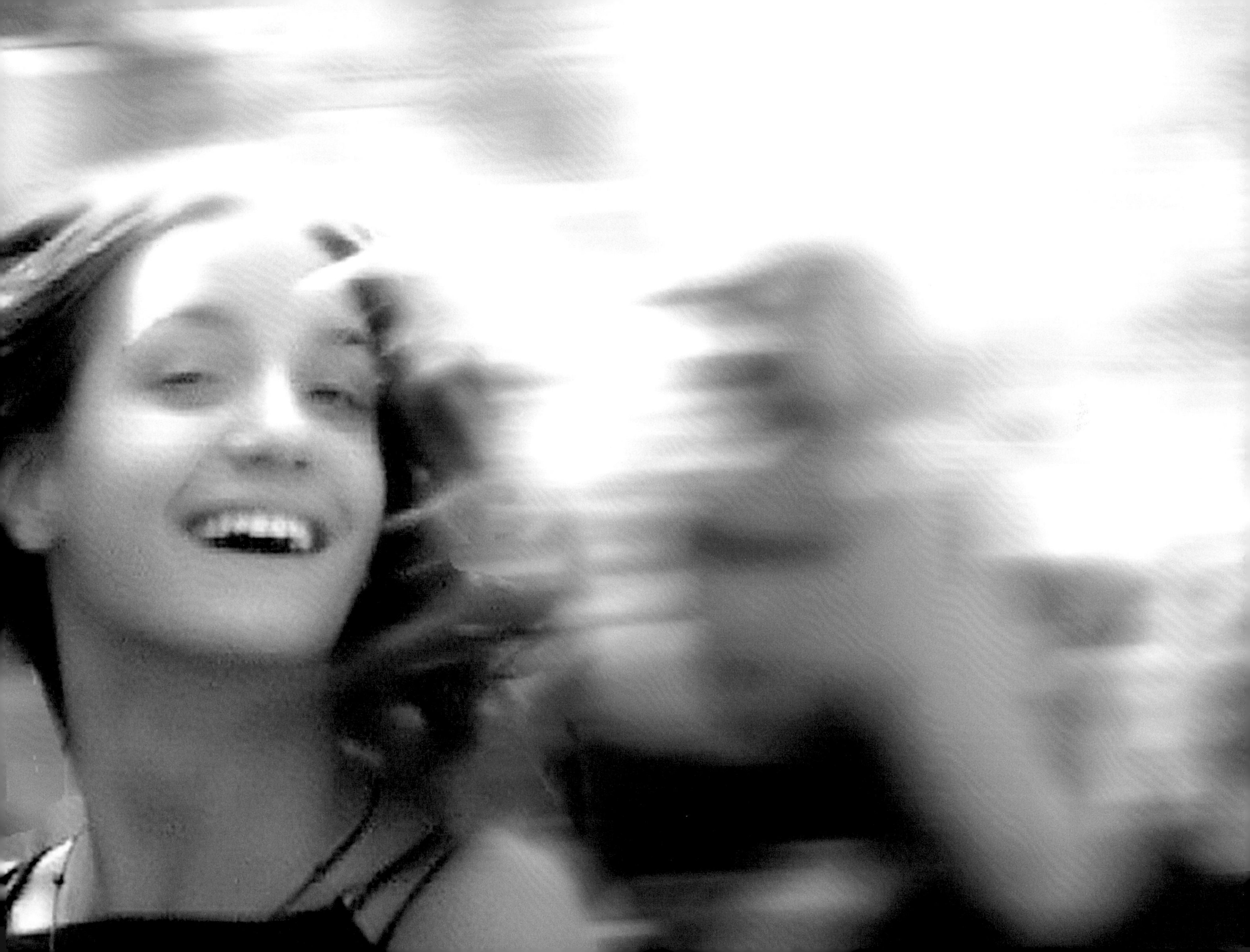

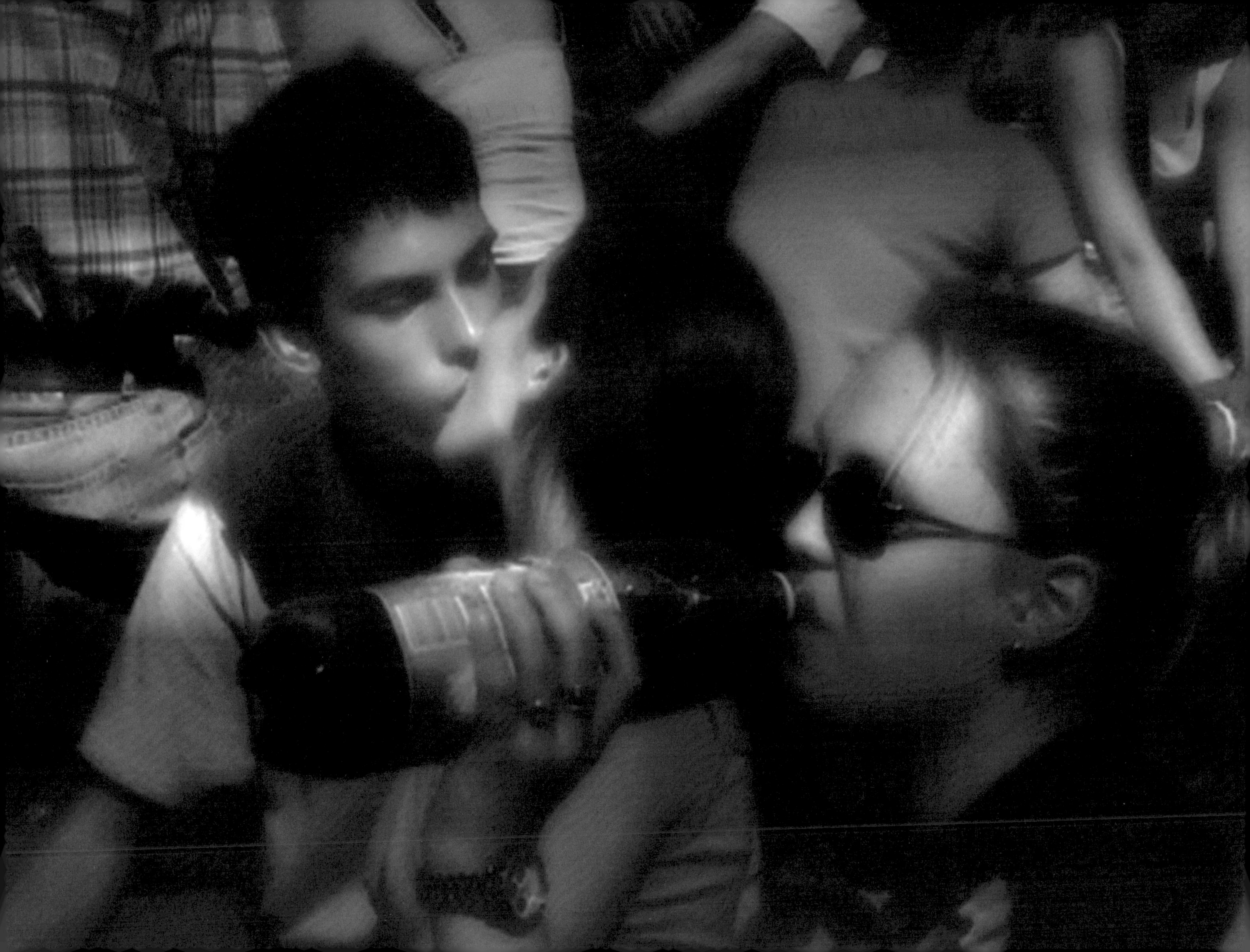

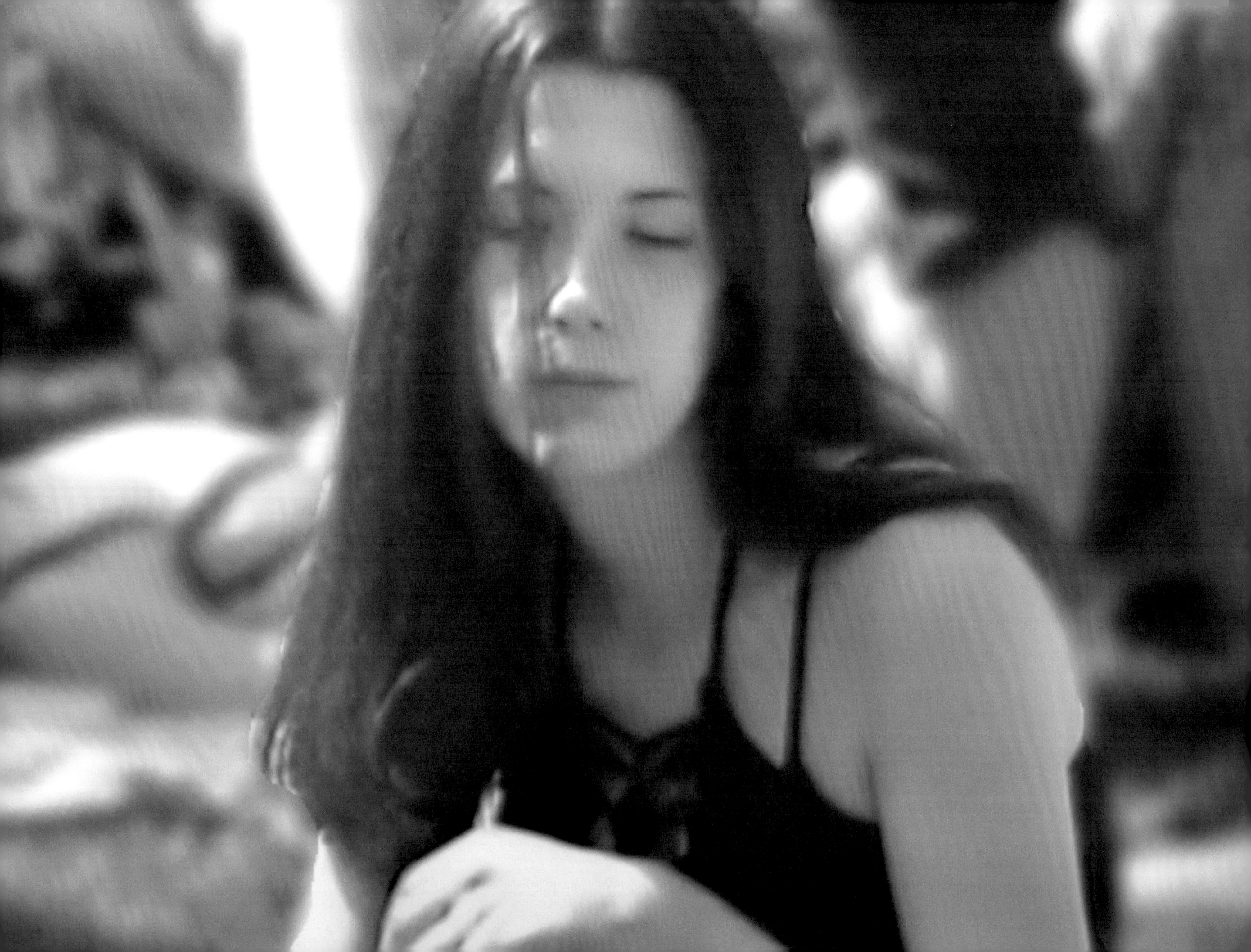

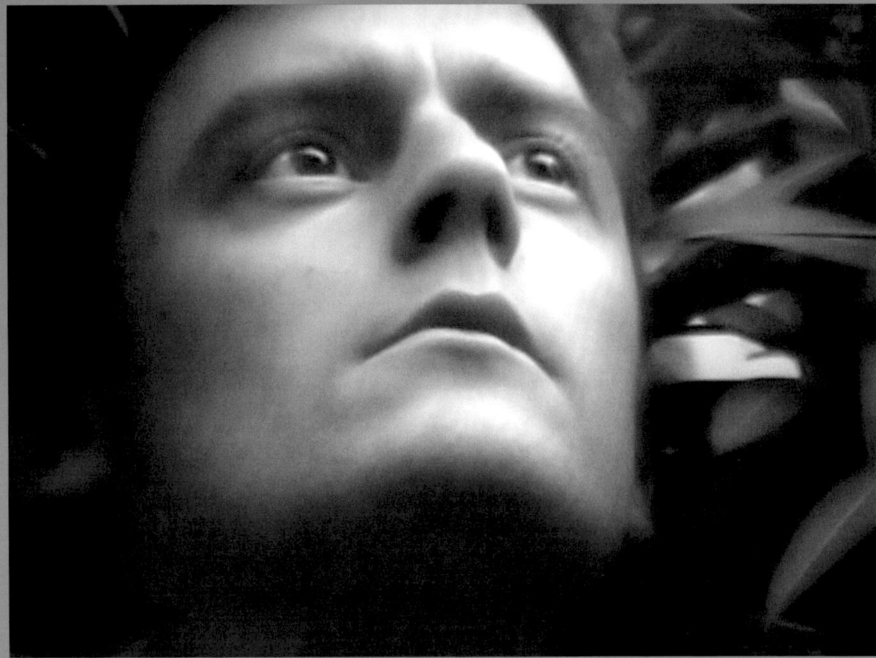

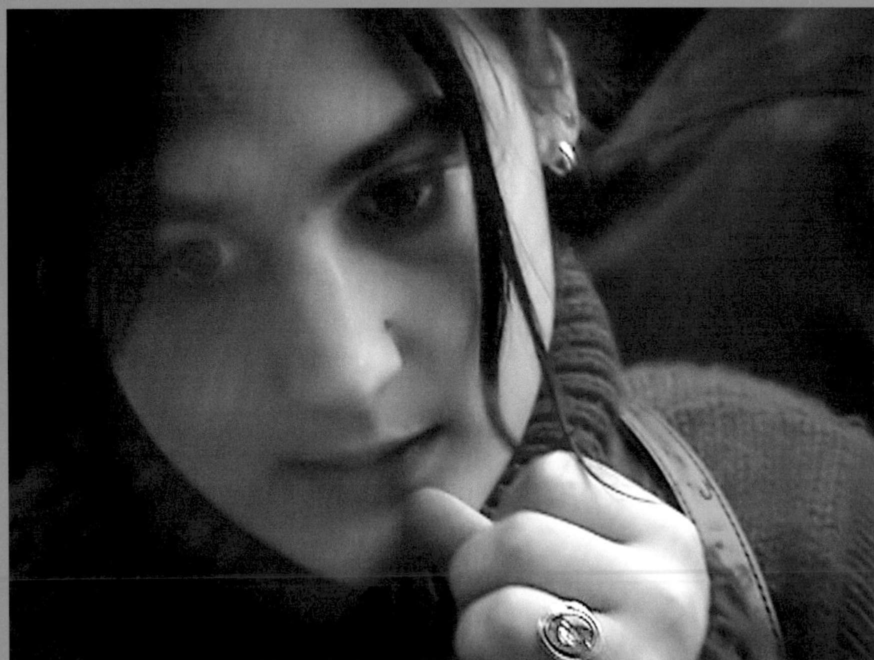

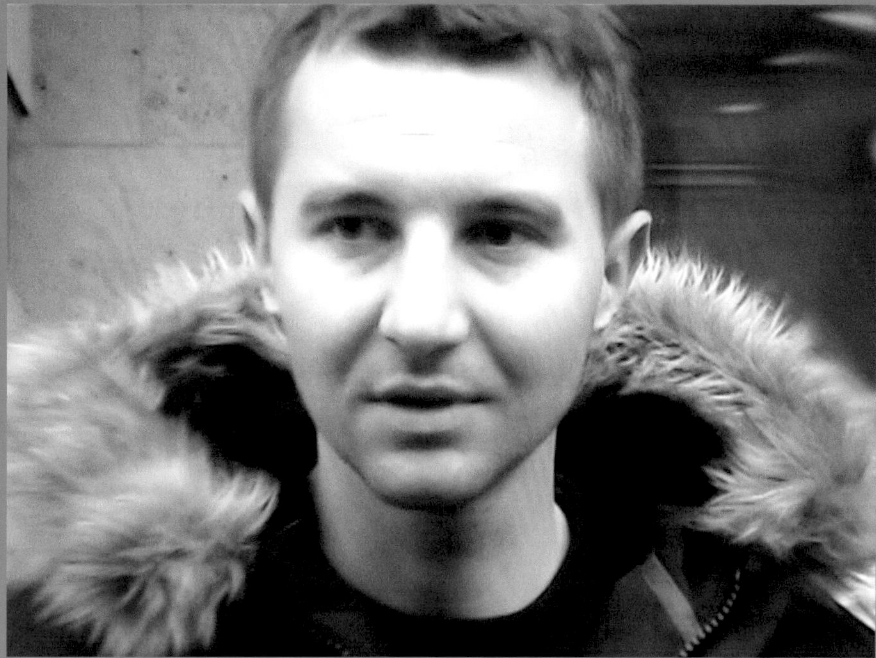

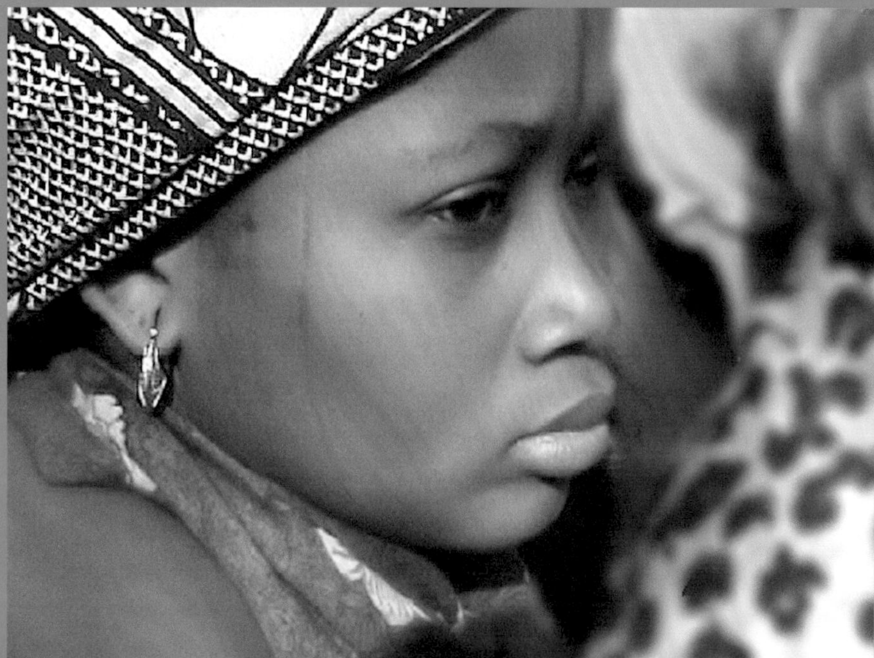

Four years later, that jubilant mood hardly shows up in my images. Yes, there are moments of joyful aggressiveness, and the prime minister gets his share of catcalls. But the fight isn't any longer against a largely imaginary fascism, neither is it about changing the world. Today's mottoes deal with unemployment, income, fears of uncertain retirement (at 20...and yet in the long run they're right). As my lens slips inside the crowd like an inquisitive snake, what it frames is, despite the apparent cohesiveness of the groups, the everlasting face of solitude.

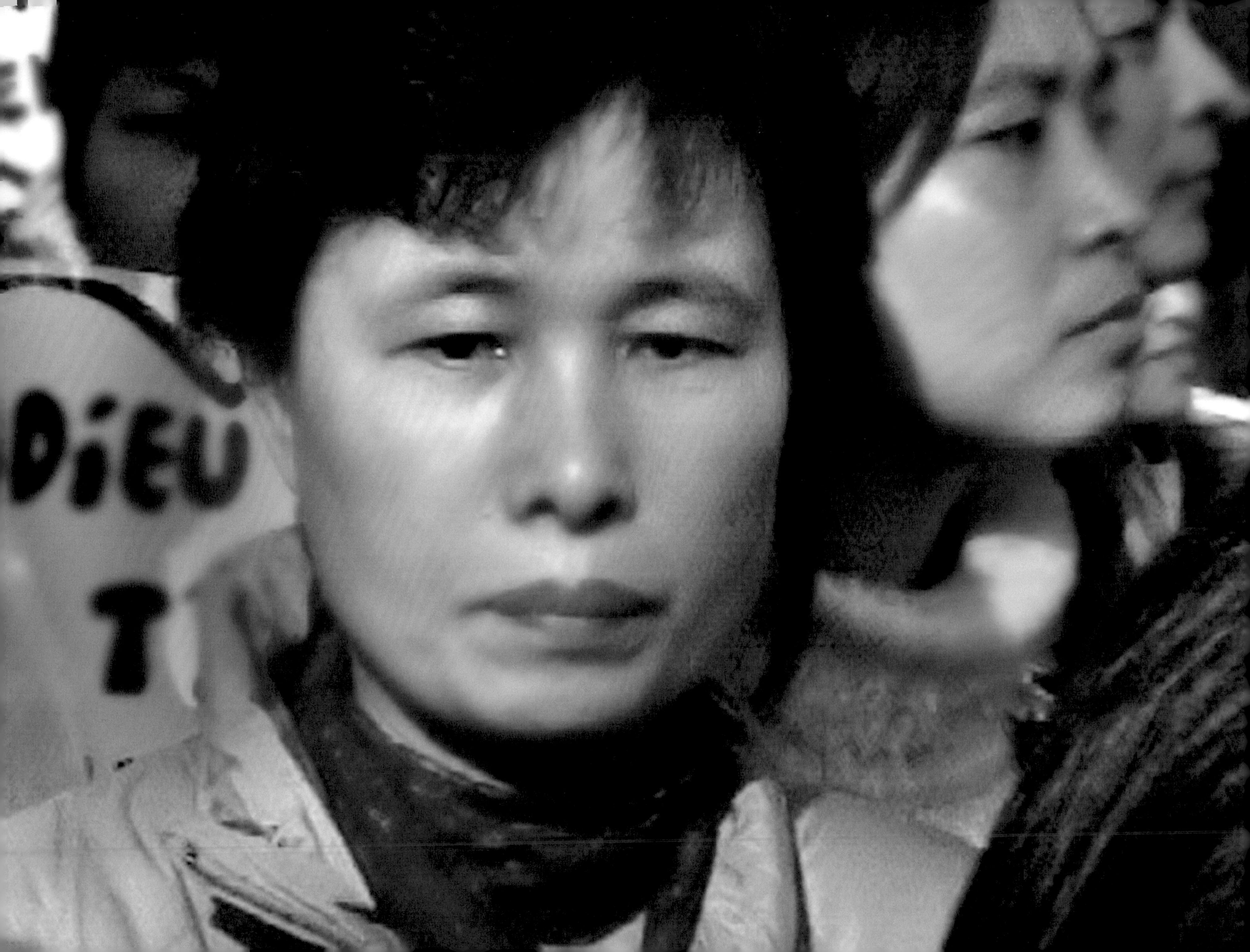

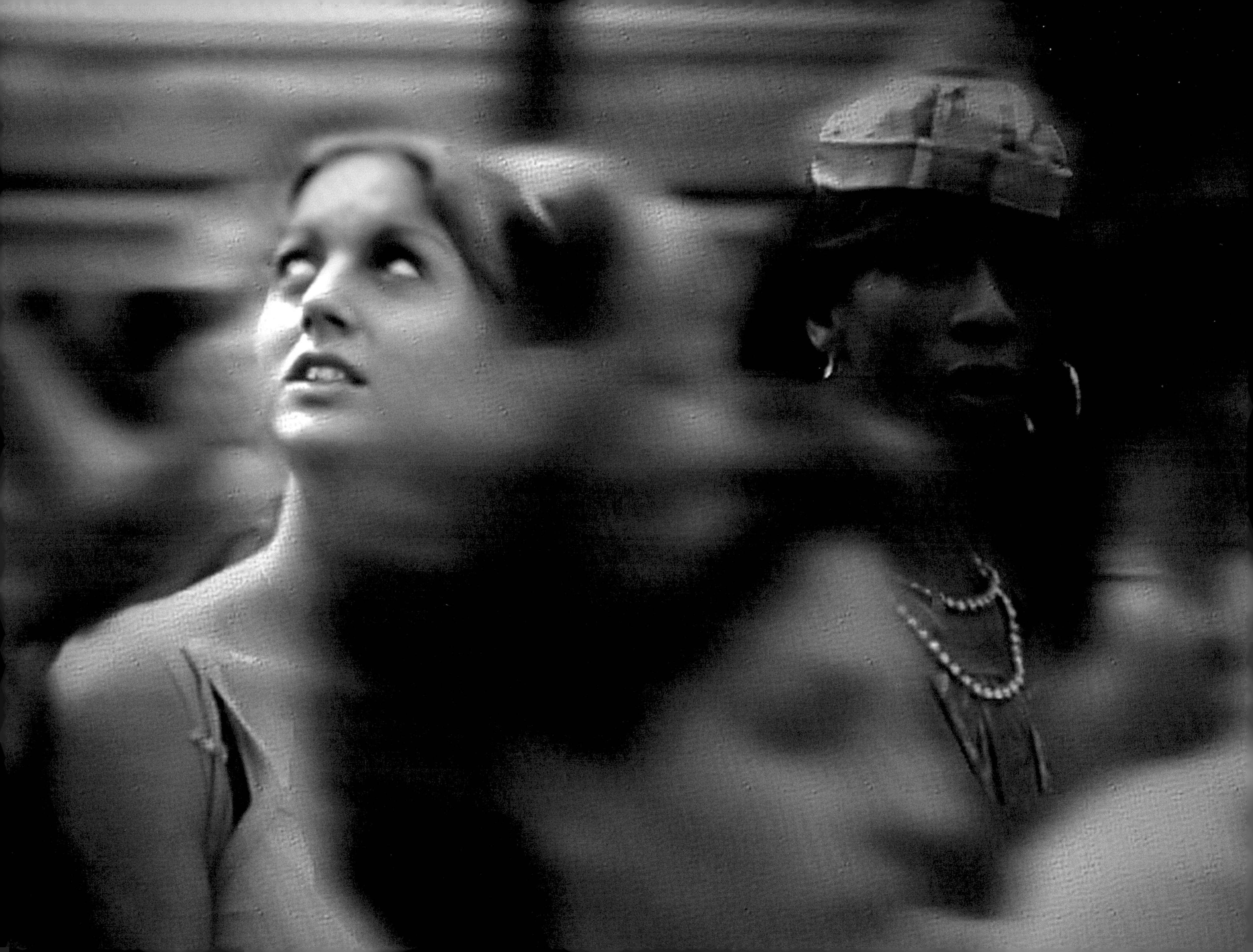

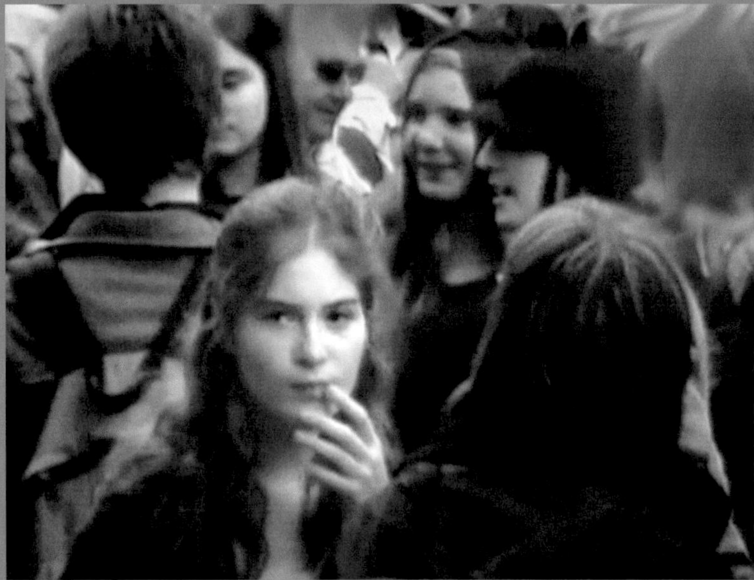

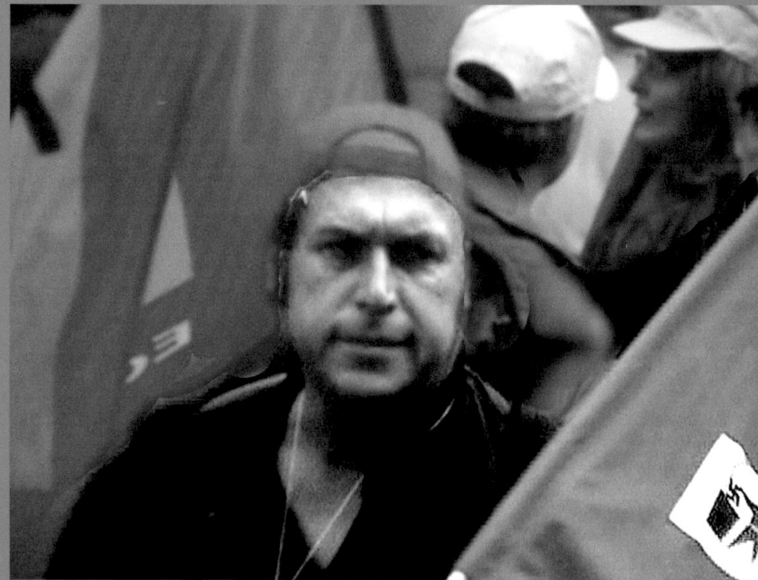

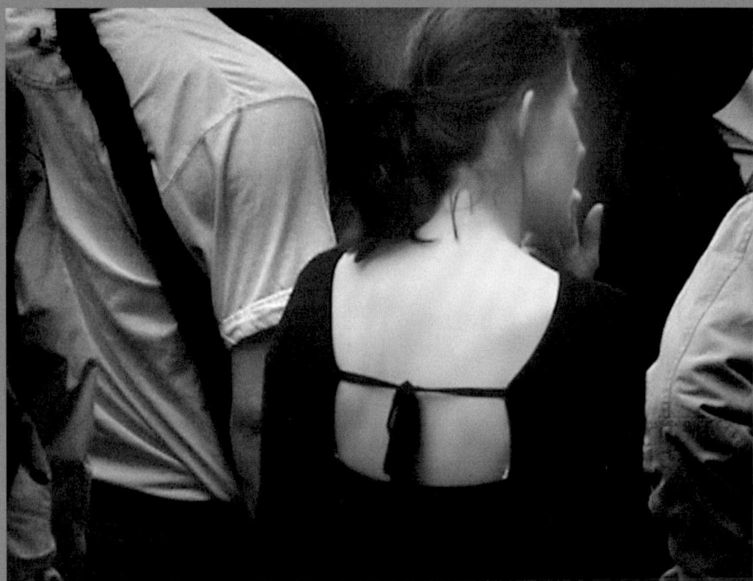

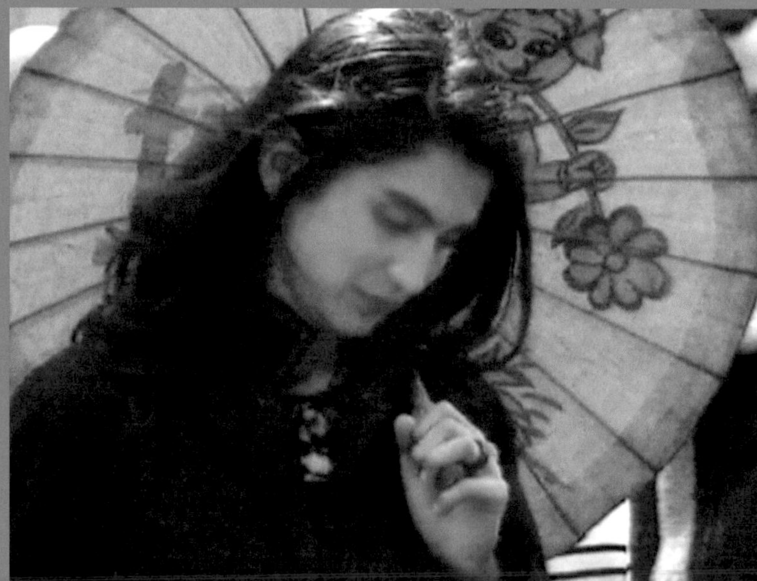

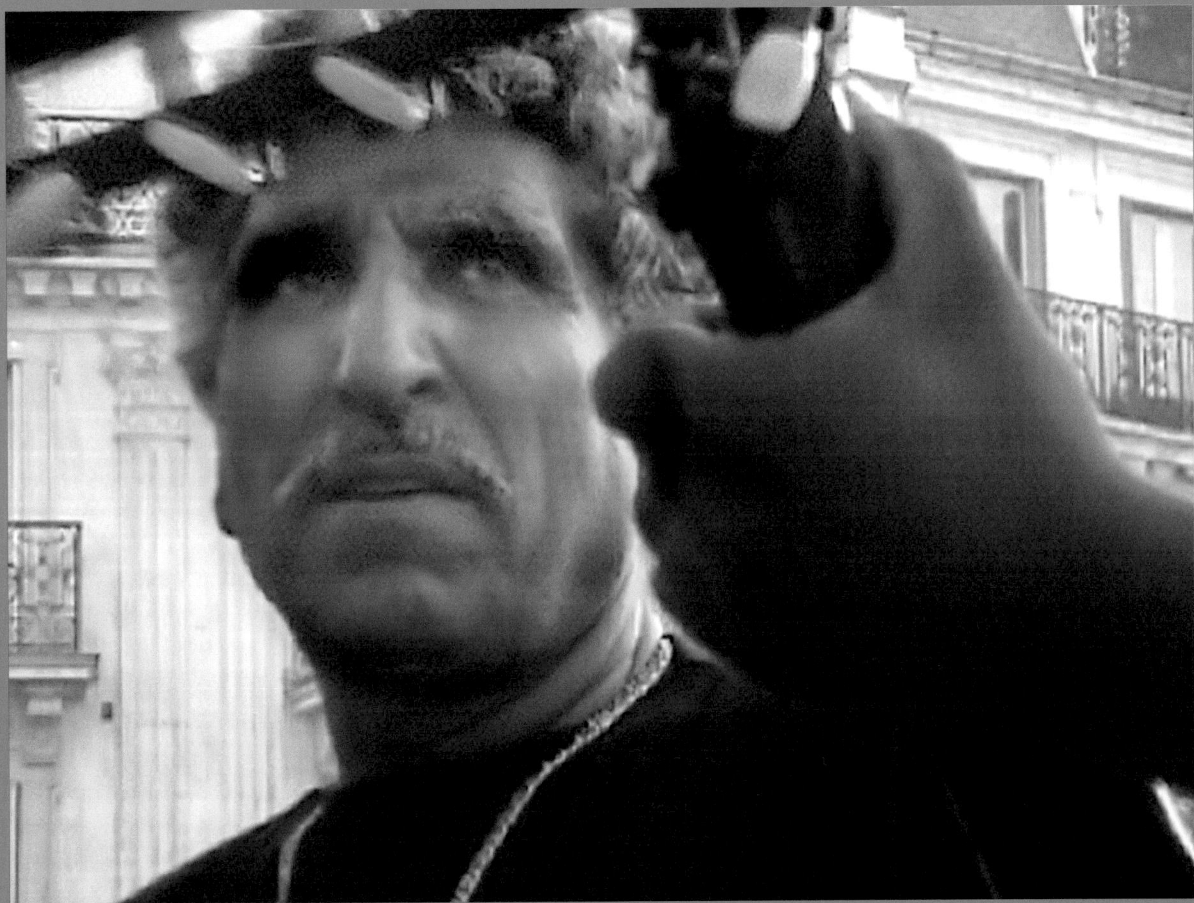

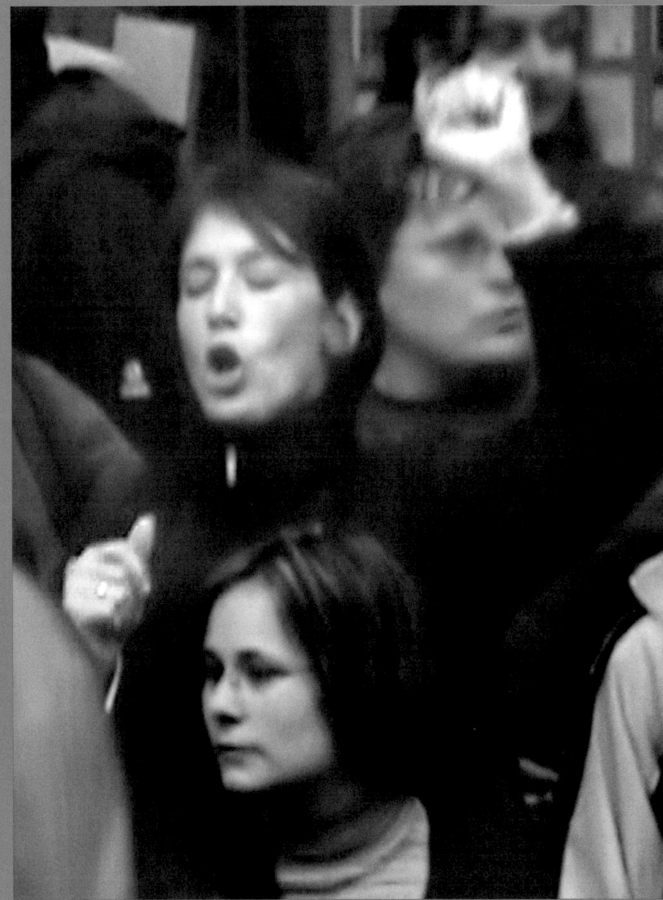

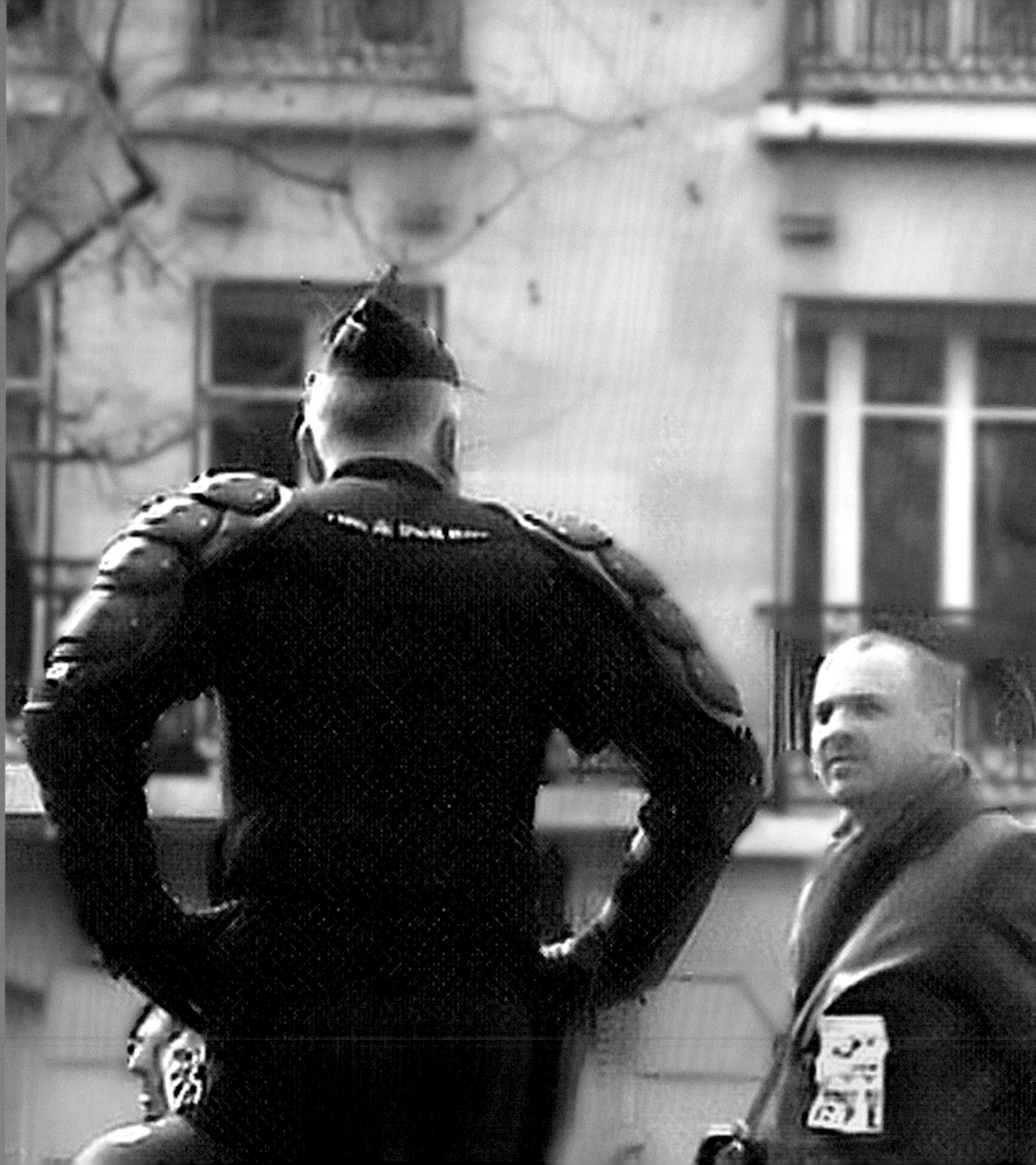

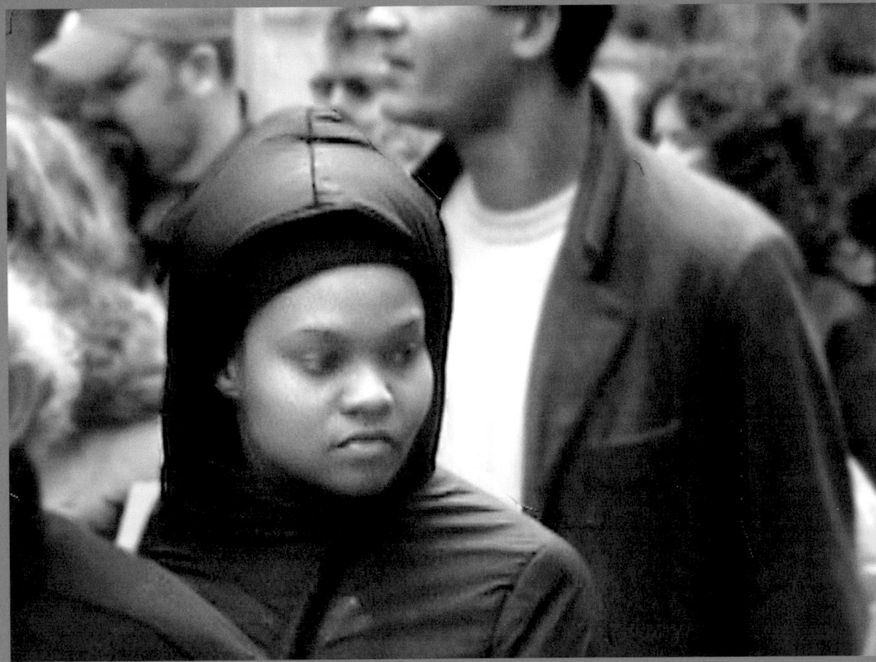

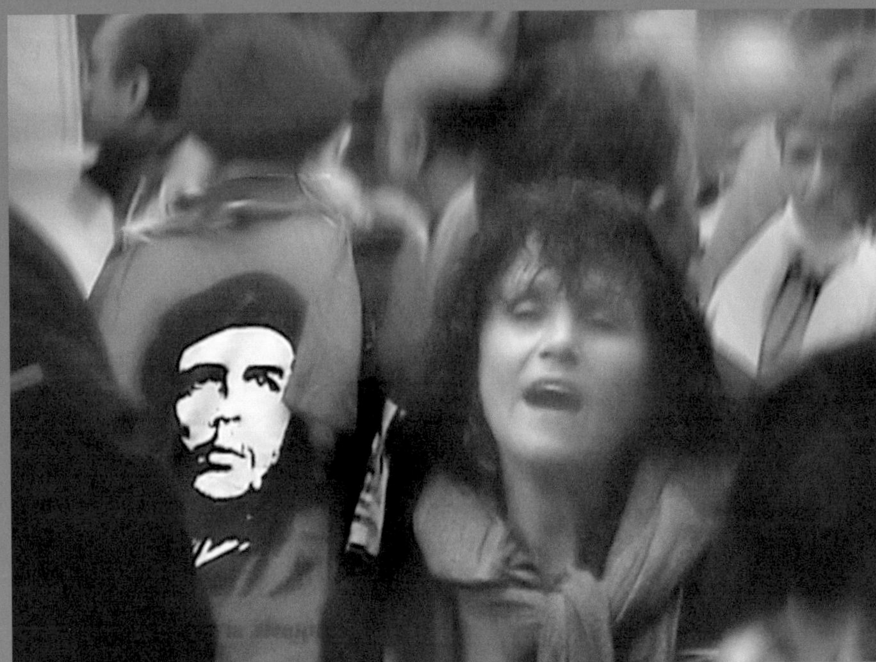

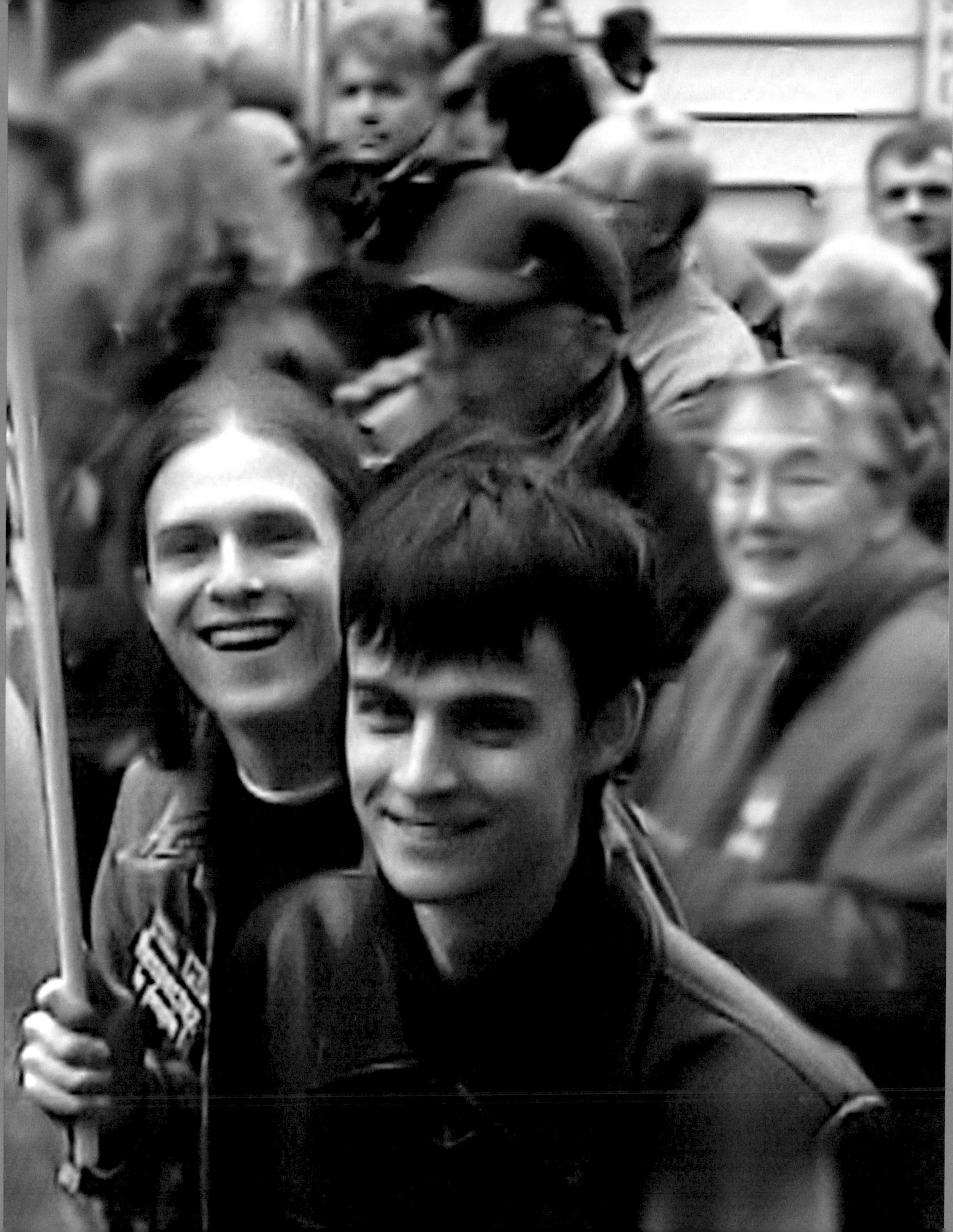

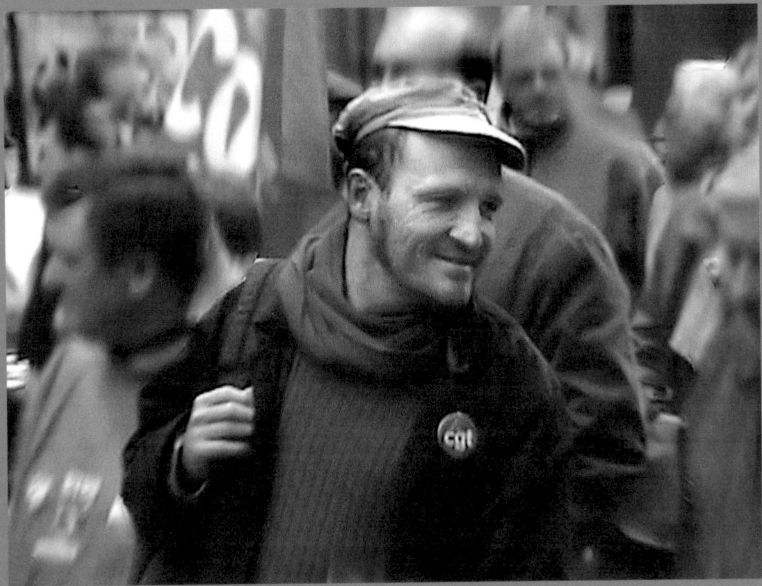
cgt

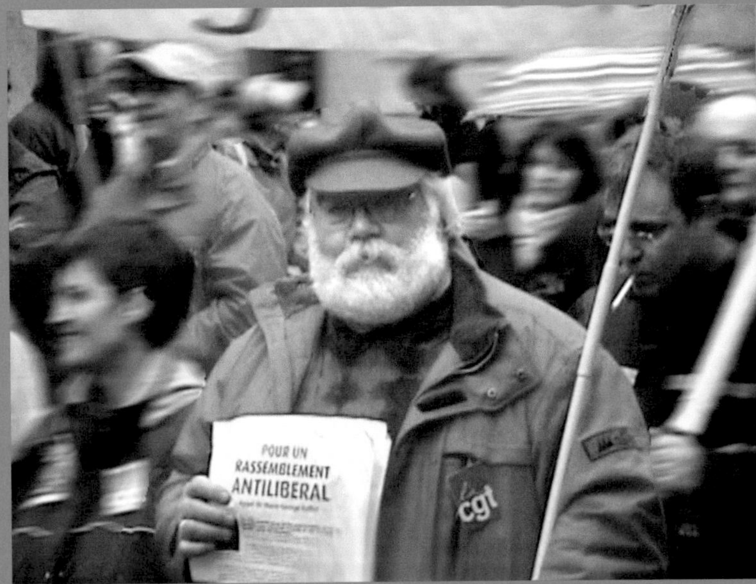
POUR UN
RASSEMBLEMENT
ANTILIBERAL
cgt

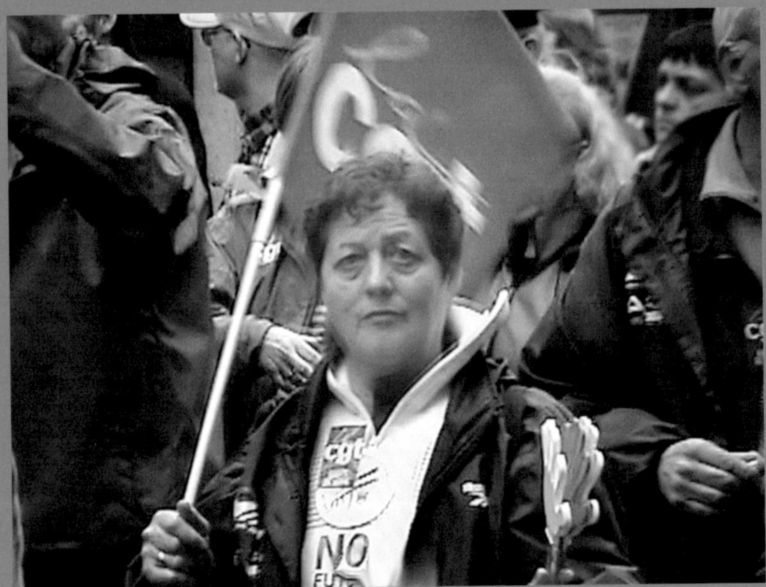
cgt
NO

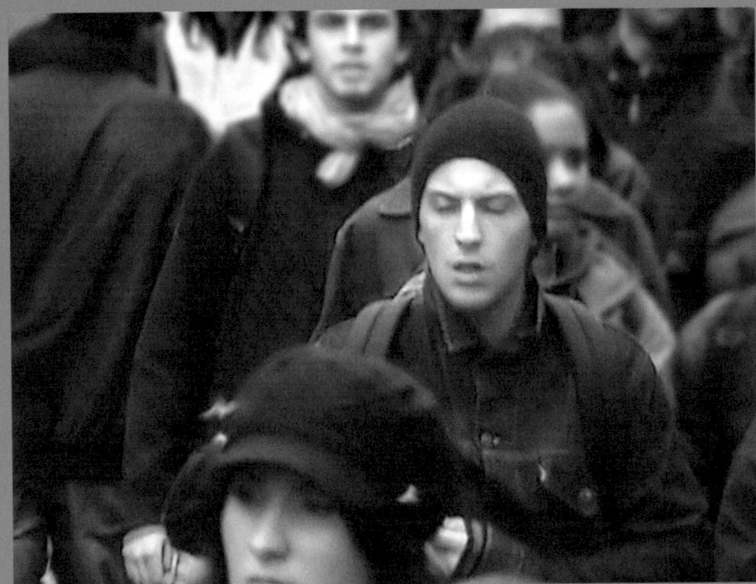

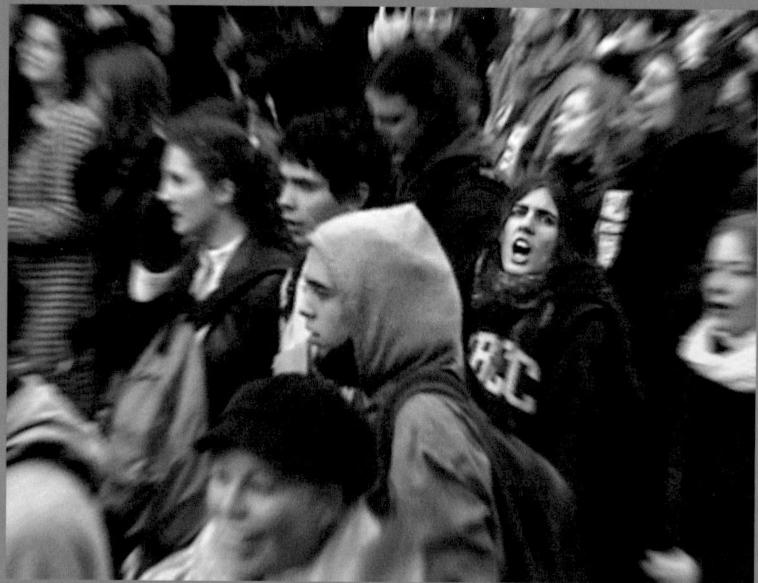

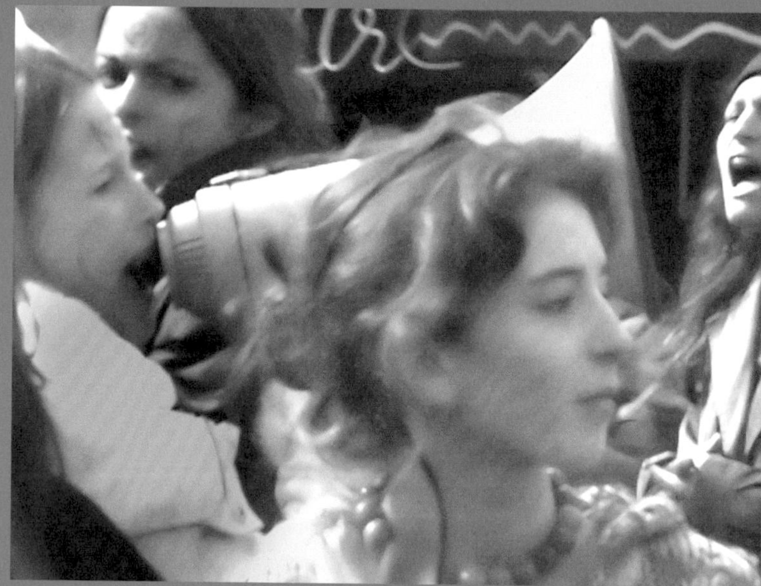

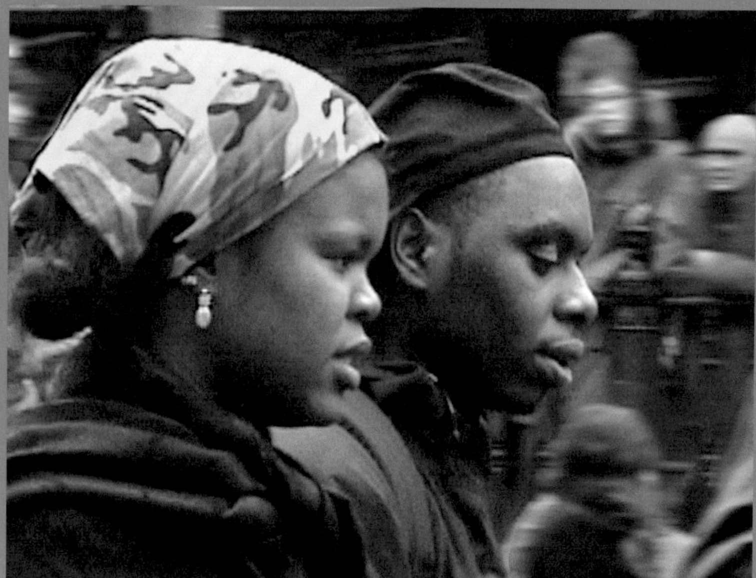

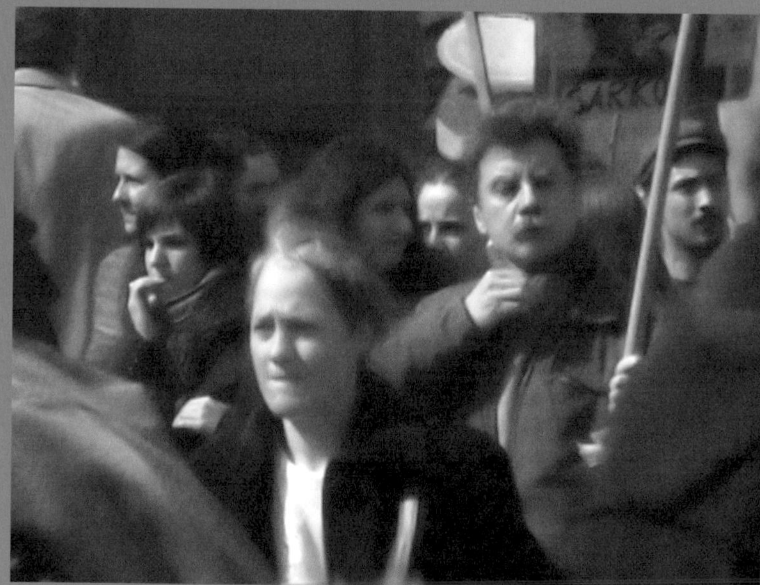

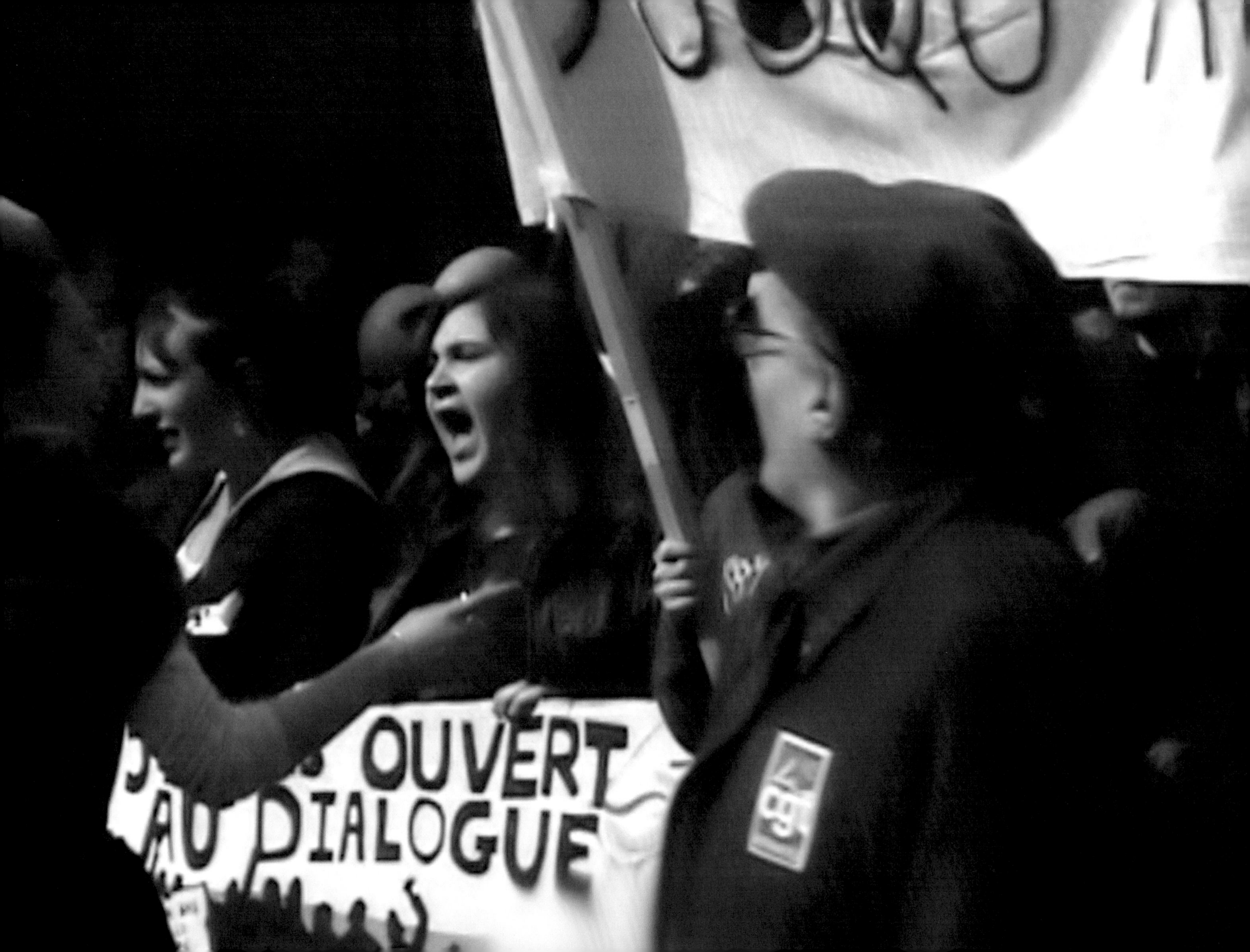
OUVERT
AU DIALOGUE

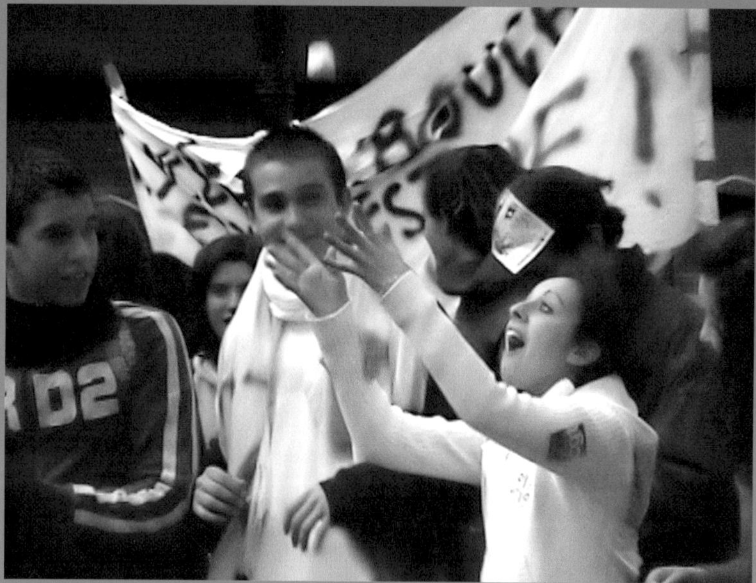

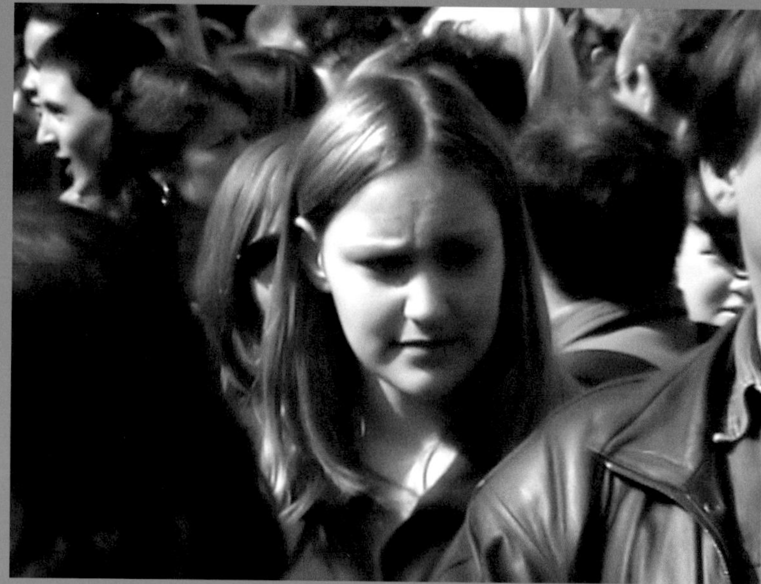

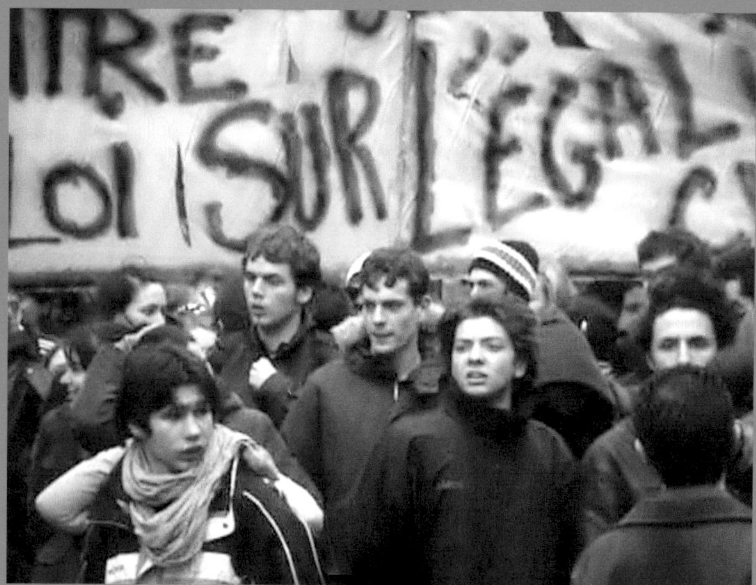
LOI SUR

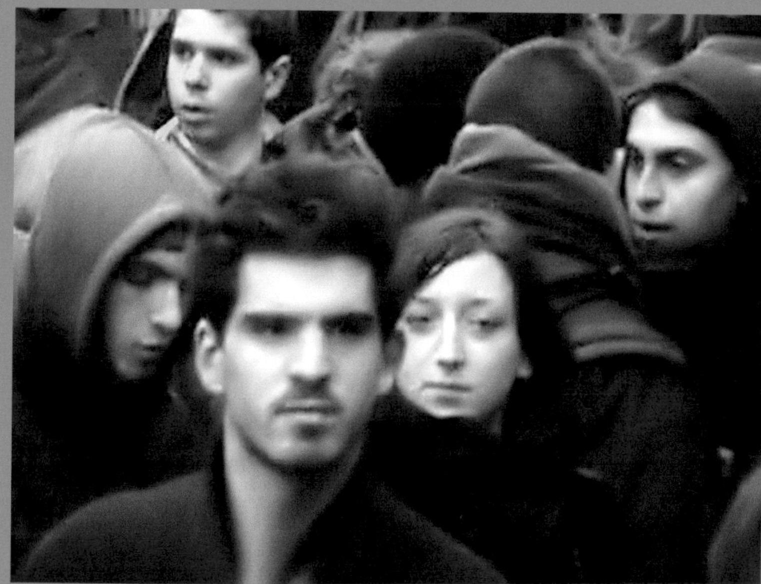

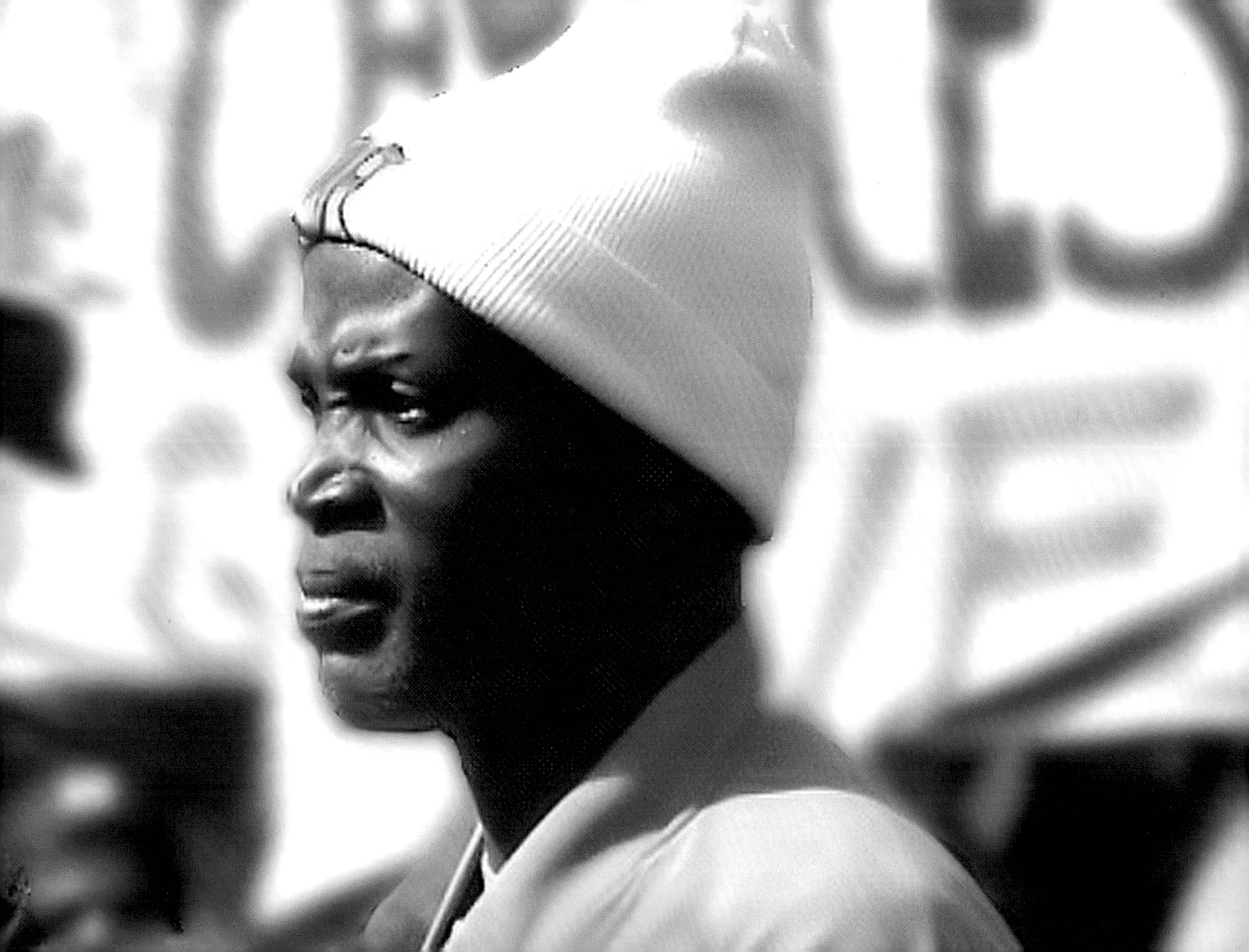

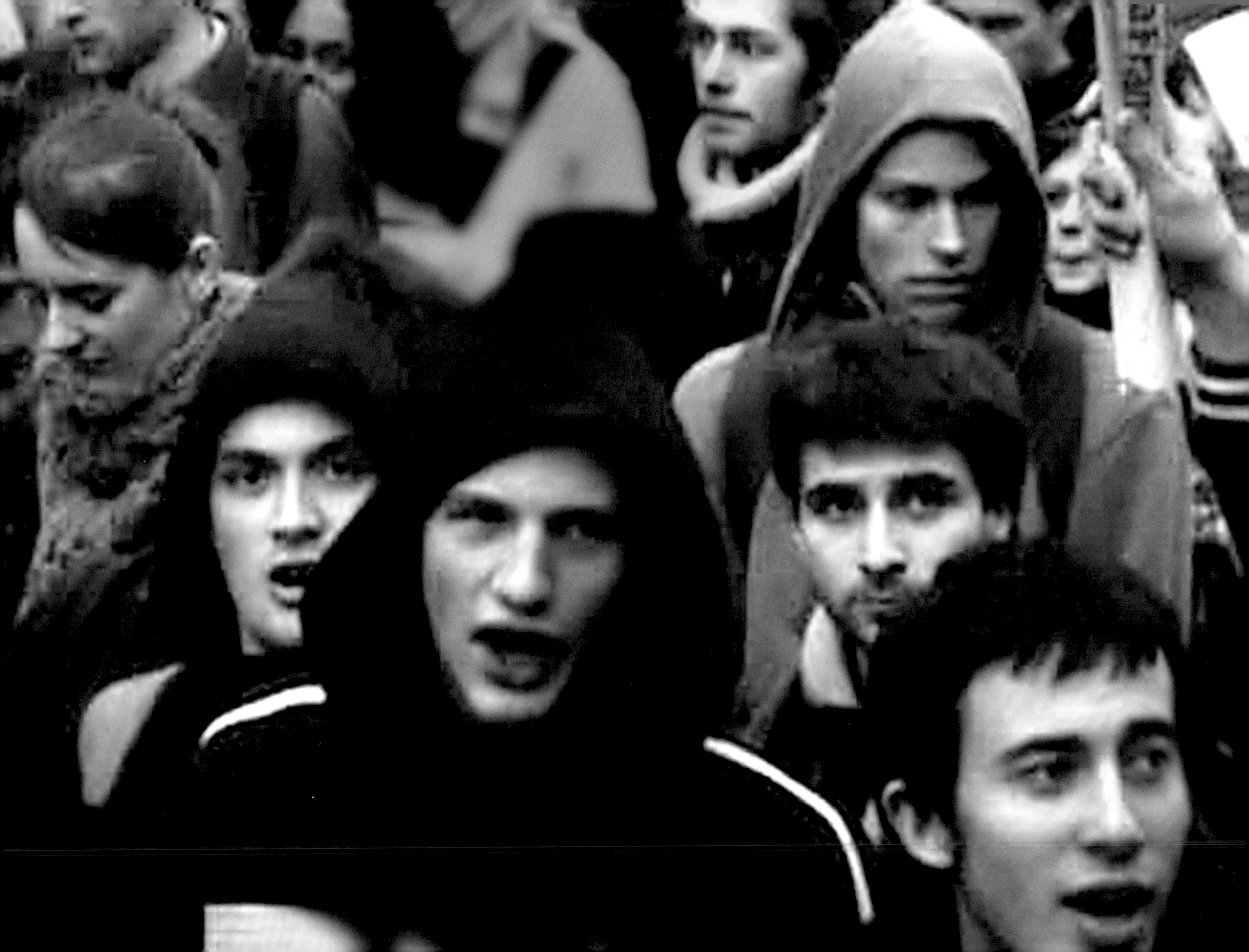

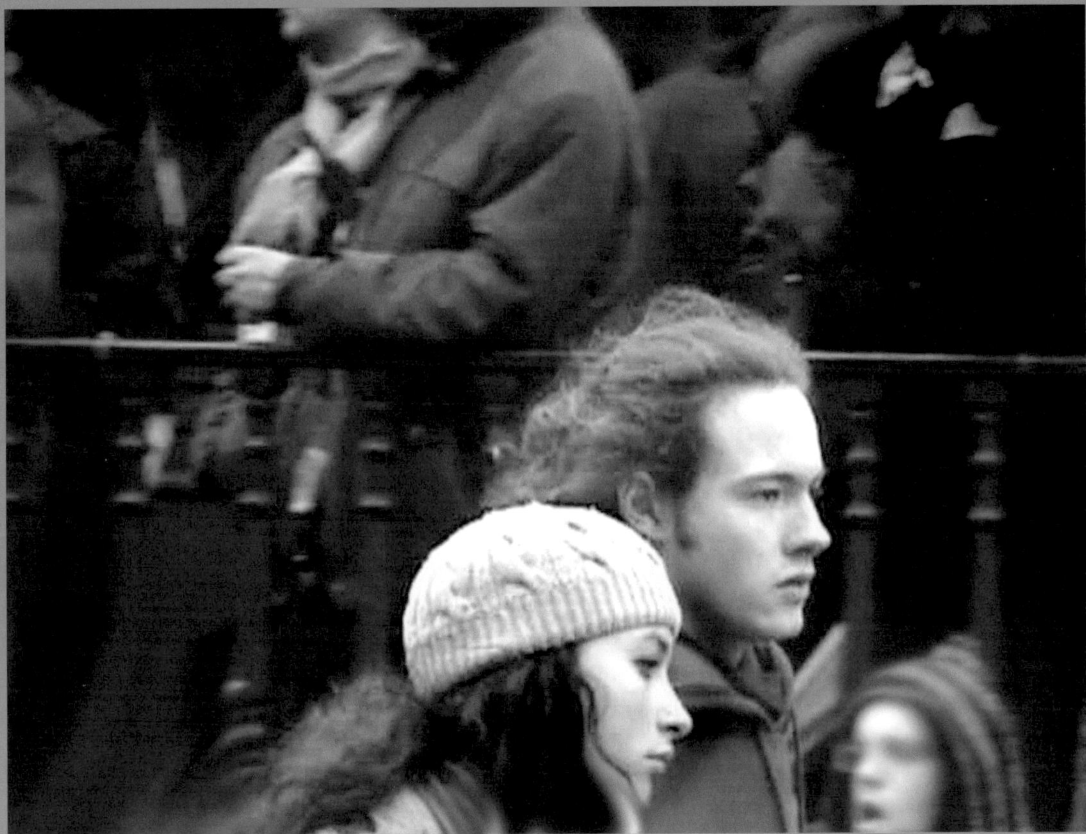

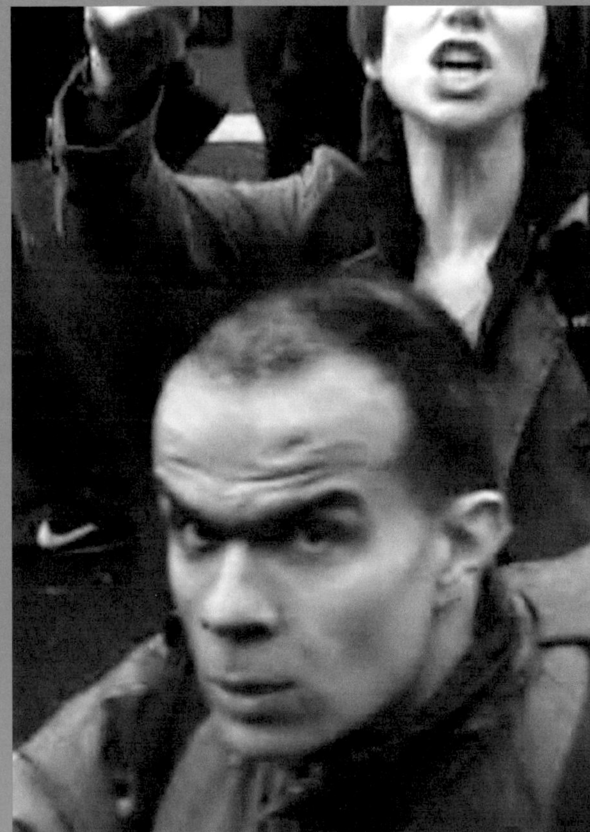

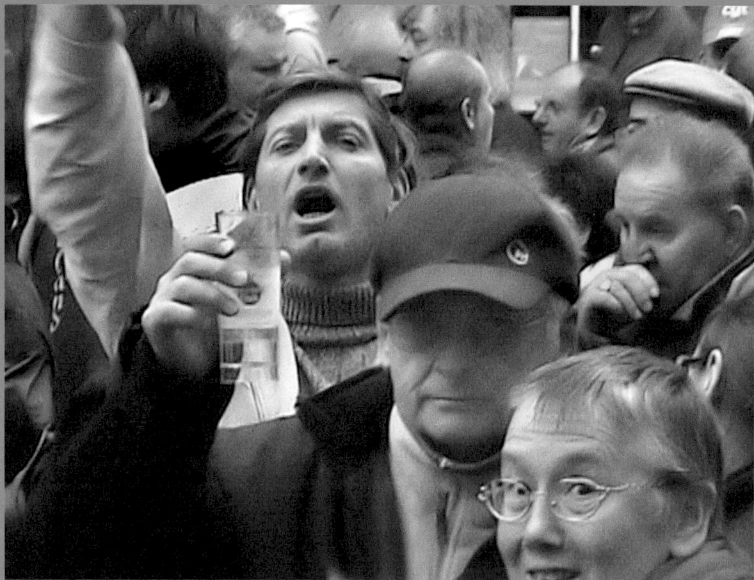

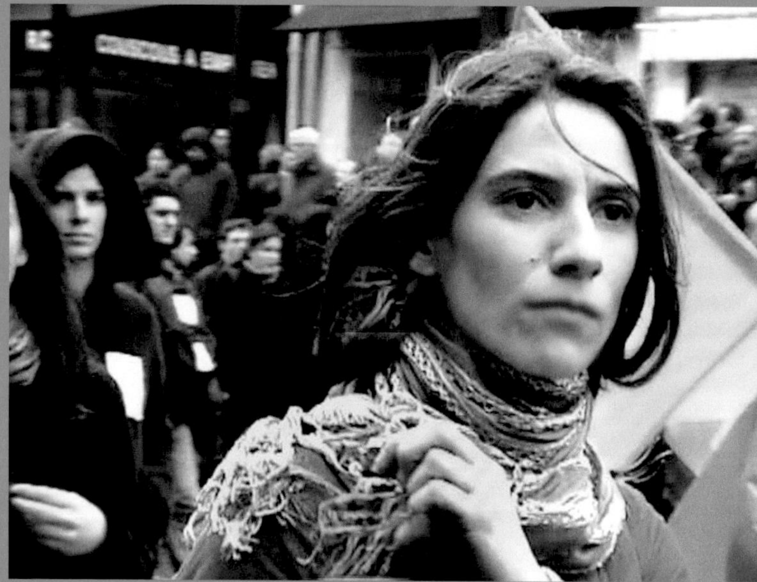

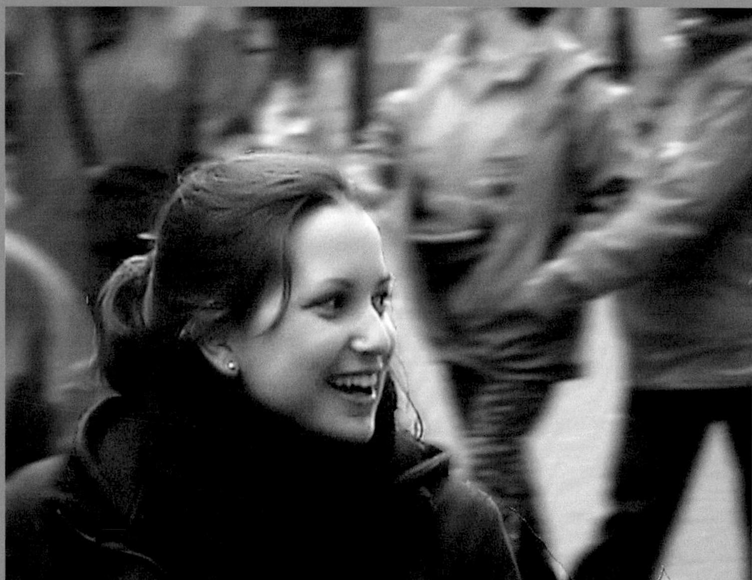

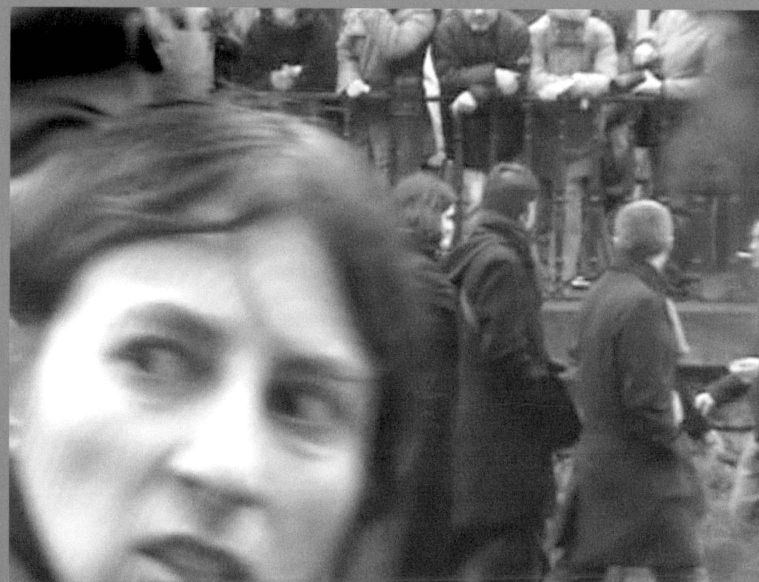

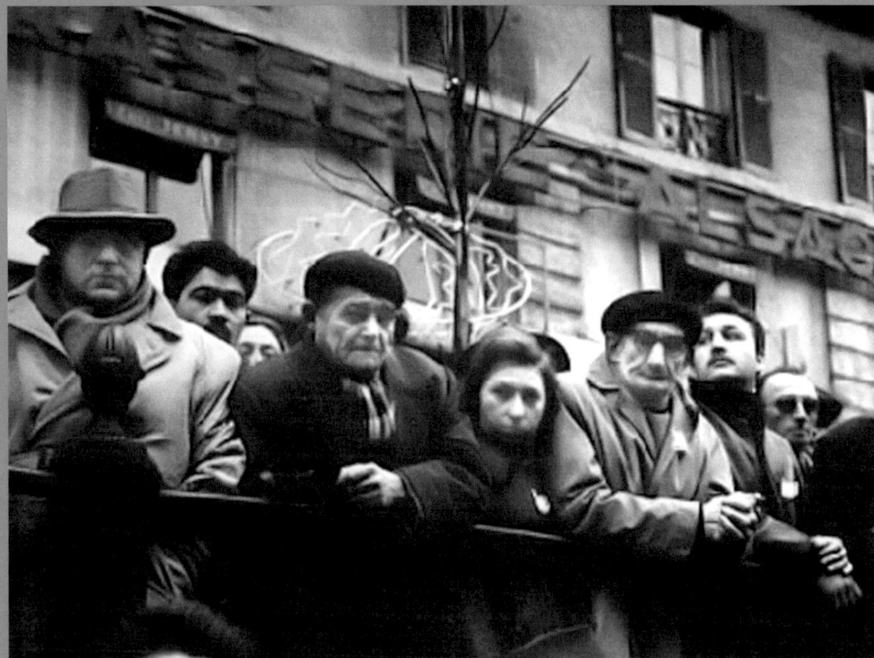

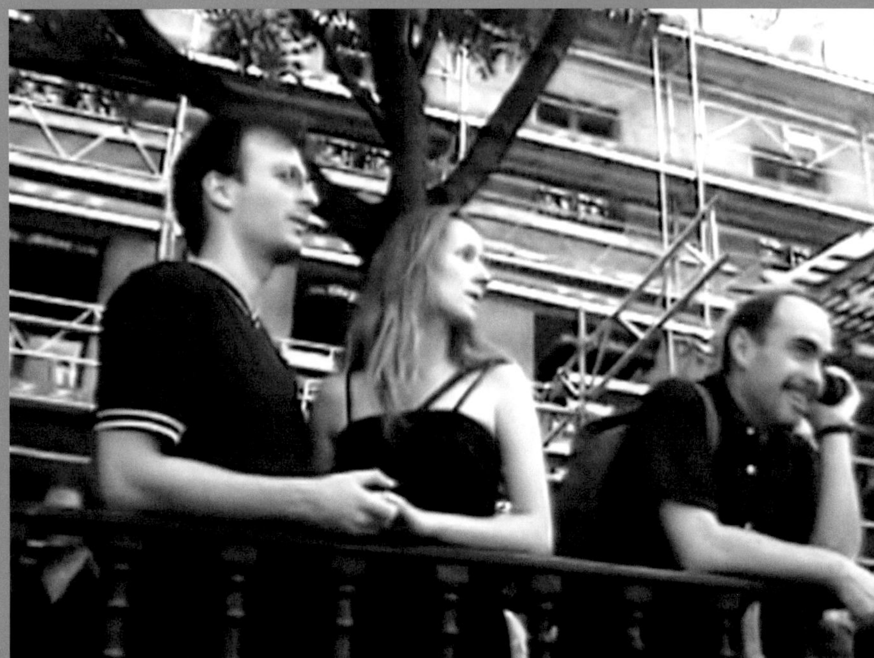

Back to that balcony at the place de la République where all huge demonstrations have always started or ended. I manage to frame again the top portion of my old photograph. In between I have been in Japan, Korea, Bolivia, Chile. I have filmed students in Guinea-Bissau, medics in Kosovo, Bosnian refugees, Brazilian activists, animals everywhere. I covered the first free elections in East Germany after the fall of the Wall, and I sniffed the first moments of *perestroika* in Moscow, when people weren't afraid to talk to each other anymore. I traded film for video and video for the computer. In the middle, on the balcony, the tree has grown, just a little.

Within these few inches, forty years of my life.

This text is the voice-over narration of Chris Marker's film *Chats Perchés* (2004) in its English-language version.

The Case of The Grinning Cat

Got a message tonight in my mailbox. It says:

"*Dear Flash-mobber,*

The second ParisMob will take place tonight. Synchronize your watch on http://www.horloge-parlante.com/fr *or your phone at 3699. Be at 50 rue Rambuteau, station Rambuteau, at 6:52* PM *with your umbrella.*

Someone will deliver the instructions to you. Start strolling quietly around the place, don't form groups, until 7:00 PM. *After 7:00 open and close your umbrella every ten seconds, still strolling. Once you're near the flower pot, start turning around, clockwise, and sing the following text in monotone: Let's walk around the pot until rain begets the golden flower...*" How poetic.

And all that under the eyes of a Cat.

A **CAT**?

This was Paris, November 2001. The sound of the September bagpipes was still in the air. Everybody felt we had entered a new age, we marveled at the way New Yorkers had faced the tragedy, and the biggest Parisian newspaper had put on its front page "WE ARE ALL AMERICANS." You would hear everywhere the same motto: let's join against the killers. The whole world was a band of brothers. Dunno who's to blame for the fact that it didn't last. Certainly not the Cats.

A cat on a roof. Then another. Then another. I picked them at random; I didn't even think that someday they would steal, catlike, into a movie. At that moment they were just signs, but comforting ones. And how we did need comforting signs in those days. So somebody, at night, was risking his neck just to have a smile floating over the city.

I wondered who the painter could be. A crossbreed of Charles Schulz and Spiderman. He was performing in the most unexpected places, you'd swear he would need a third arm—or was it a paw?—just to keep his balance between brushes and buckets. On occasion he assigned a task to his cats. Some were in charge of welcoming the travellers in the rail stations. To someone who landed in that gloomy city where smiling had become a kind of secret cipher between affiliates, the grin of the Cat was the gate to a different Paris, as it used to be in merrier times. And it was no wonder that, following its path, you would encounter the traces of that past. In fact, the first Cat I had spotted wasn't on a roof, but in one of the rare locations that had not changed for sixty years. The locks on the canal, a legendary site of prewar cinema. *Hôtel du Nord*, Louis Jouvet, Marcel Carné, holy names for a film maniac.

SUBTITLES

> *—I need to change atmosphere*
> *and you're my atmosphere*
> *—I've been called names before*
> *but never Atmosphere!*
> *(cult dialog from* Hôtel du Nord*)*

Then I discovered I wasn't alone in my hunt. Some newspapers heralded the Cat. "An army of yellow cats is invading the city." Which was a clear overstatement. That army was made of a few sentinels, but strategically disposed. Some of them did climb down from their roofs to appear at human eye's level, and one even went to the ground. The author craftily used the texture of a tree, on the banks of river Seine, to make the critter look like an owl in its nest, thus illustrating my favorite slogan "The Owl is to the Cat what the Angel is to the Man." But as soon as they were within reach, they became vulnerable, and the Enemy was watching.

A Grinning Cat appeared on the wall of the church at St. Germain des Prés. Within a month he was erased. Does that iconoclastic rage ring a bell? Sure, the Taliban blowing out the Buddhas in Afghanistan. I'm not joking. Given their respective environments, both obscurantisms show the two faces of the same coin.

To the soundtrack of the Metro,
I wander across the city...

...and I'm looking for the Cats.

The musicians get a standing ovation. Of course, those people were standing anyway, but don't forget that probably not one of them ever entered a concert hall. That's why I love the Metro. I have some good friends there. Meet Bolero, the cat at Strasbourg Saint Denis, and his human companion, Elizabeth. No cat in Paris is better groomed than Bolero, even in the upper-class districts. In the Metro you come across the derelict and the tourist, equally lost; you too get lost at times, unless you join the society of those who are simply lost in their thoughts, sometimes with good reasons....And naturally it is just when after so many apparitions of gremlins, zombies, and griffins you're ready to give up your hunt, that the Cat deigns to materialize. The next surprise is to watch a pigeon transforming itself into a man....

Once outside, the real world strikes back.

While I was hunting cats downstairs, honorable men on the first floor were cooking the presidential election. This one promises to be especially mind-boggling. The Left, which had a good chance to challenge the incumbent president, Mr. Chirac, is in pieces. As the saying goes: one Trotskyite, a militant; two Trotskyites, a party; three Trotskyites, a split. We have all three, plus the Communists, plus the Greens, plus a few mavericks, while the Socialist Party desperately tries to make out of this cacophony a coalition. So begins the New Year.

Chirac was the first to draw. To confront him, Socialist Jospin would be the best choice. But there is an obvious lack of support from his own allies. They reproach him not to lean ostensibly enough on the left side, and at times he doesn't help to clarify the debate—when, for instance, in a TV interview he declares that if he himself is a Socialist, his program is not. Hence a certain confusion, which doesn't escape the piercing eye of Mr. Le Pen, the extreme rightist contender. He says, "Jospin is threatened by the six candidates of the radical Left. My intention is to beat him in the first round." Nobody then pays attention to that prophecy.

It may sound a bit strange to hear some leftists throwing fiercer barbs to the candidate of the Left than to his opponent, when they don't accuse him blatantly of being a slave to Capital. The Trotskyites are within their own logic, but others who pretend to be only critical supporters begin to play with fire. The catch is, they all are absolutely sure that there is no risk playing the tough guys. "Imagining that Jospin wouldn't be present at the second round is pure nonsense."

Now let's go back to a more familiar world, the world of cats, which has its own share of troubles. Take for instance that Saturday afternoon, when the cat Caroline got stuck on the top of a tree and couldn't descend. Even the firemen gave up. That was enough of a drama to keep the whole neighborhood aghast. But the Parisian soil begets heroes when they're needed, and this one saved the day.

On April 21, catastrophe.

The cat Bolero pinched his paw in the escalator. Elizabeth brought first aid.

And as misfortunes never come singly…

Yes, the unthinkable happened. For the first time in a modern democracy, the extreme Right comes in second in a presidential election.

To a kinky situation, a kinky answer: the whole political spectrum from Left to Right supports Chirac in the second round.

The polls deliver their prediction. Chirac should get around eighty percent of the vote. "It's a gag," says one of Le Pen's cronies. "There will be a national uprising!" Mr. Le Pen himself announces "a big surprise" for the next round—and he goes specific: getting less than thirty percent, says he, would be "a bitter failure."

The answer of the street is immediate. As Le Pen's favorite ground is the danger of immigration, the youngsters loudly claim their immigrant origin.

SUBTITLES

We—all—are
Immigrants' children
First—Second—Third generation

Obviously an old activist. How many May Days does he stock inside his memory?

Here I've got a scoop:
Le Pen bashing—in Esperanto.

I didn't miss a word.

Let's face it: these girls with their war paint are lovely, but the fascist legions are not besieging our gates. And if Le Pen is a dictator, it's mainly against his own people. Yet what we see here coming onstage is an entire generation that was spoken of as being apolitical.

Chirac is elected. Eighty-two percent! Mao Zedong rolls in his grave. A real statesman would have seized that unique opportunity to build up a kind of New Deal, but this is not about a real statesman, it's about Mr. Chirac. On the spur of the exhilaration, he promised his voters they could count on him, then he went back home, and the rest is NOT history.

But the second round surprise was not what Le Pen had predicted.

I was there, watching PPDA [Patrick Poivre d'Arvor], the most celebrated anchorman of French television. And whom did I spot in a corner of the screen?

SUBTITLES

FREEDOM

So the Cat himself had chosen to reappear at that moment.

Was he suddenly titillated by political ambition? My own cat, Guillaume, immediately designed an acronym: humanistic-anarchistic confederation of workers…

…or was it enough for him to continue to publicize his grin?

And by the way: where did that grin come from?

The Cheshire Cat of course.

Also Miyazaki, the manga, Japanese ads…

Found in my files: an archive from the year 2000, when the author still was testing his style.

But when you search deeper into art history, you can make surprising discoveries. An expert speaks.

How true.

Thus you could follow the path of the Cat through the ages, from cave painting until constructivism.

Some metamorphoses of the Cat.

The Cat advertises himself in the Metro.

The Cat uses *Amélie* for his own benefit.

The Cat rates high at the Stock Exchange.

The Post Office issues stamps representing the Cat.

The Cat makes the front page in the tabloids.

The Cat squats on the Web.

When the Cat entered the White House official site, I knew that something serious was at stake. For in the meantime, a War was boiling up.

On March 17, President Bush gives Saddam forty-eight hours to leave Iraq. He also compares him to Hitler.

Good. Let's just imagine Churchill giving forty-eight hours to Hitler to get out of Germany.

SUBTITLES

Enough—enough of this society
that only brings war
and misery

In Vietnam
the napalm
wasn't Saddam
wasn't Islam
It was Uncle Sam

And the gassing of the Kurds, who was it?

The Kurds.
Always caught between two enemies.

March 19. President Bush announces the war.

My fellow citizens, at this hour, American and coalition forces are in the early stages of military operations to disarm Iraq, to free its people and to defend the world from grave danger....

Voice of Tony Blair: *"...it concludes that Iraq has chemical and biological weapons, which could be activated within 45 minutes..."*

UN inspectors don't find a trace of the famous weapons. Yet here a well-known French personality asserts that they did, and quotes a newspaper. "The only wish of the people in Baghdad is to be protected by Americans and Britons. Bush senior liberated Kuwait, Bush junior liberates Iraq. Someday the oldest street in Baghdad shall be named after him." Who said all Frenchmen were traitors?

March 20. The bombing of Baghdad.

A people's representative addresses the Americans. Not very smart.

Pierre Lellouche: *"The flood of anti-Americanism in which this country is swimming these days is incredible....We are on the verge of the canonization of Saddam Hussein!"*

Not smart, but mainly not true. These youngsters don't canonize anyone, they'd rather demonize everybody. With a peculiar dislike for President Bush perhaps, but in this they won't remain lonely for long. They think globally, and their slogan is: to each his own.

SUBTITLES

Bush has Iraq
Chirac: Ivory Coast
Putin: Chechnya
and Sharon: Palestine…
They want a worldwide war
Let's have a worldwide wrath

The pattern of these demos is as multifaceted as a Rubik's cube. A group deliberately aligns Israel in the war camp, and a few yards away you meet the supporters of the "Jews for peace" movement. You hear that young Jews have been attacked by rabid anti-Zionists, yet you see here and there the badge to fight anti-Semitism. Why should the streets of Paris be less chaotic than the rest of the world?

"Are you filming us?" says the cop.
"Of course not!" say I.
Almost no lying…

But my main reason to be here has nothing to do with the intricacies of world politics. Since his coup on election day, everybody wonders when the Cat will strike again.

So I wander from demo to demo with a single question:

Where are the Cats?

Where are the Cats?

Where are the Cats?

One more time…and I don't finish my question.

SUBTITLES

MAKE CATS NOT WAR

Bush: *"Any outlaw regime that has ties to terrorist groups and seeks or possesses weapons of mass destruction is a grave danger to the civilized world.…We've begun the search for hidden chemical and biological weapons, and already know of hundreds of sites that will be investigated."*

And yet—no Weapons of Mass Destruction. The correspondent of Skynews beautifully phrases the question.

"They haven't been deployed. They haven't been discovered. Will this war make history by being ended before you found its cause?"

UNESCO had warned against the risks of plundering in the Baghdad museums.

On April 11, the archeological museum was plundered.

If someday I had the opportunity to plunder the Louvre,…

I know damn well what I would pick.

A visit to the Street Museum.

At the end of my stroll, I happen to be back where we started, where the people used to open and close their umbrellas—that debatable golden pot in front of which I did show you the first Cat. What is the Cat up to by now? After his triumph in the demos, he seems just bound to relax, or fly.

But his reputation keeps growing.

He is sighted everywhere.

Except that sometimes the French language plays tricks. For "cat" we say "chat": c.h.a.t.—which means that when you look for cats on the Web, you have to get rid of all the *chatting* sites.

But one thing is for sure: with all that glory, the Parisian street has ceased to interest him.

SUBTITLES

SEE YOU SOON

On the Parisian street by now, you can hear the backlash of the unkept promises. The new prime minister, Mr. Raffarin, may learn that he's finished—in stronger terms. We had left Mr. Raffarin in the euphoria of the 2002 victory. Let's remember what he said that night...

SUBTITLES

Does the Republic
always keep its promises?
Where is Liberty nowadays?
Where is Fraternity in the neighborhoods?
People want to share that Republic
and new ways of governing are needed
to be closer to the people
and more efficient...
Politics may become powerless
So tonight we're happy
for this republican upsurge
but we have been challenged
so we have to draw some lessons
and change our politics...

Fine. But one year later, *nothing* has changed.

Rhythm is what keeps the demos running. This one was born during the Vietnam years. Johnson then was the target. Then we heard it in May 1968. And today again, adapted to a new mood. Don't forget what the Spanish Republicans used to say after they were crushed by Franco: "*We had the best songs.*"

The crowd here chants a call for a General Strike—something totally unrealistic in this time and place. But that kind of political jujucraft has a tremendous appeal; it goes back in history and evokes the great ancestors, the heroic strikers as we used to watch them in Eisenstein's movies. One more step, and we're in 1936, the Popular Front...There we shift from unrealist to surrealist. Who could believe that the loudest demonstrators, those who boldly sing the Internationale, are the members of a union, the FO, created in 1948, at the outset of the Cold War, with American money, to challenge the Communist-controlled CGT? The times, they're a-changing.

SUBTITLES

Raffarin you haven't won
We're not tired
We're resolute

June 1. A "*die-in*" for the victims of AIDS:

SUBTITLES

We're angry at the leaders
who may spend 200 billion
to wage war in Iraq
and can't find ten billion
to fight AIDS

In these times, we the people gathered to watch eleven billionaires kicking a ball.

What about the French team?

Stalinesque-sized posters, as we had never seen the like of in Paris —and not one goal recorded.

A tiny concert, to remember the people who die in the street...

Some demonstrators are more equal than others. When they themselves belong to show business, like the casual workers who complain about their status, they have a better chance to attract attention than, say, garbage men. They too crave for historical models. Somebody's got the brilliant idea to unearth a song composed during the German occupation, and by changing names, adapt it to poor Mr. Raffarin. There is a lot to deliver about the prime minister's deficiencies, but comparing him to Marshall Pétain is, shall we say, far-fetched....It's a great asset in life, not to know what you're talking about.

Komandantur, really...

Anyway, causes are a matter of fashion. In summer the cause of the showbiz temporary workers had been fashionable; in autumn the Islamic scarf would have its say.

SUBTITLES

O beloved France
Where is thy Freedom?

You trustworthy people
respect our differences!

Don't forget: for the journalists
the spokesperson is Wahiba!

Thank you gals.

But when the Tibetans made a *pray-in* to protest the visit of the Chinese premier, nobody winked.

Oops! Seems that someone goofed in the sound department. Let's get the right track. And when I say right...

SUBTITLES

No to Unions' dictatorship

Next chapter: Raffarin's revenge.

SUBTITLES

Hold on, Raffarin!

A curious moment. I catch a piece of dialogue: "This government is a mess." Some supporters. This looks even more tricky than in the other camp. Let's try to locate ideology.

Ah, there it is.

SUBTITLES

Striker, you're a pain in the ass!

Once more, the reference to the past accompanies a certain fuzziness in the symbols. These conservative youngsters picked their logo in a famous wartime poem, "Liberty I write thy name," whose author was Paul Eluard, a communist, who would be surprised to side with the strikebreakers. Their leader aims at being the rightist counterpart of peasant leader José Bové.

Bové periodically goes to jail, and periodically there is a demo to ask for his release. I browse through these faces, until I recognize a friend. Léon Schwartzenberg, celebrated physician and activist, who ranks regularly among France's most-beloved personalities. While sick and not too young, he is there to support his friend. And it is also the last time I see him.

SUBTITLES

Professor Schwartzenberg was 79
He passed away this morning
He will be buried this Friday
at the Cimetière Montparnasse

Through his whole life, Léon sided with the underdogs. A famous battle was in favor of immigrants, specially those who fall victims of inextricable red tape, the "paperless."

SUBTITLES

We have lost a friend
The warm-hearted professor
So long Léon
We loved you

In 1999 there had been a concert in favor of the "paperless." I happened to be there, and filmed a young singer who was also a sort of counterculture icon, Bertrand Cantat.

Five years later, when he reappears in this movie, he has become the main character of a tragedy. He was madly in love with actress Marie Trintignant. Then one day he was madly angry at her, he struck her, and she died.

There were hideous attacks ("we told you these radicals are murderers"), there were lame defenses, yet he was indefensible, and yet he would have to carry this burden during his whole life, and words were powerless. For a moment we forgot about other dramas. The war was going on, the misery of the world was going on. Perhaps there was a kind of bitter symbolism in the fact that those two years full of sound and fury had climaxed in the story of two star-crossed lovers.

And then, as usual, the tragedy turned to merchandise. A famous singer kills a famous actress, what a bounty for the scavengers. It has happened in Vilnius, Lithuania, a place nobody knows, which adds to the mystery. "The crime of Vilnius," that sounds better than Brighton. Over this quagmire, all I can do is to keep a small silent place for Marie and Bertrand, and through editing, for a flimsy moment, bring their faces together.

And you wonder why the Cats abandon us?

For months I haven't seen the
cat Bolero on his steps.

What if they left us for good?

"We were the Freedom Cats. If you didn't catch the message, just move on!"

And then—comes a sign.

The same unknown hand has painted
circles of Cats on the sidewalk,
to watch over our sleep.

Thank you, Cats.

We will badly need you…

…wherever we go.

"Legend has it that duke Gediminas, the founder of Vilnius, had a dream in which a wolf howled on a hill. A priest deciphered the dream: the duke must build a city whose name would be heard throughout the world, like the howling of the wolf."

(*Courrier International*, June 19, 2003)

The Case of the Grinning Cat

Video
Chris Marker

Voice
Gérard Rinaldi

In homage to
George Sanders
(1906–1972)

Soundtrack
Michel Krasna

Cats theme
Anton Arensky
(1861–1906)

Musical quotes
Giovanni Fusco
Jean-Claude Eloy

Mix
Florent Lavallée

Production
Les Films du Jeudi
Laurence Braunberger

In association with
Arte France
Thierry Farrel
Luciano Rigolini

With the involuntary
concourse of
Frederic Taddei
Akosh S.

Additional footage
Courtesy "Amis du Chat"

Still photography
J. F. Dars

No cat has been
impolitely treated
in this movie

This film is dedicated
to M. Chat
and those who, like him,
are creating
a new culture

They Stare

We exchanged looks, as one says,
but what did they get in exchange?
Sometimes a fraction of a second,
sometimes a long, serious look;
sometimes friendly, sometimes (rarely)
hostile; and me like a fast pickpocket
running away with my bounty, sure to
find a quiet place to unpack it at will,
and rejoice. And now all of 'em are
aligned on this wall like they're waiting
for the firing squad or the final Examiner
united as they will be on Judgment Day
supposing there will be one and God
won't be tired of all that brothers and
sisters at last though some of them
hated the guts of the guy next frame
the French cop and the Japanese
Trotskyite for instance the very last
generation of cops who still showed a
human face behind their goggles after
which they began to put on bubbles that
made them look like Martians and my
driver in Siberia who no doubt was a
stoolie next to Kurosawa who...

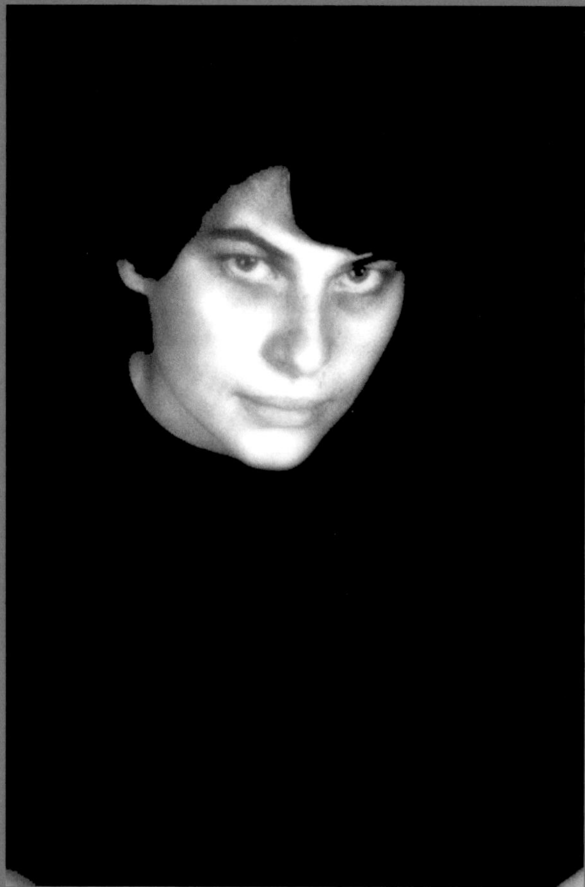

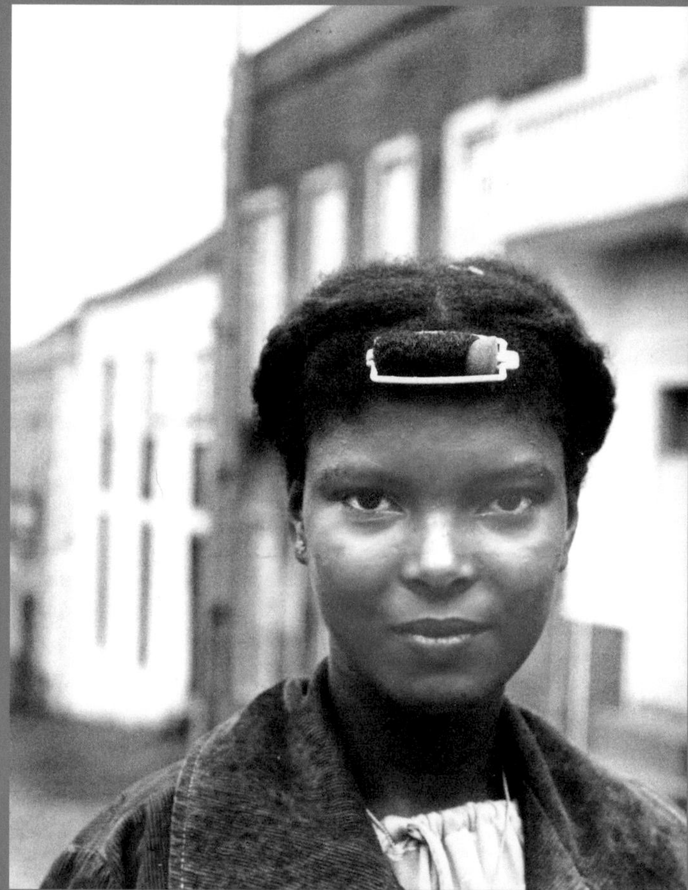

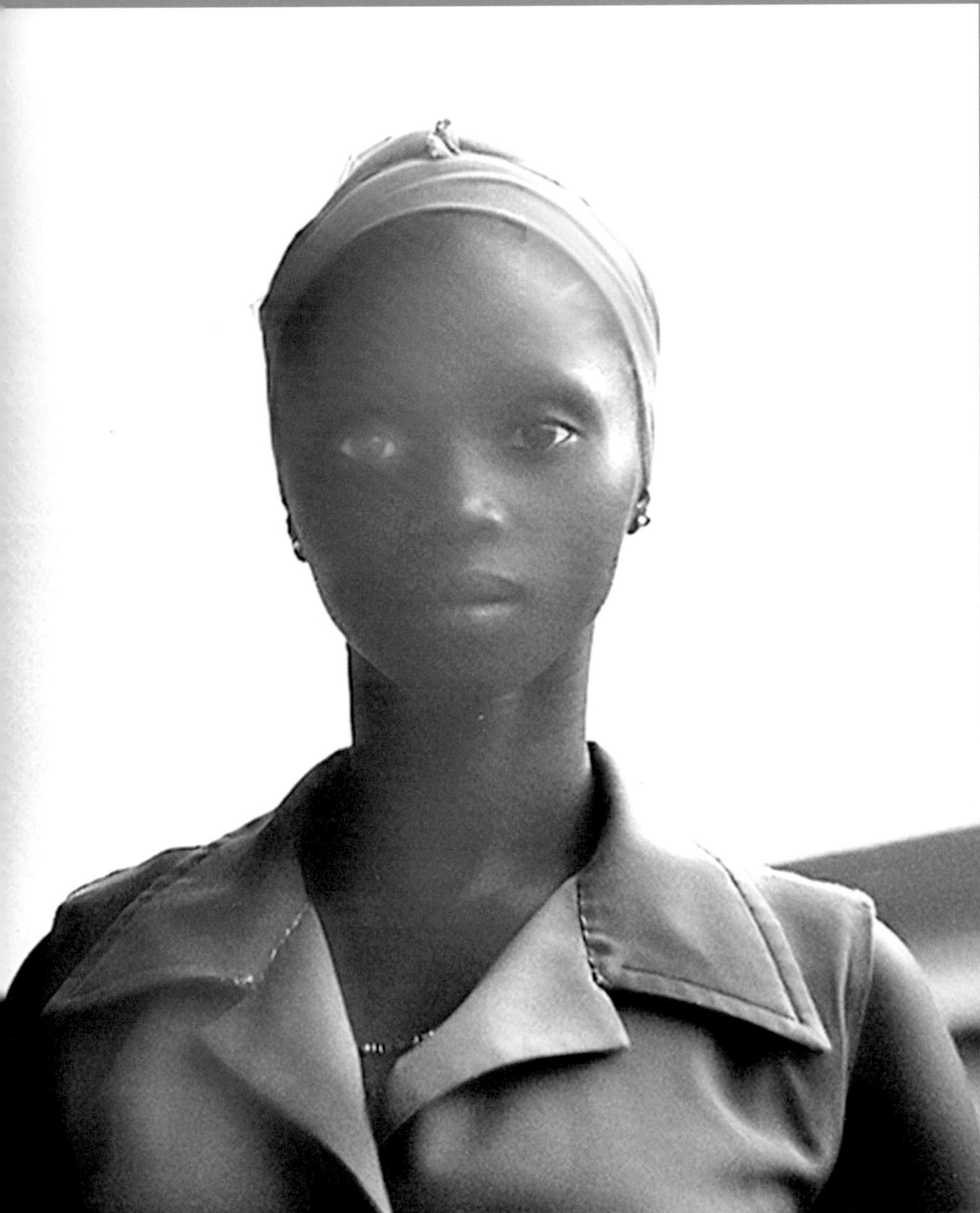

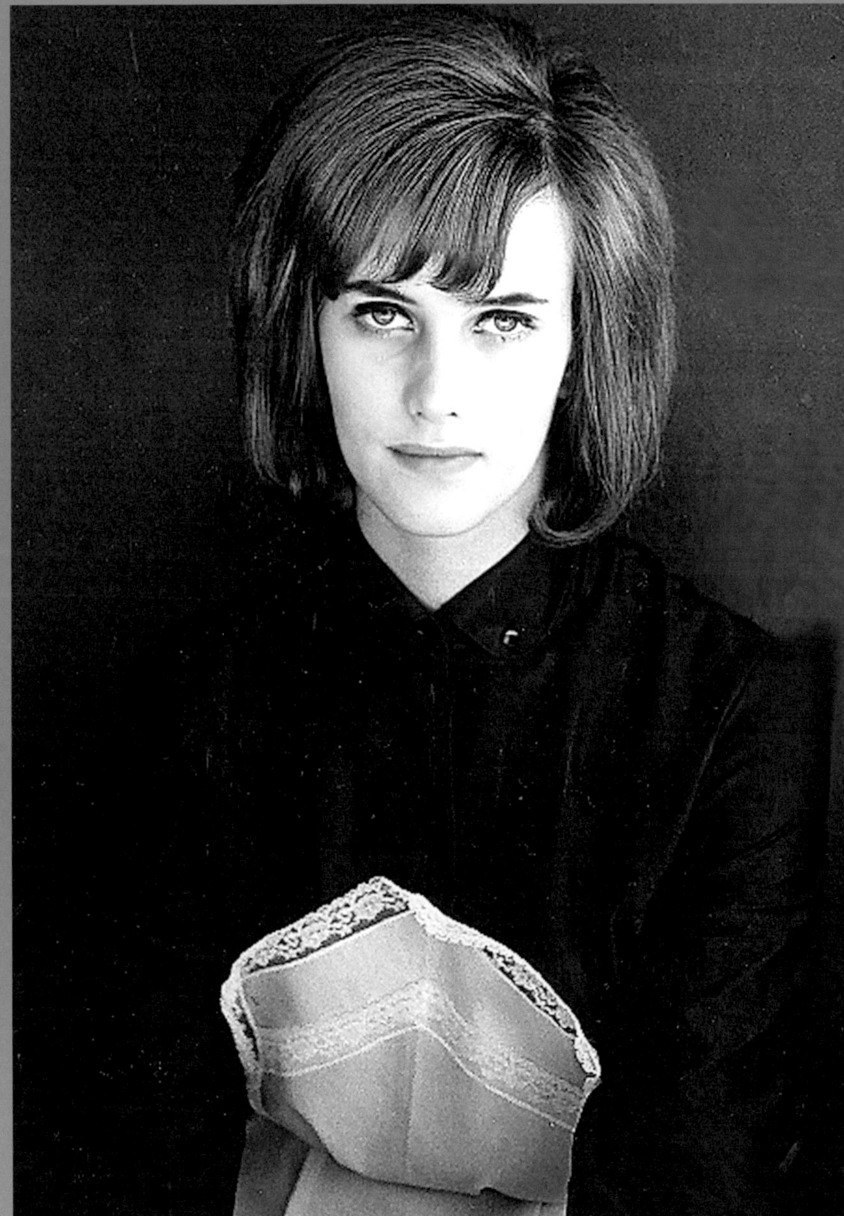

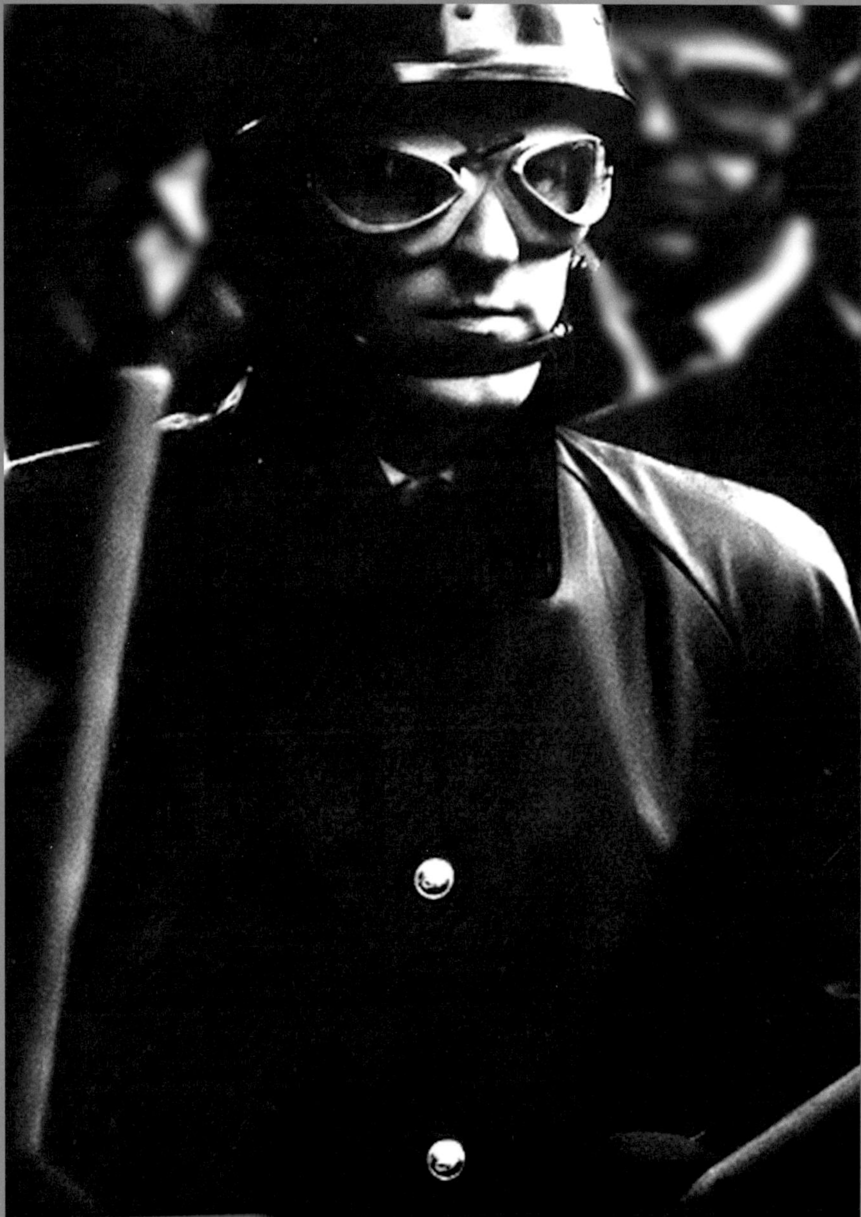

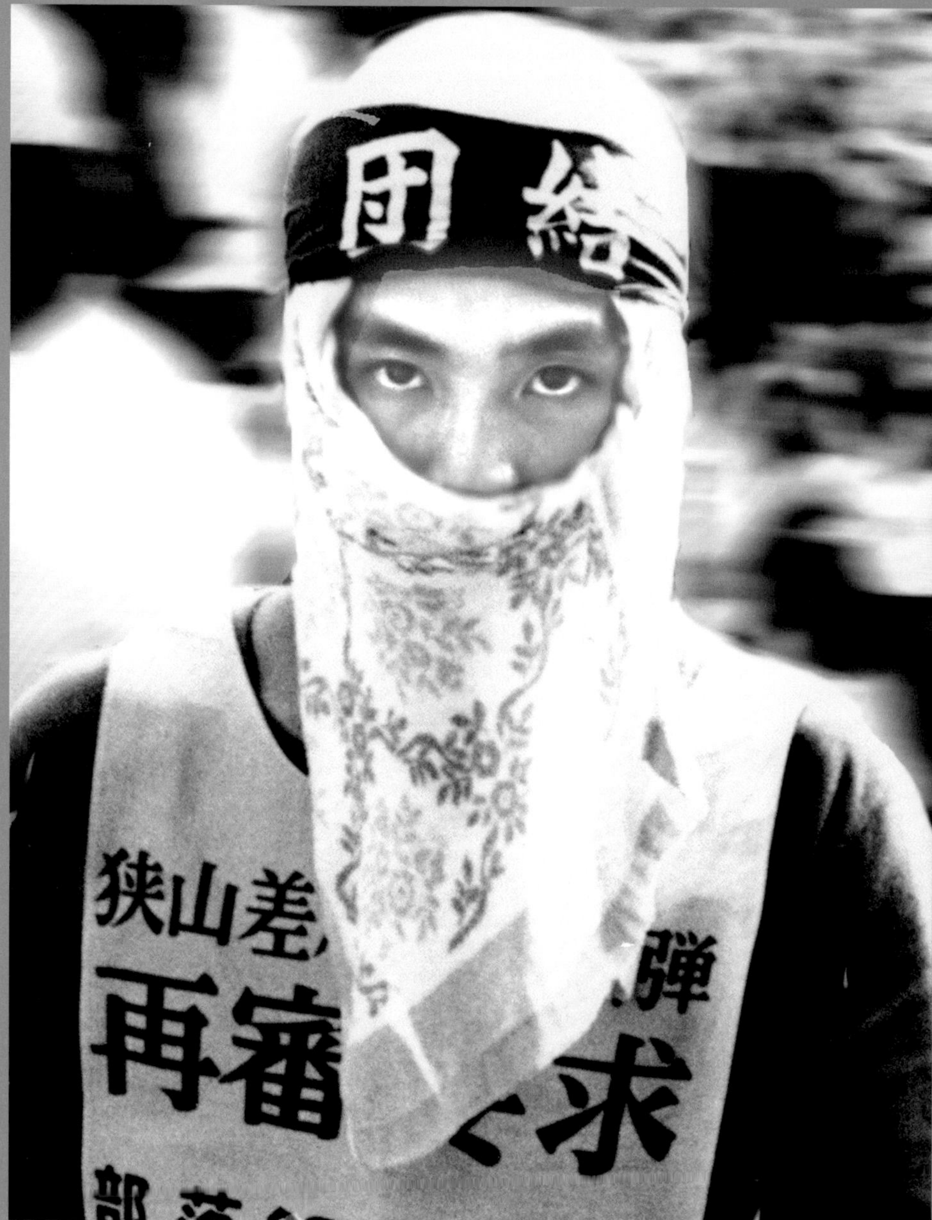
団結
狭山差
弾
再審
求

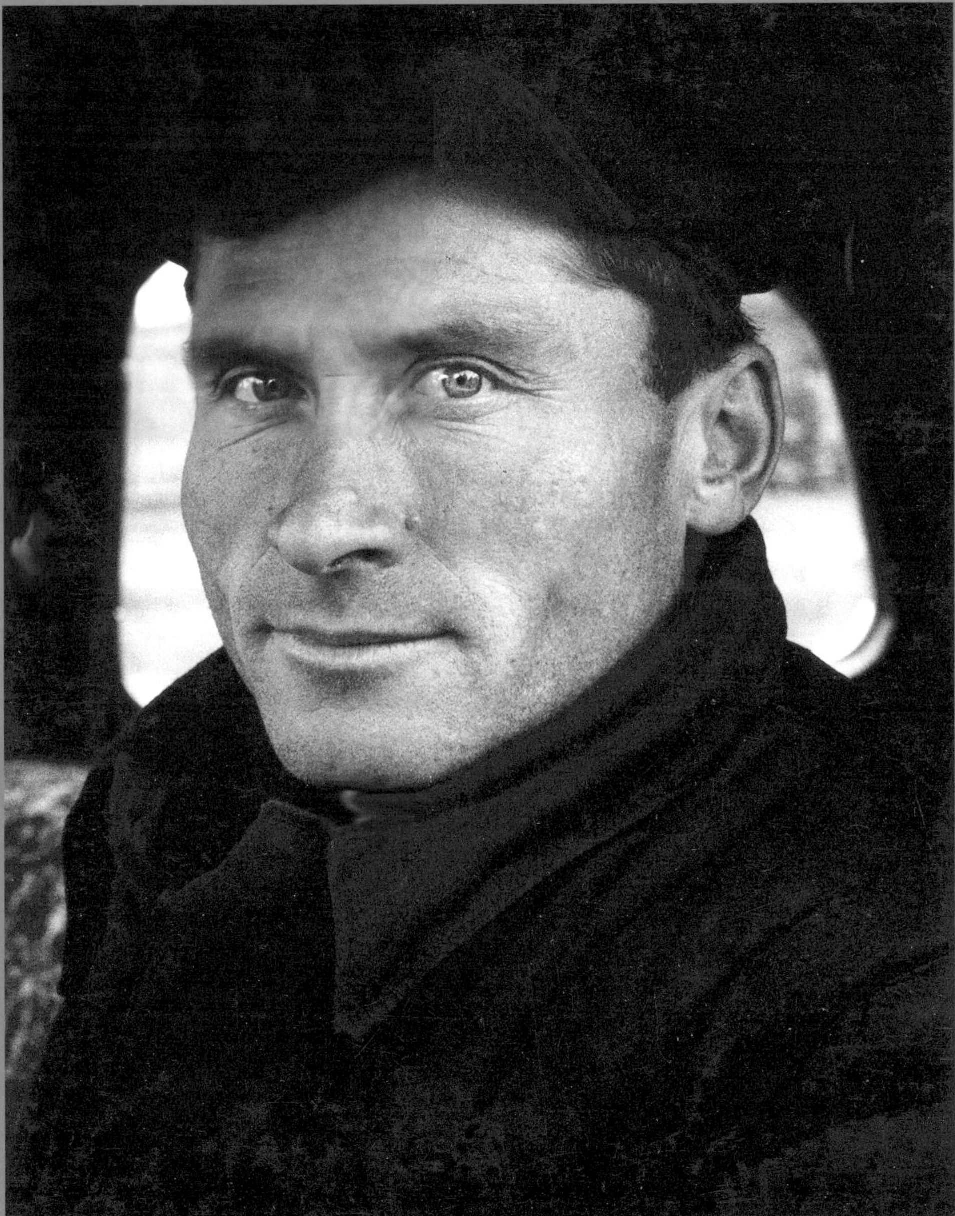

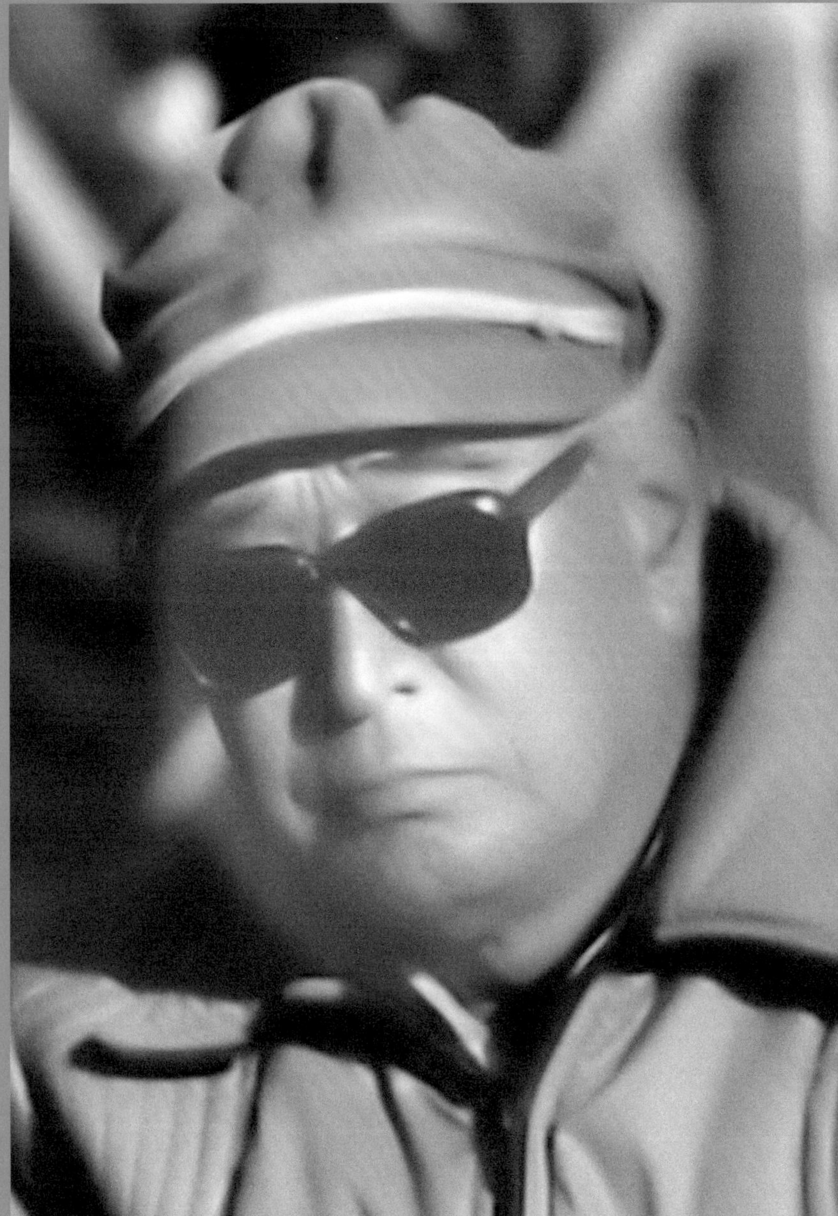

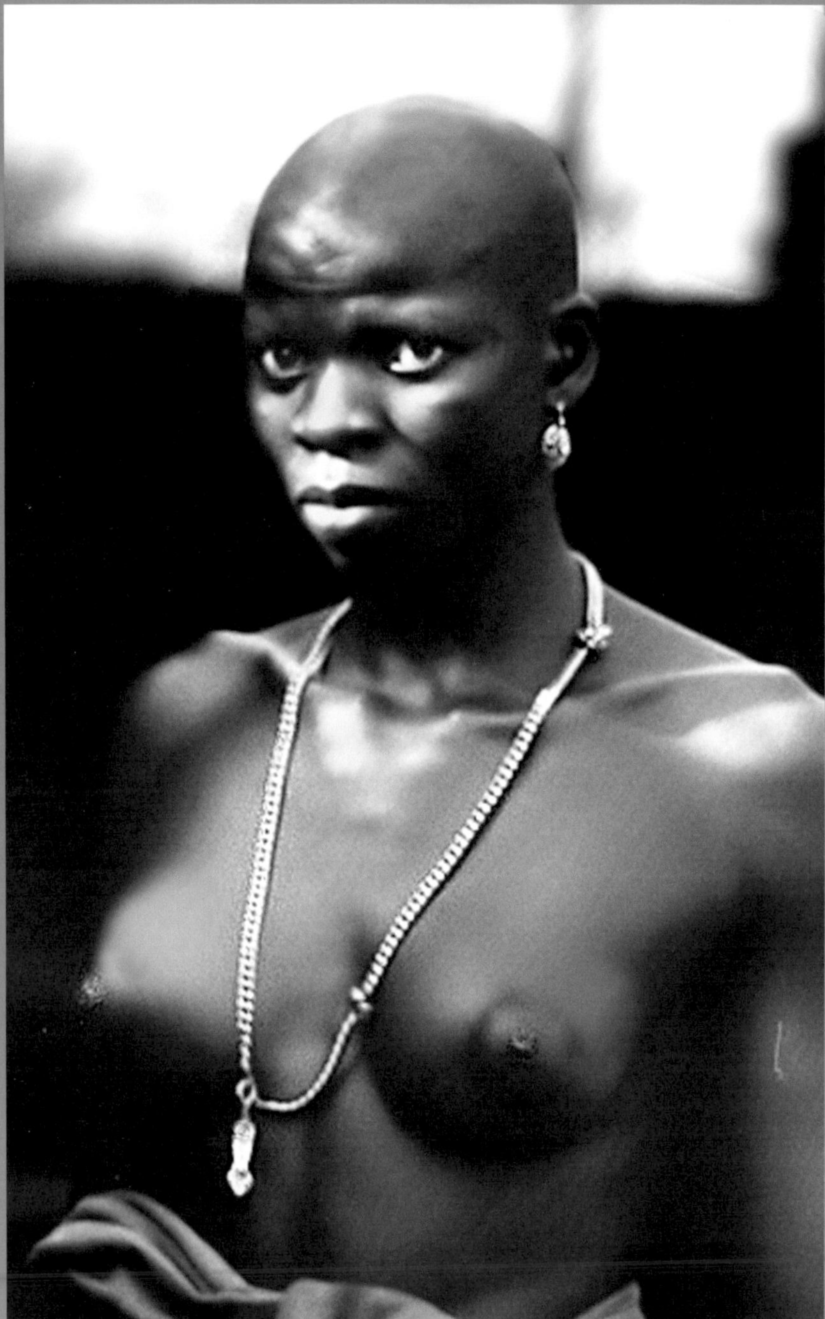

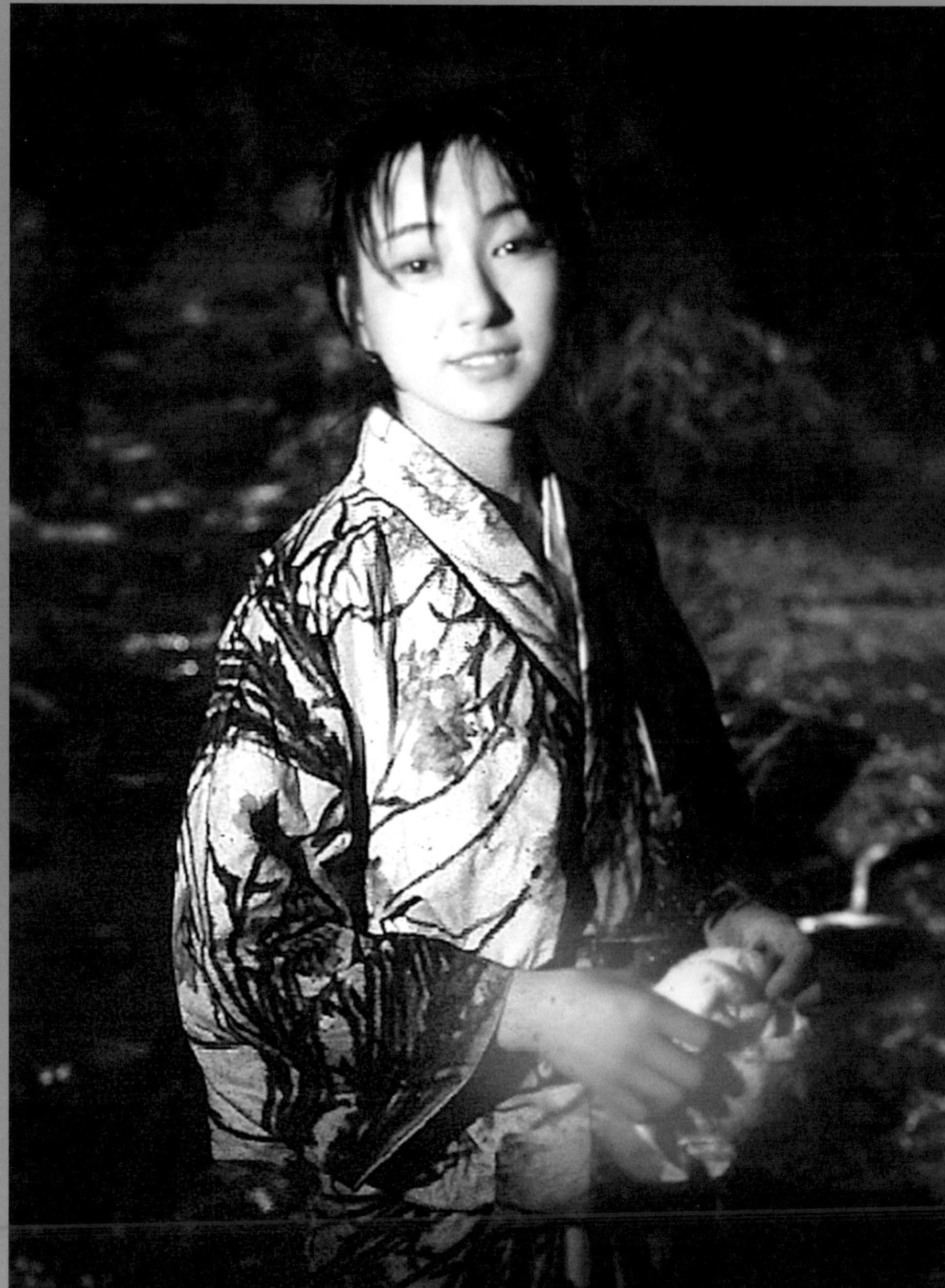

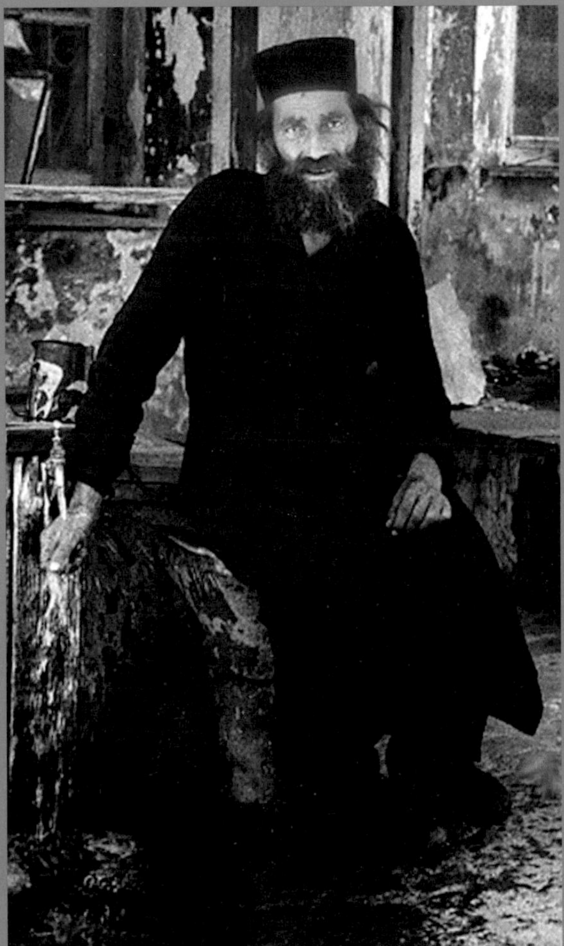

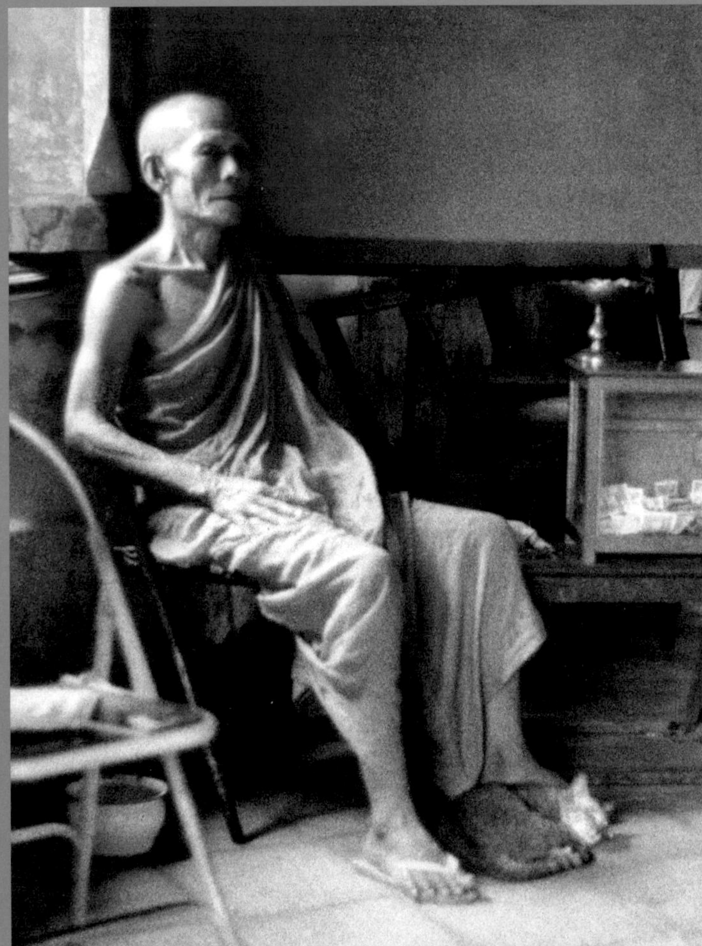

Acedia, the word monks invented to describe that state of utter dereliction. I caught it on Mount Athos and also in Canton with that boy thrown ashore by the wreckage of the Great Cultural Revolution....Perhaps in the look of the Mummy too, while I wonder what she should care about now. From that extreme to the beaming fashion model in Moscow we cross the whole palette. Sad women in Bissau don't smile; others do, yet their smile is the promise of a smile. Such are the young Mexican, the Parisian cover girl, the Japanese actress who specializes in *chambara*, these TV epics where everybody dies at the end, but her. The Siamese monk doesn't smile, neither does he know *acedia*. He, of all people, has something to live for. The proof is between his feet.

A cat.

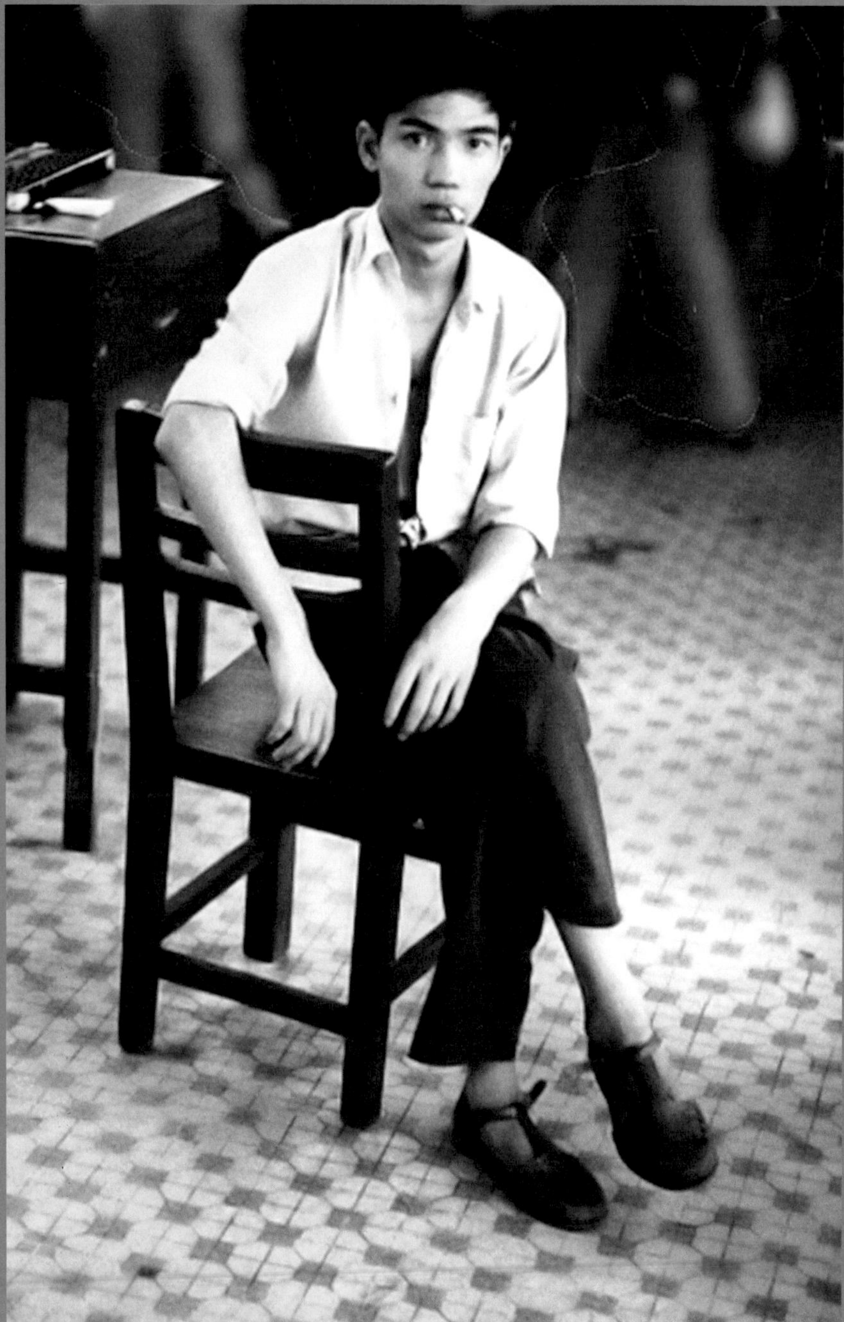

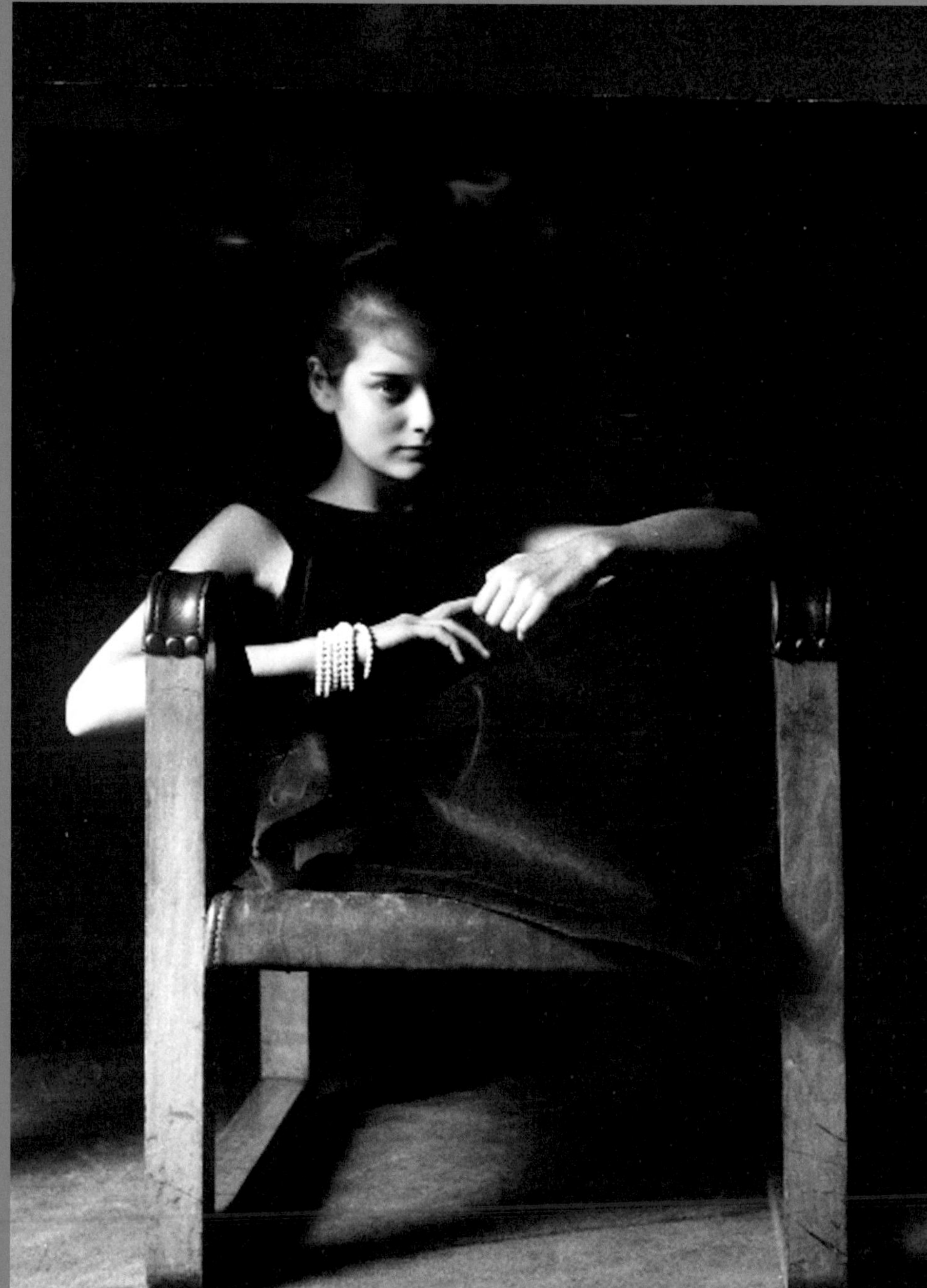

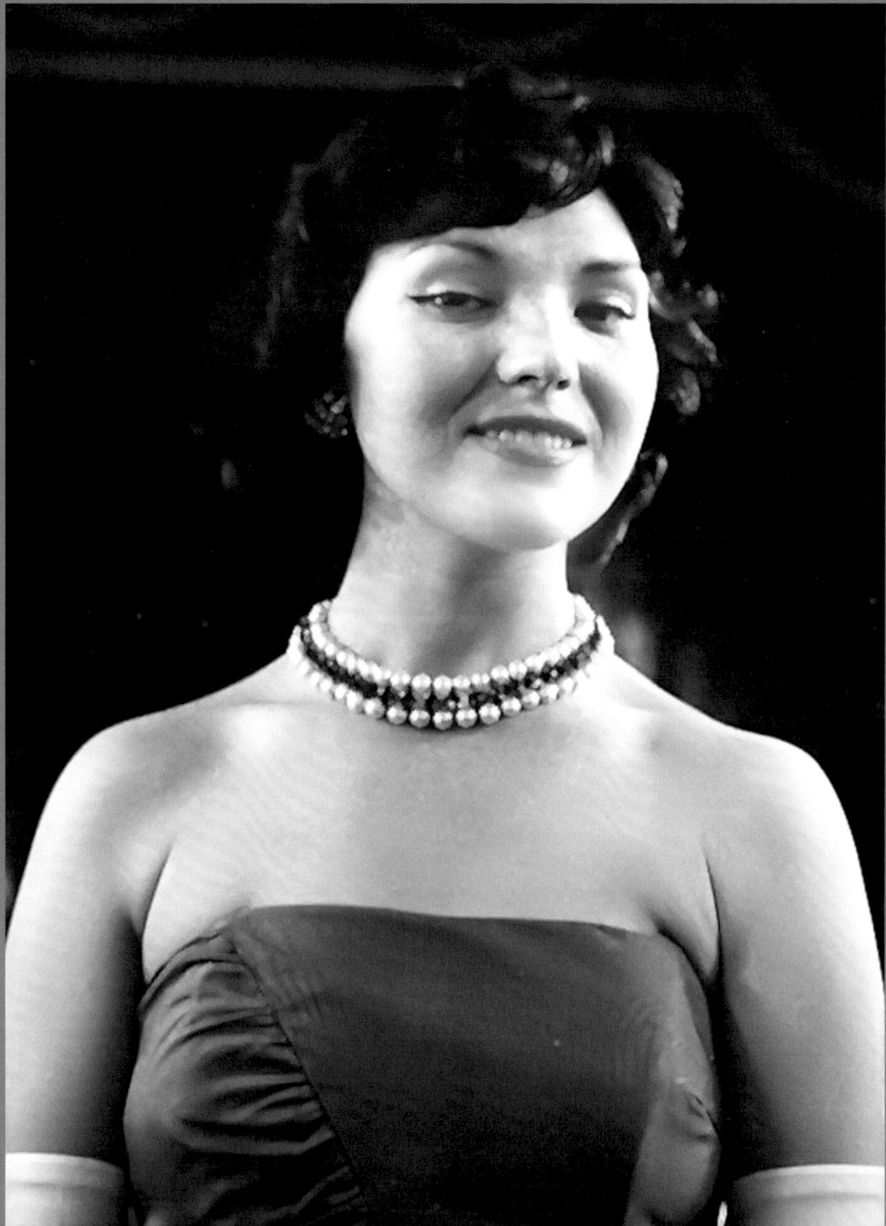

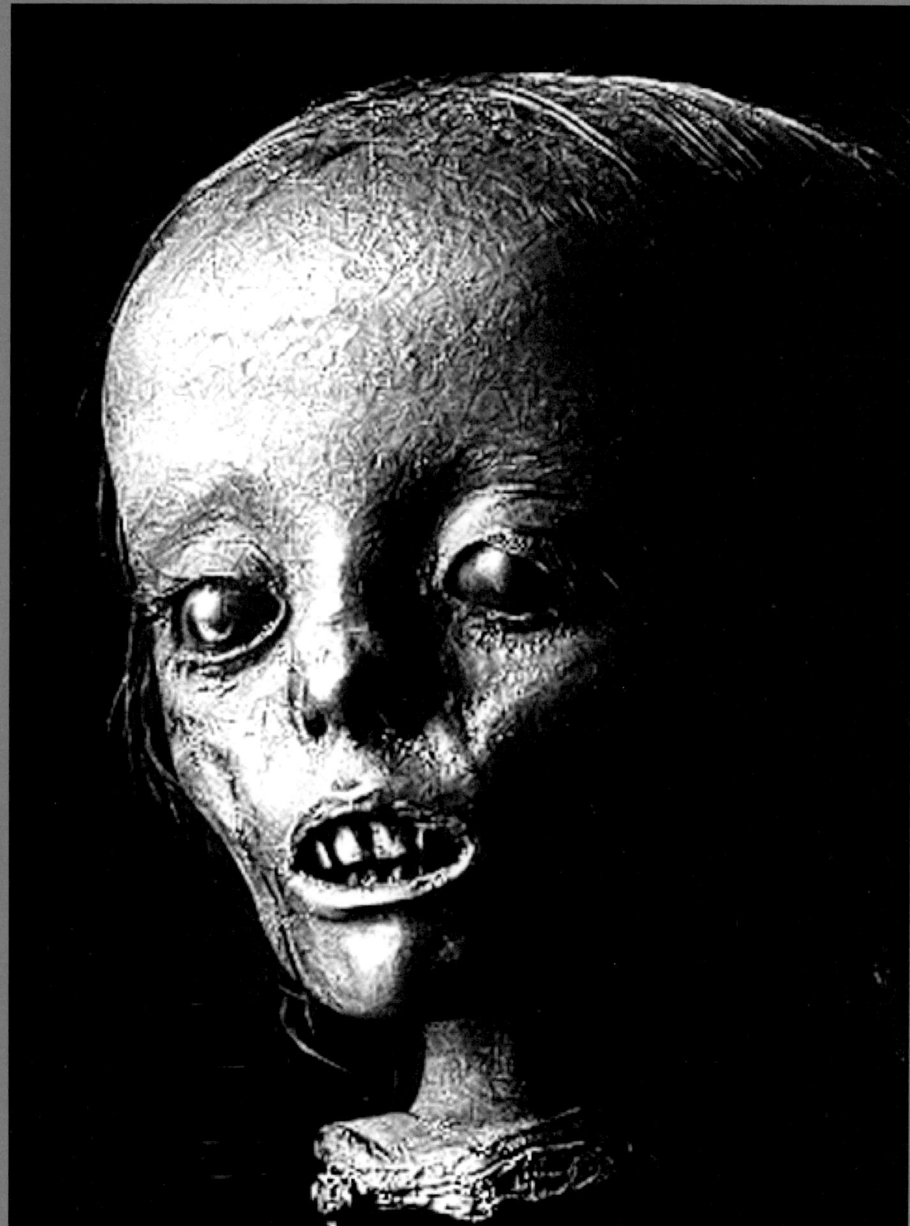

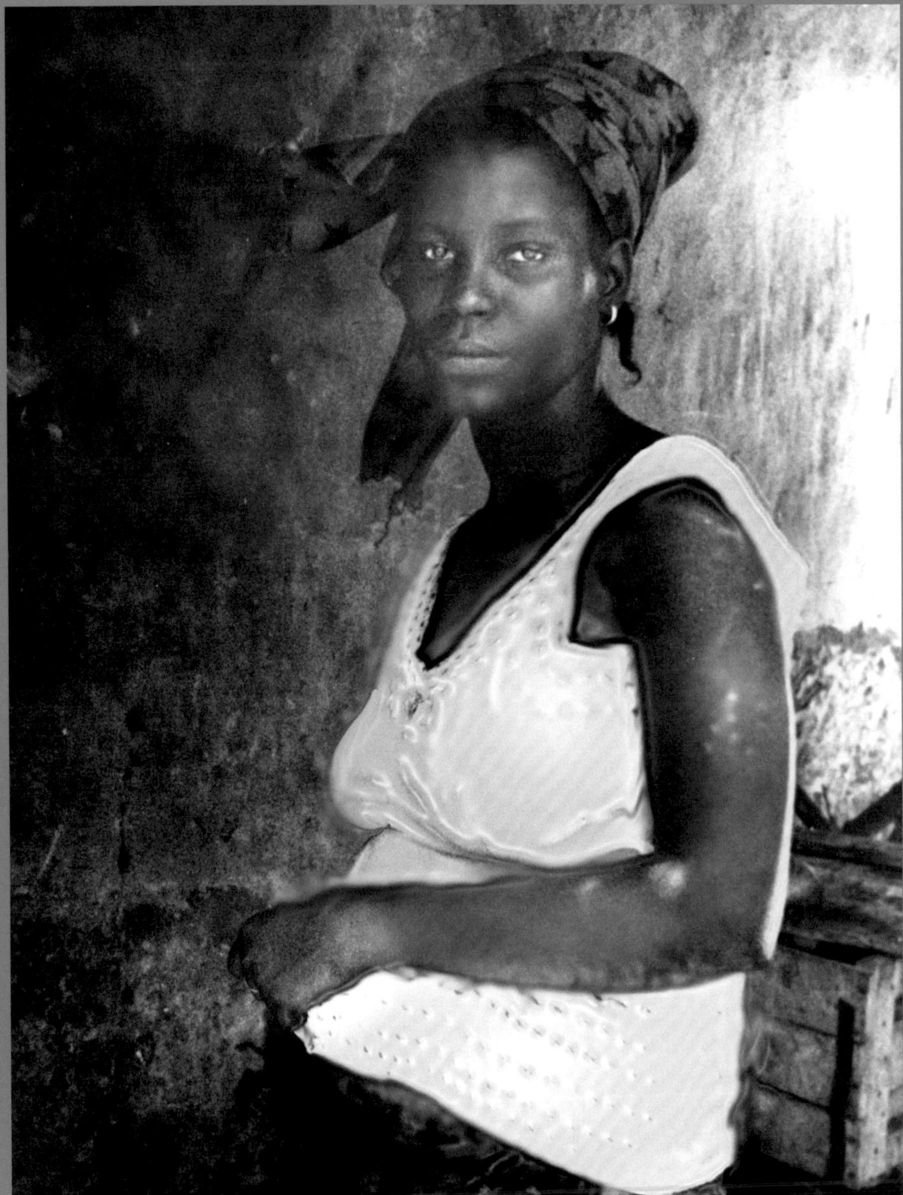

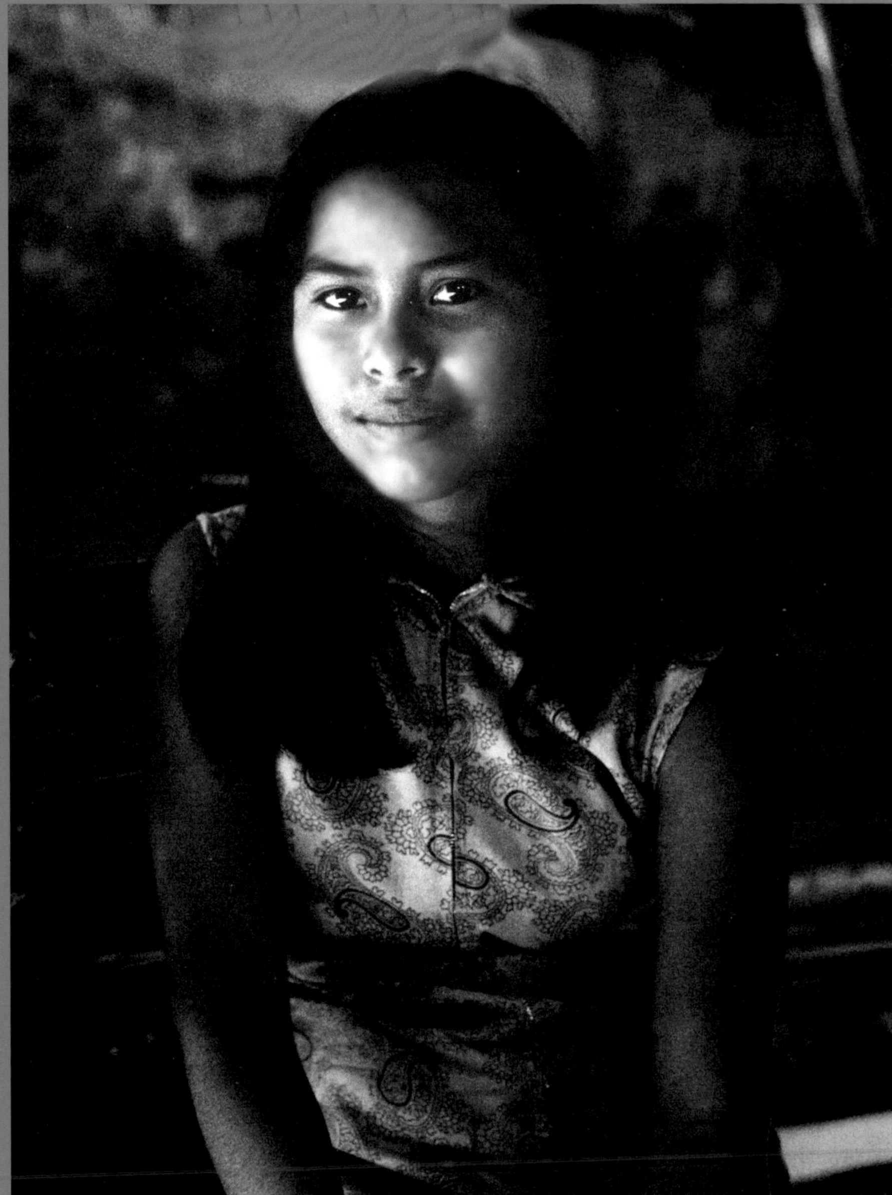

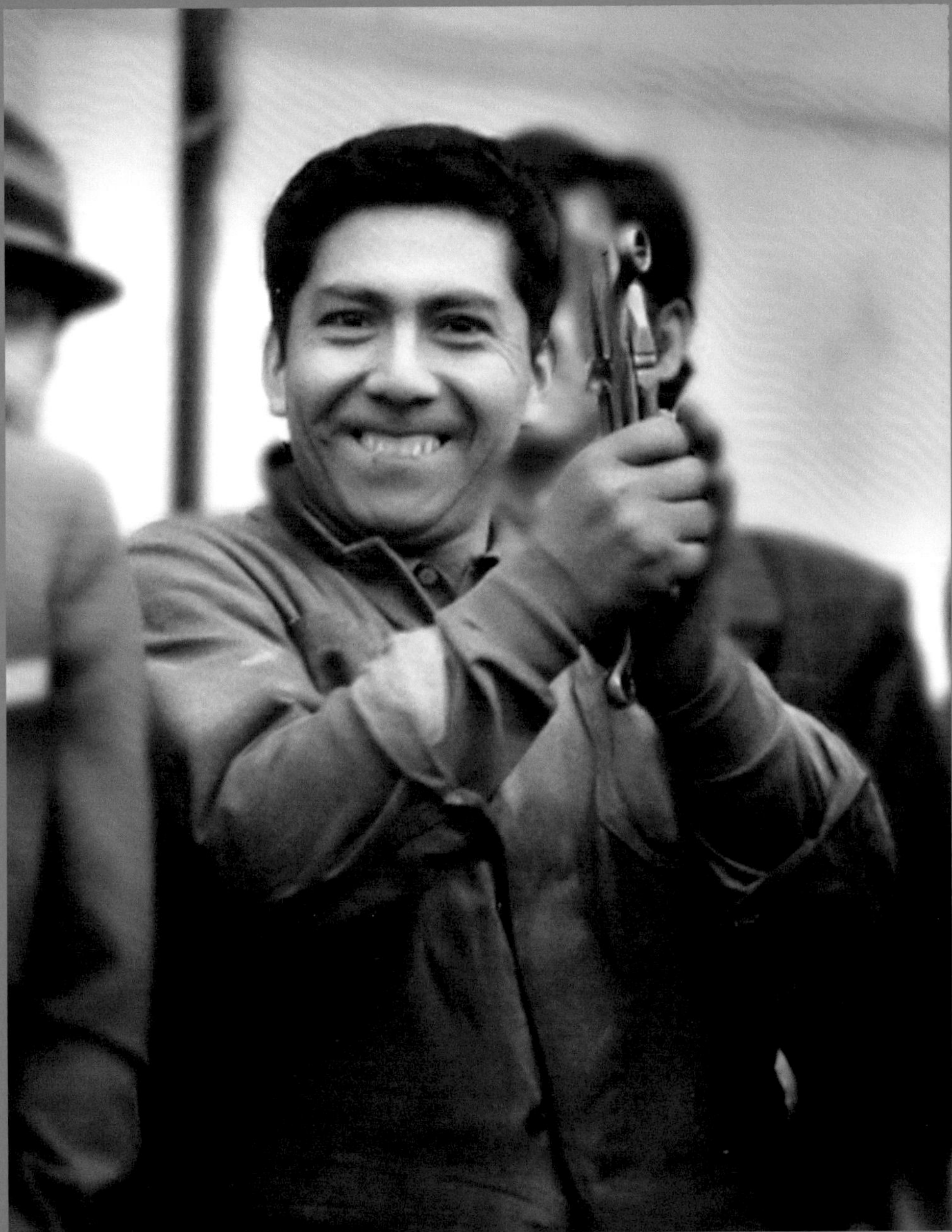

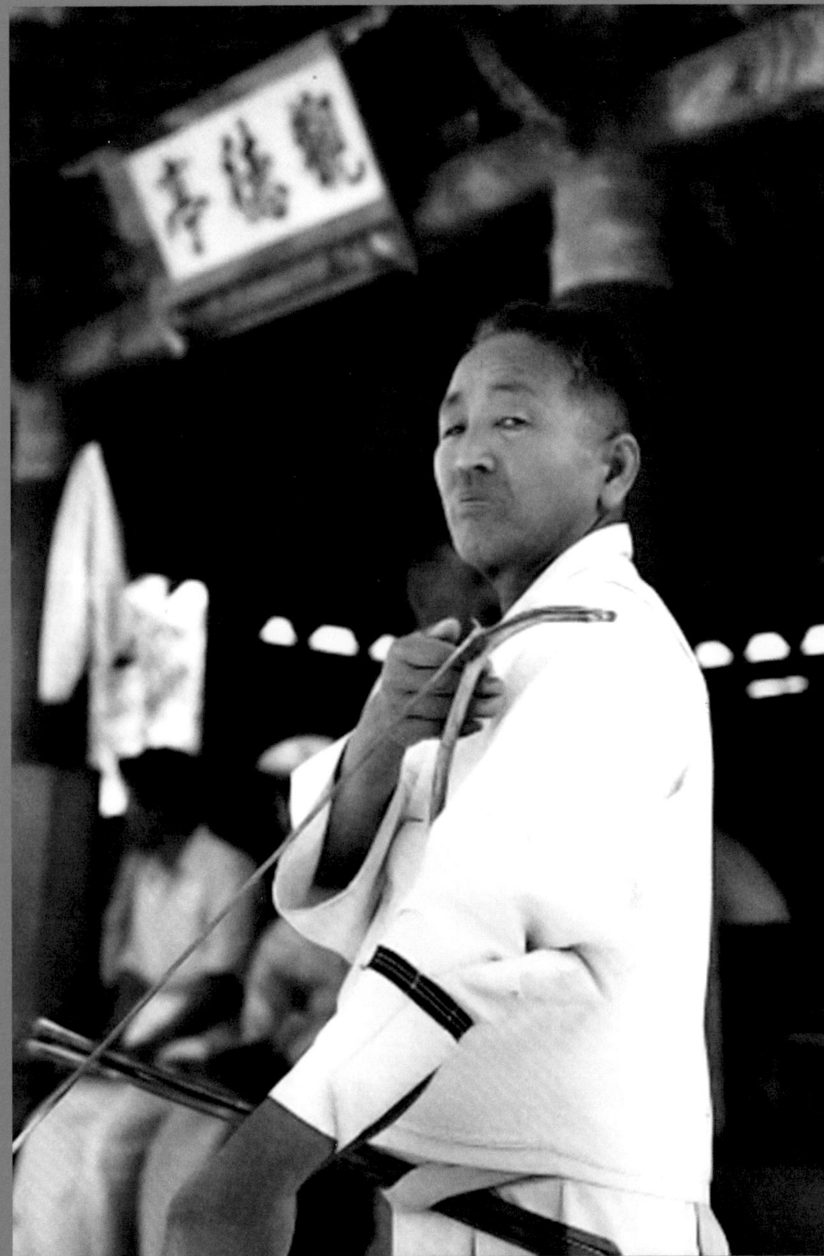
觀德亭

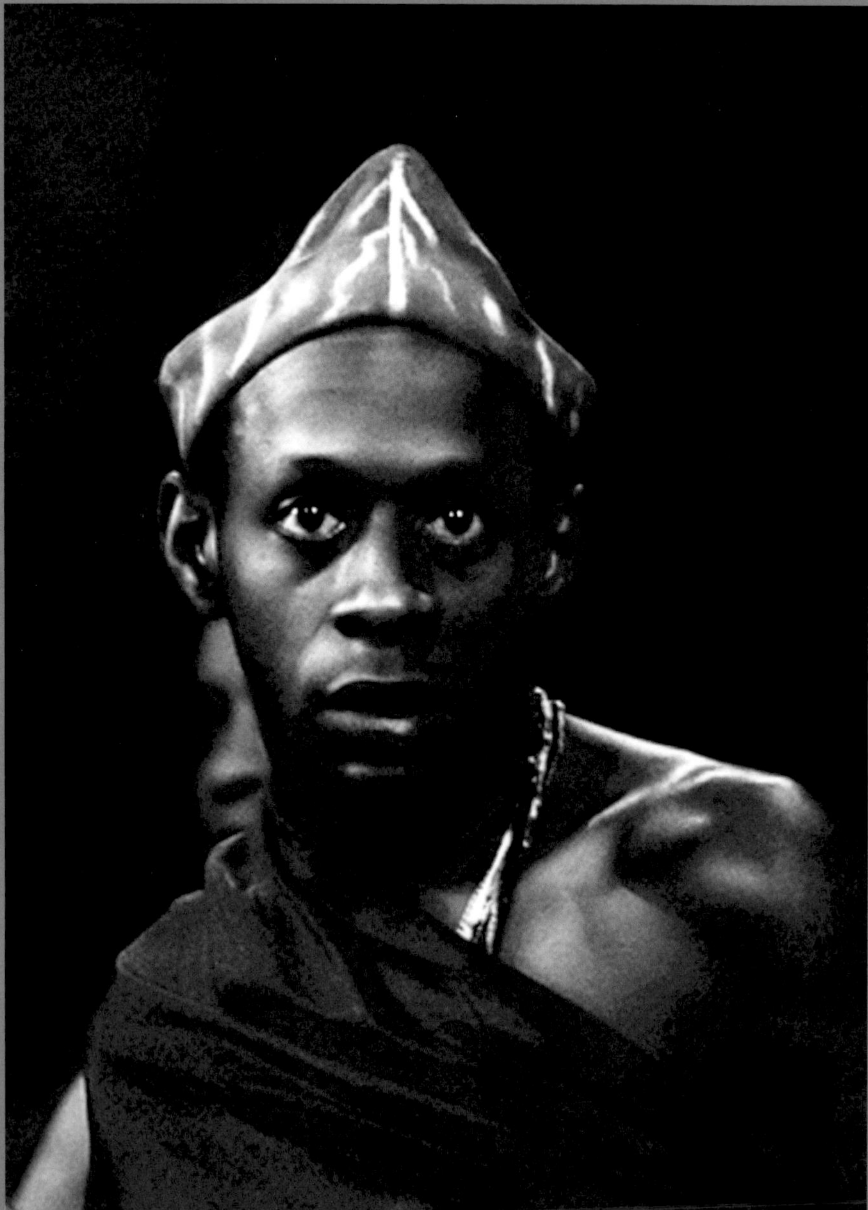

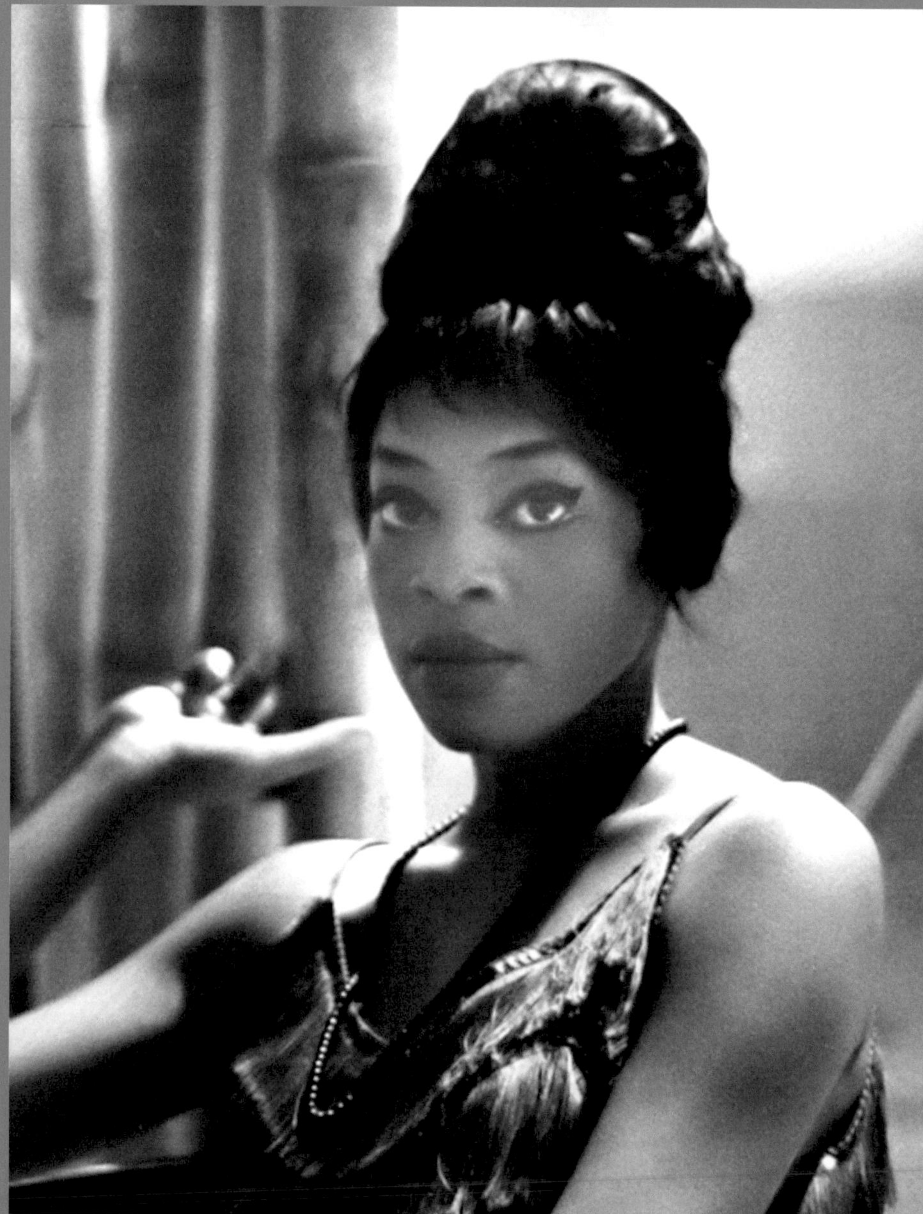

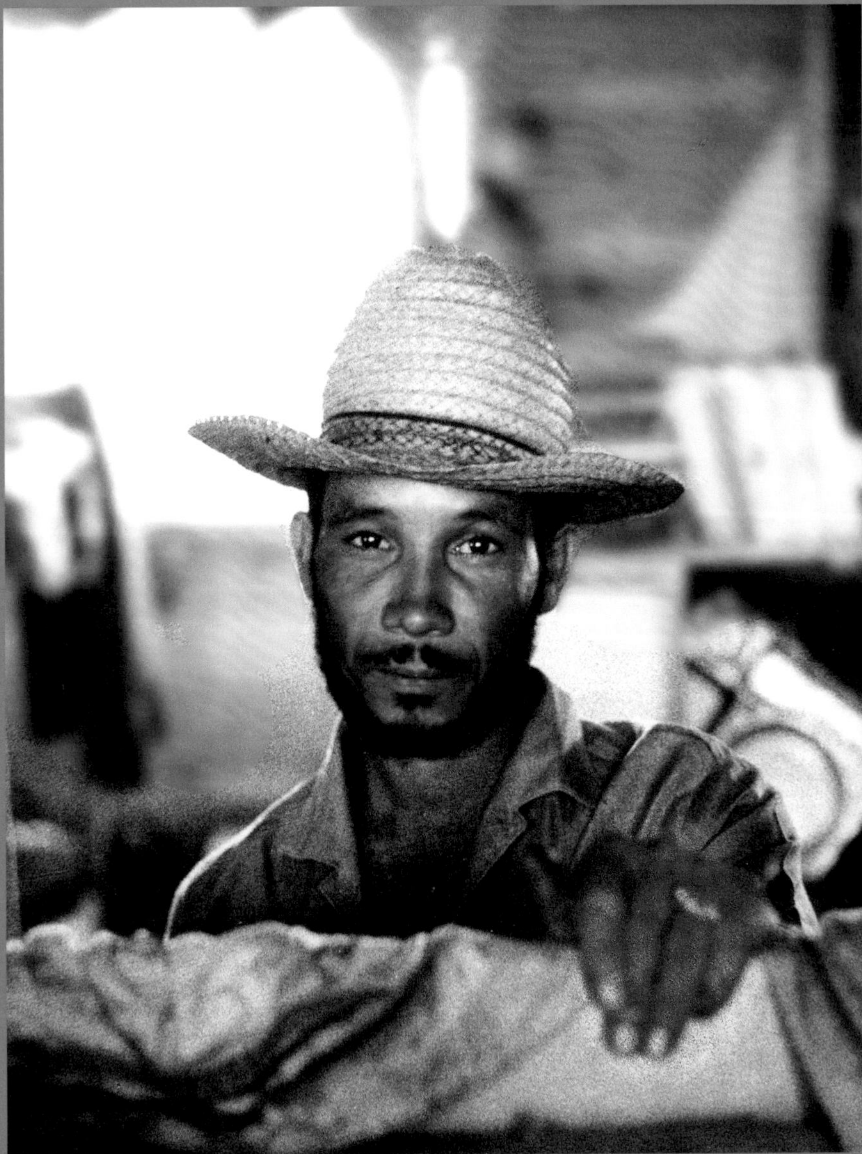

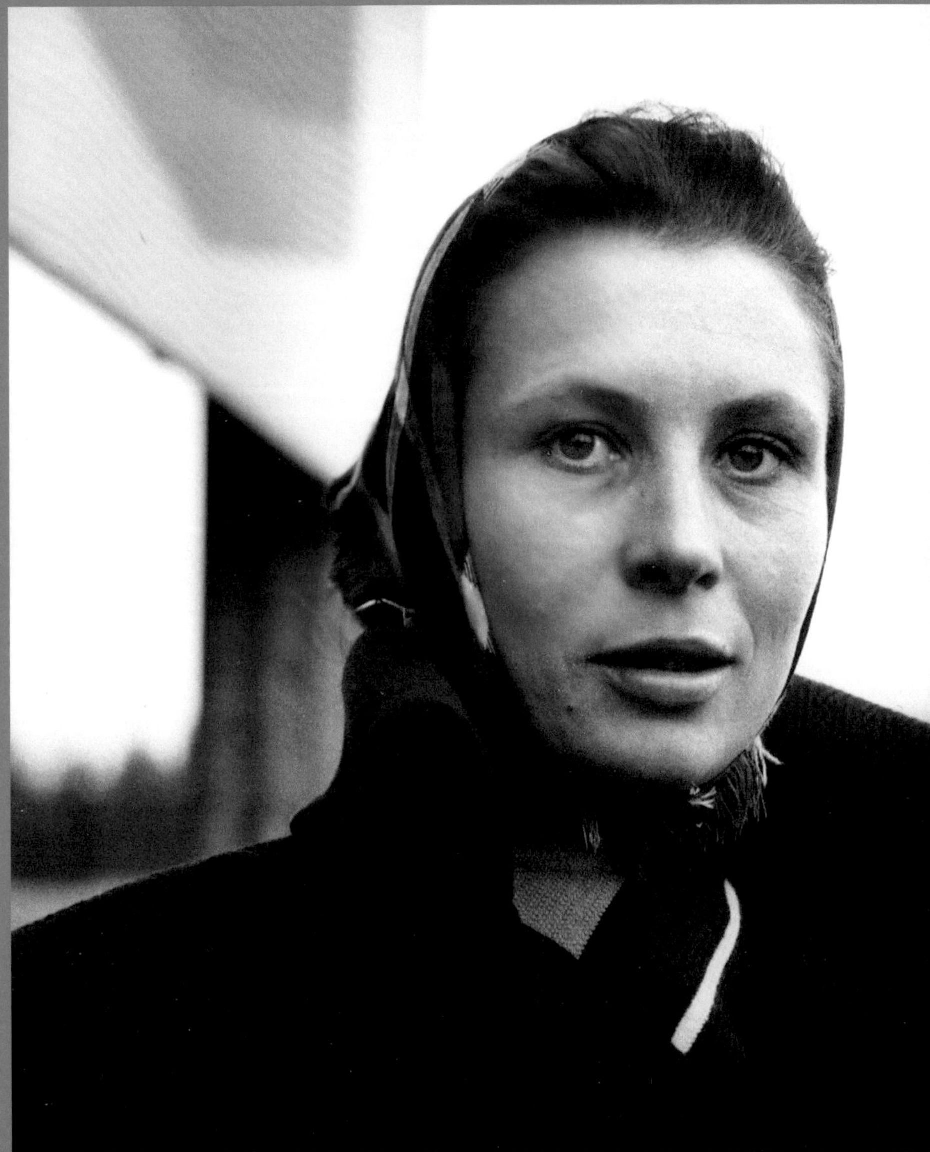

In this 1/50th of a second the Chilean worker under Allende knew that the nationalized factory now was his property, the Thai boxer on the canvas knew that he had lost, the Cuban cane-cutter knew he would meet the challenge of the Ten Million (they didn't), the German leftist knew her side had been severely beaten at the polls, the Korean bowman knew he was the best in his category, the three Chinese migrants knew that without the man they came to bury, their life would become harsher every day. In this malignant, undefinable world, the speed of the shutter stopped the rarest moment, a moment of certainty.

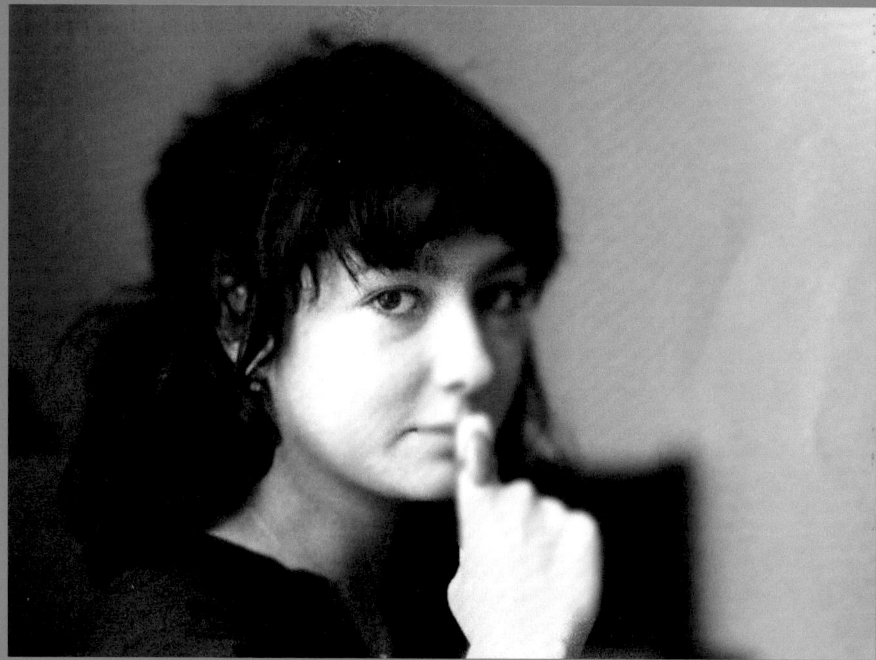

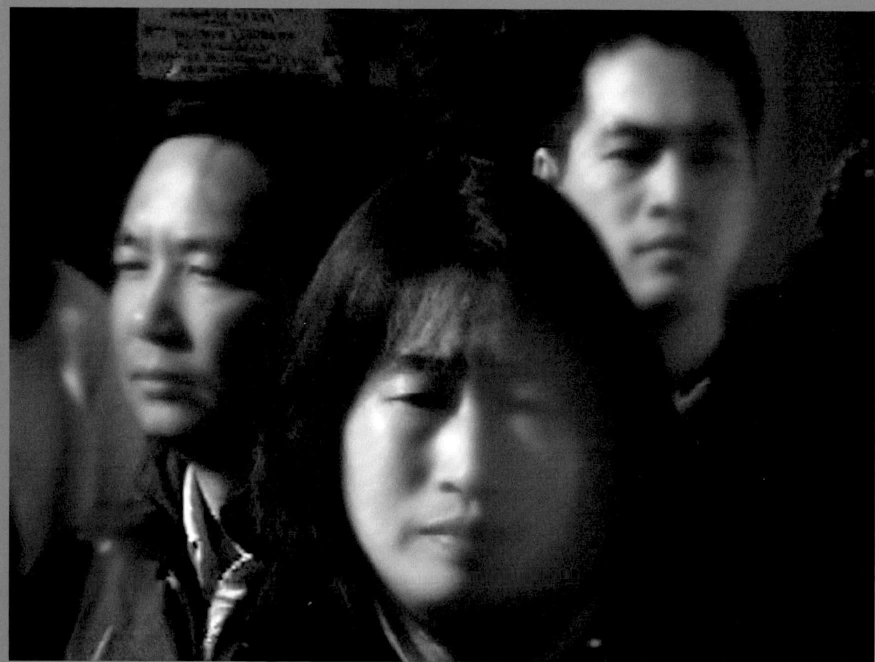

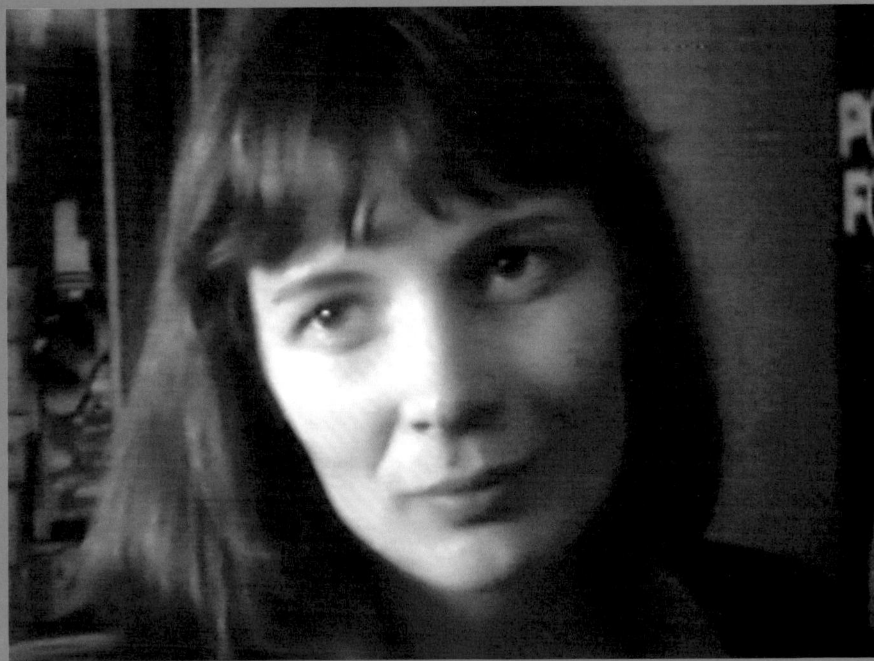

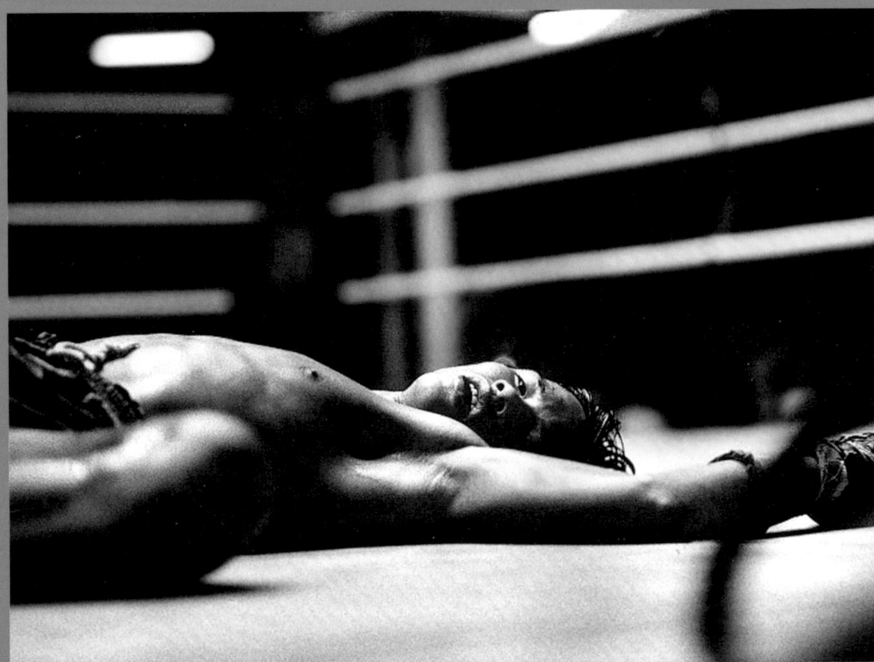

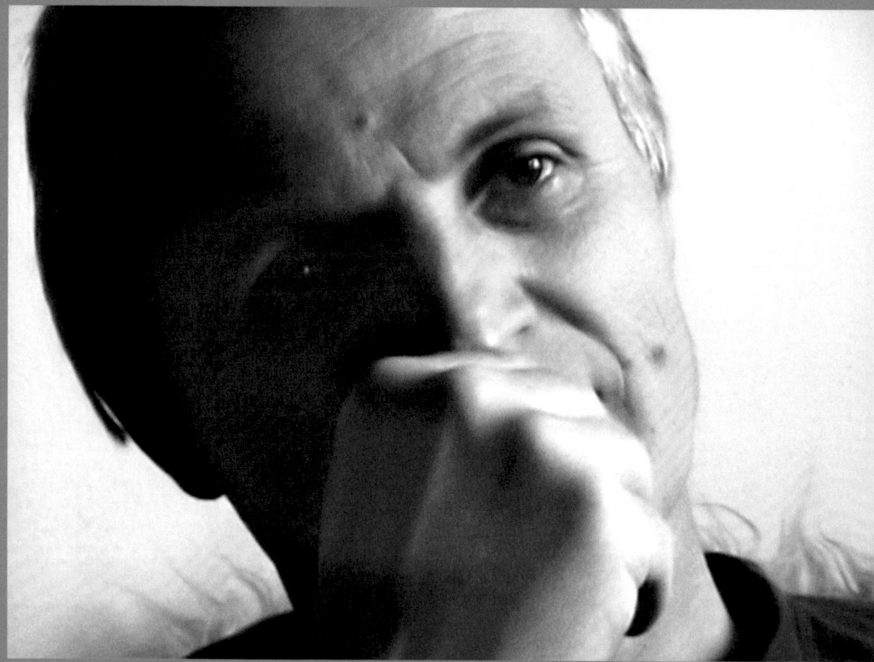

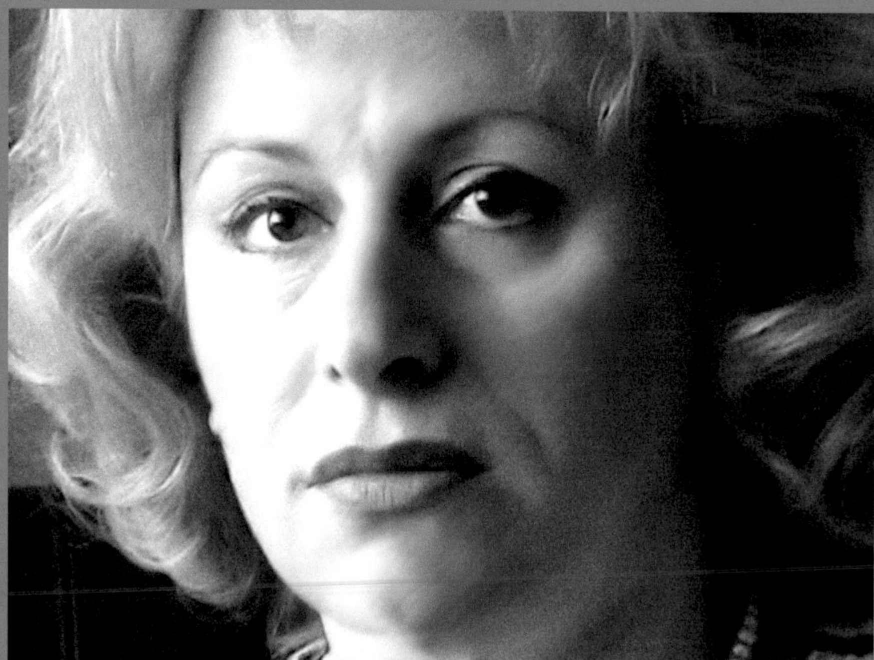

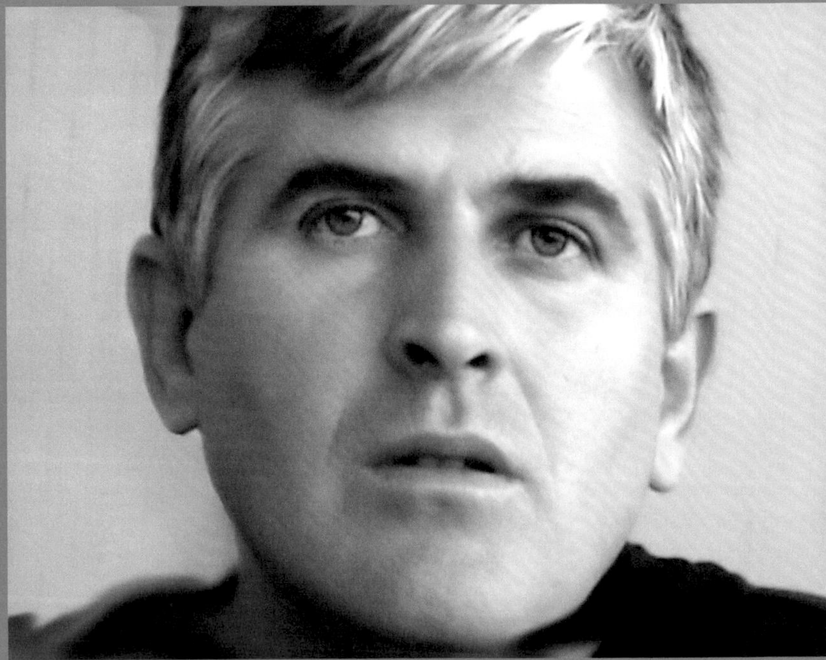

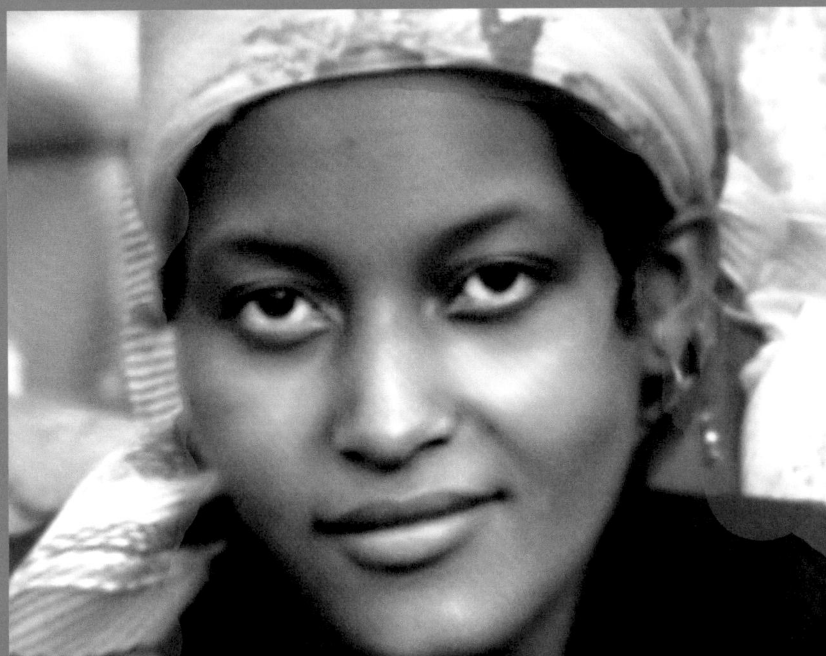

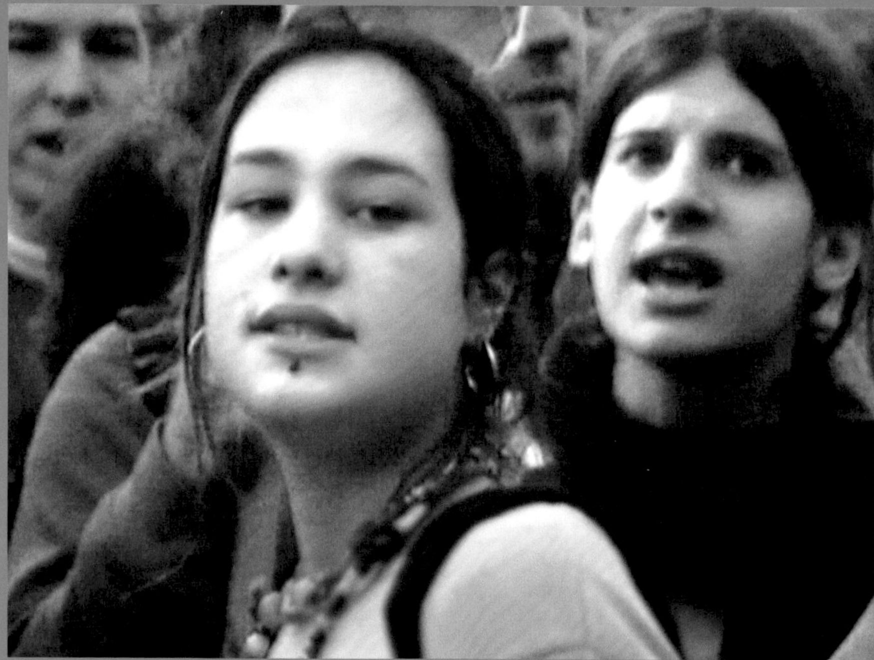

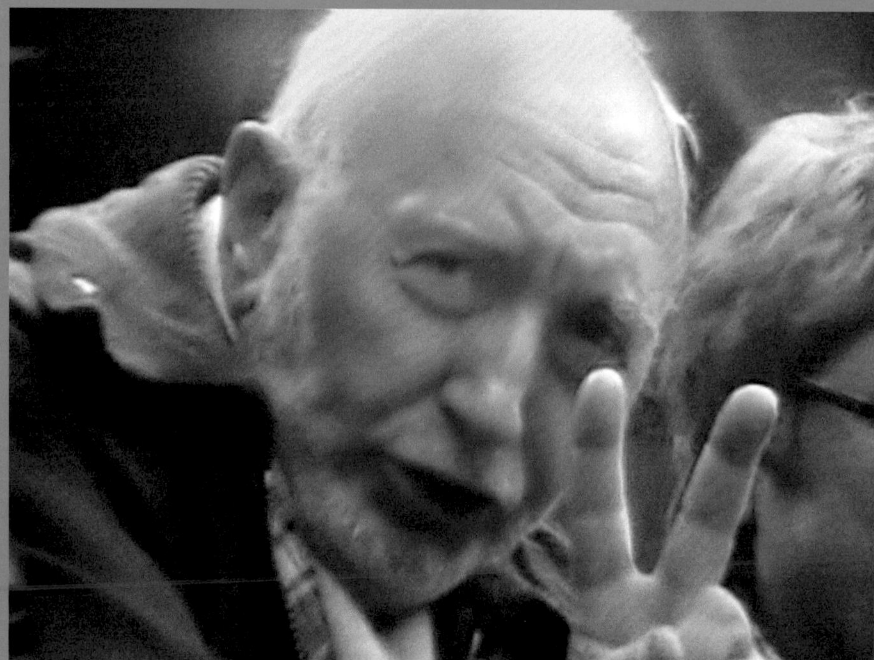

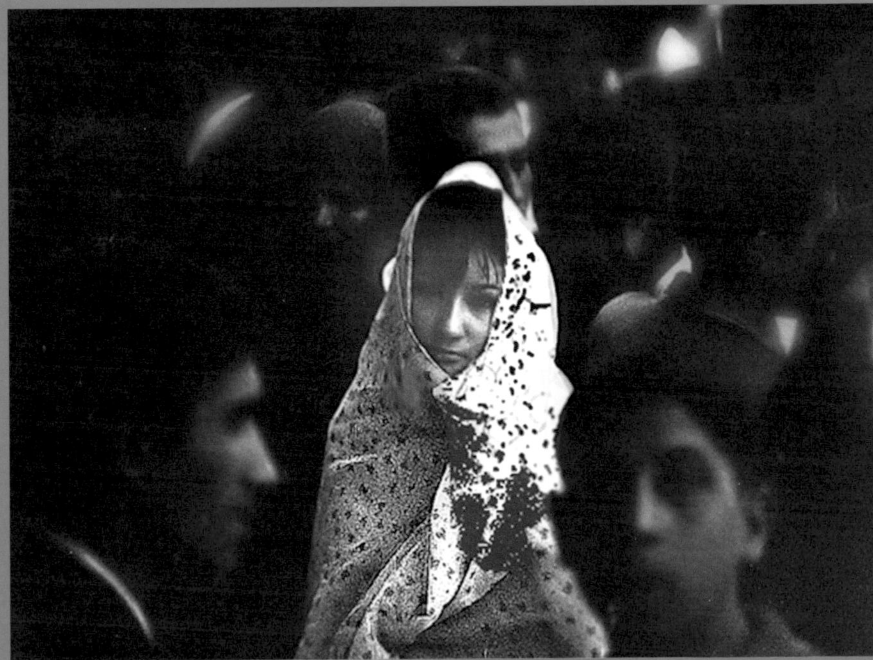

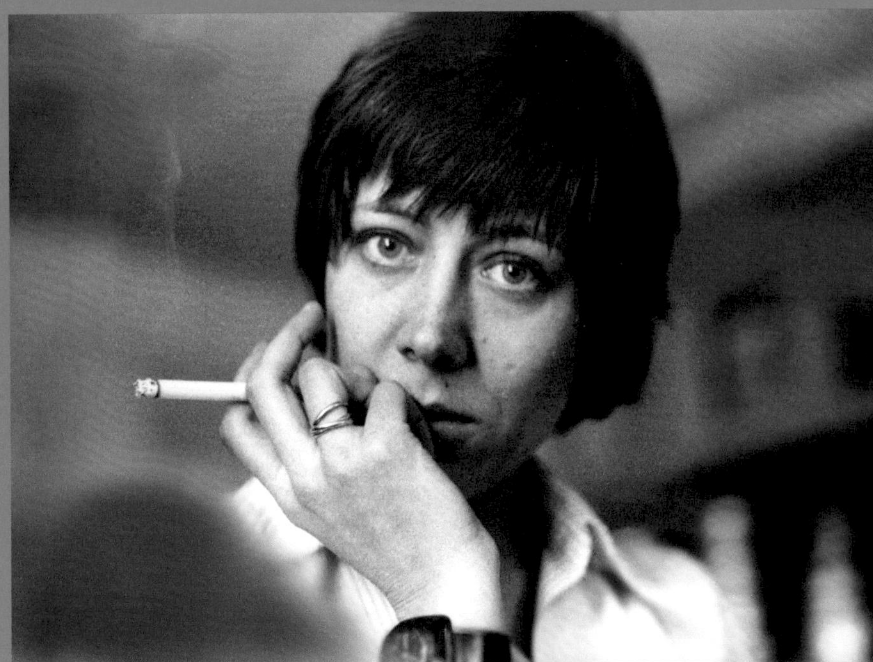

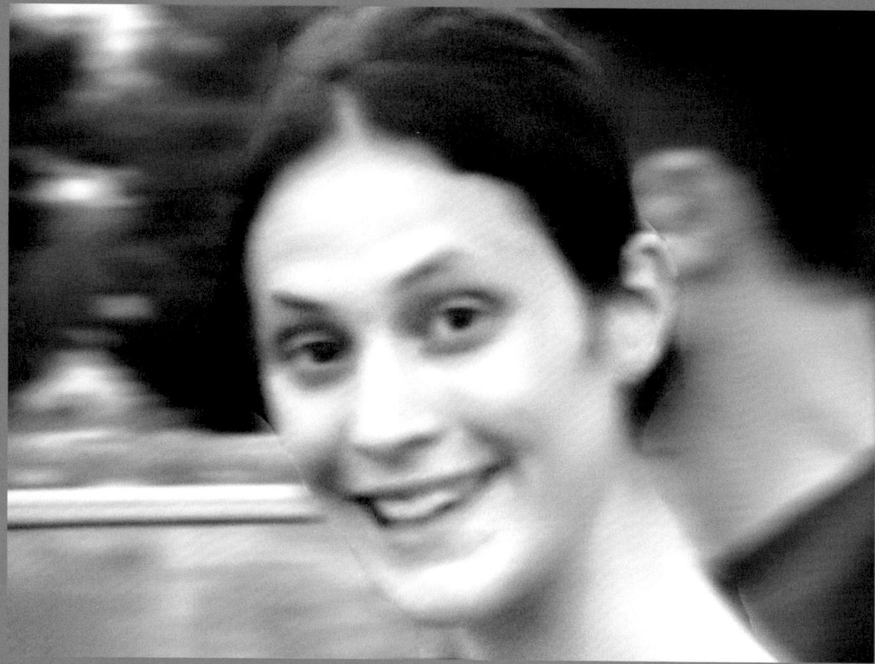

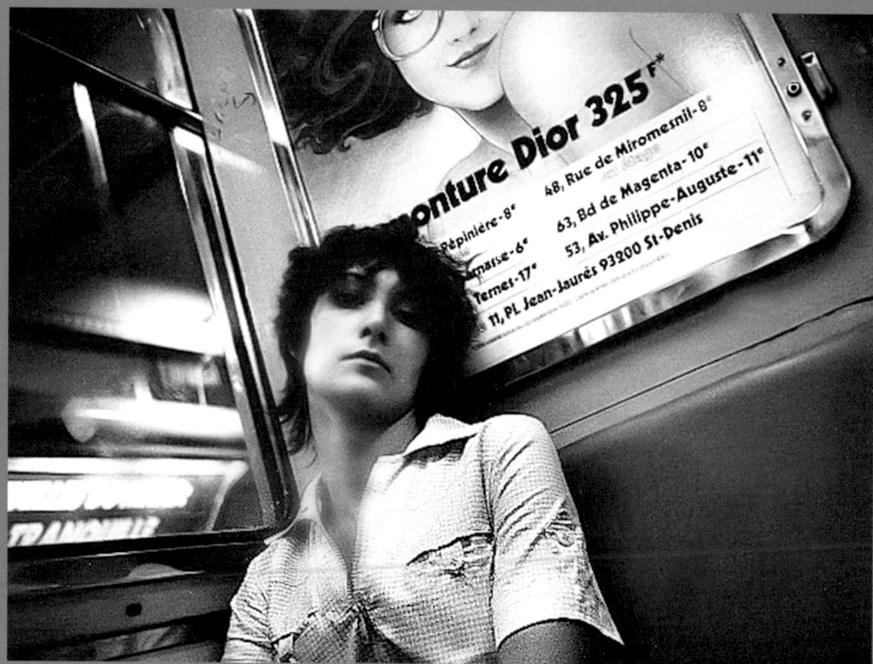
onture Dior 325F*
Pépinière-8e
48, Rue de Miromesnil-8e
63, Bd de Magenta-10e
Ternes-17e
53, Av. Philippe-Auguste-11e
11, Pl. Jean-Jaurès 93200 St-Denis

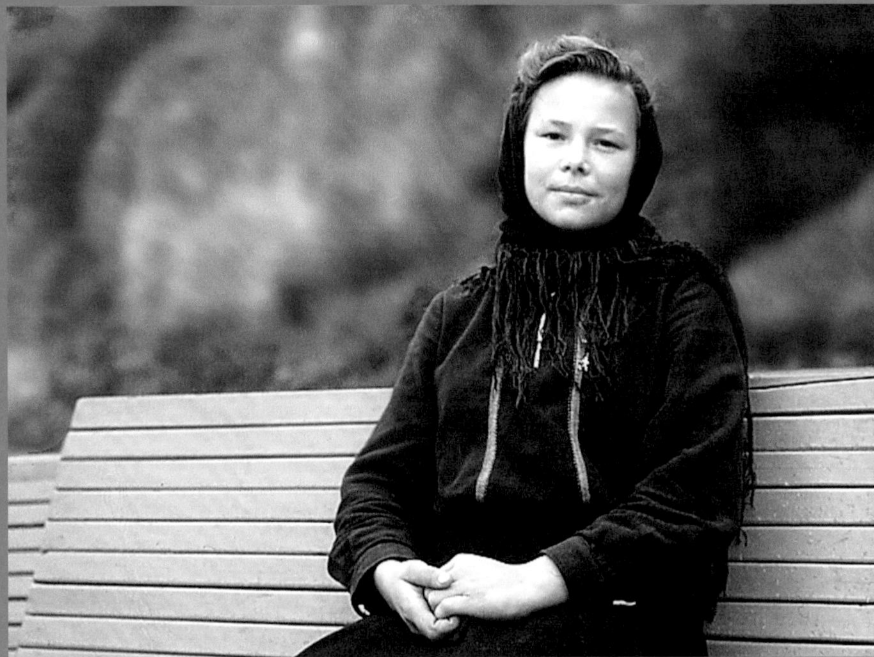

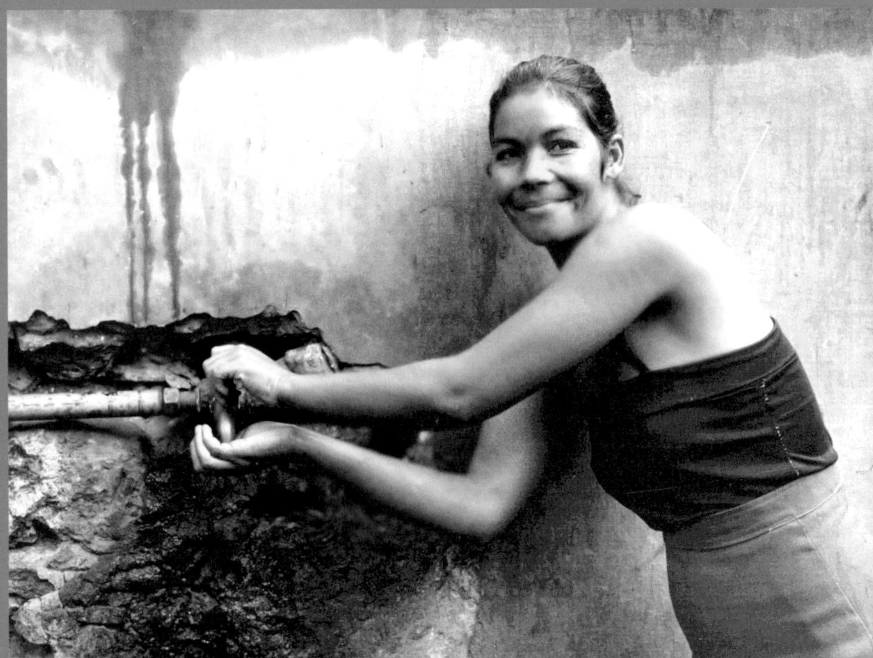

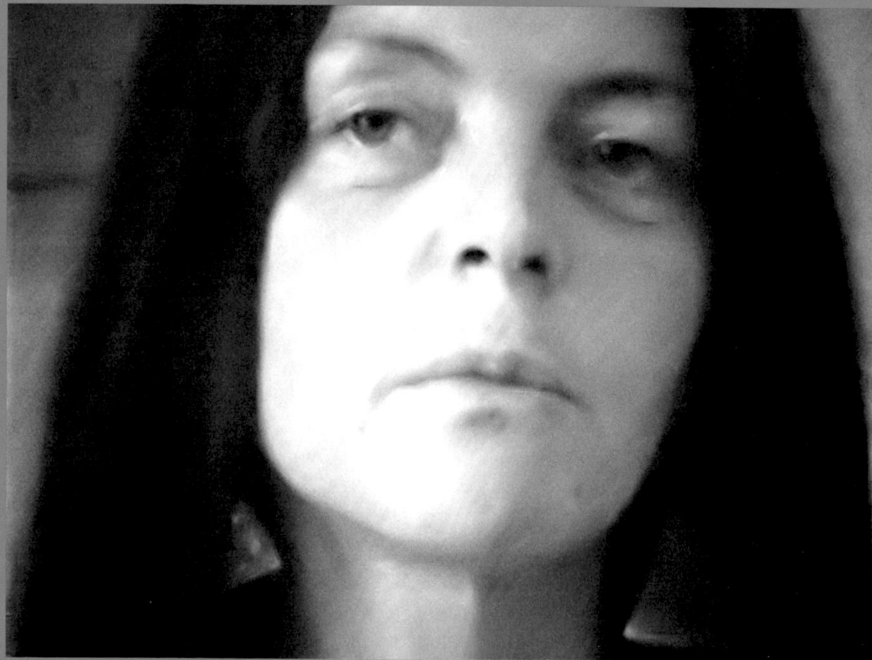

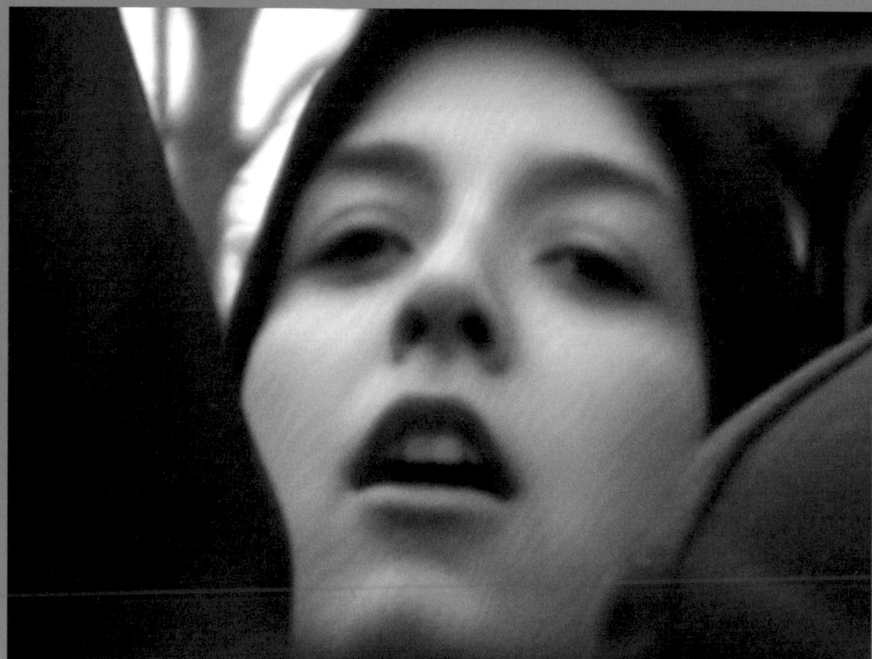

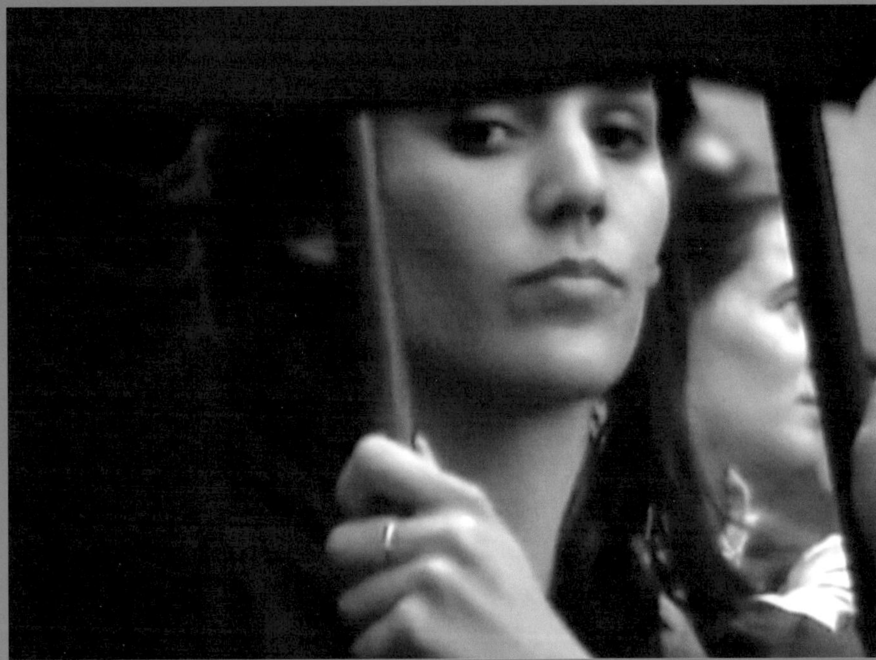

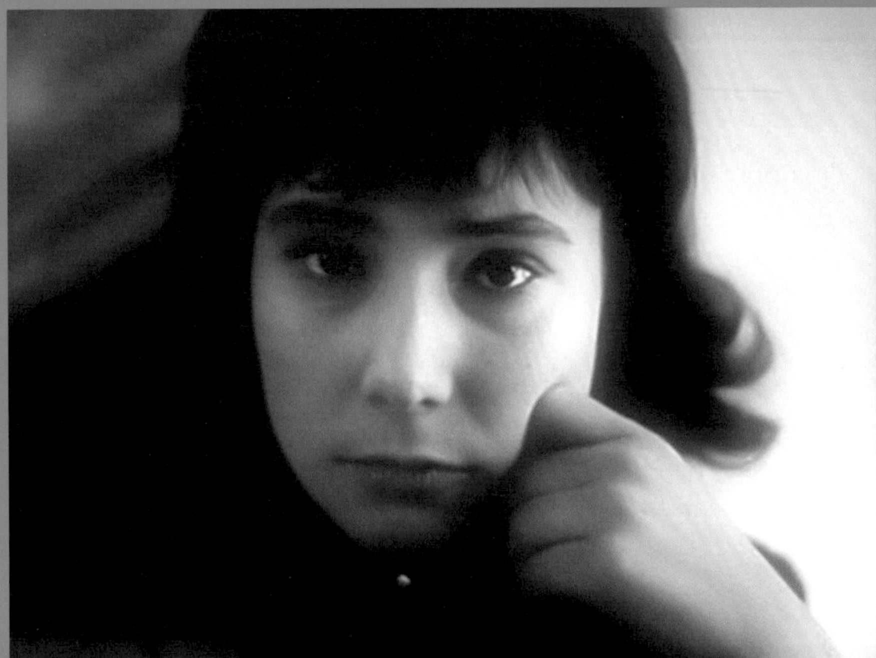

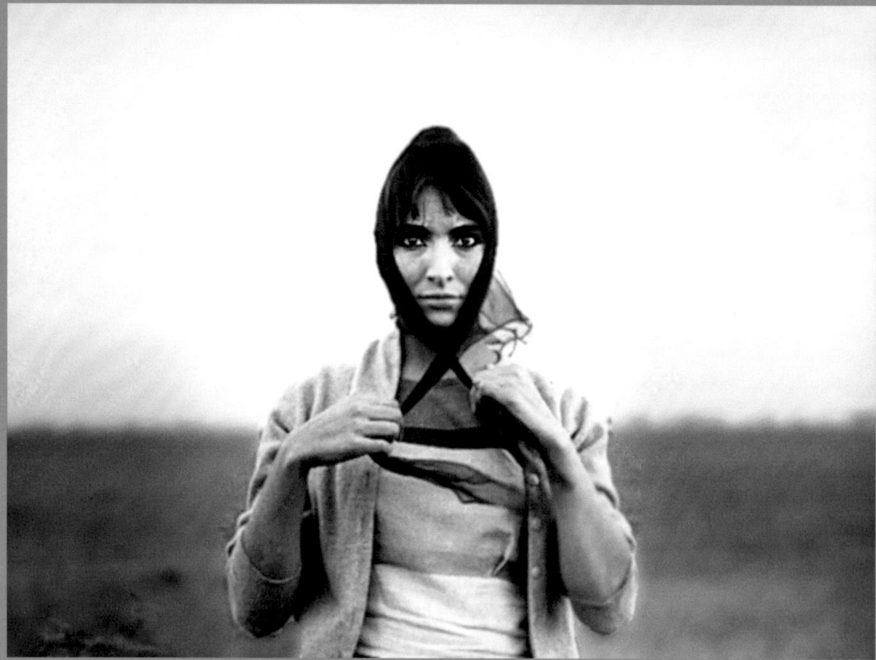

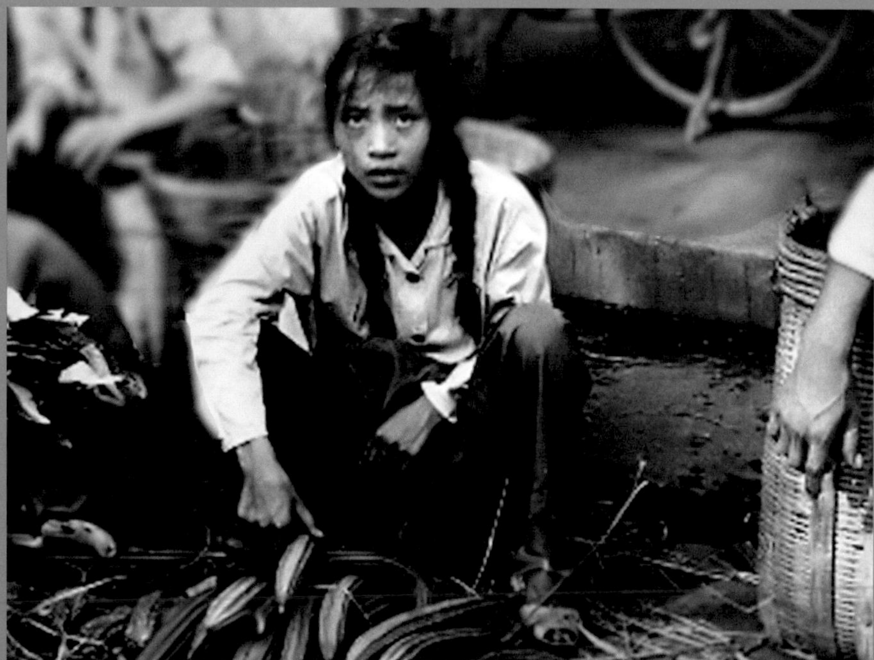

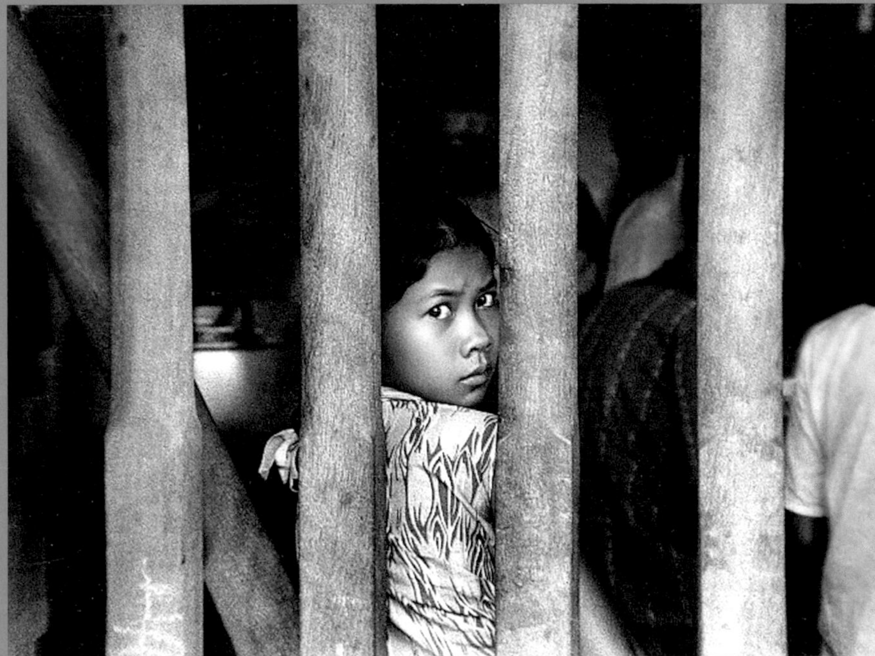

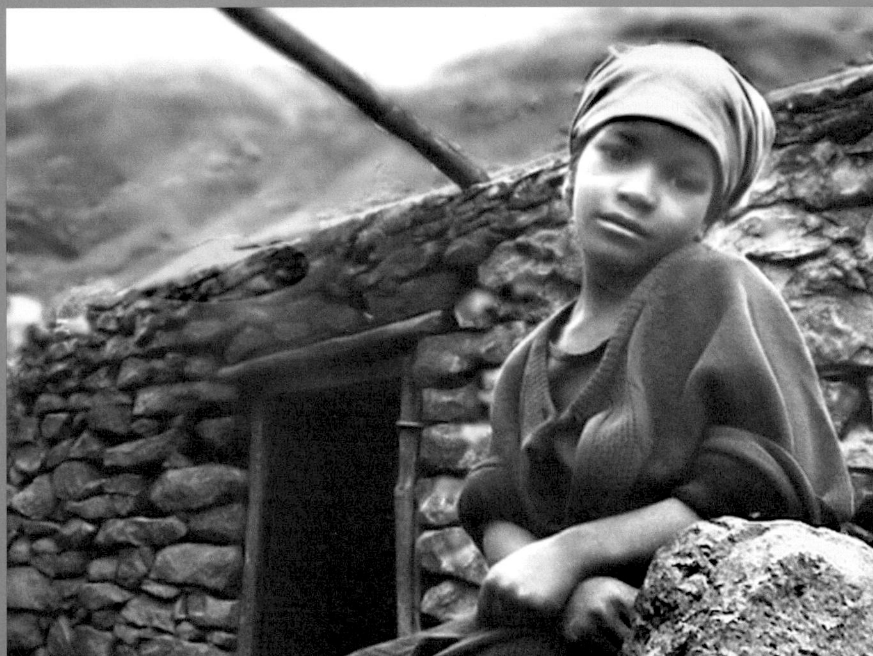

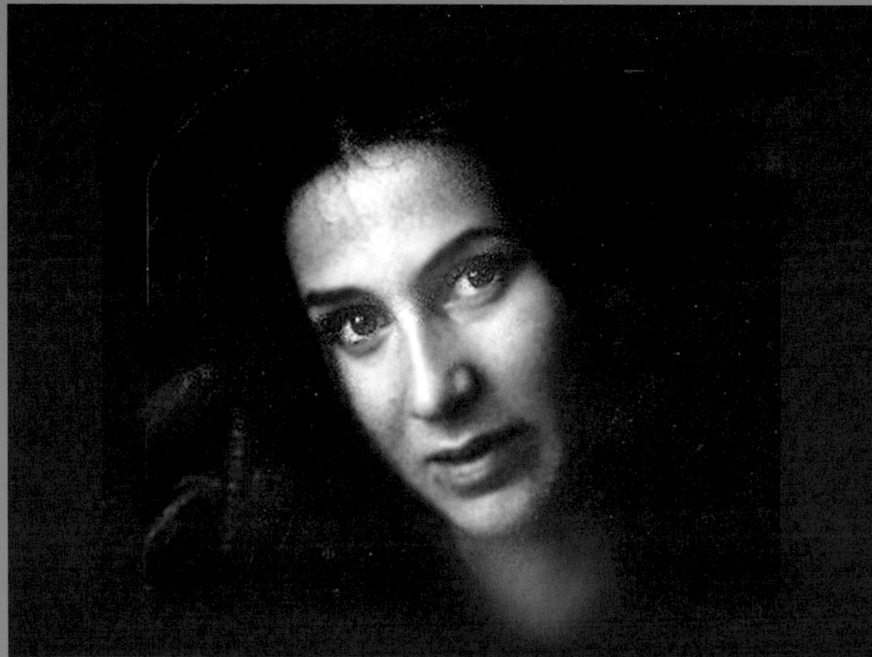

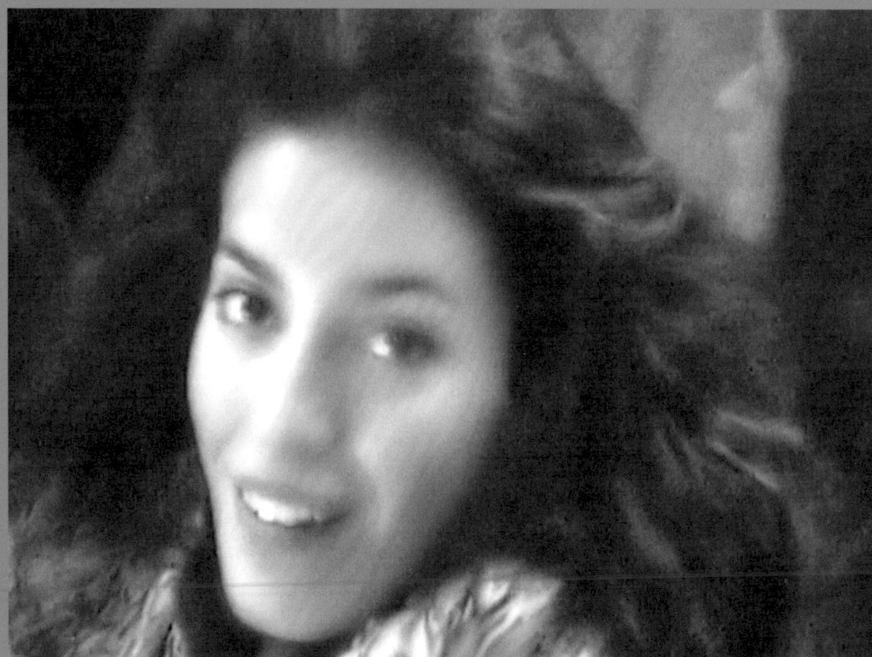

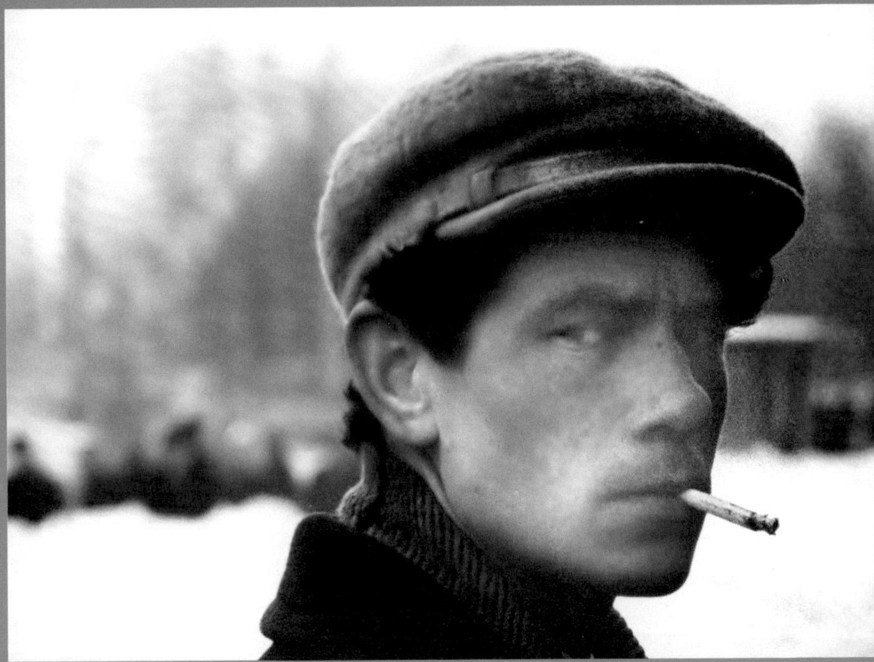

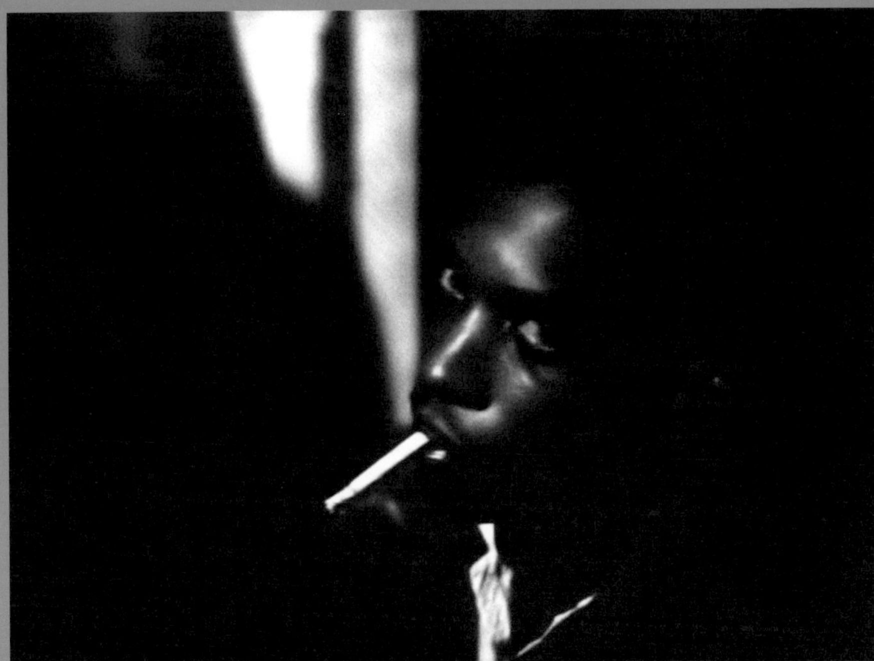

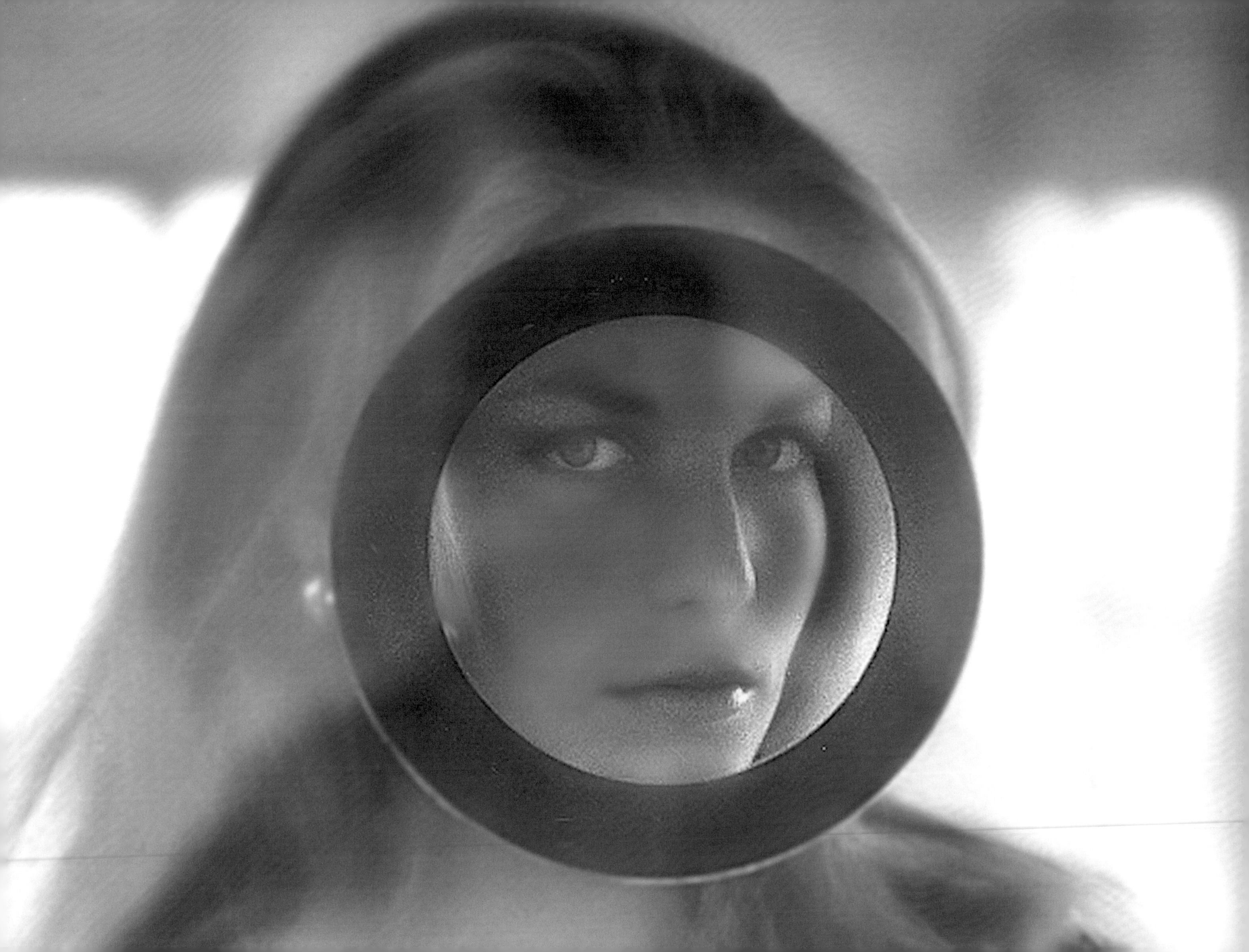

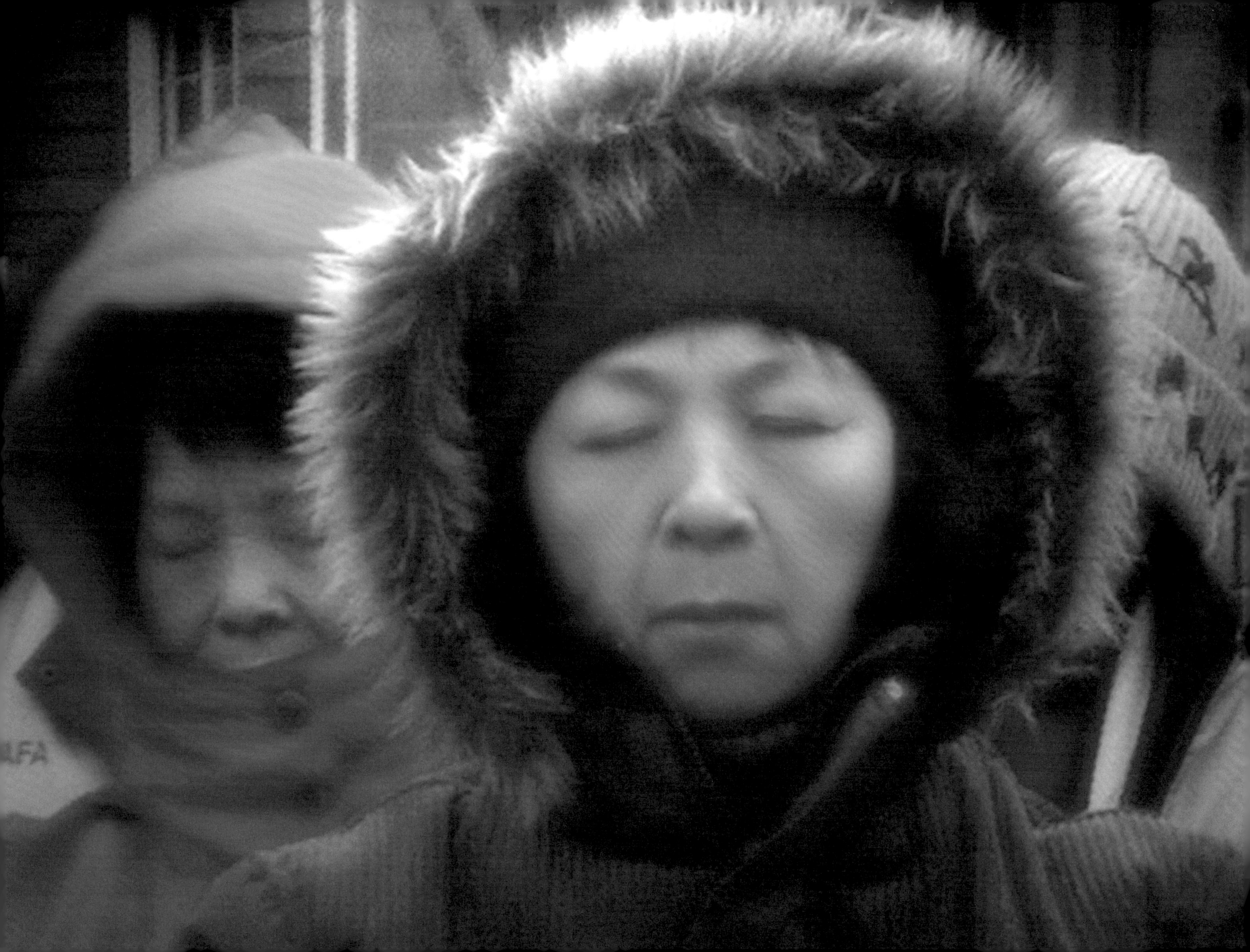

I Stare 2

I STARE at them, but not enough, not long enough. There is a beautiful poem by Valery Larbaud, who evokes four young women he caught a glimpse of during his journeys, and he laments not being able to reach them now. *"For, I don't know why, it seems to me that with them I could conquer a world."* There is something of that megalomaniac melancholy in the browsing of past images. Perhaps, if I could catch up with that absolute beauty in Cape Verde, the violinist in Stockholm lost in her thoughts, the grandmother in Corsica kissing the sacred stone, the exhausted Chinese laborer, the Japanese extra sleeping between two takes, the two Russian girls listening to poetry, the young woman dozing in the train, and the old man with his paper toys, perhaps I could conquer a world. Or rather, they would conquer a world for me.

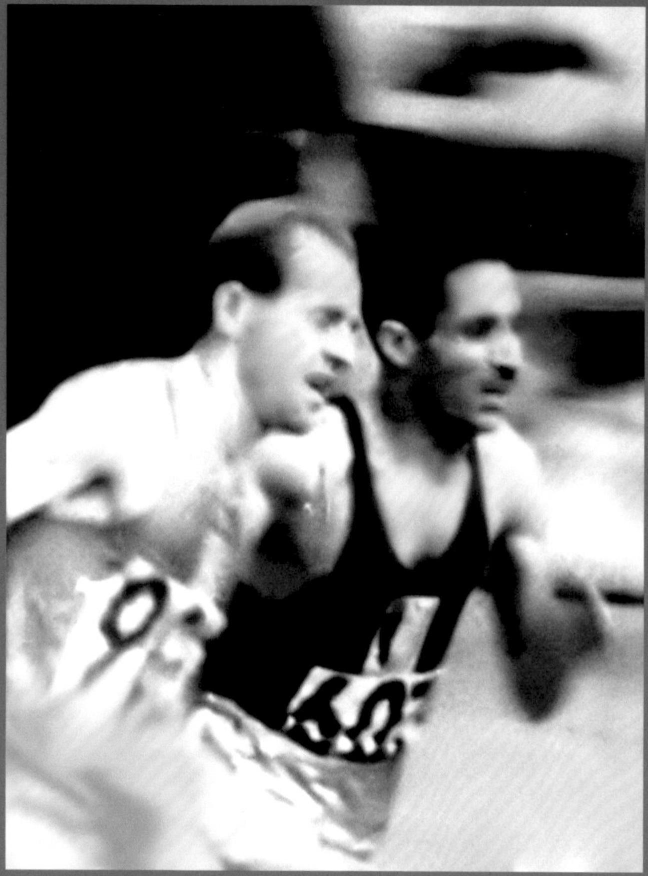

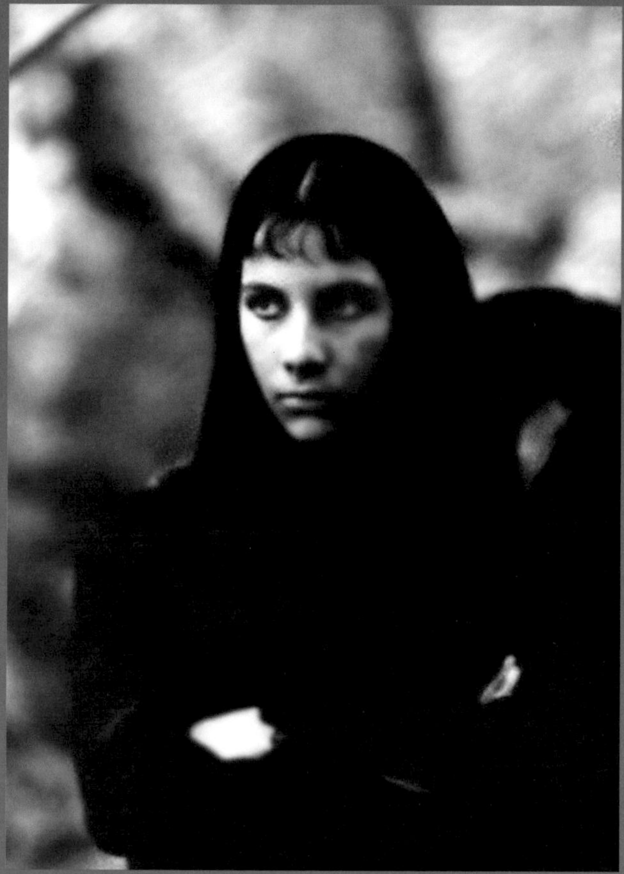

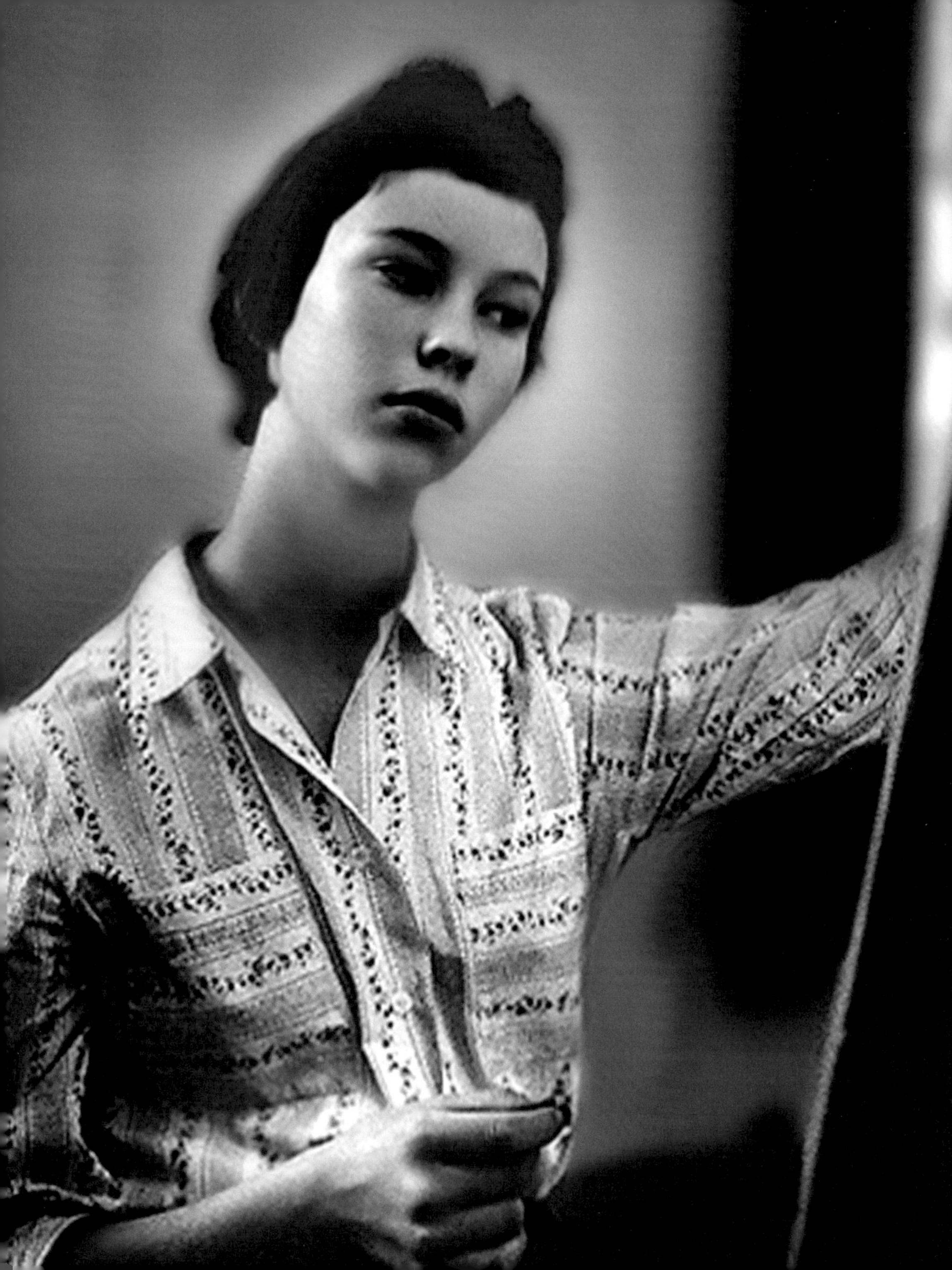

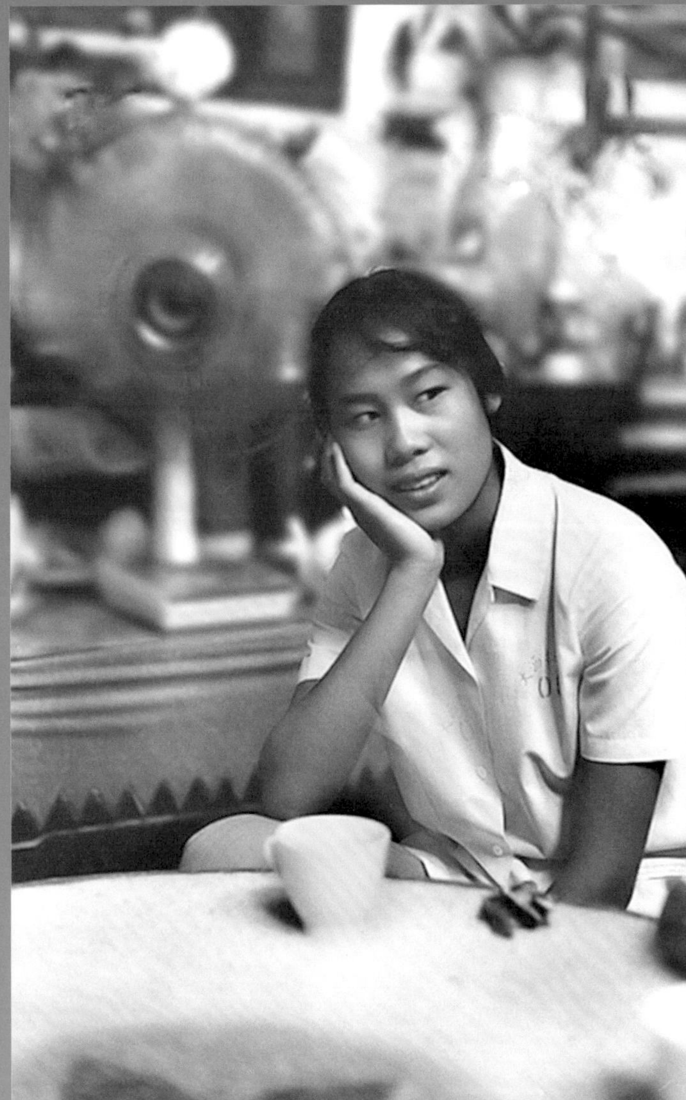

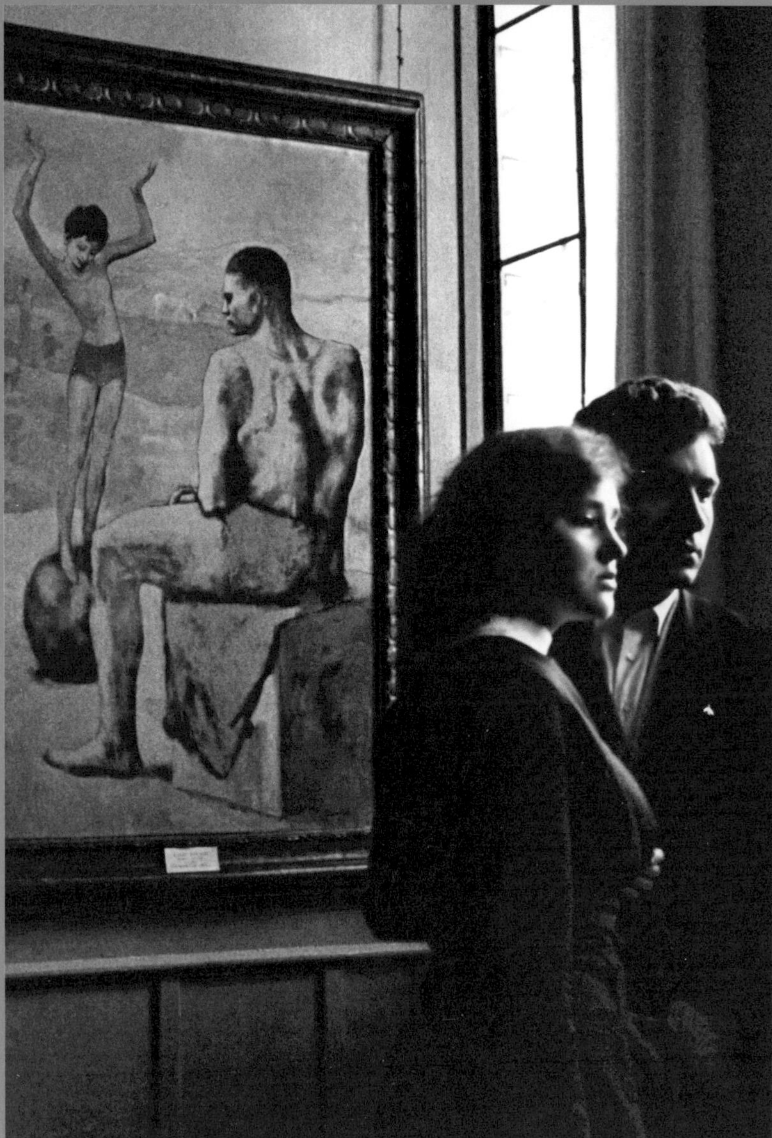

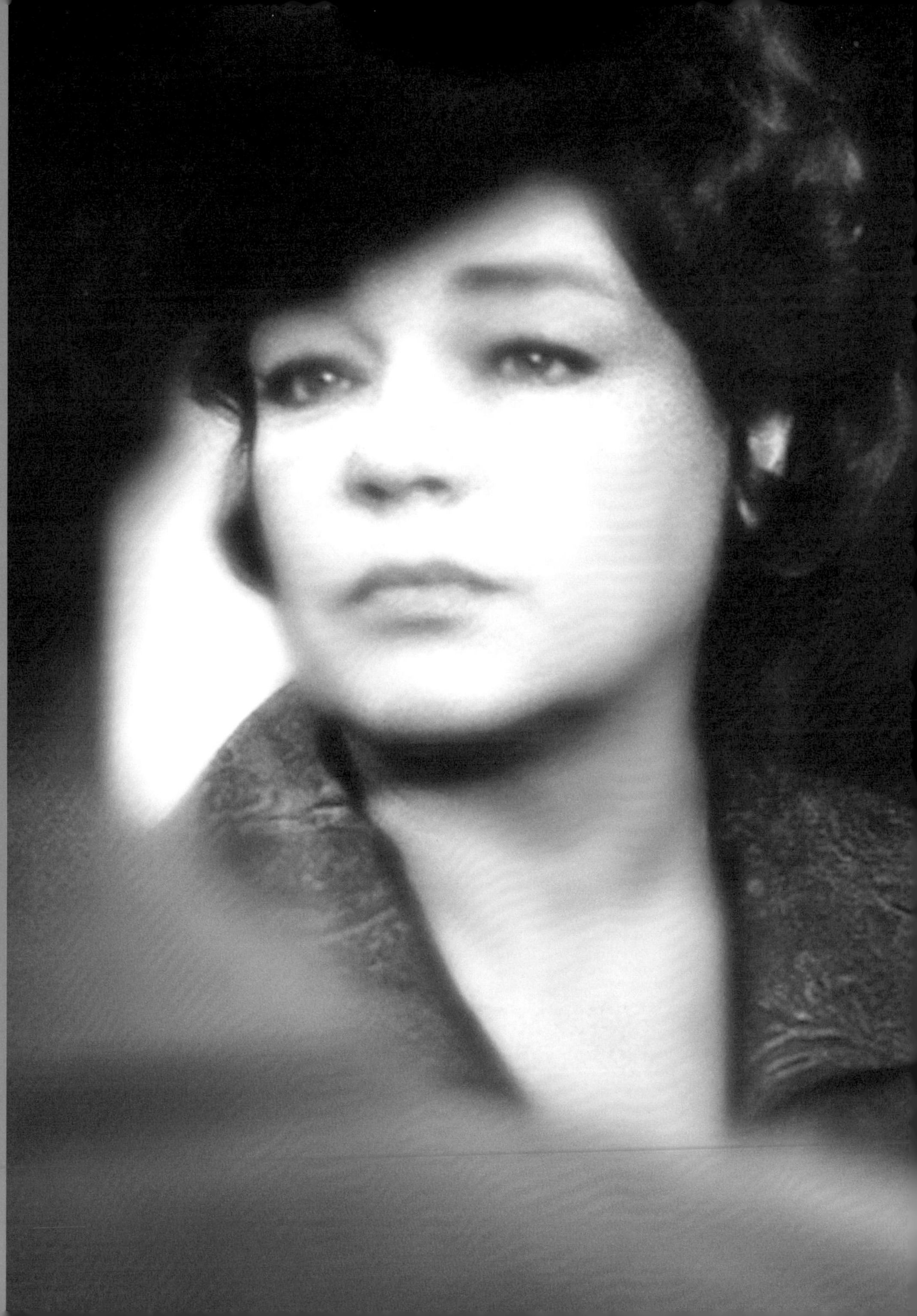

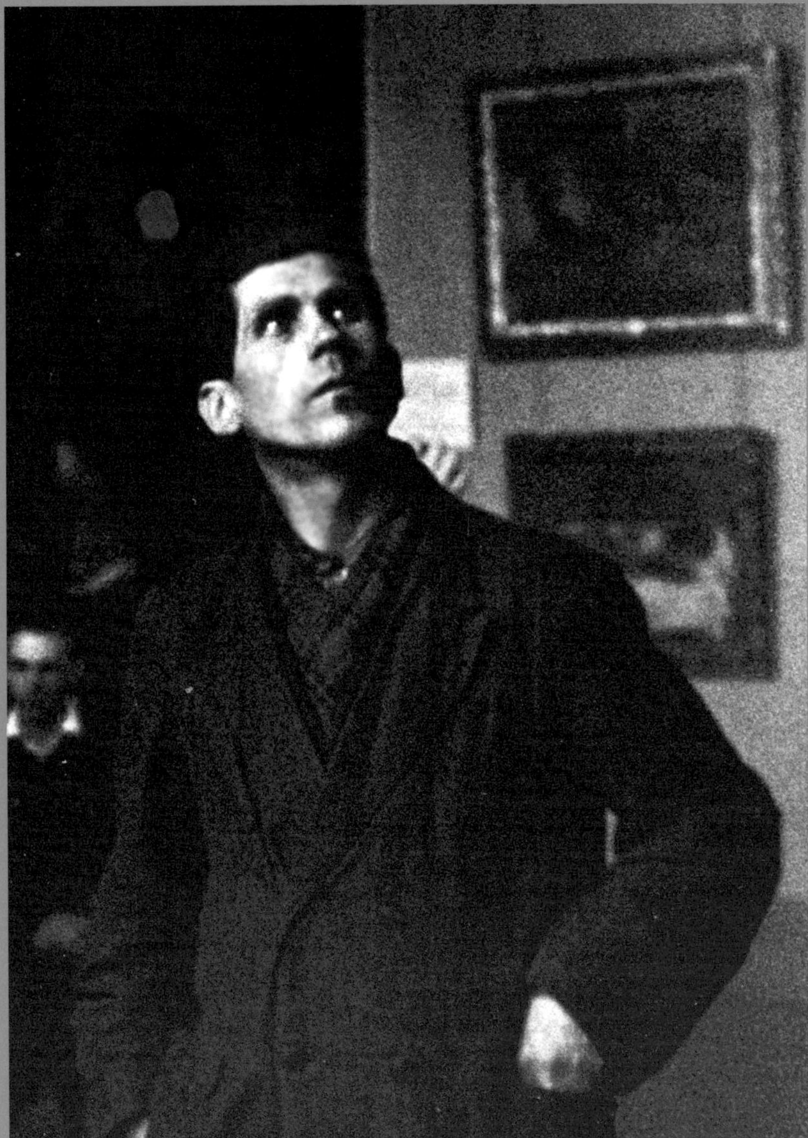

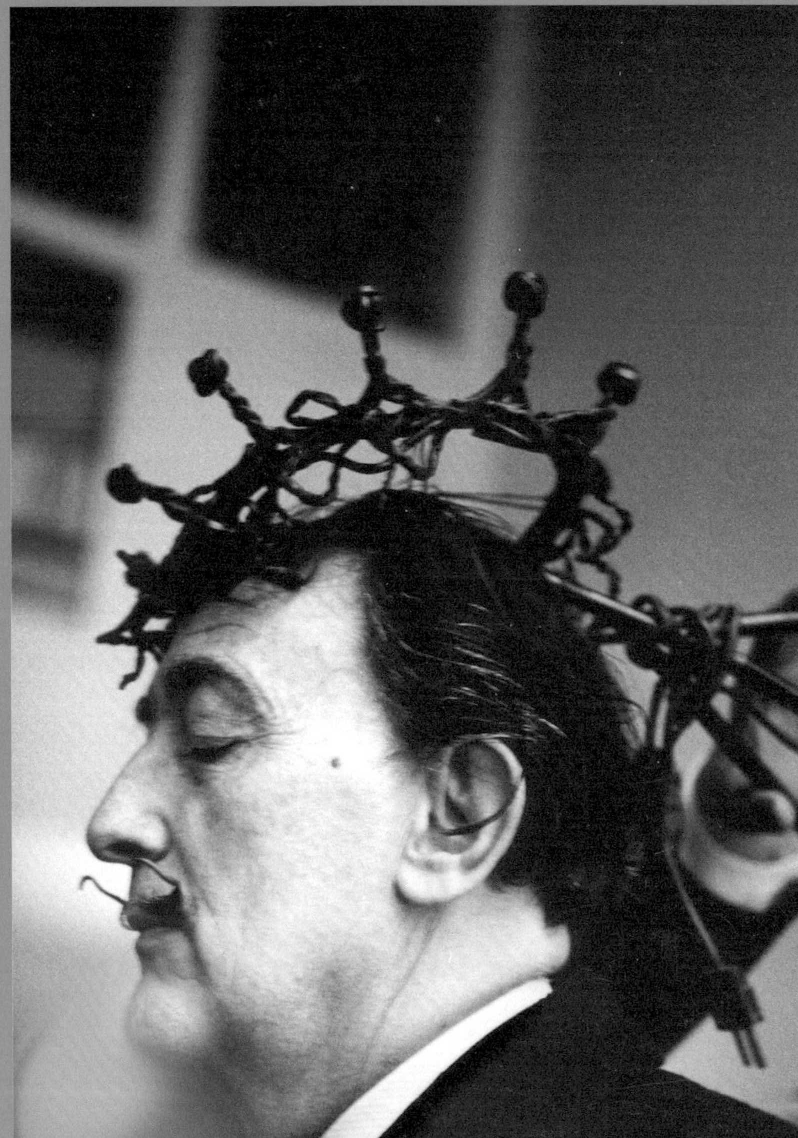

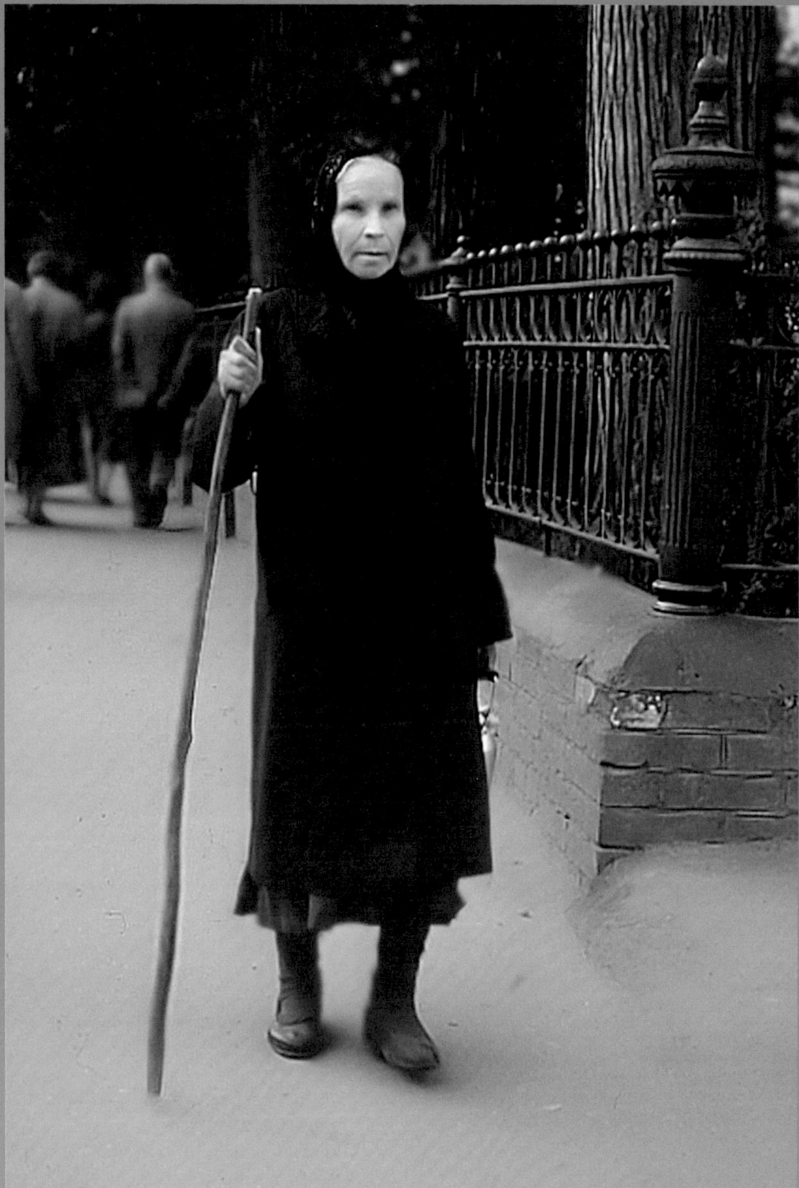

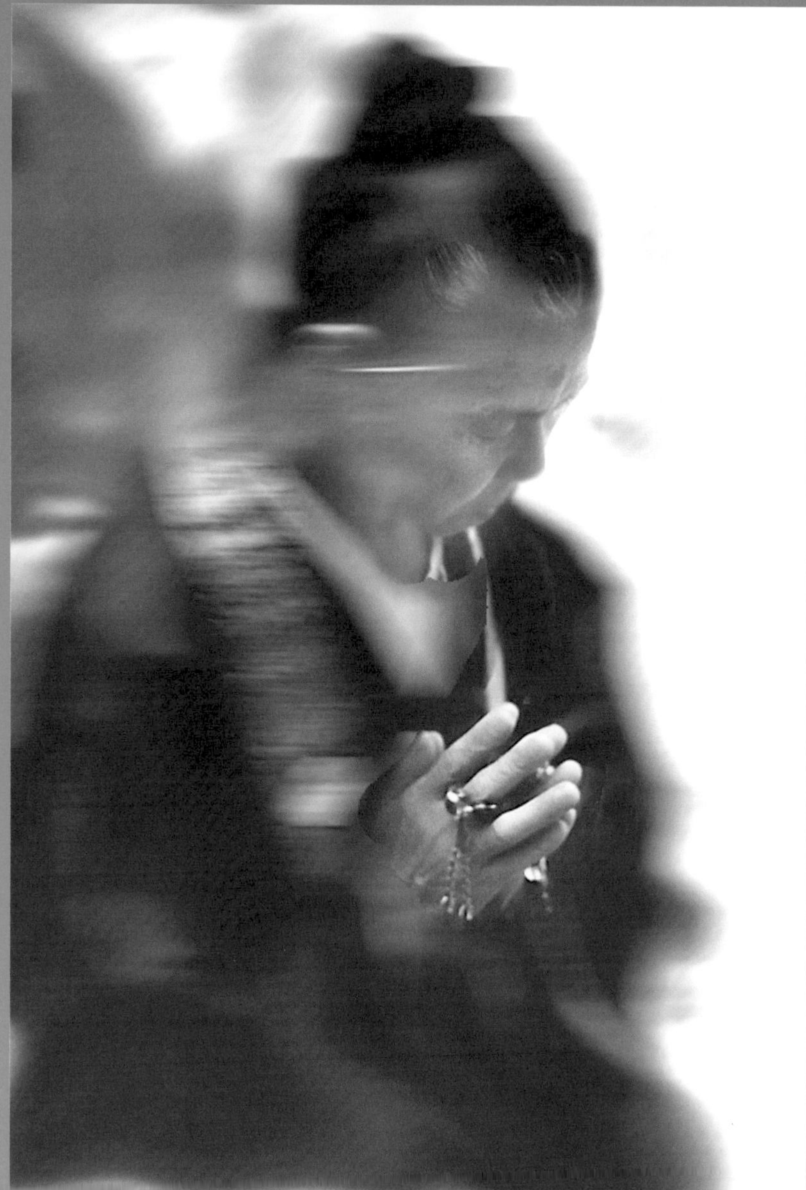

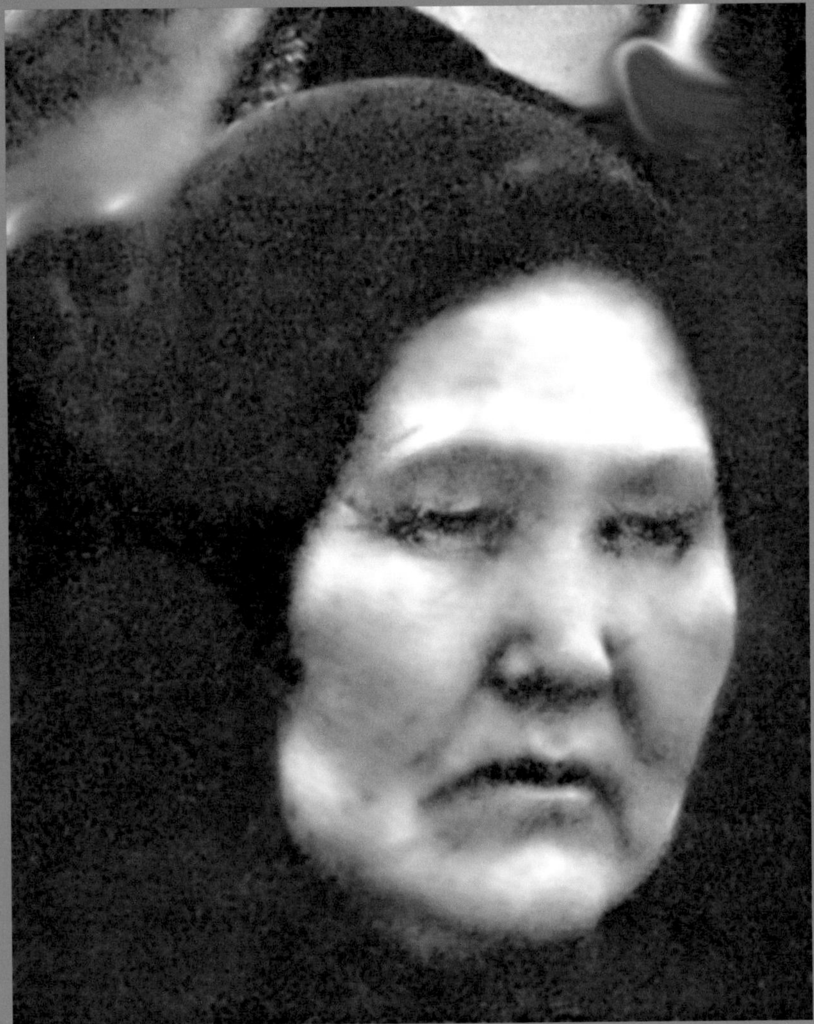

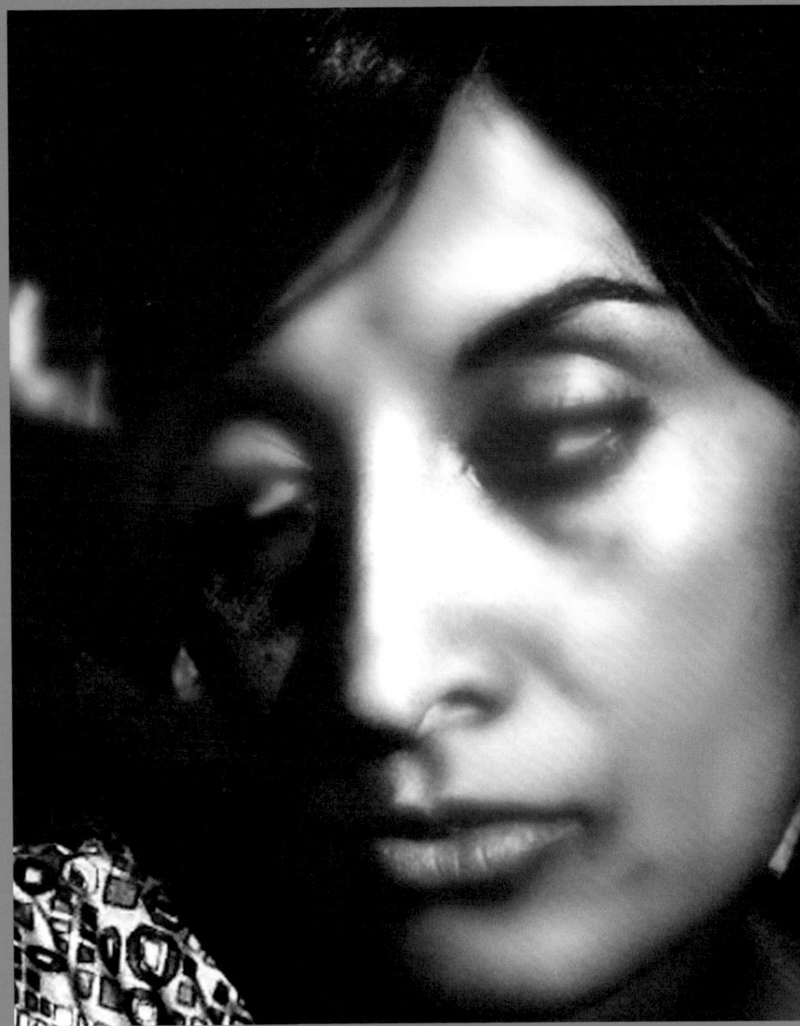

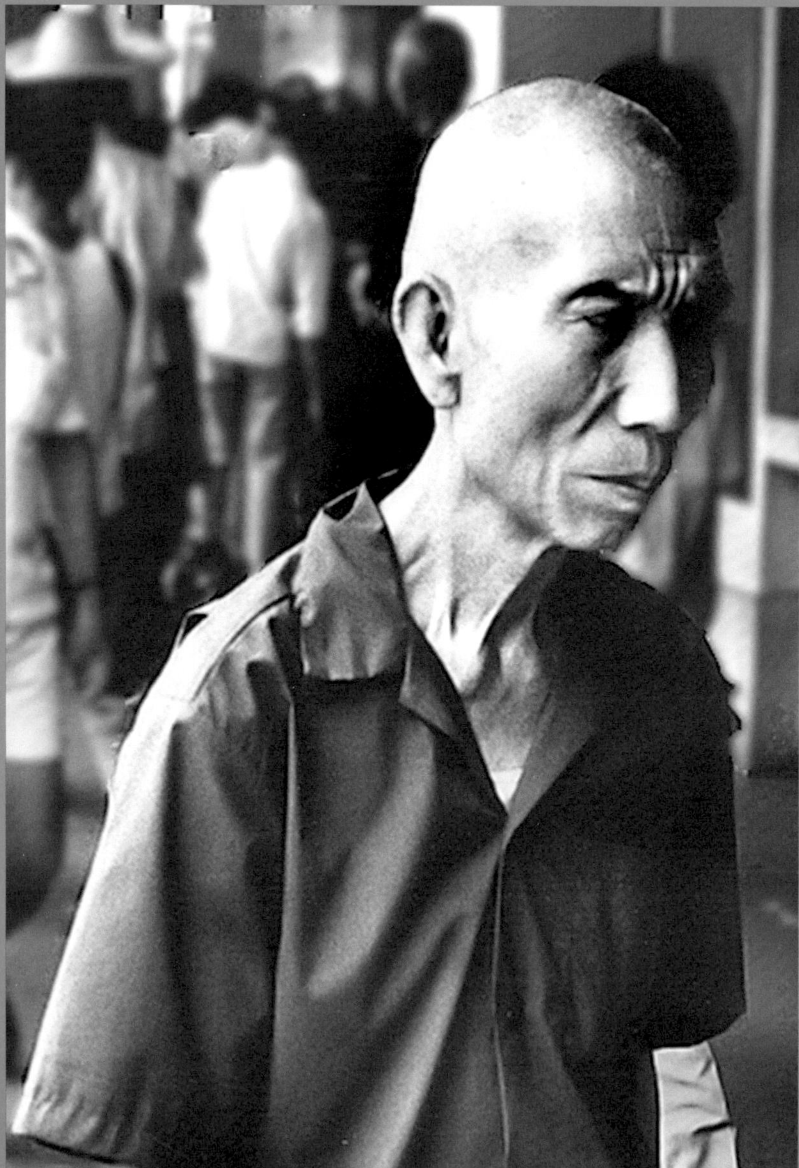

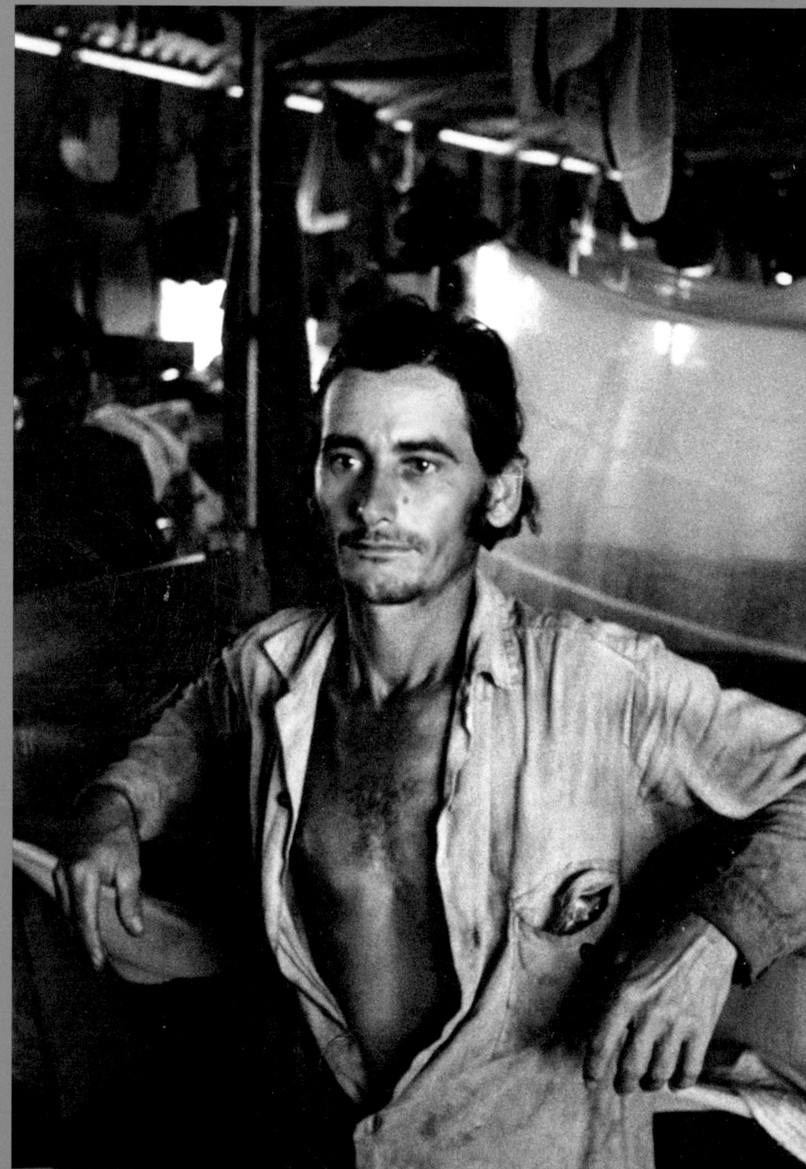

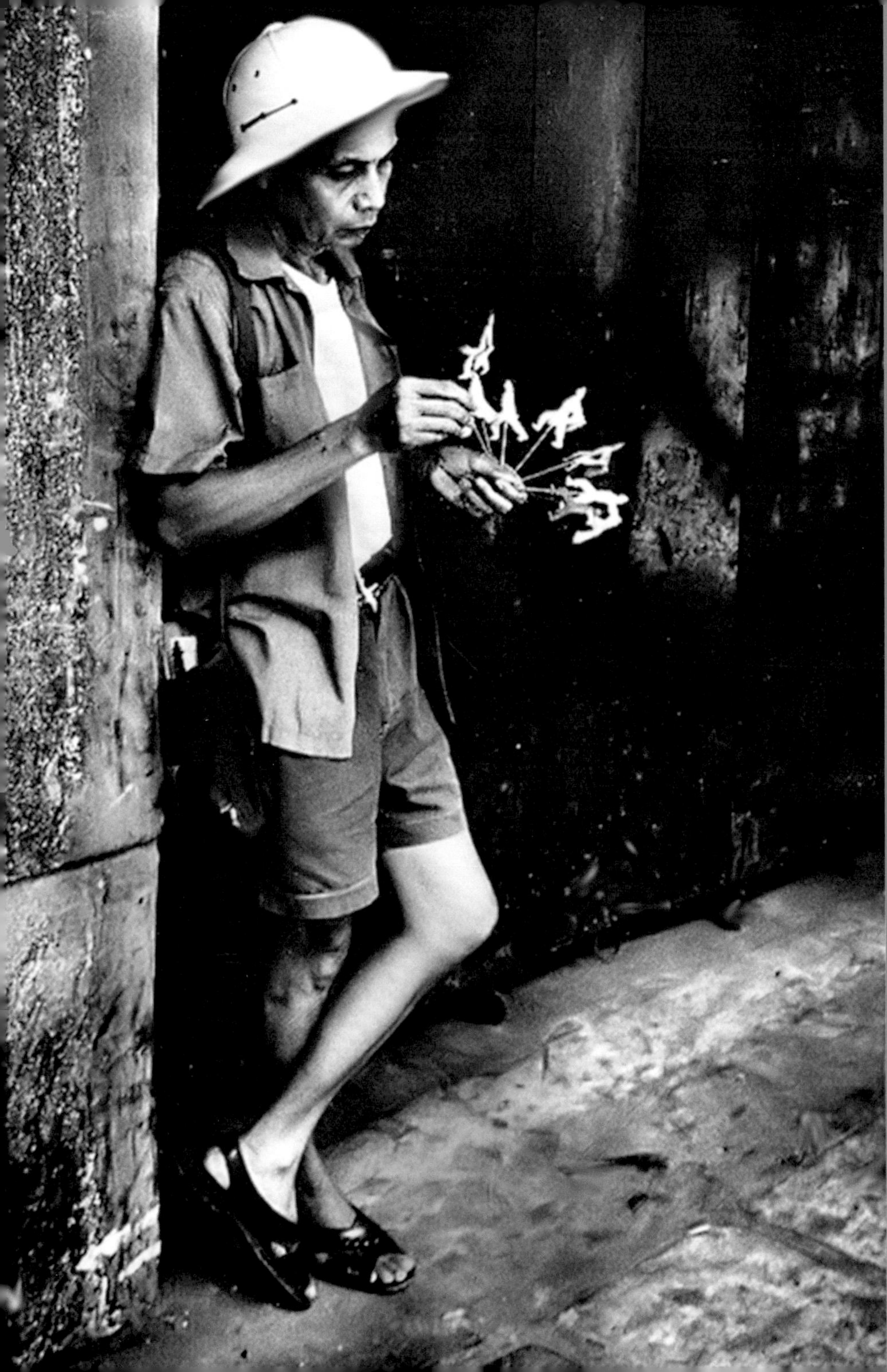

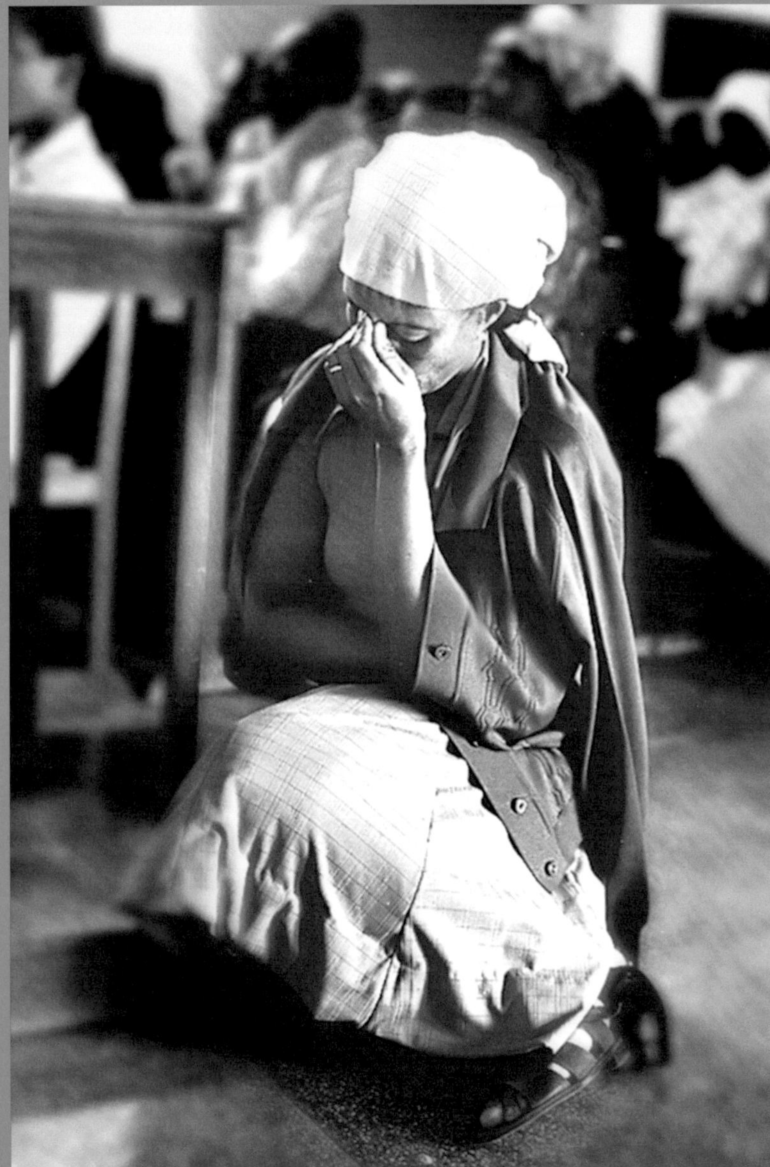

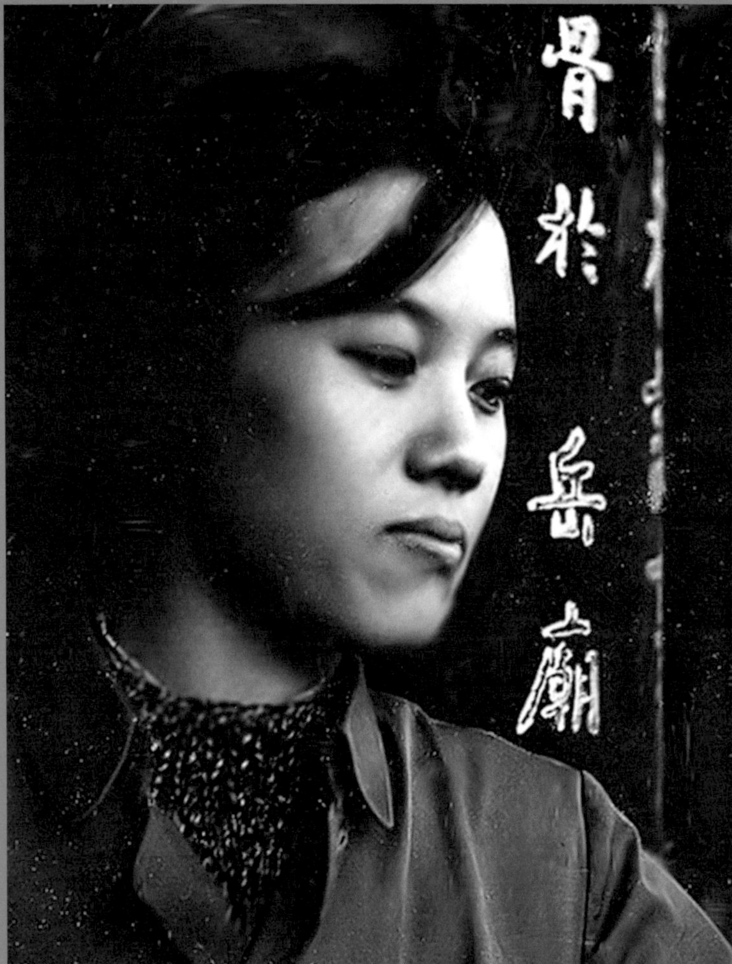
骨於岳廟

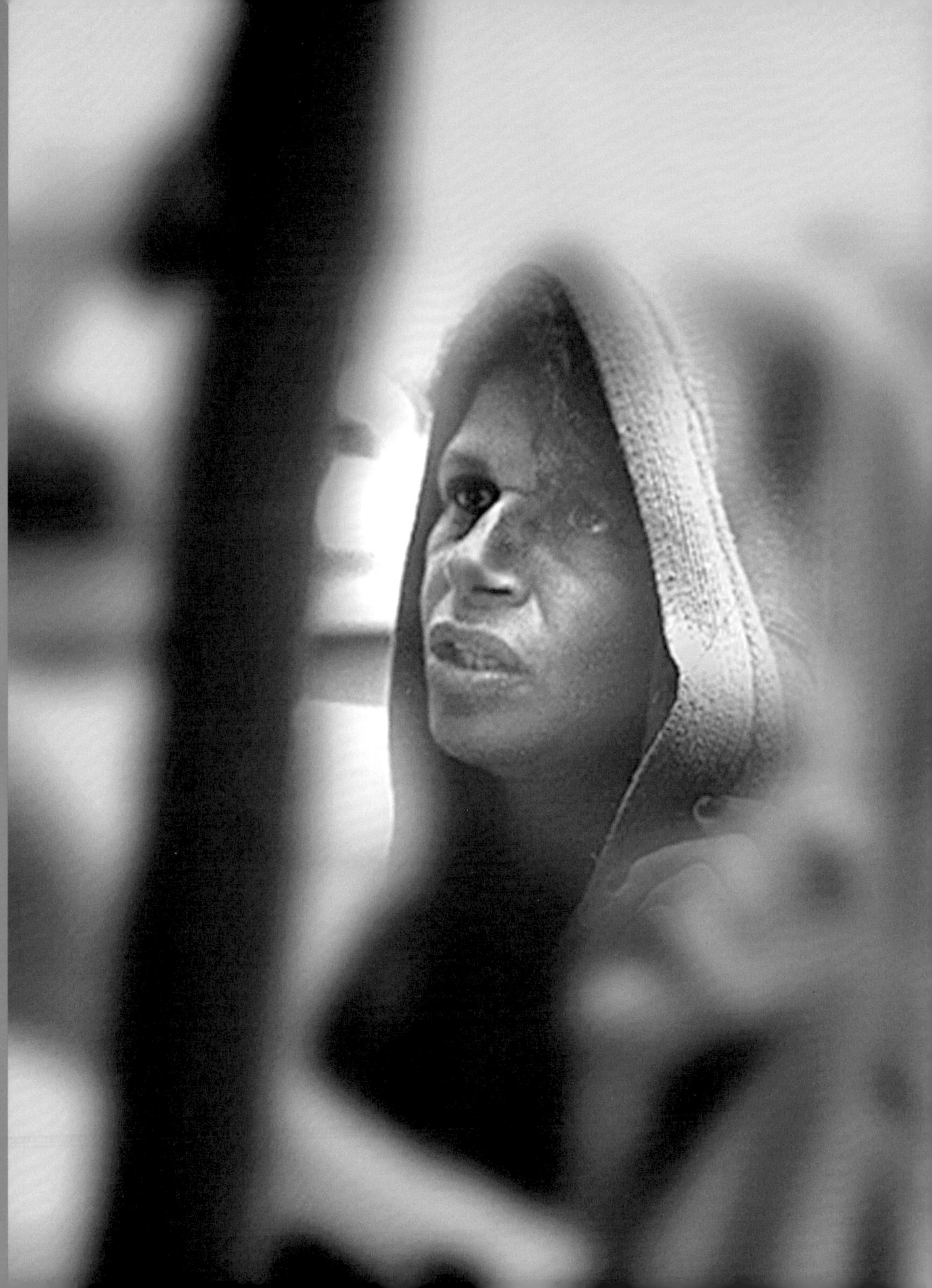

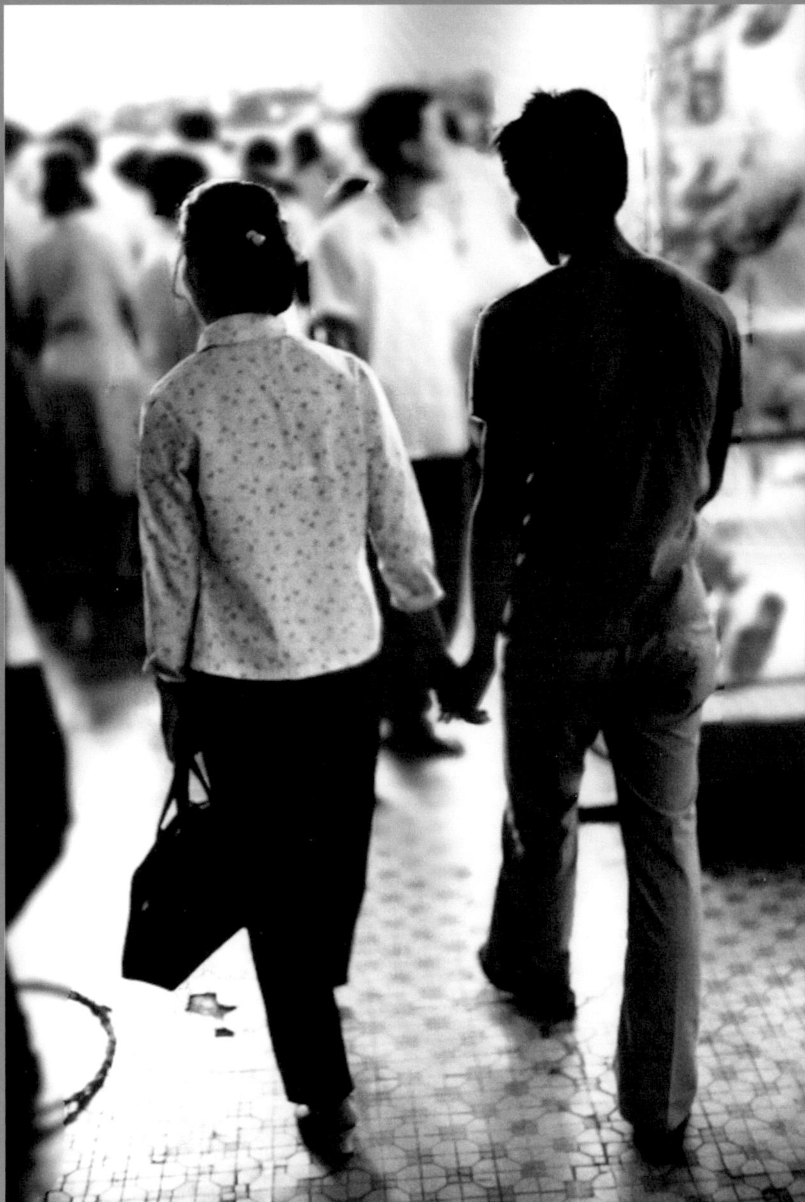

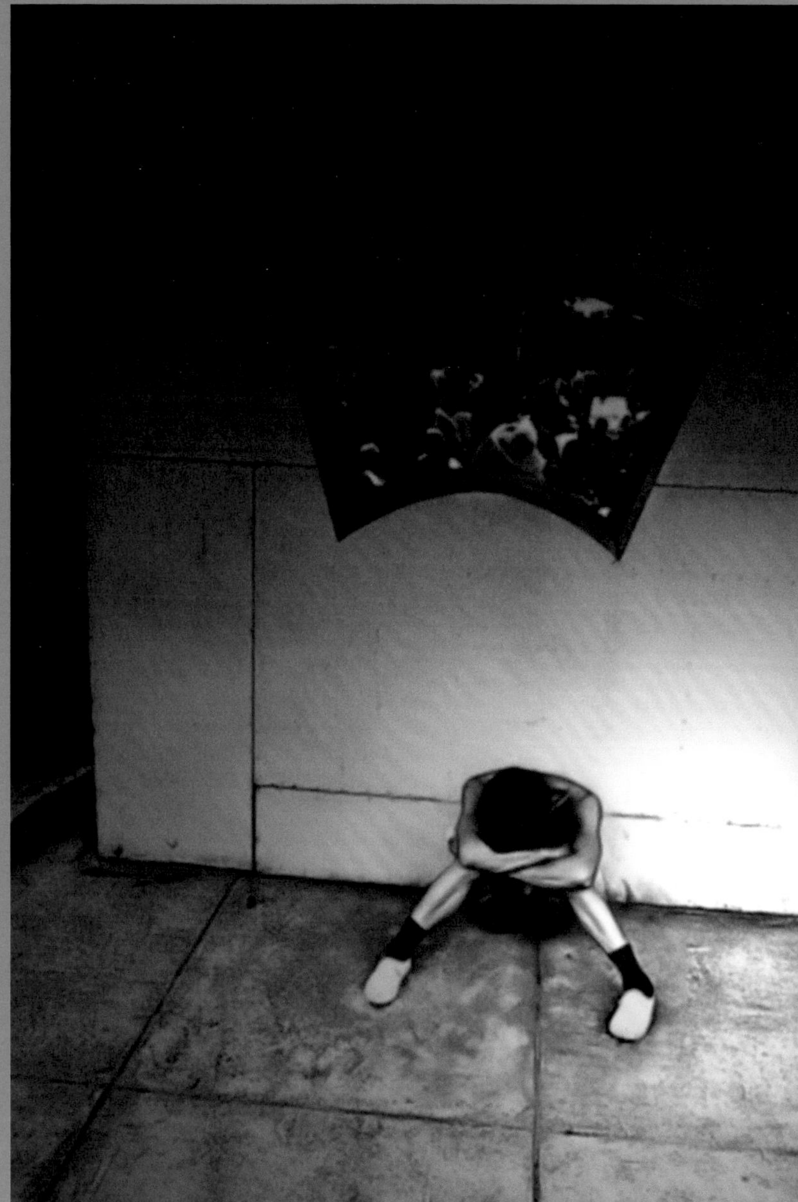

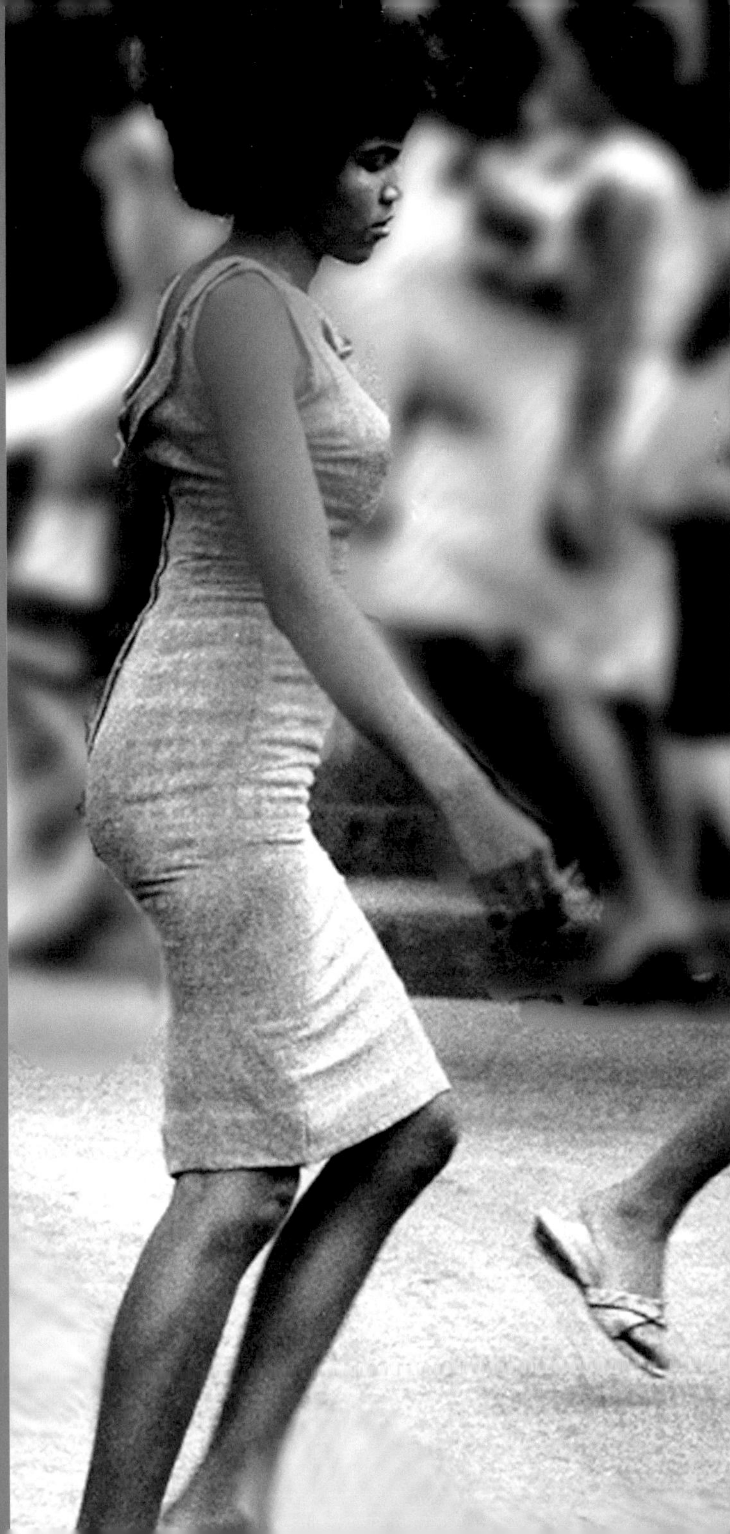

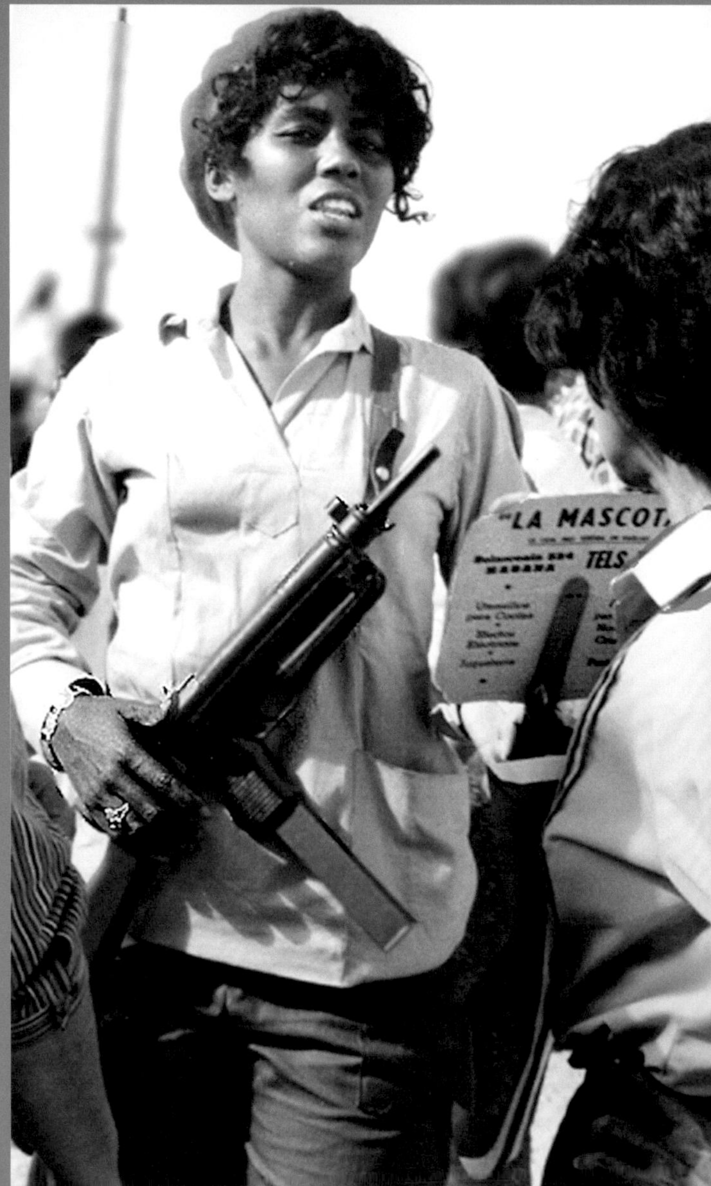
LA MASCOT
TELS

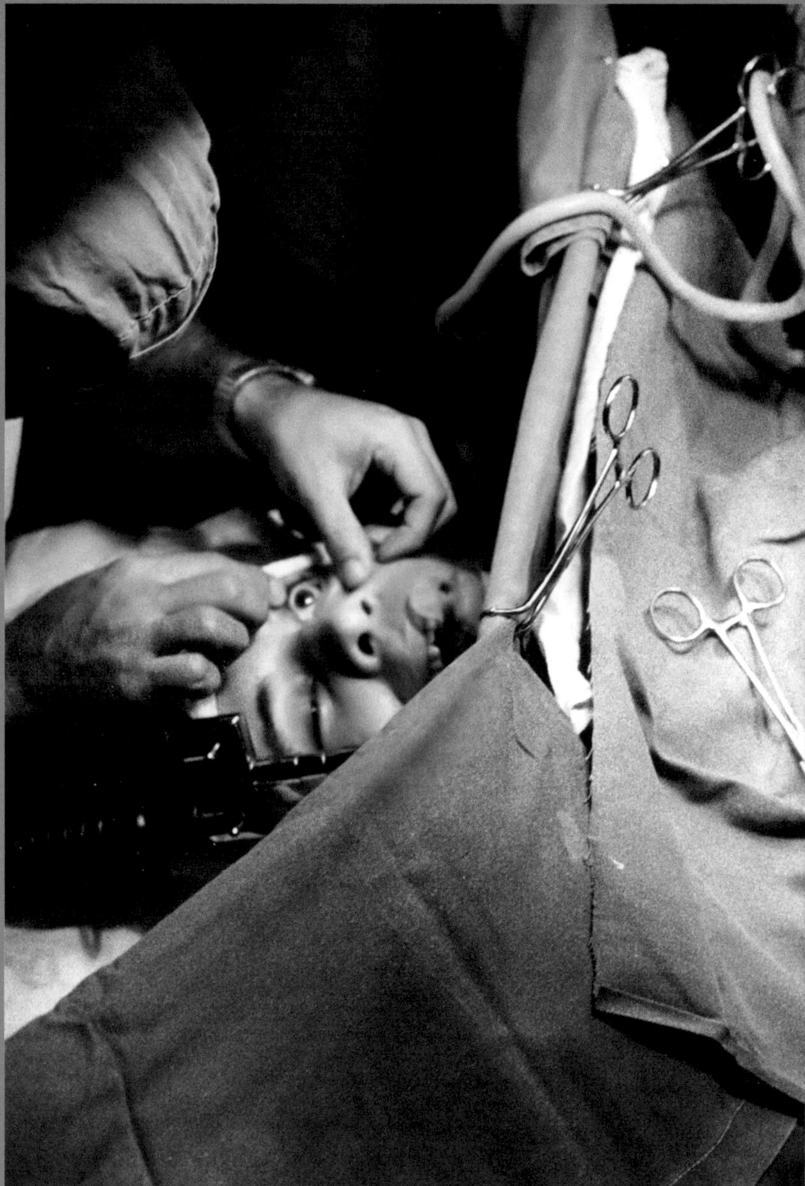

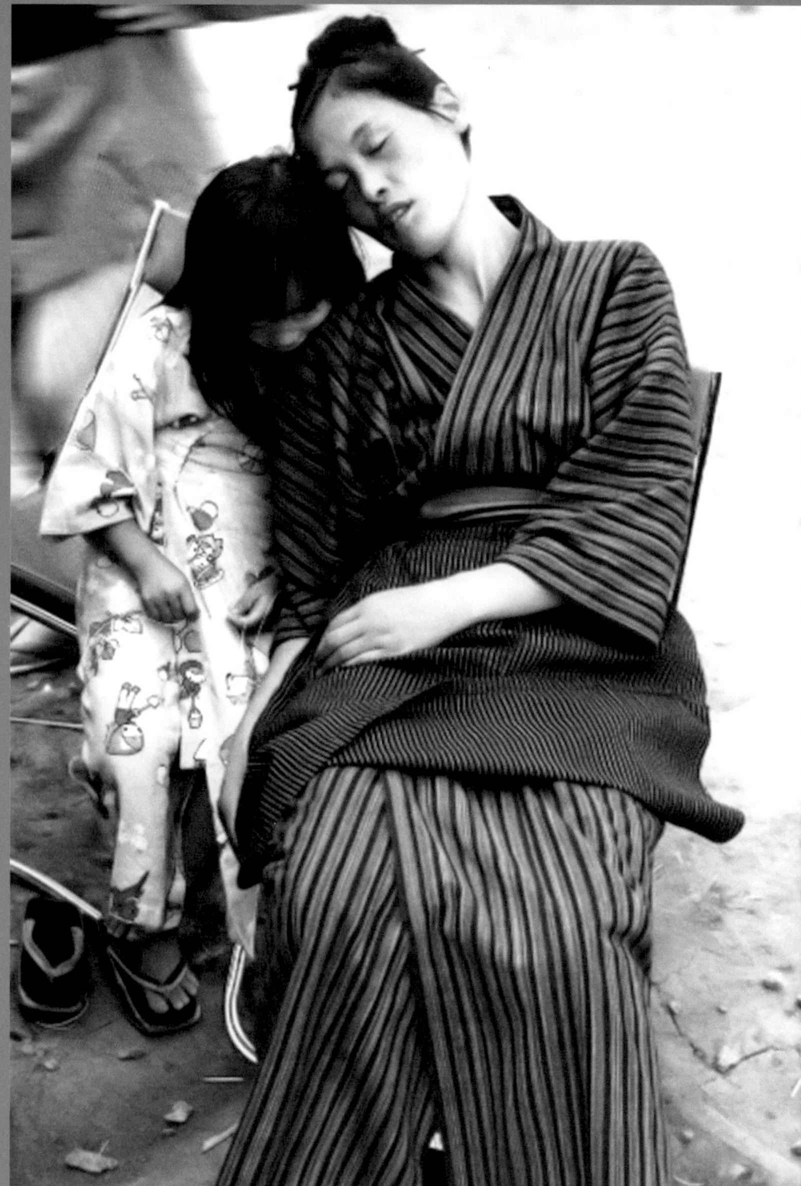

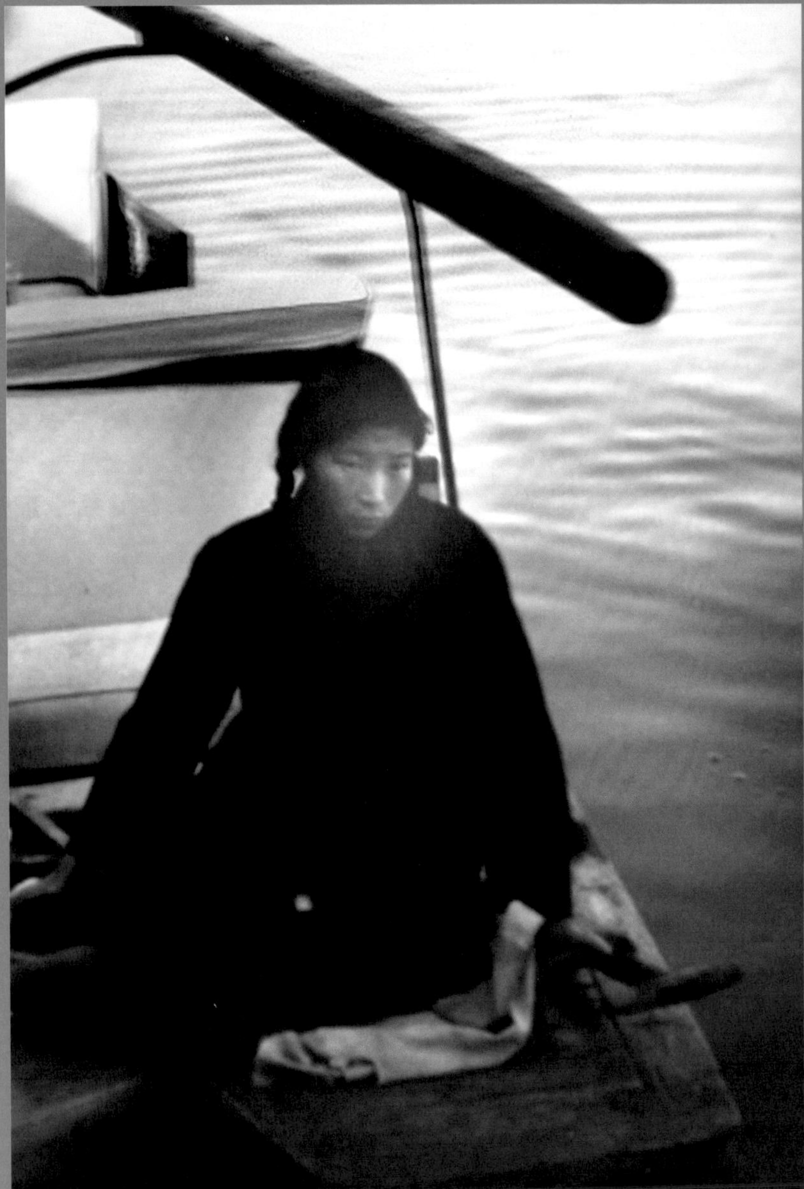

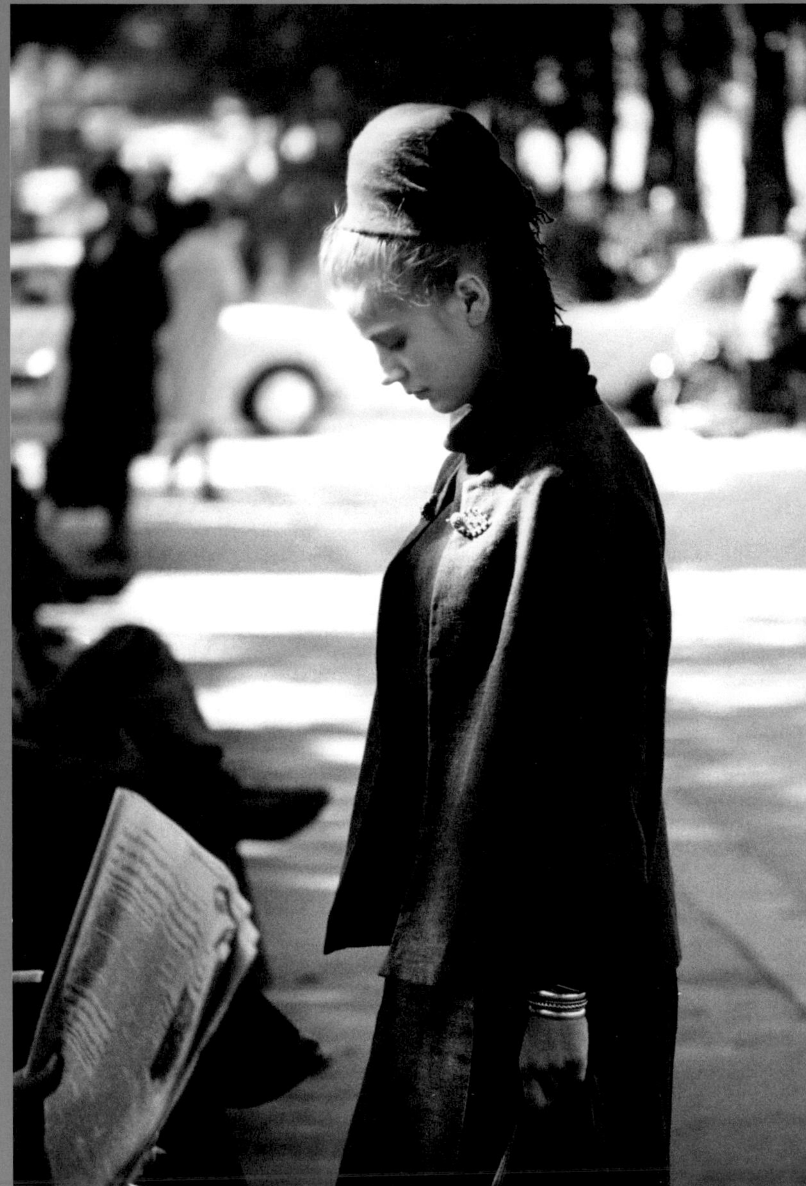

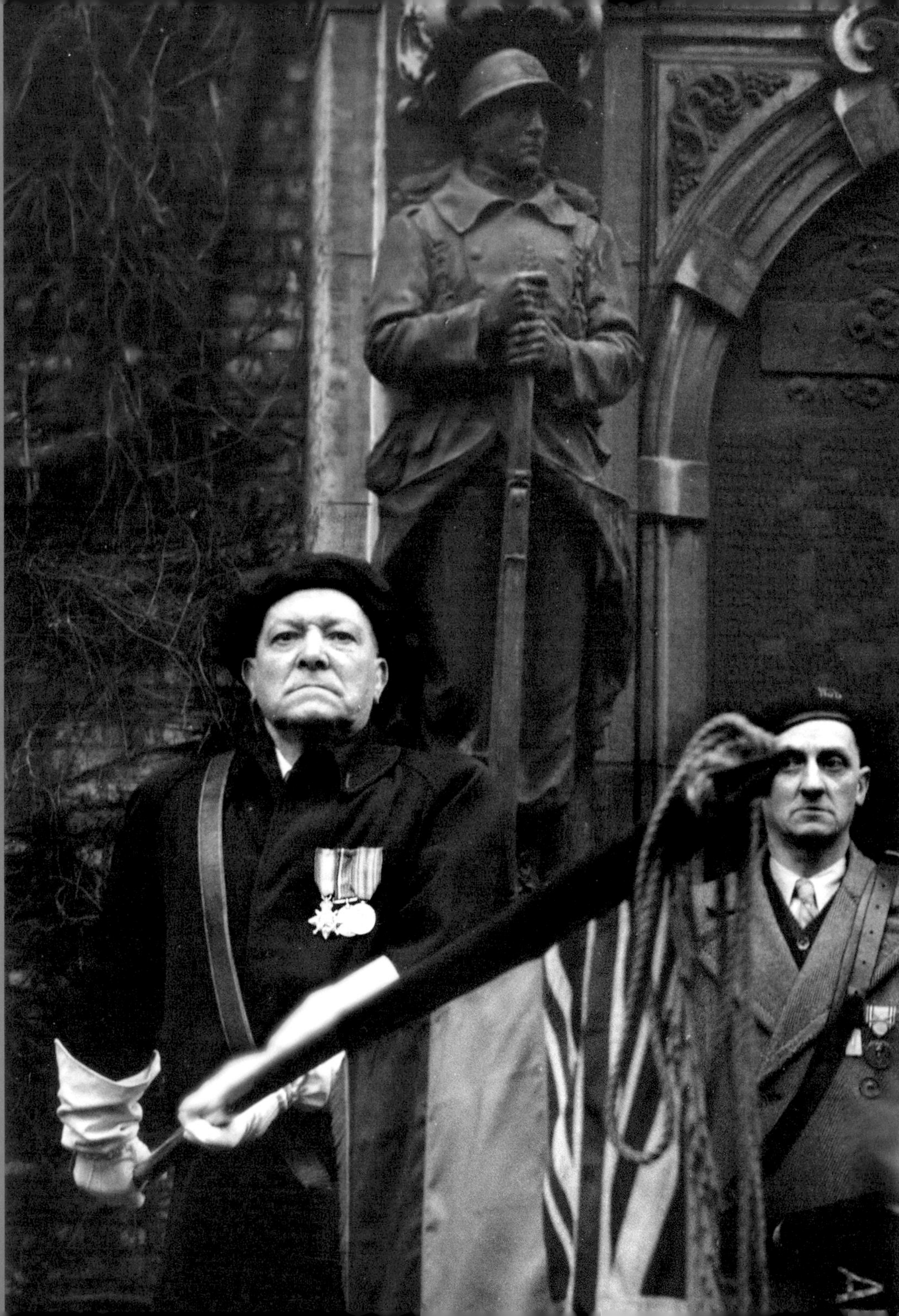

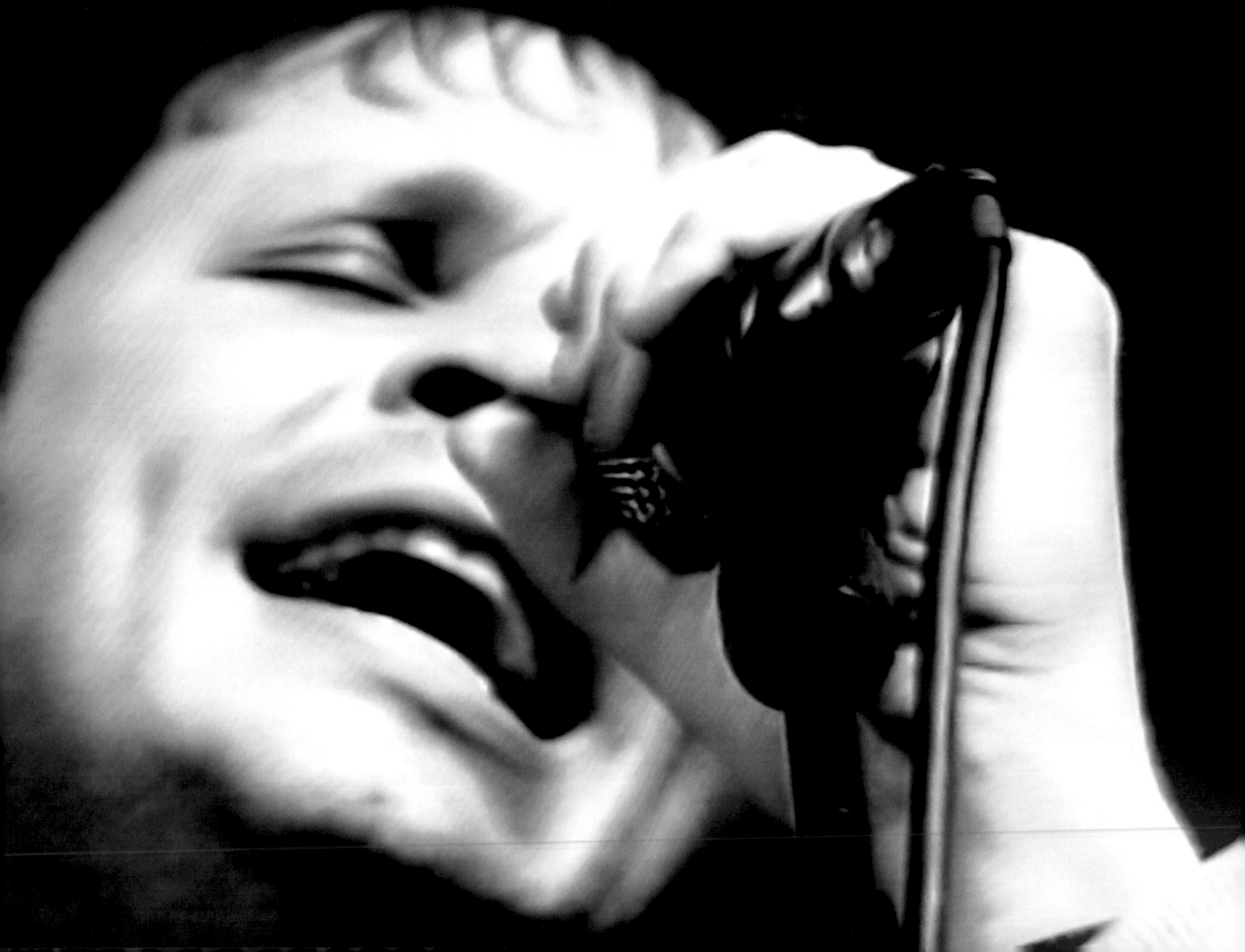

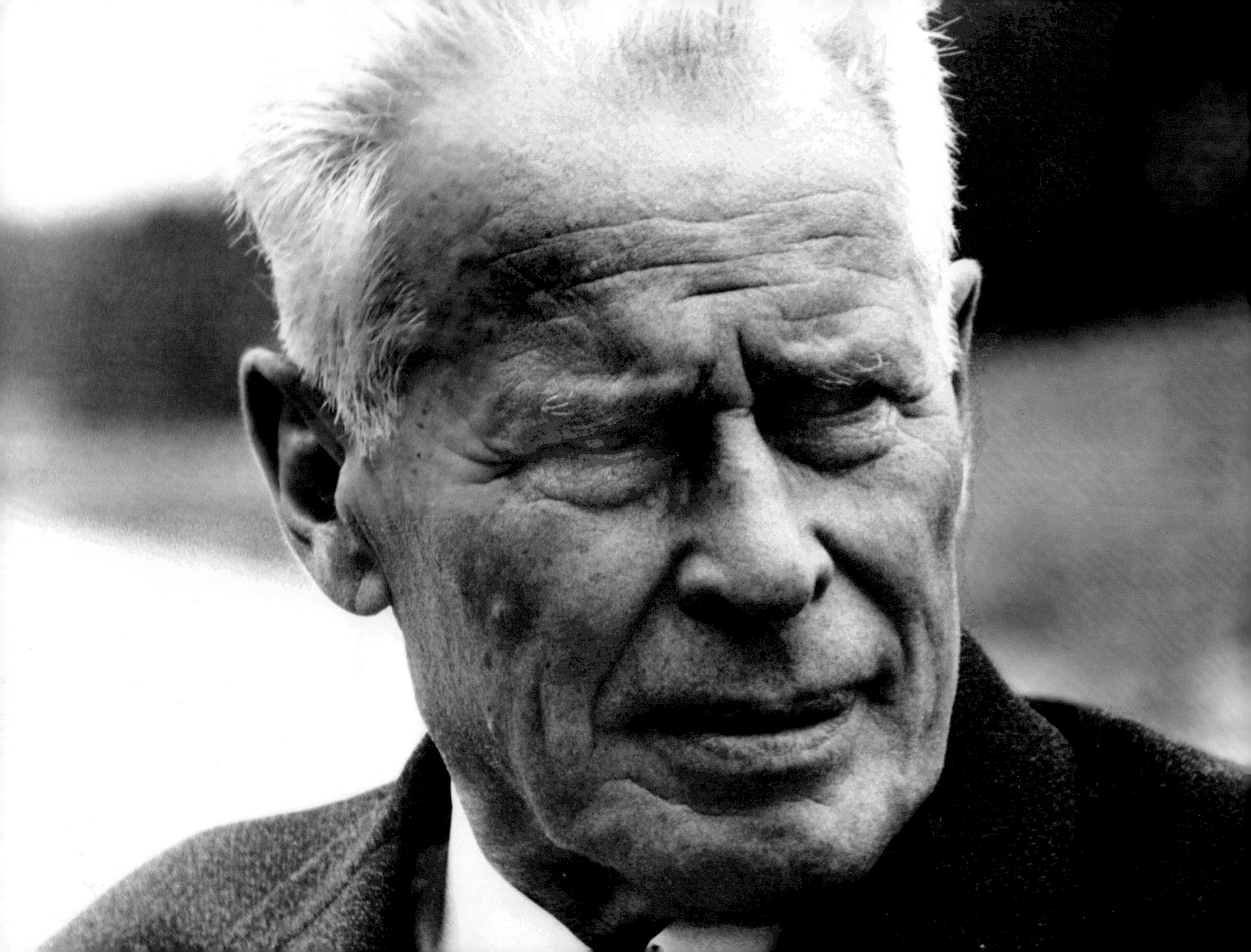

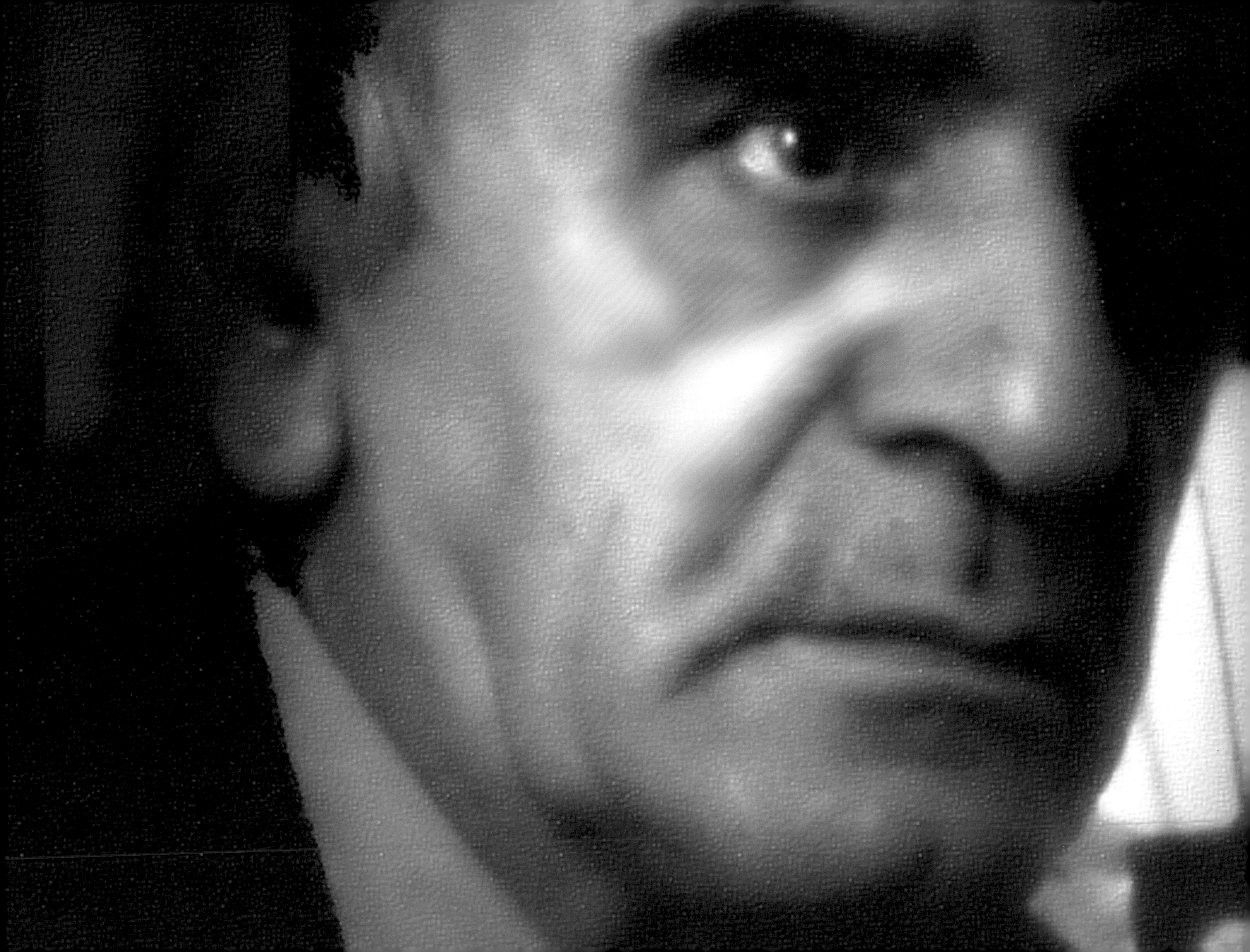

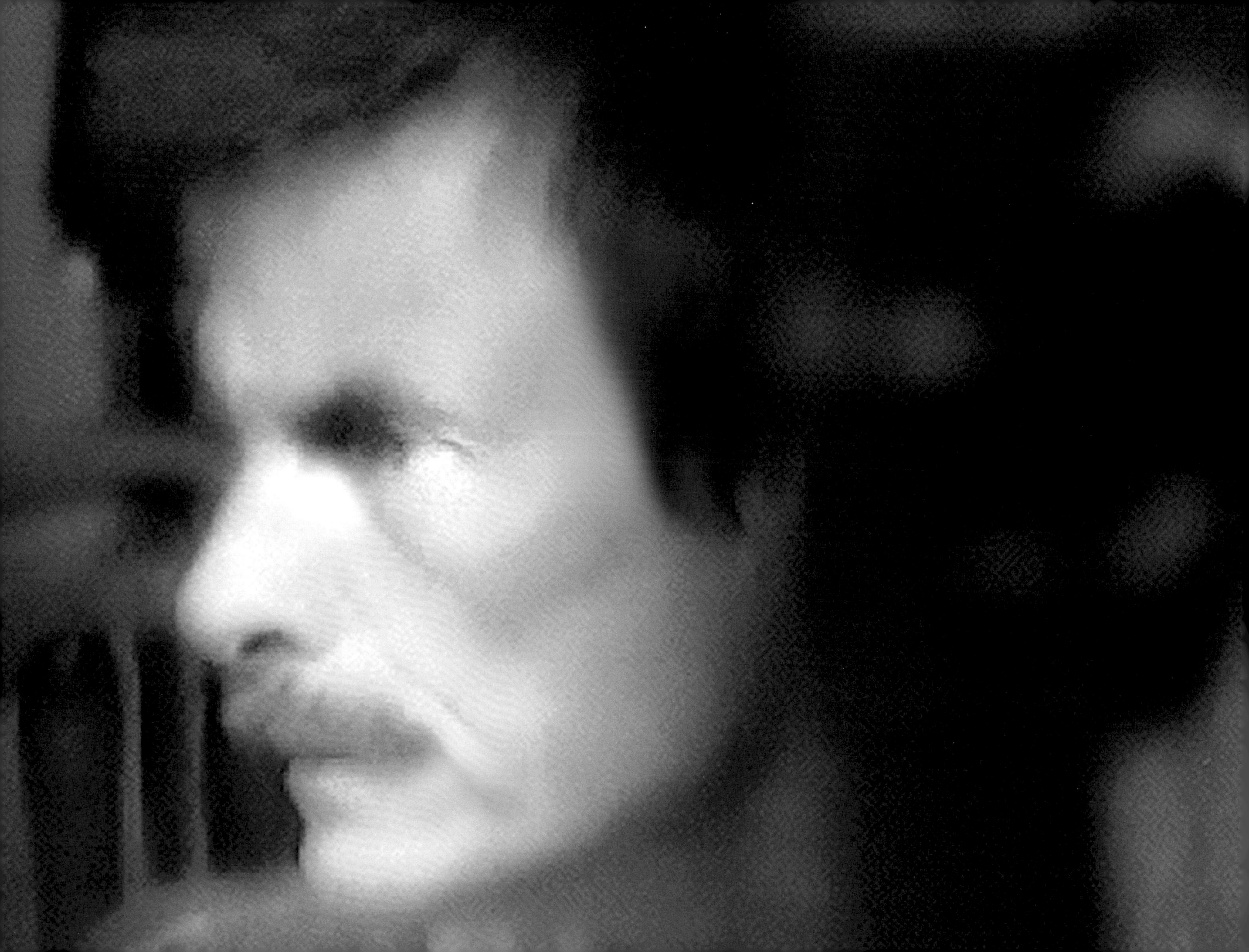

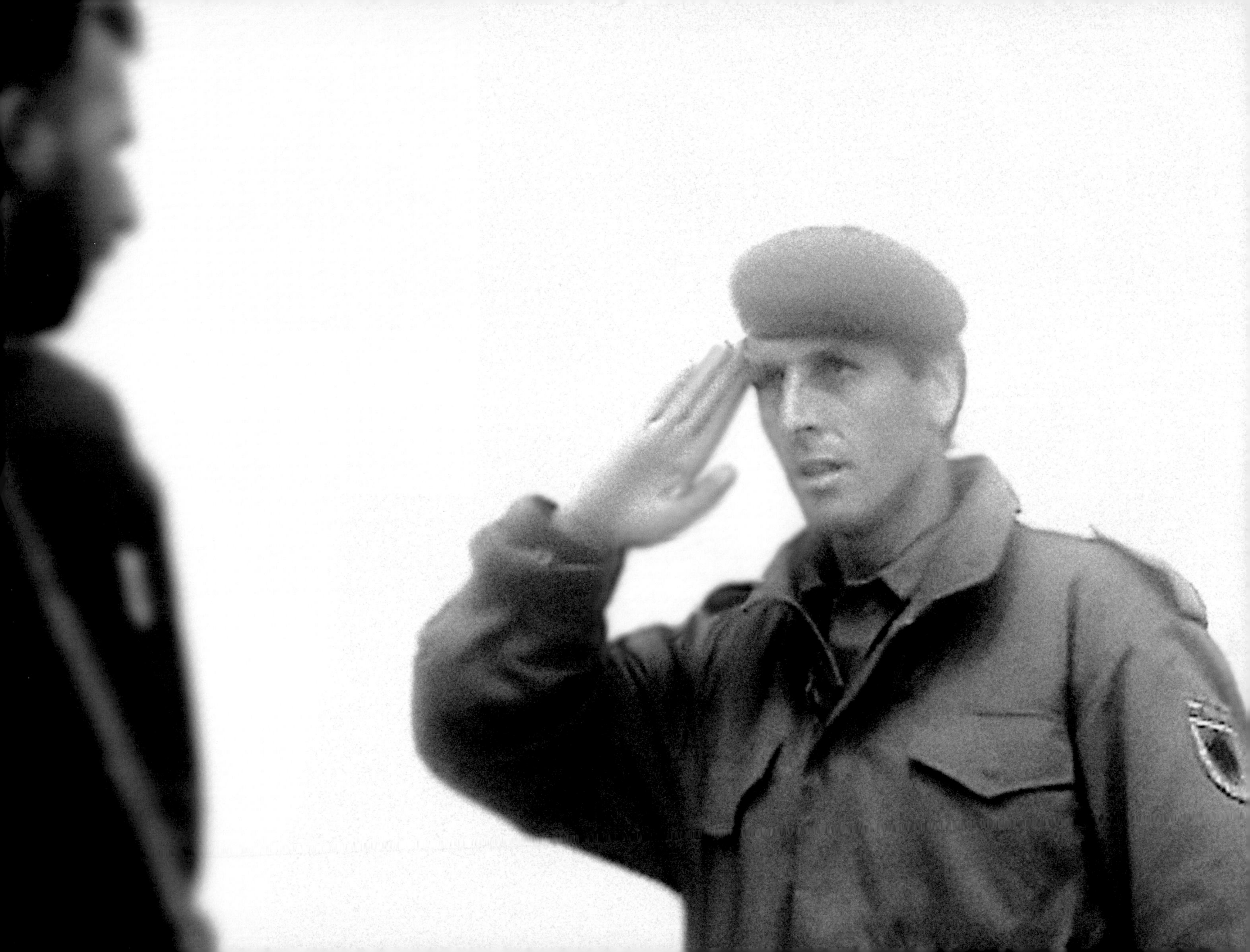

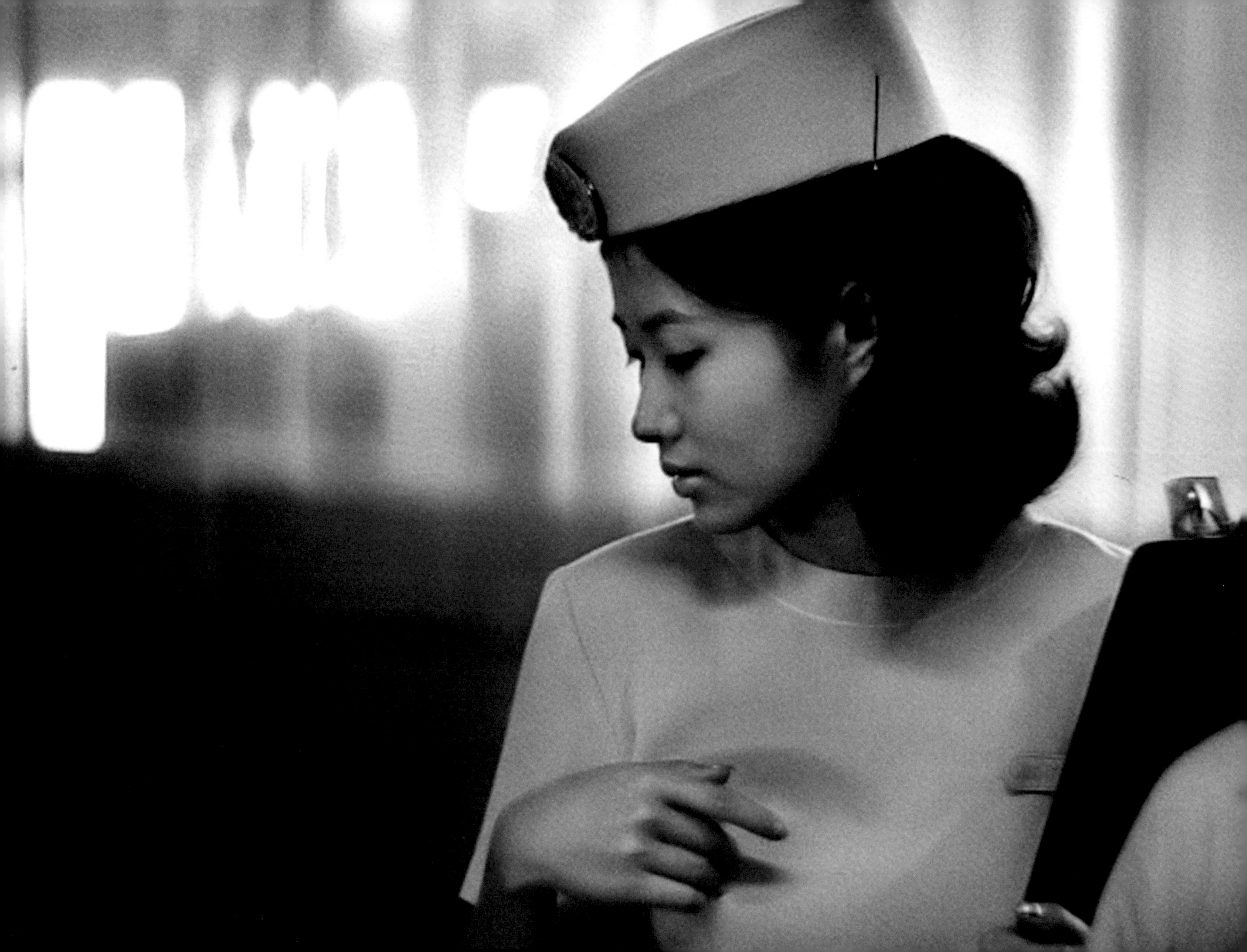

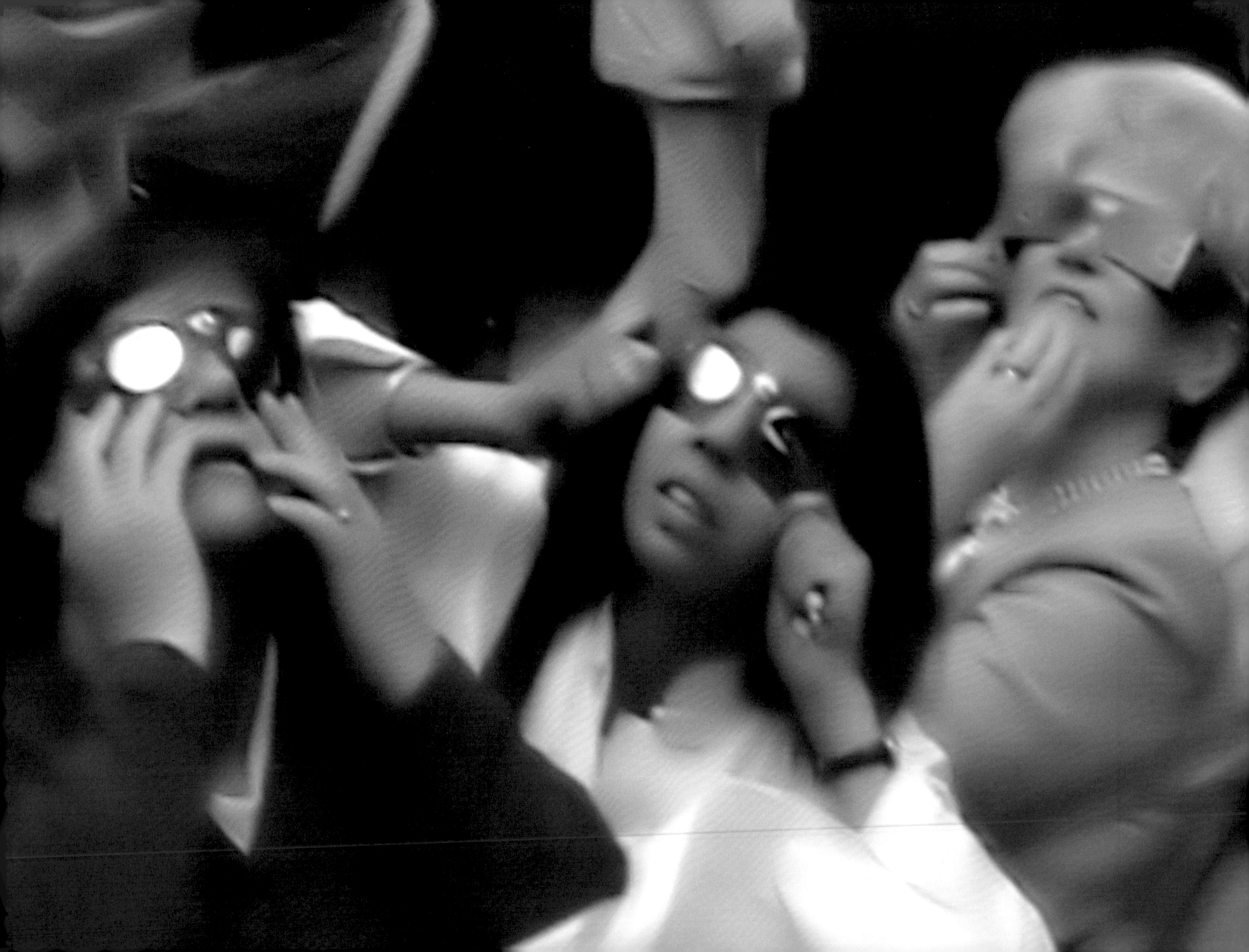

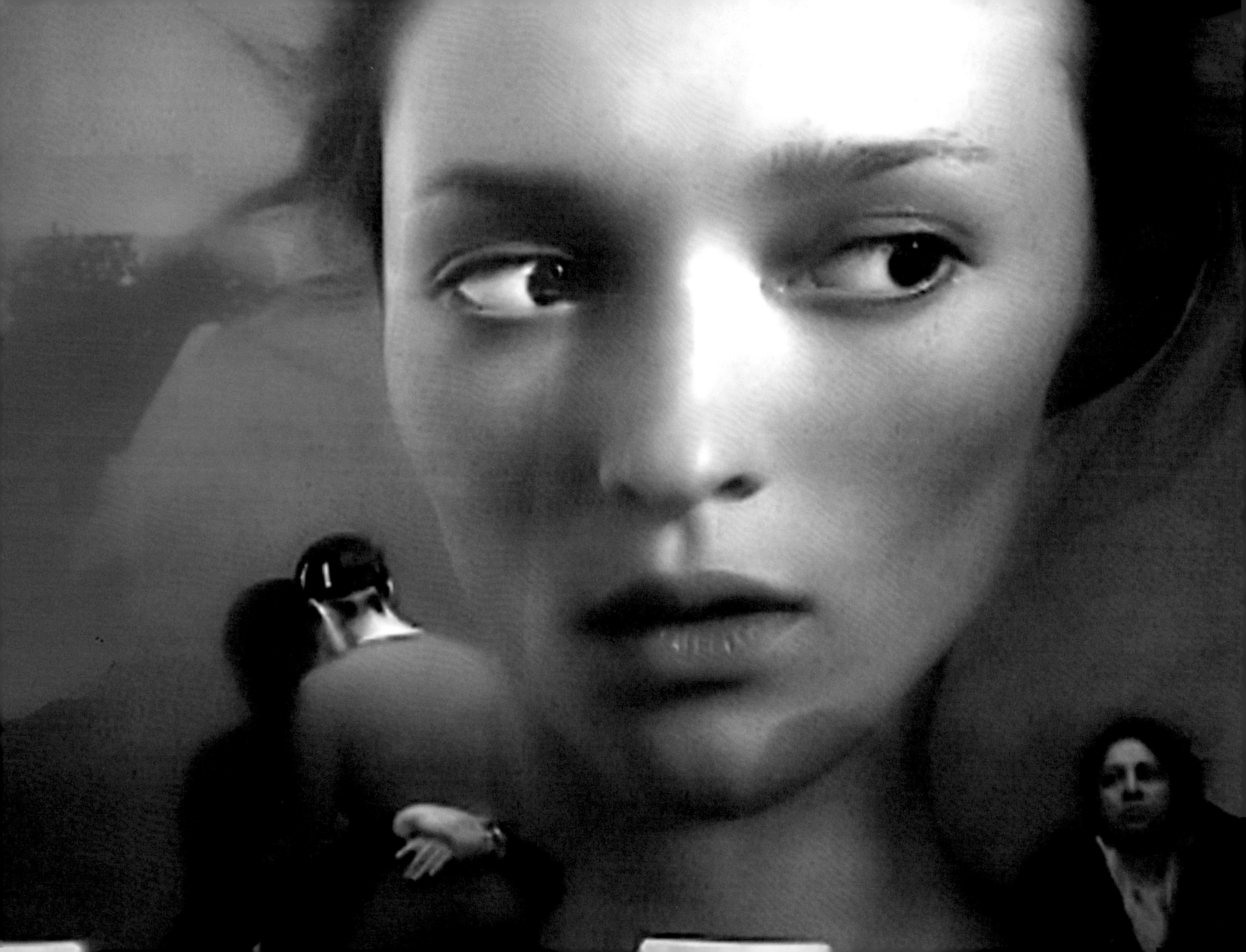

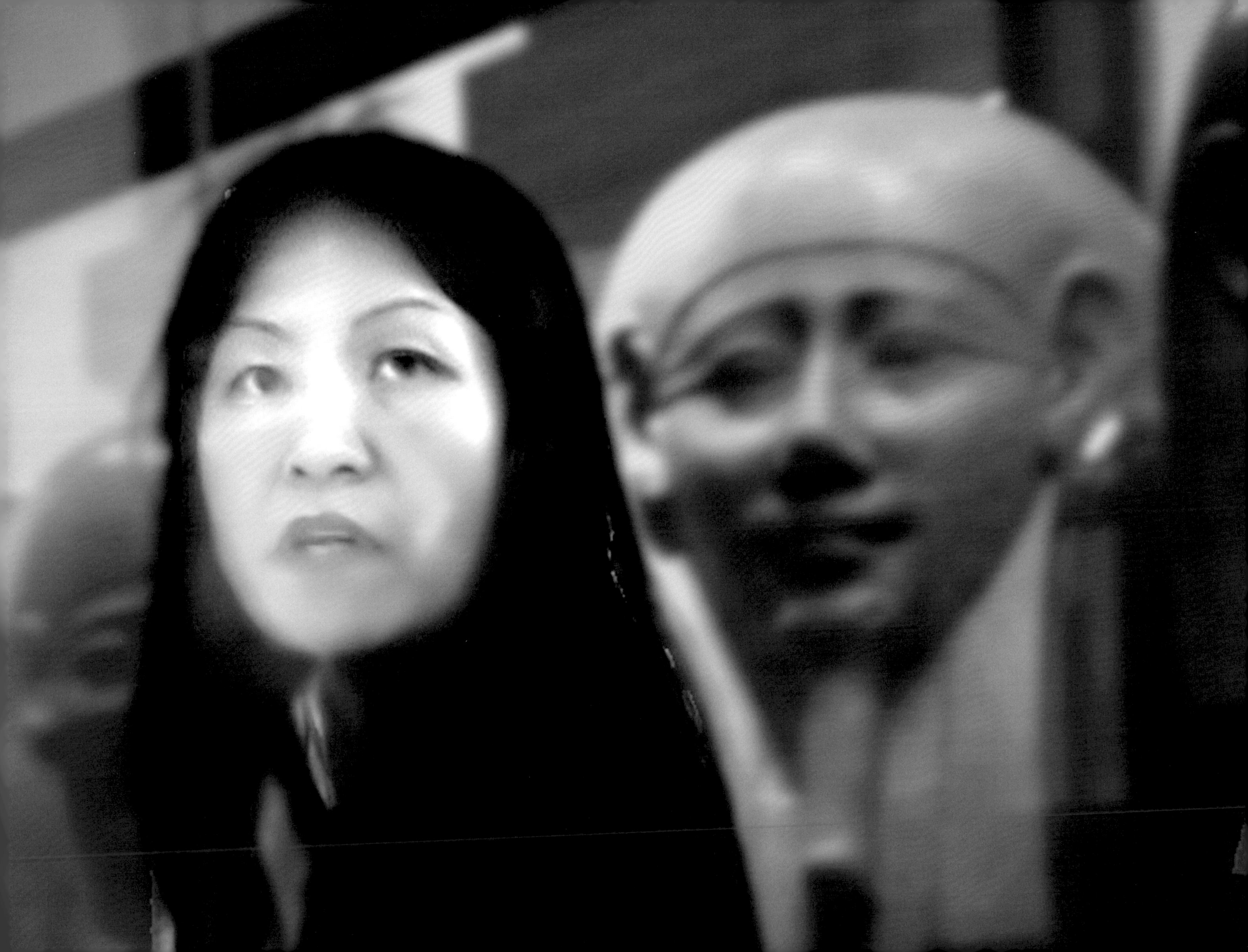

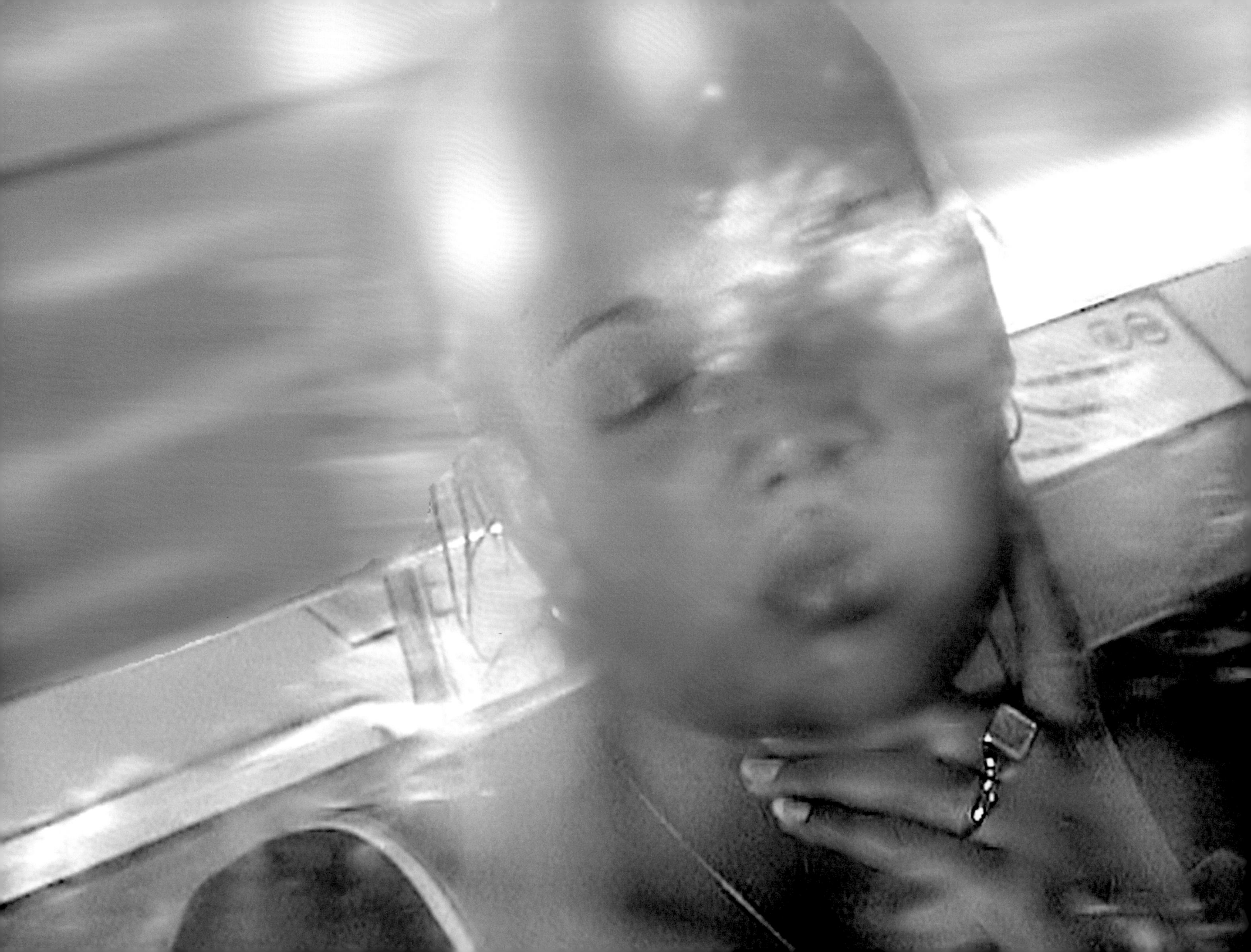

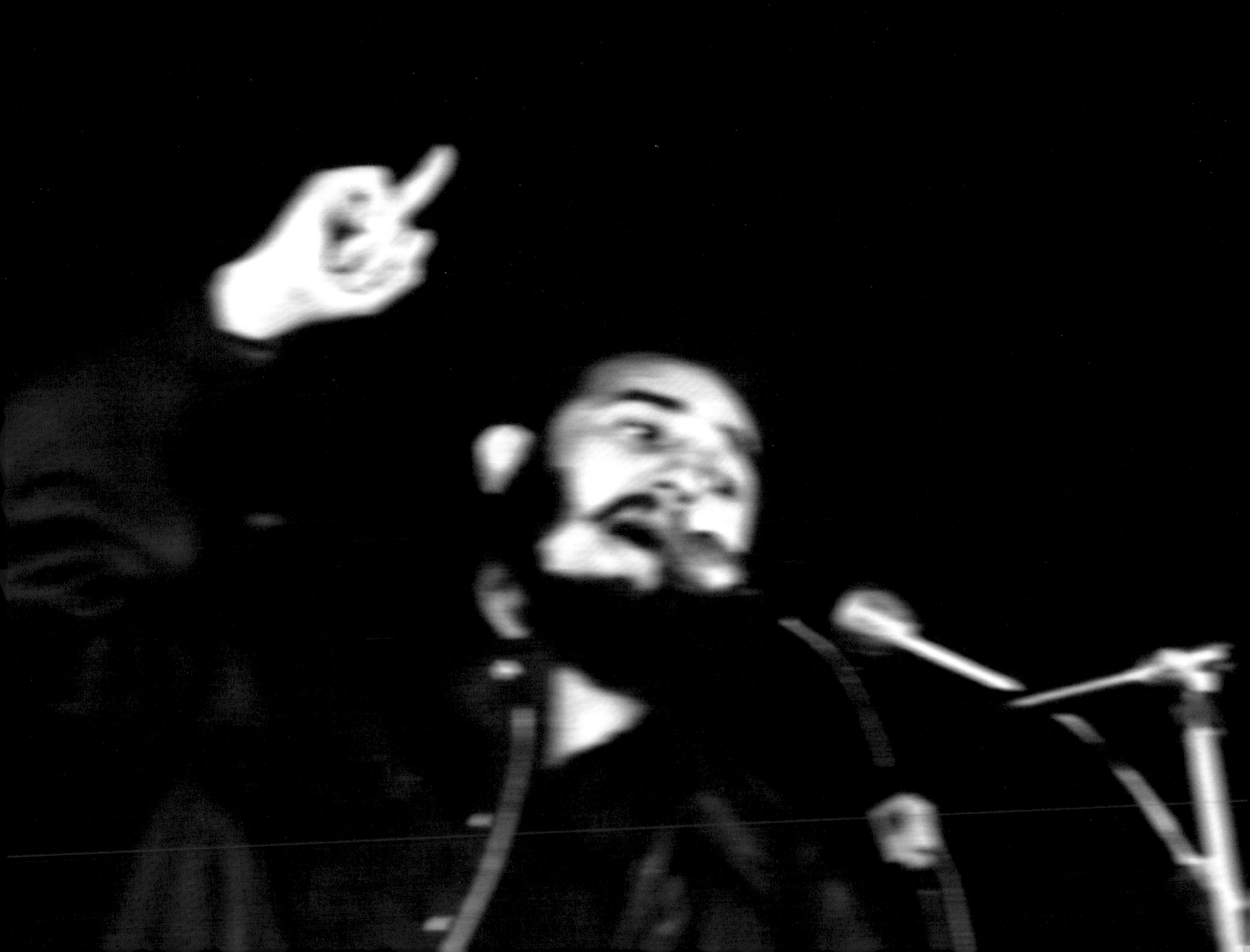

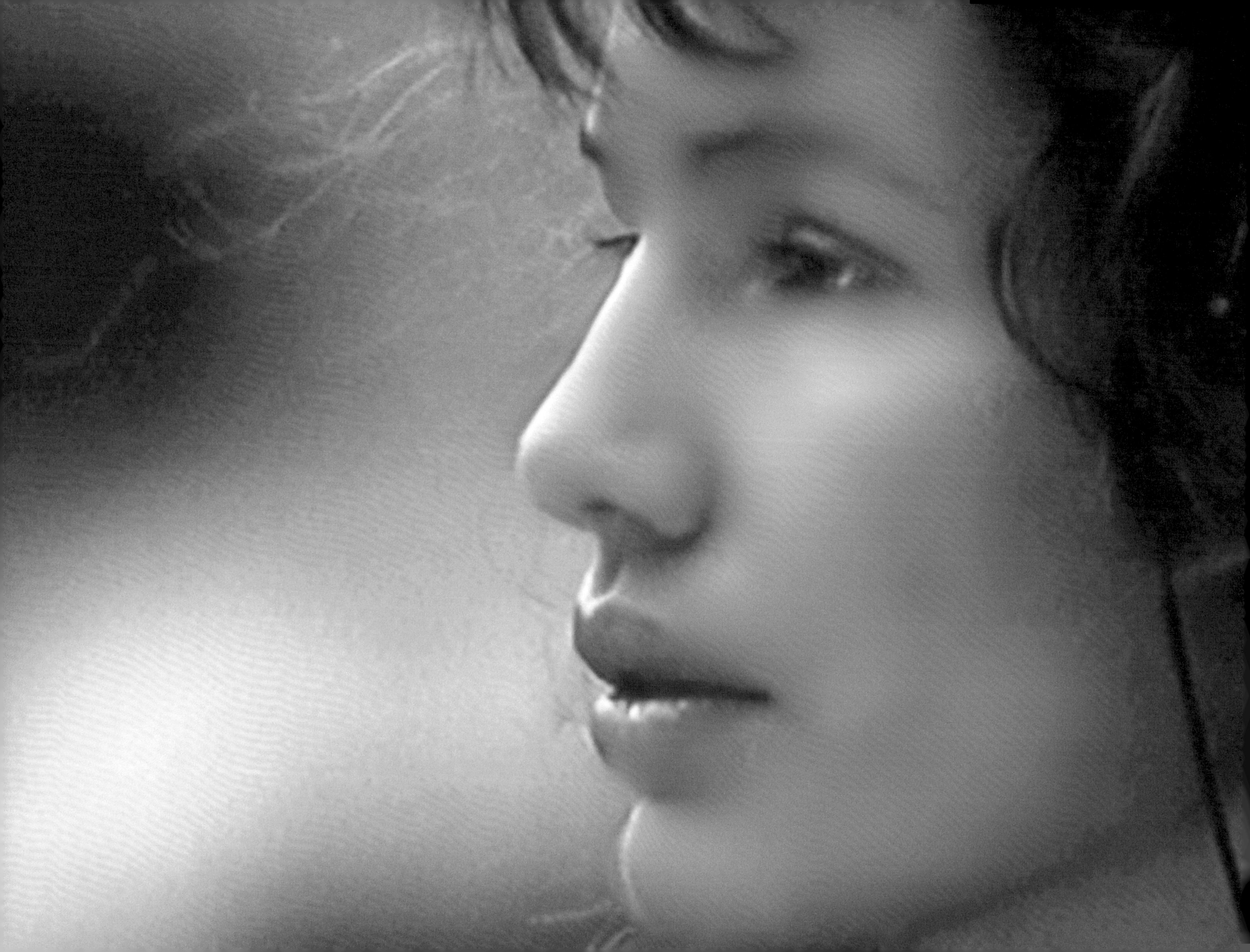

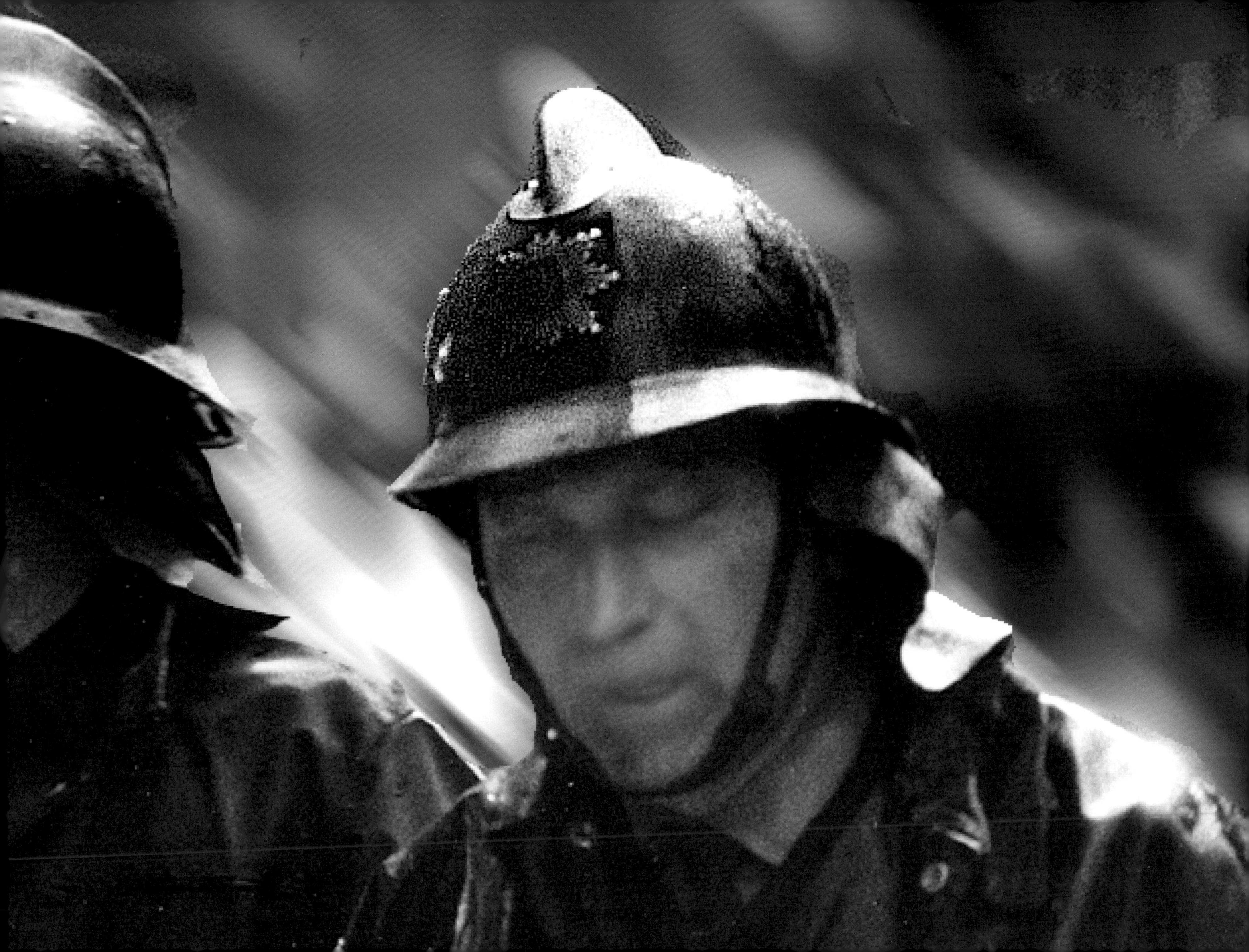

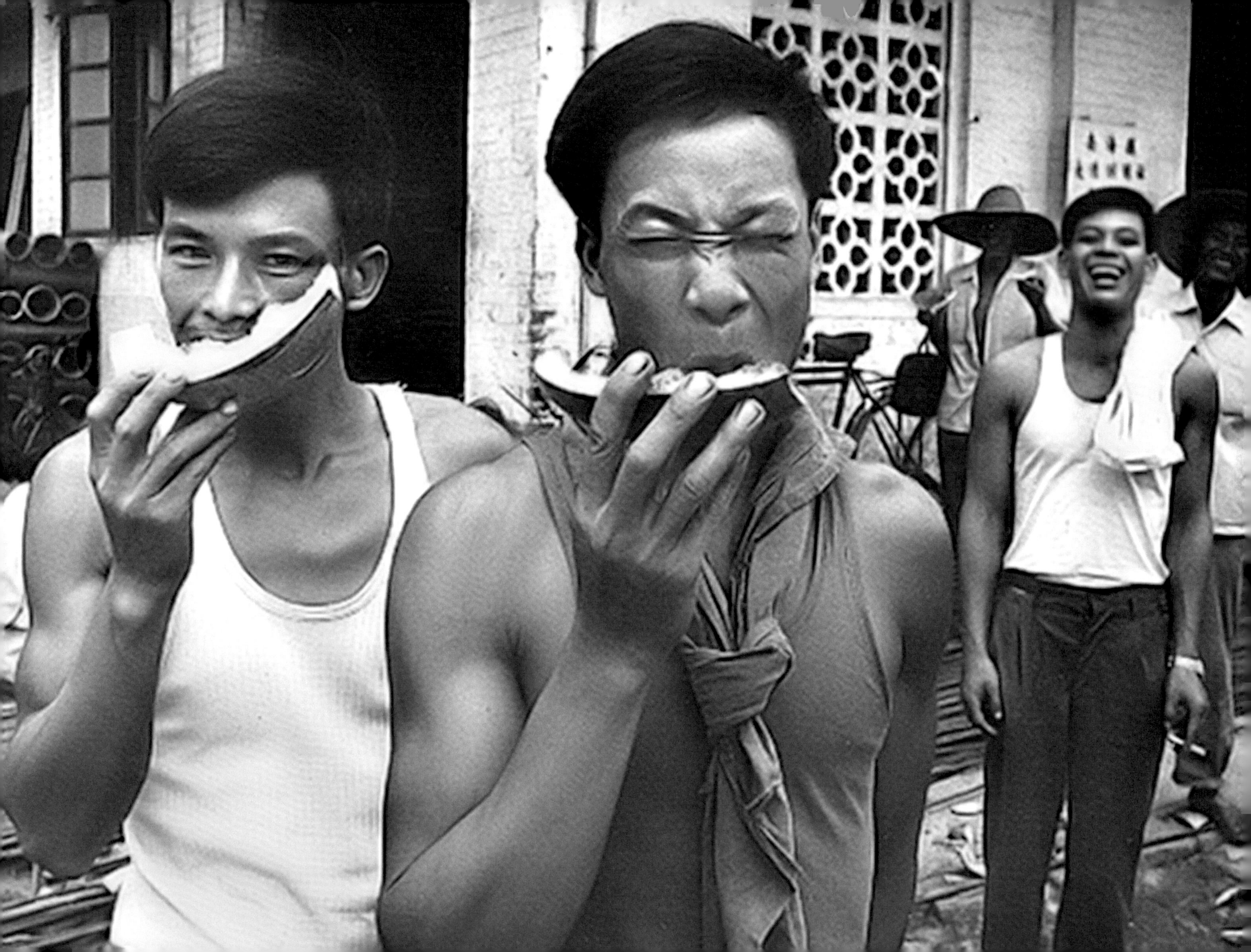

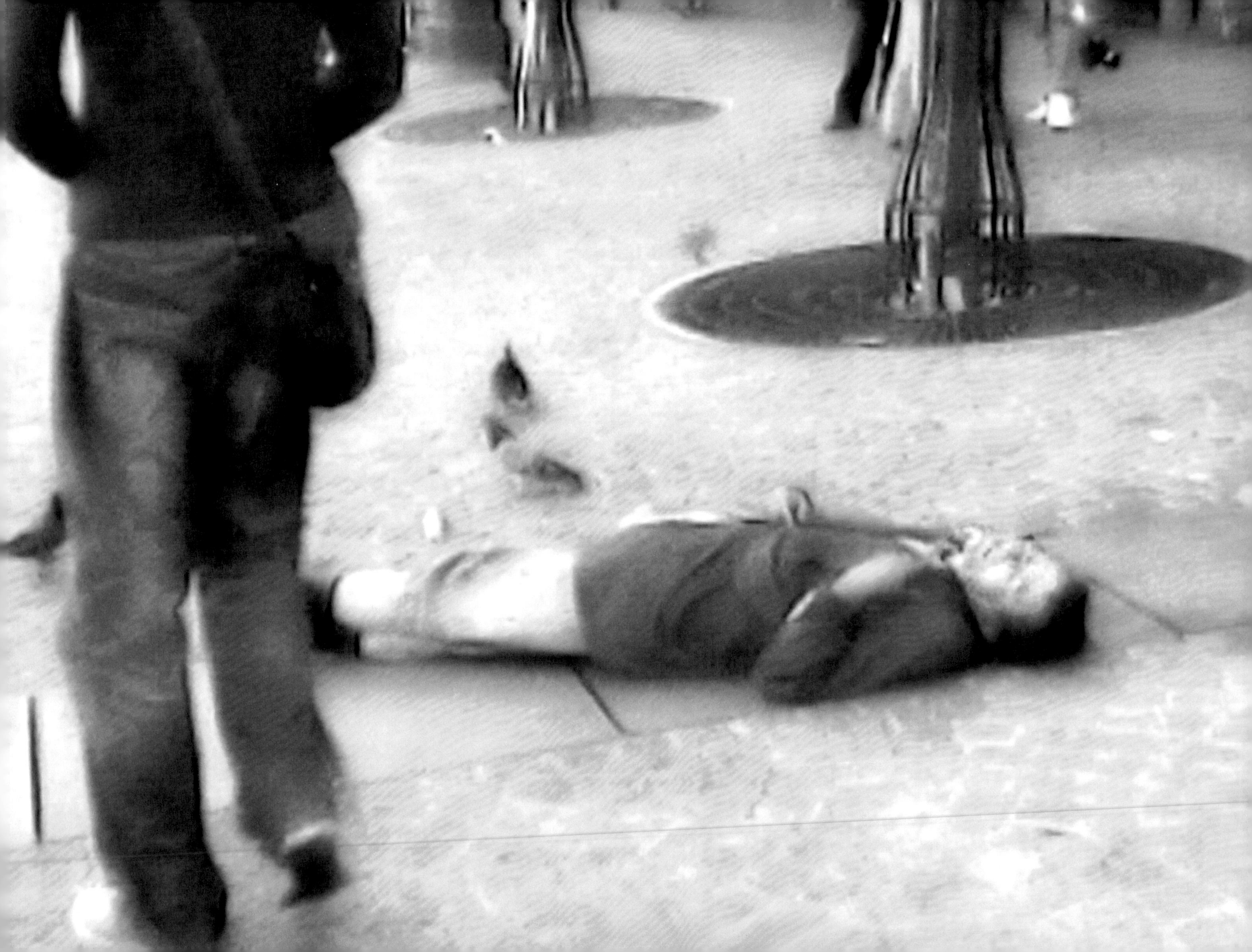

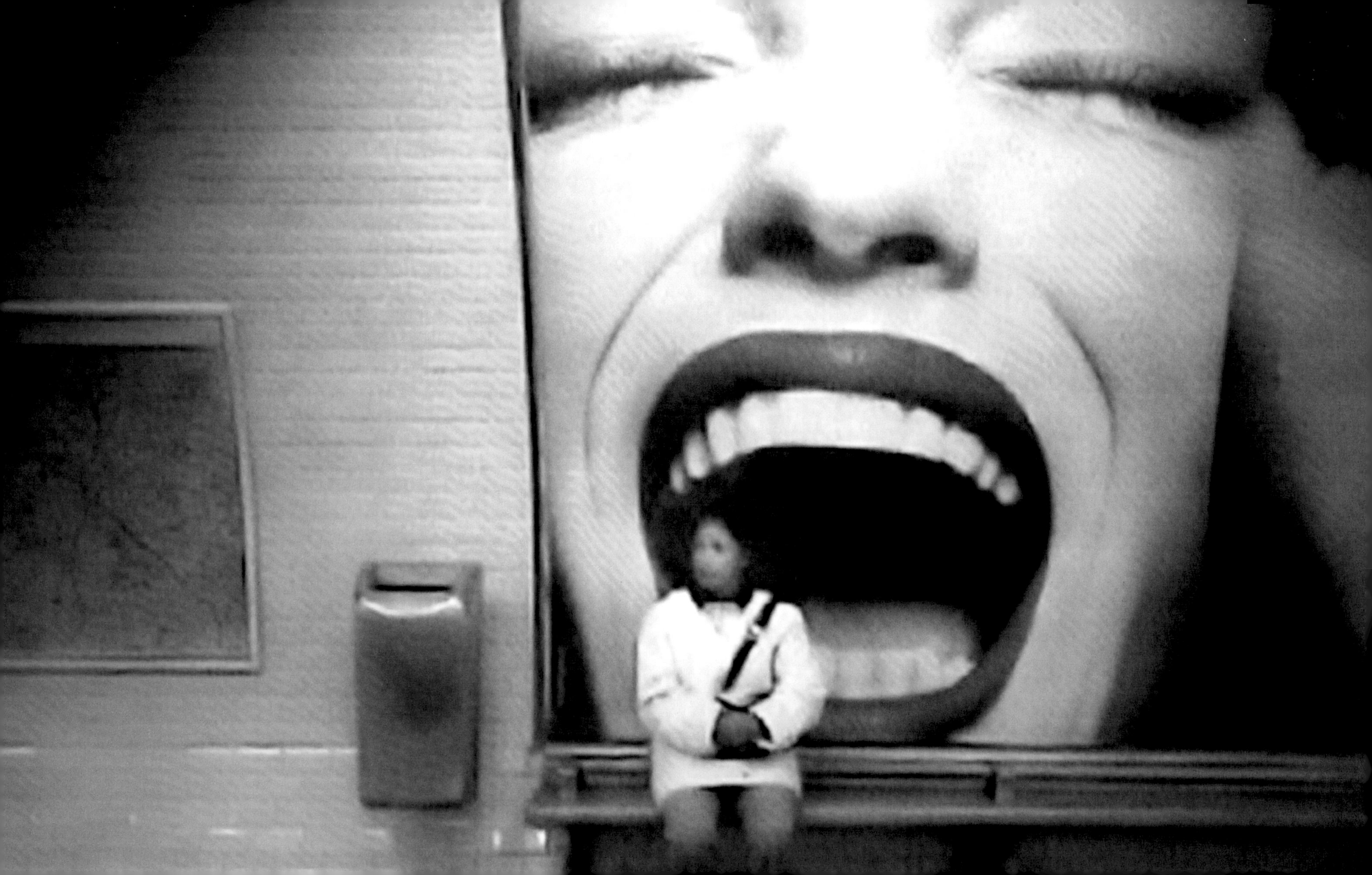

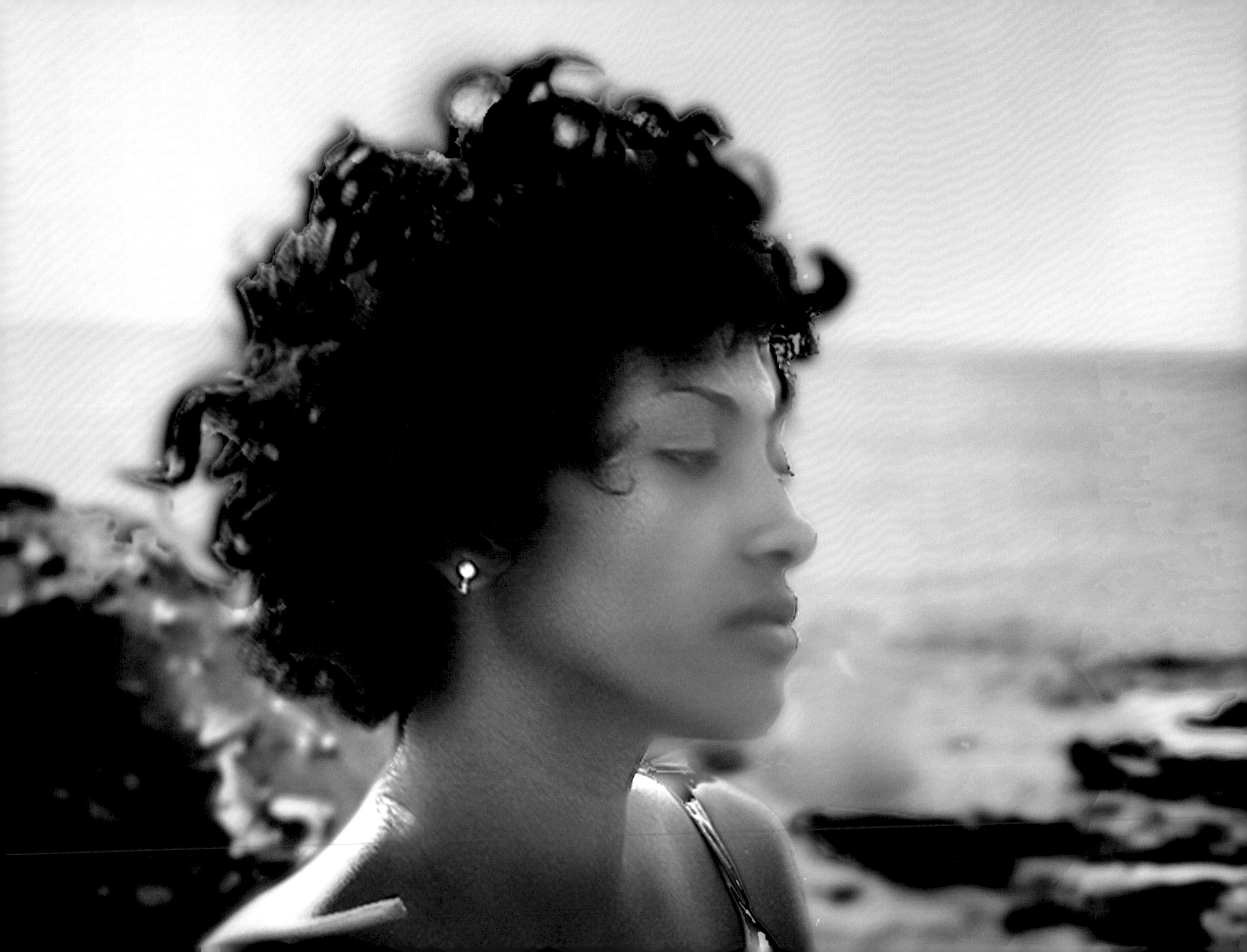

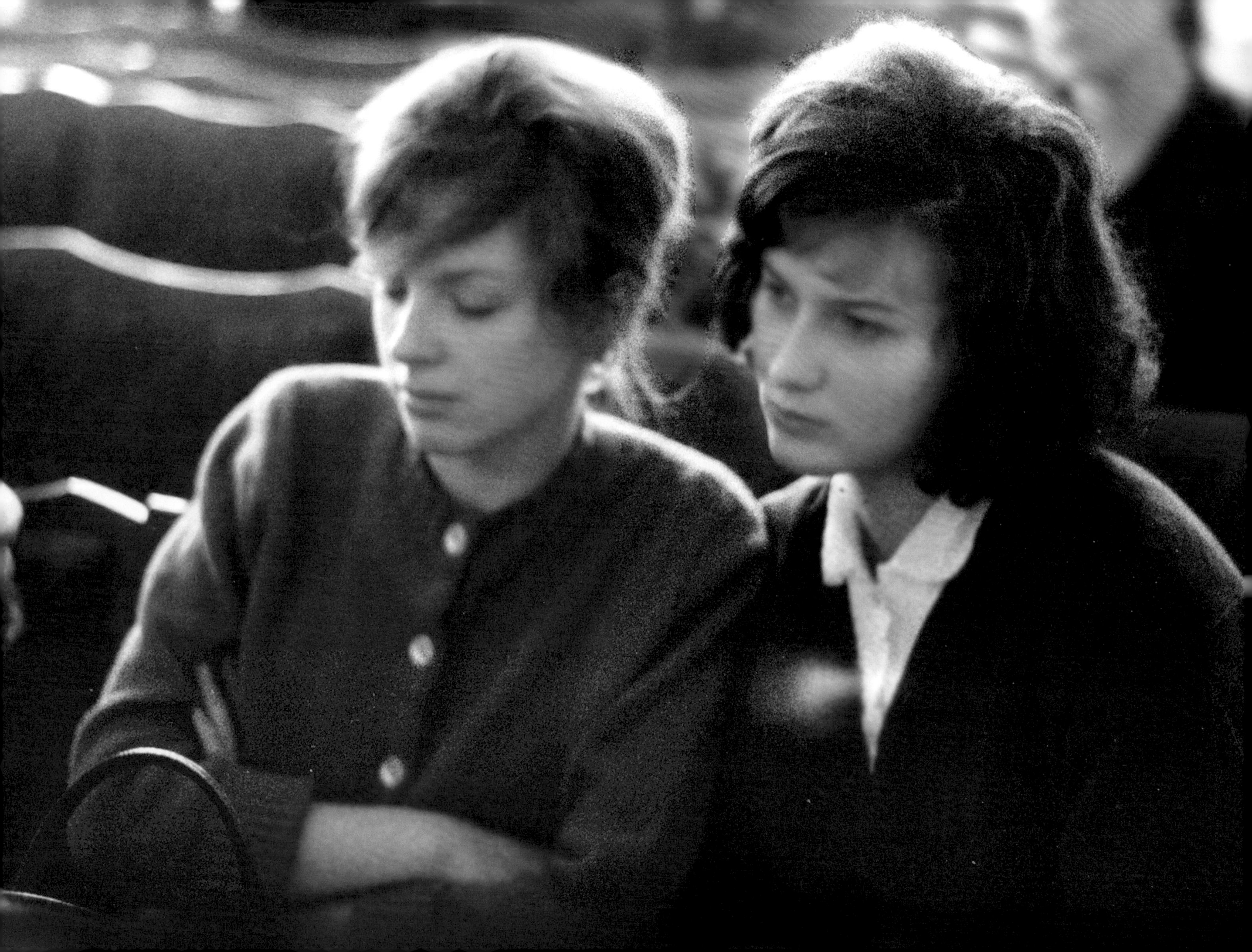

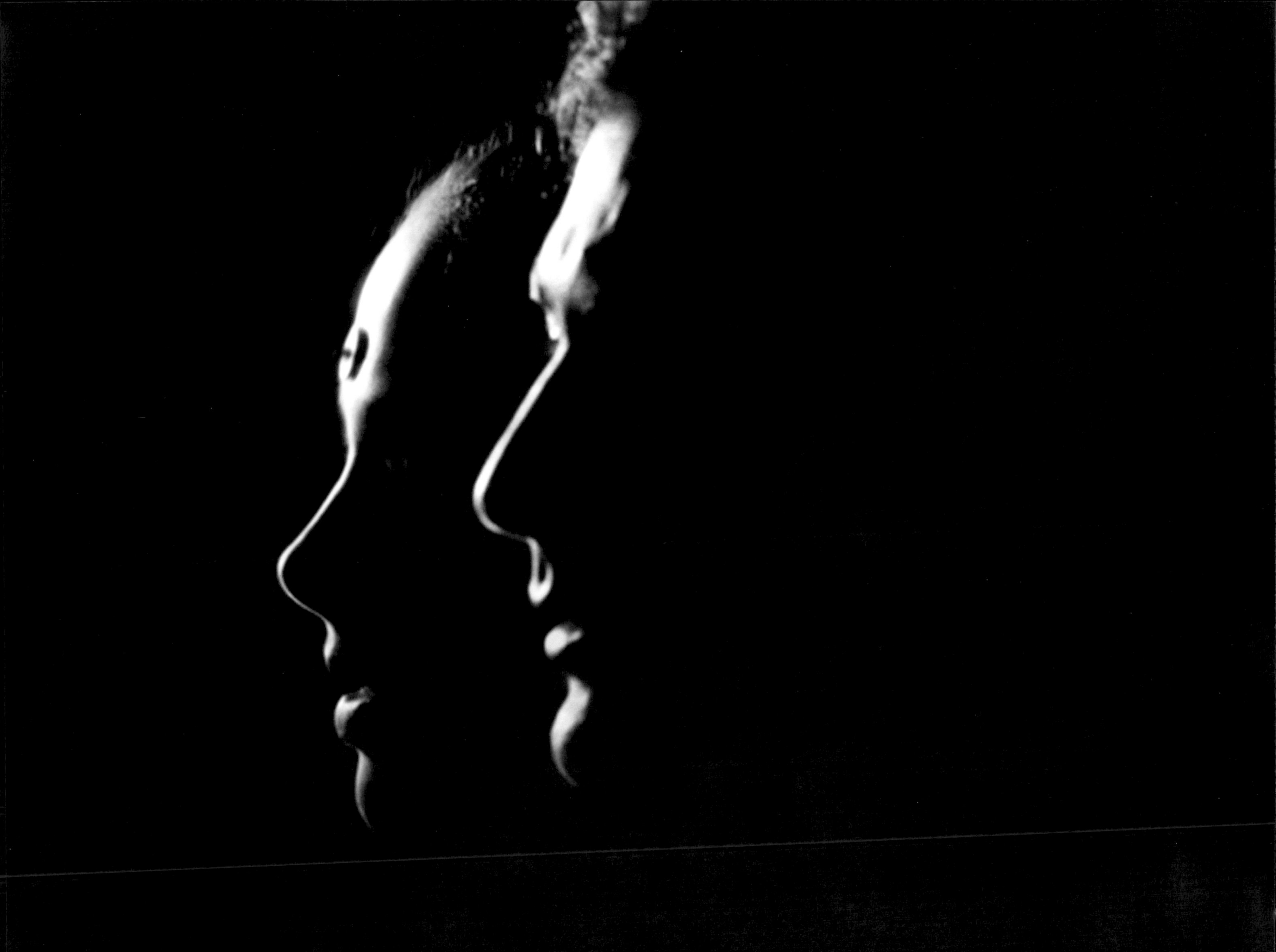

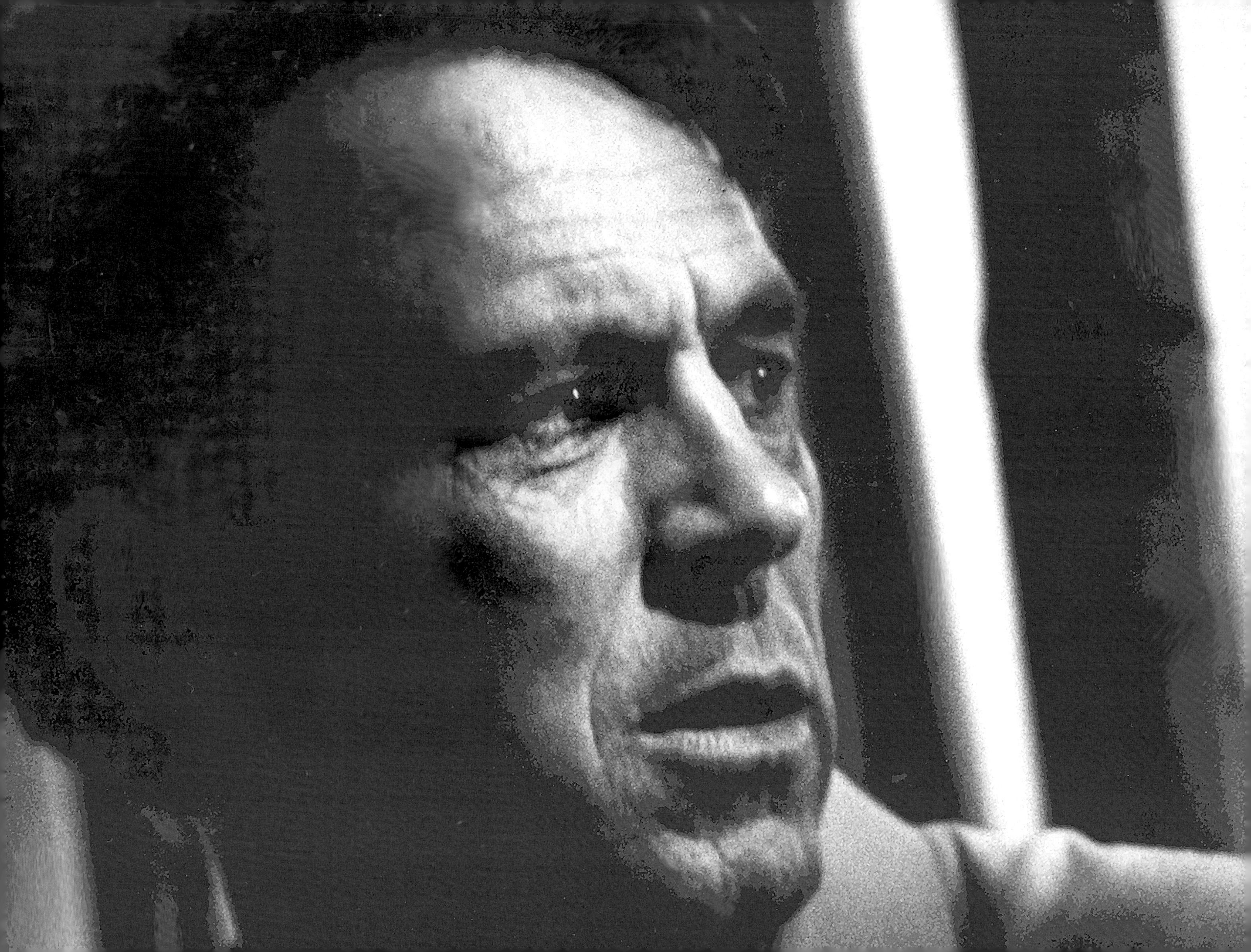

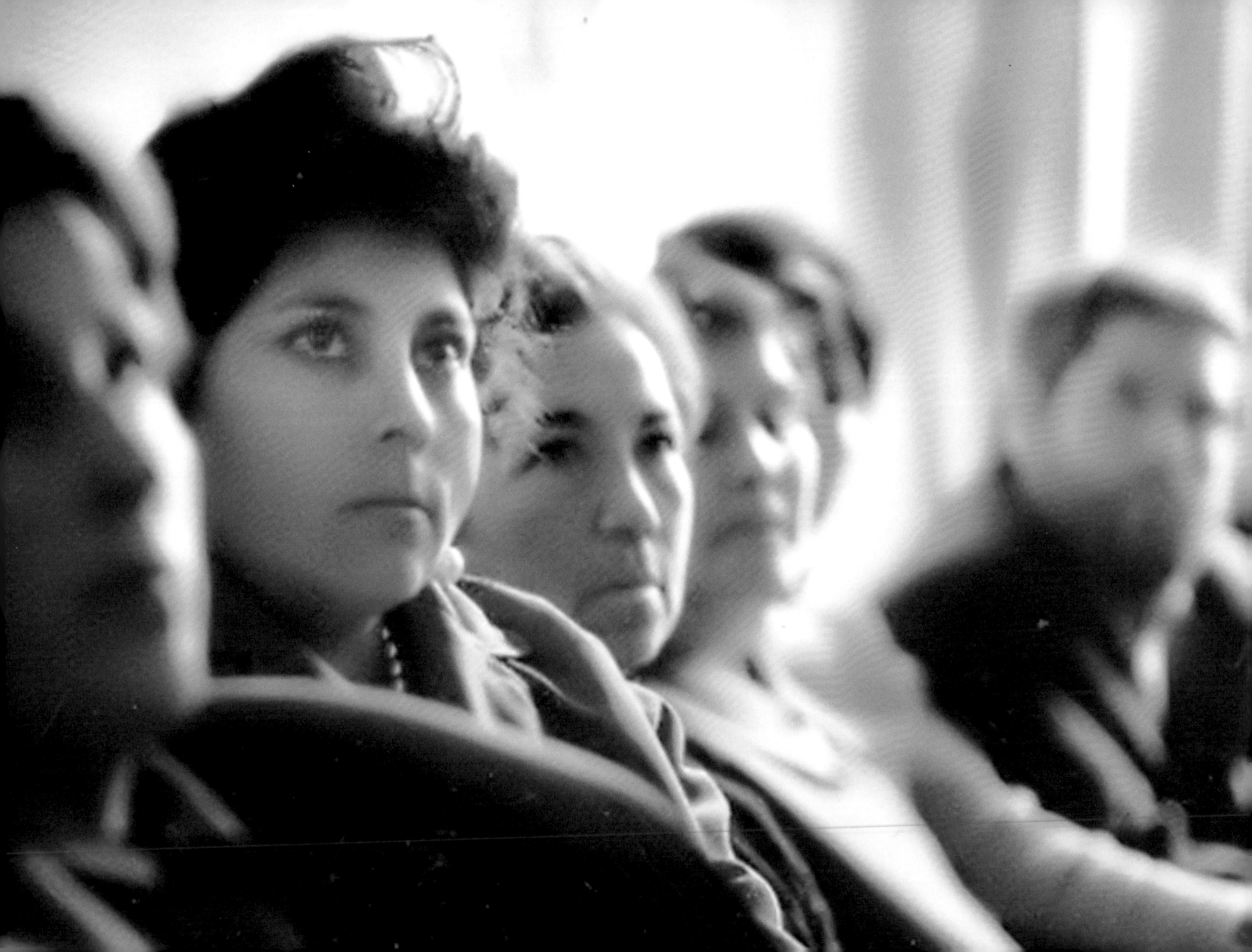

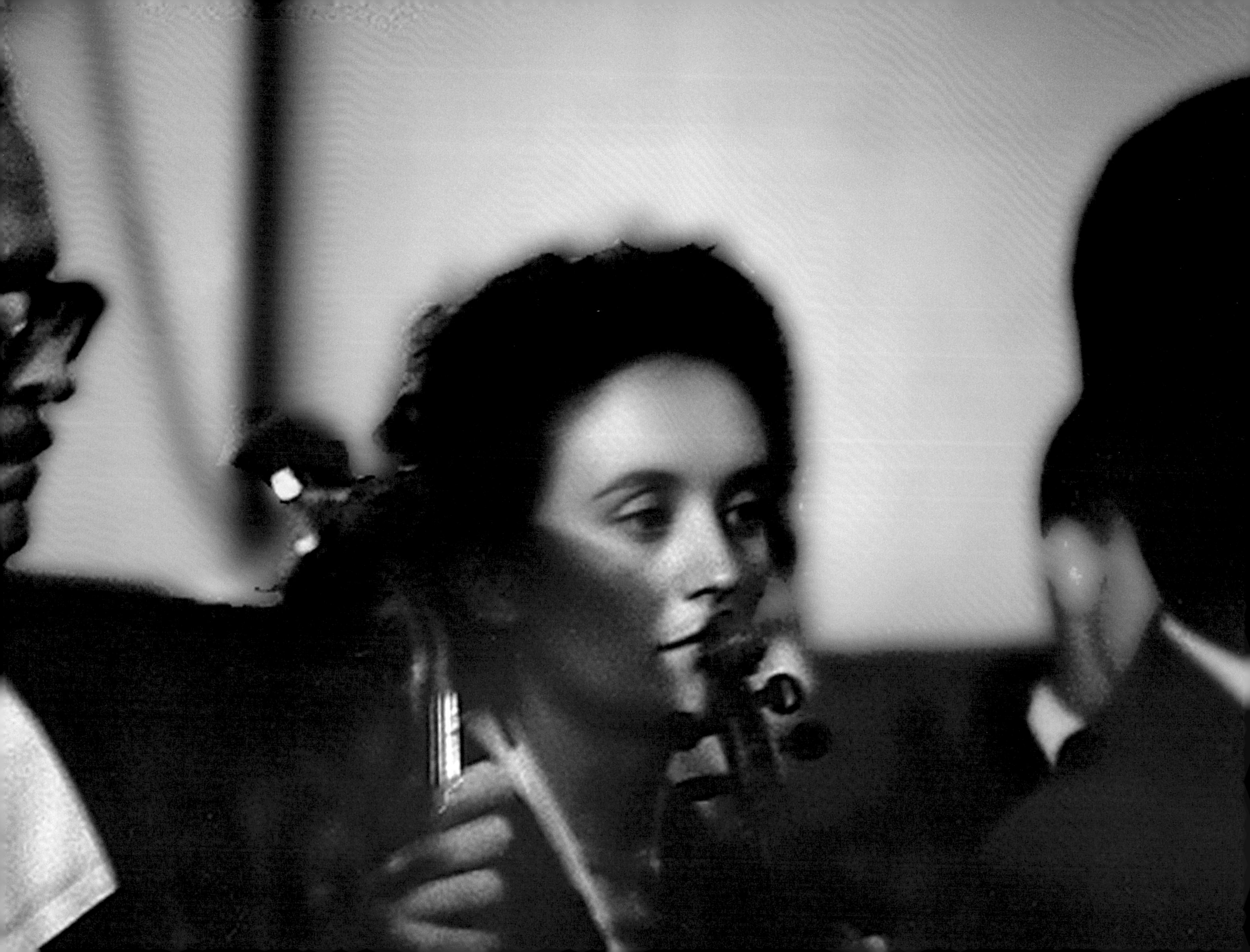

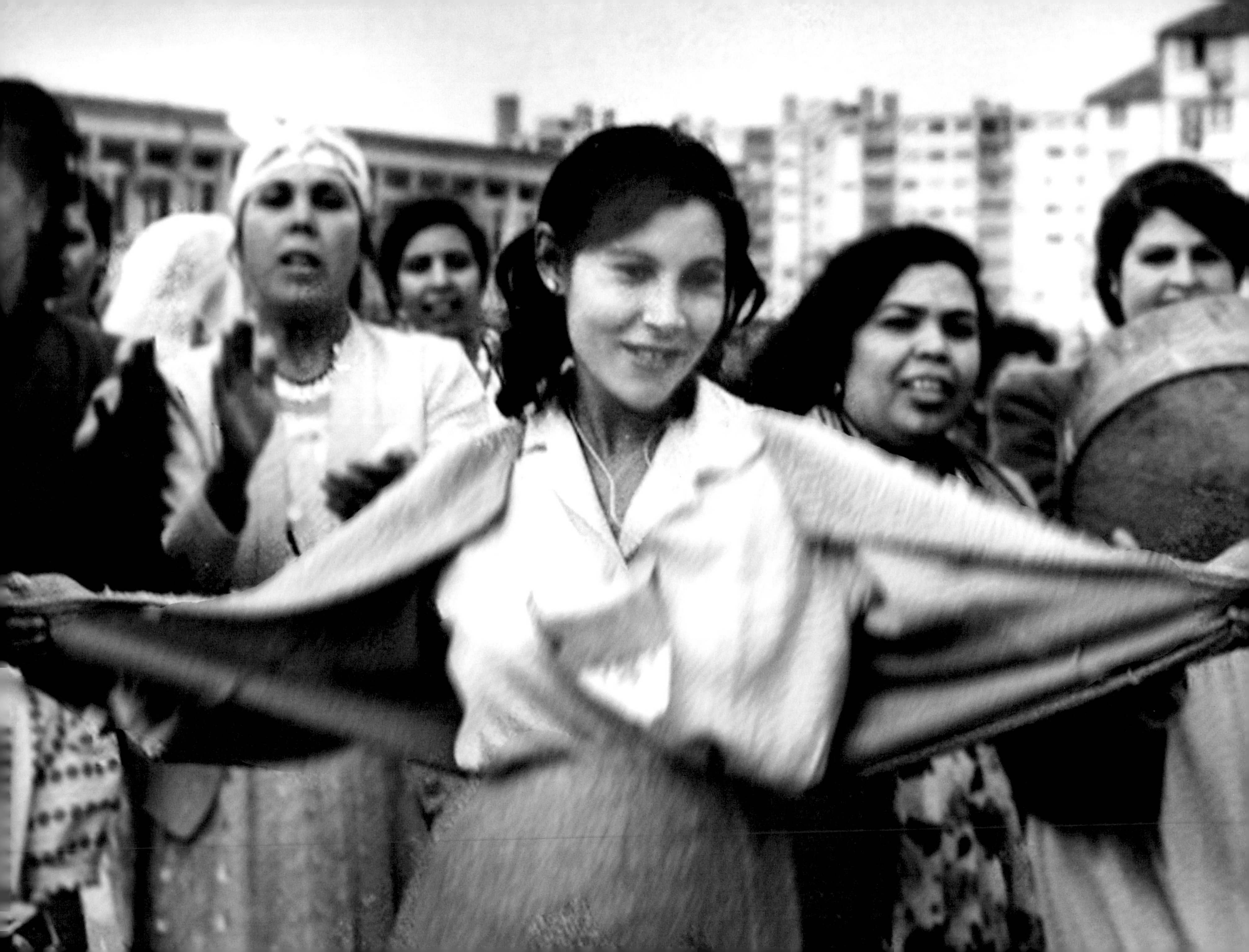

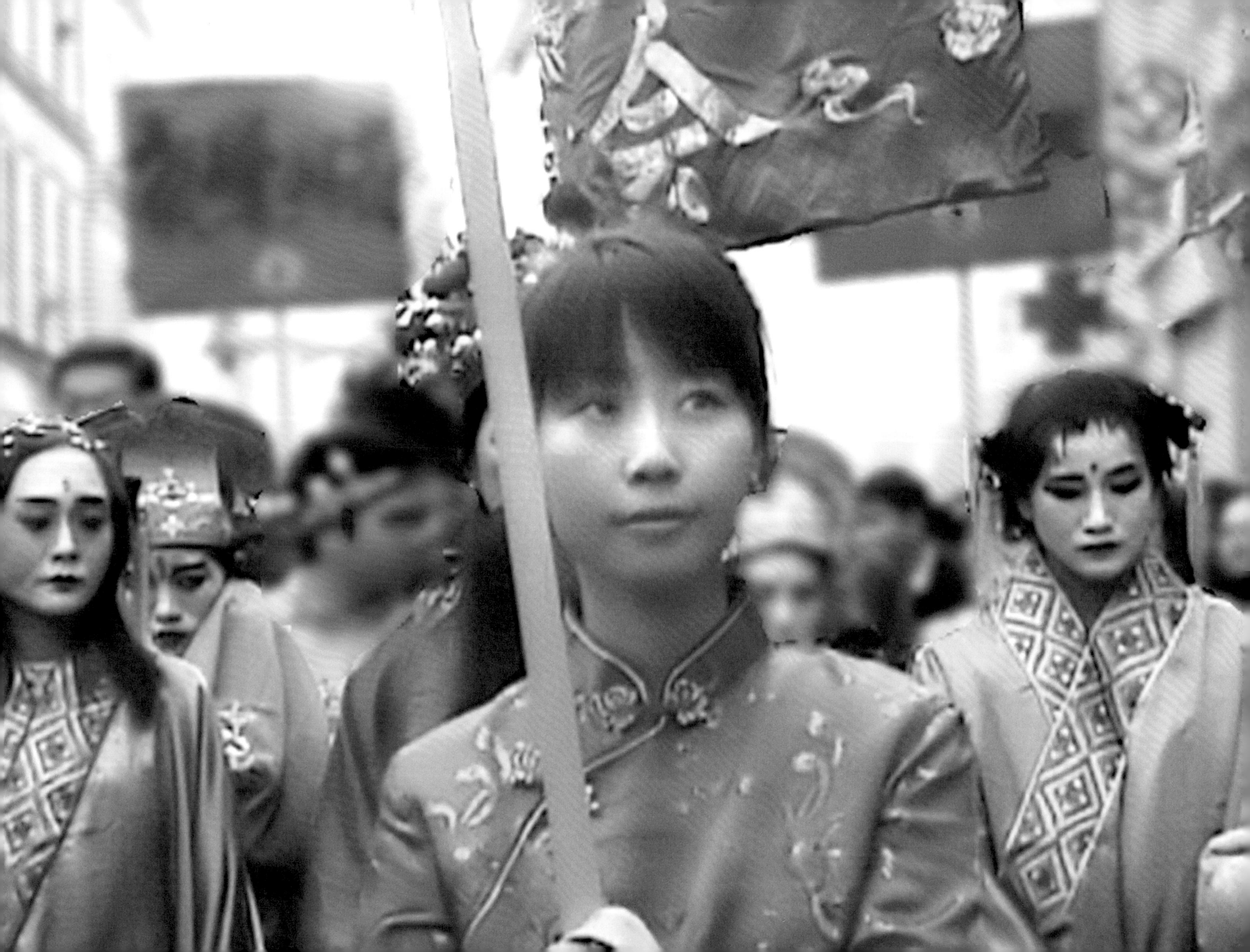

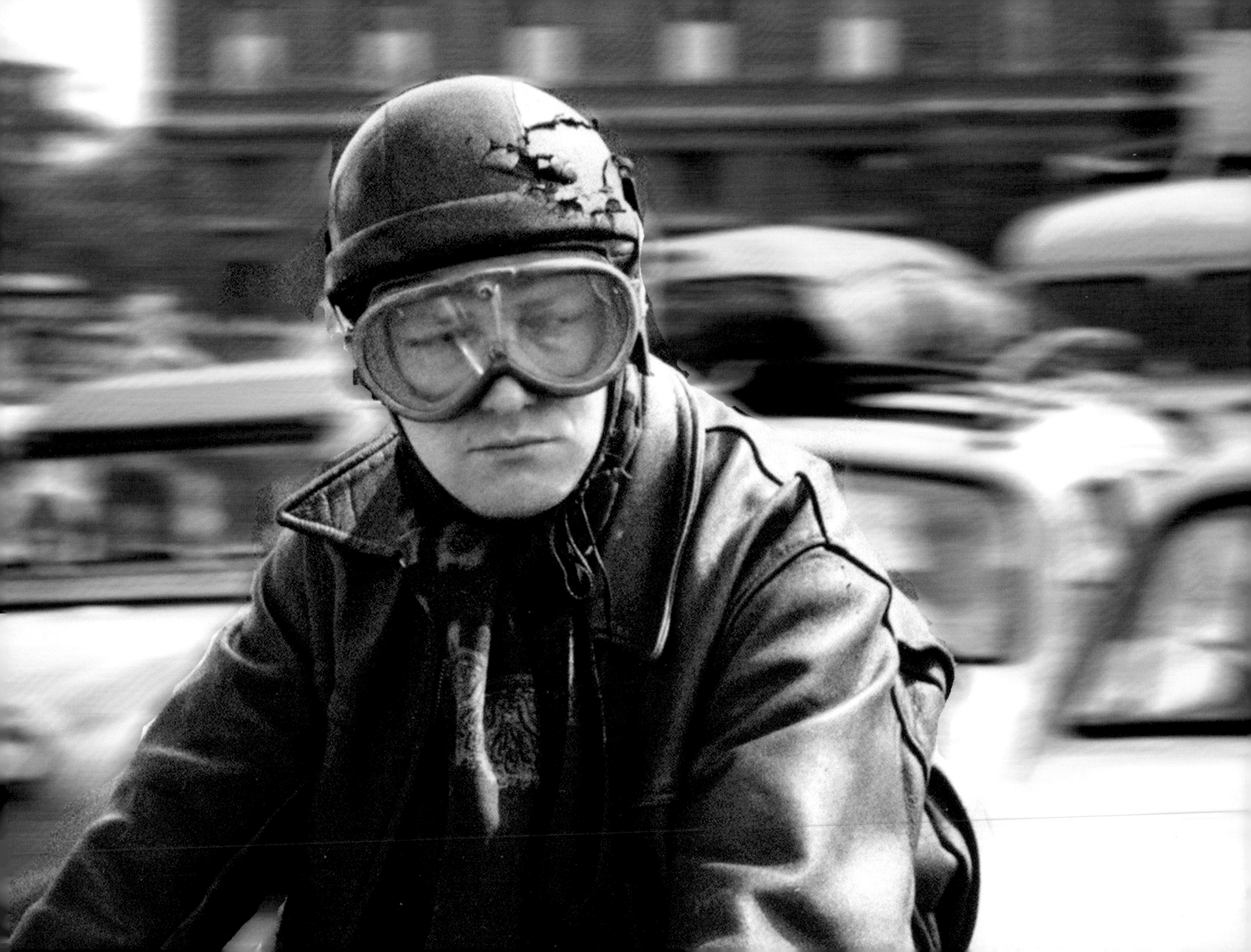

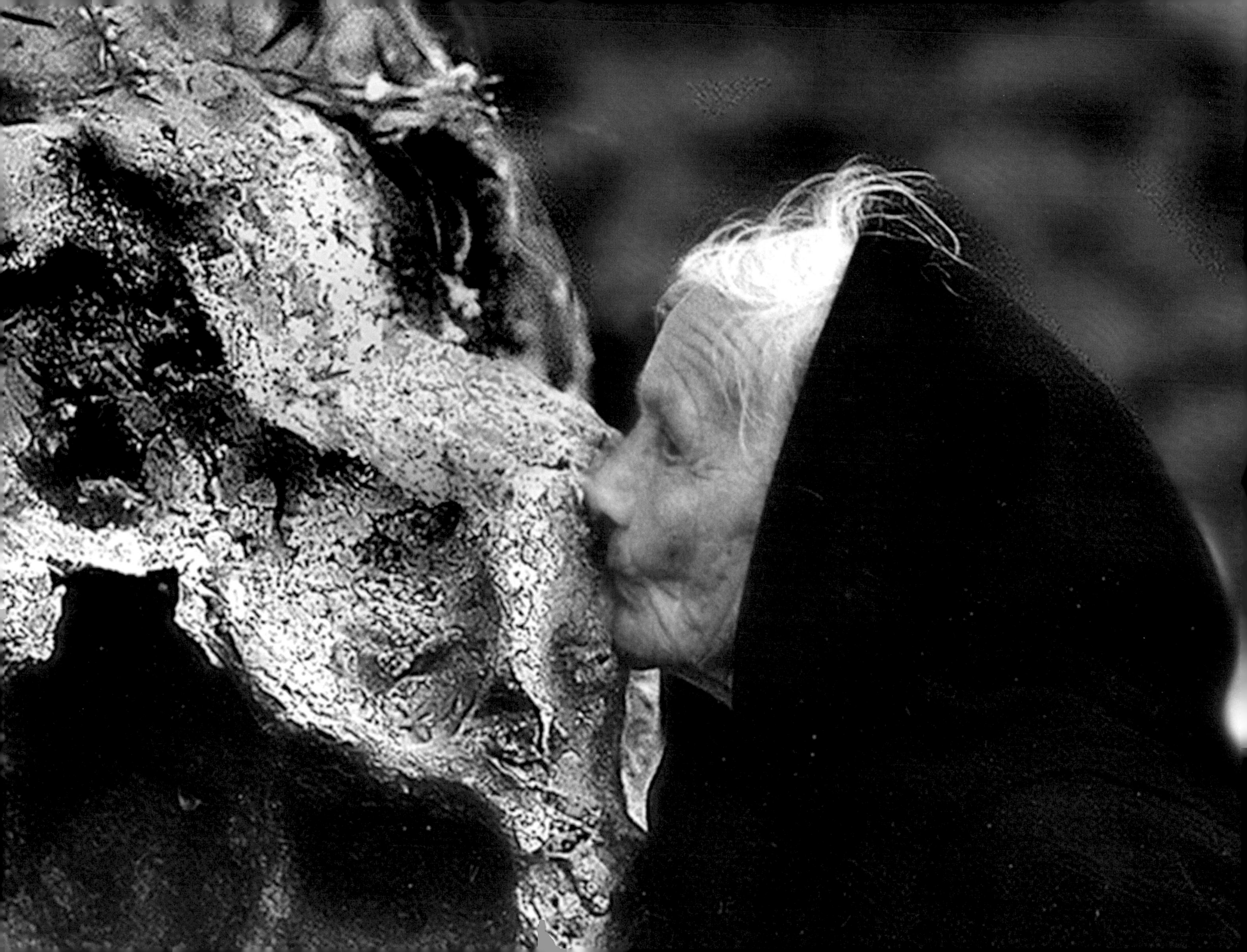

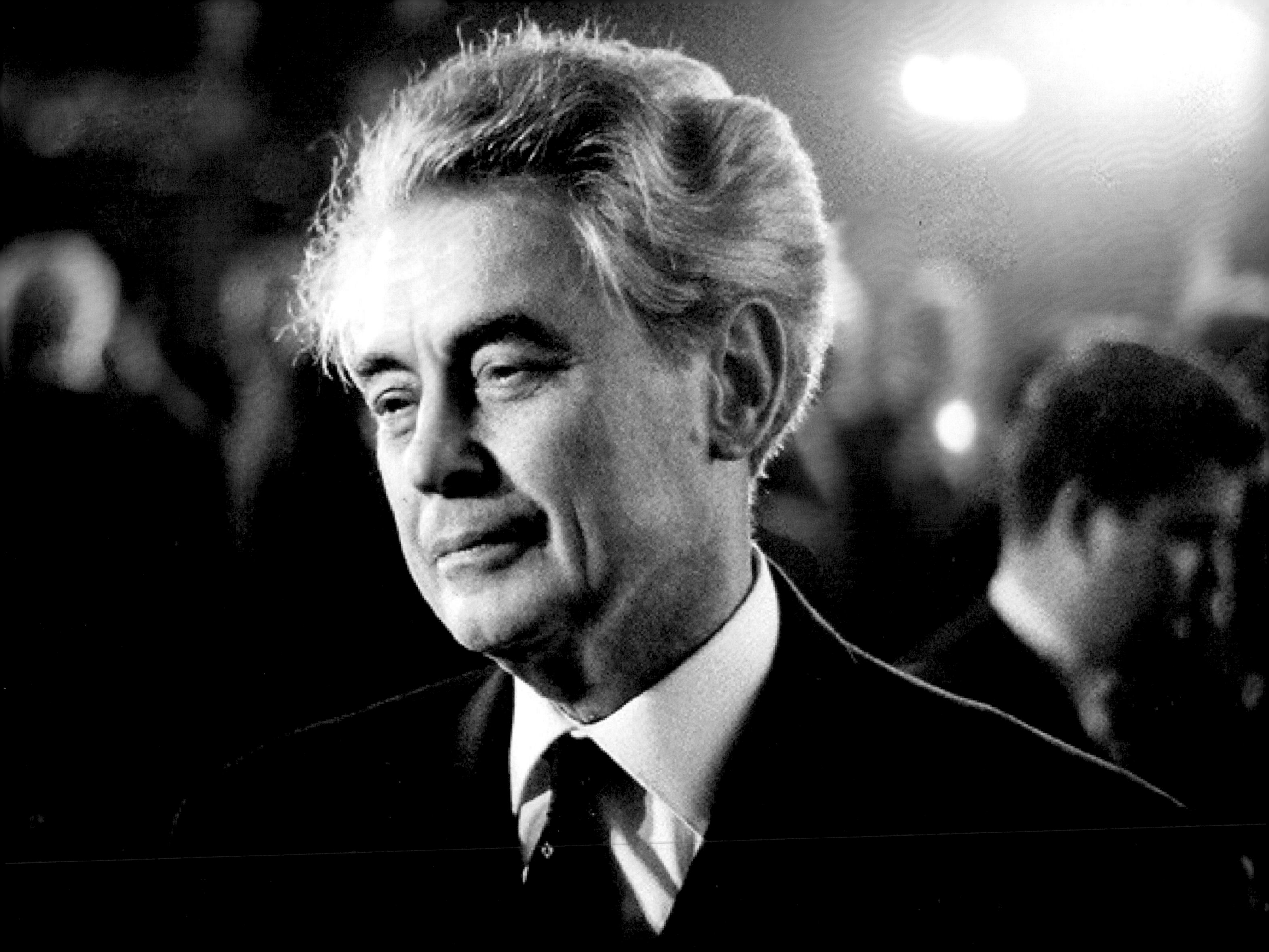

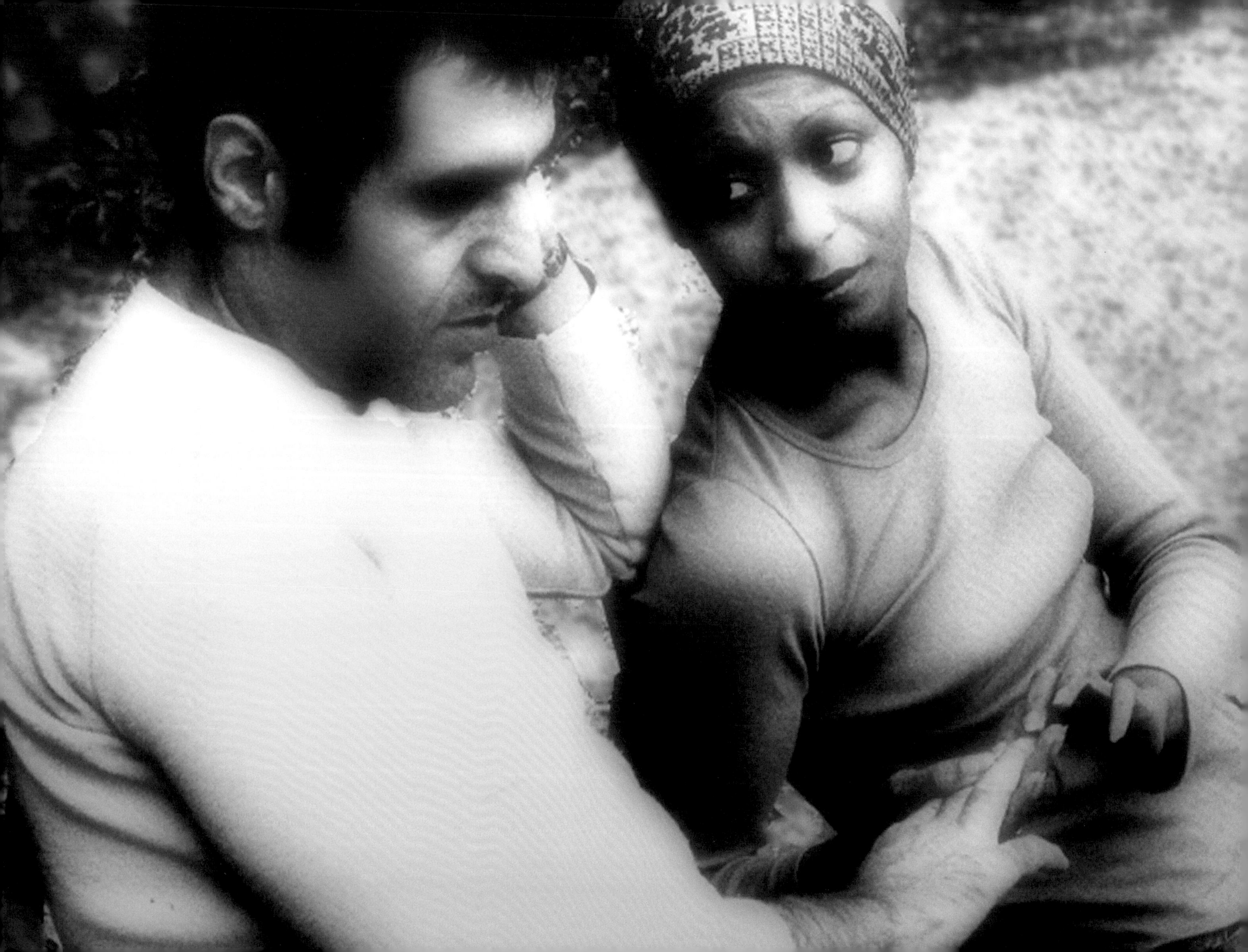

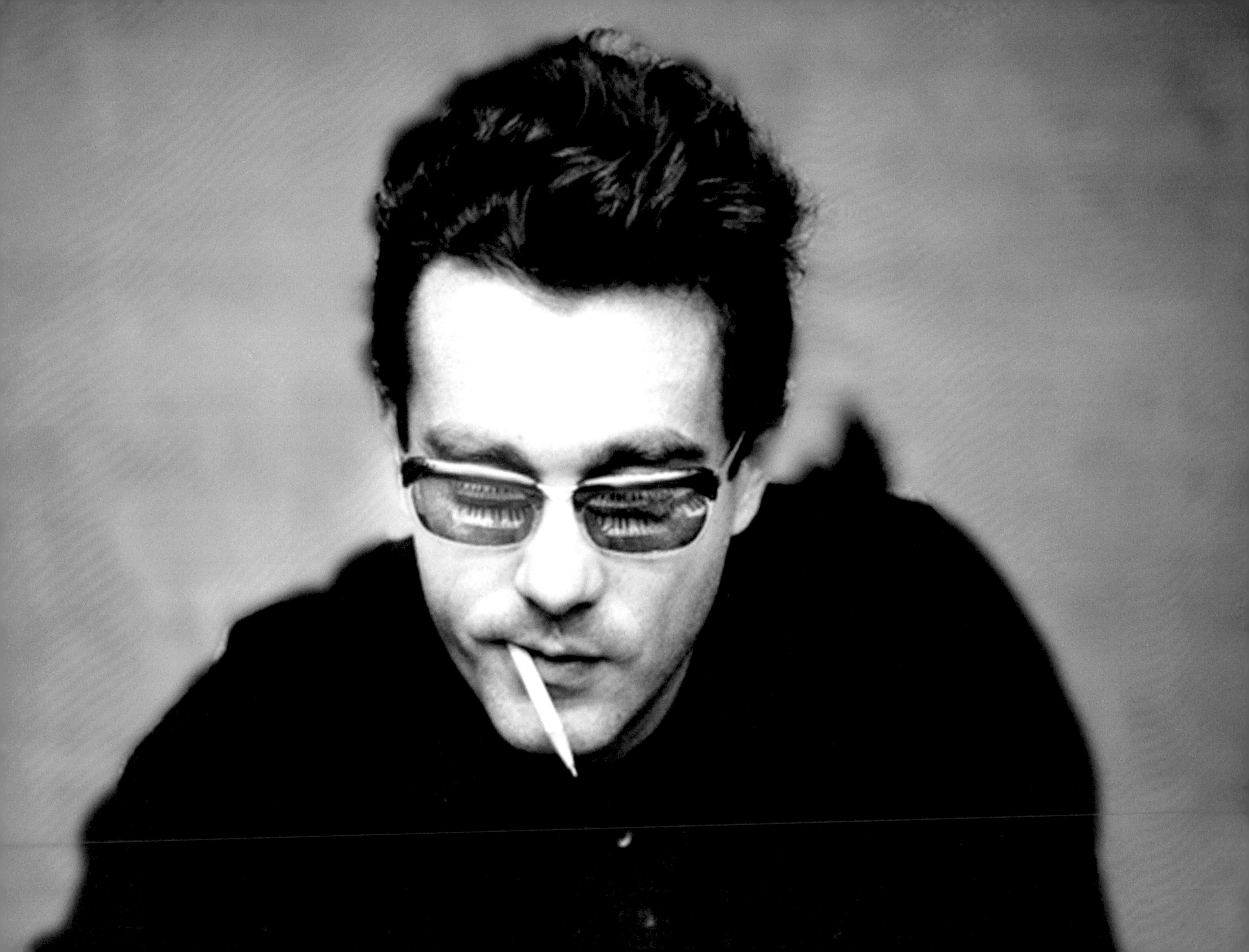

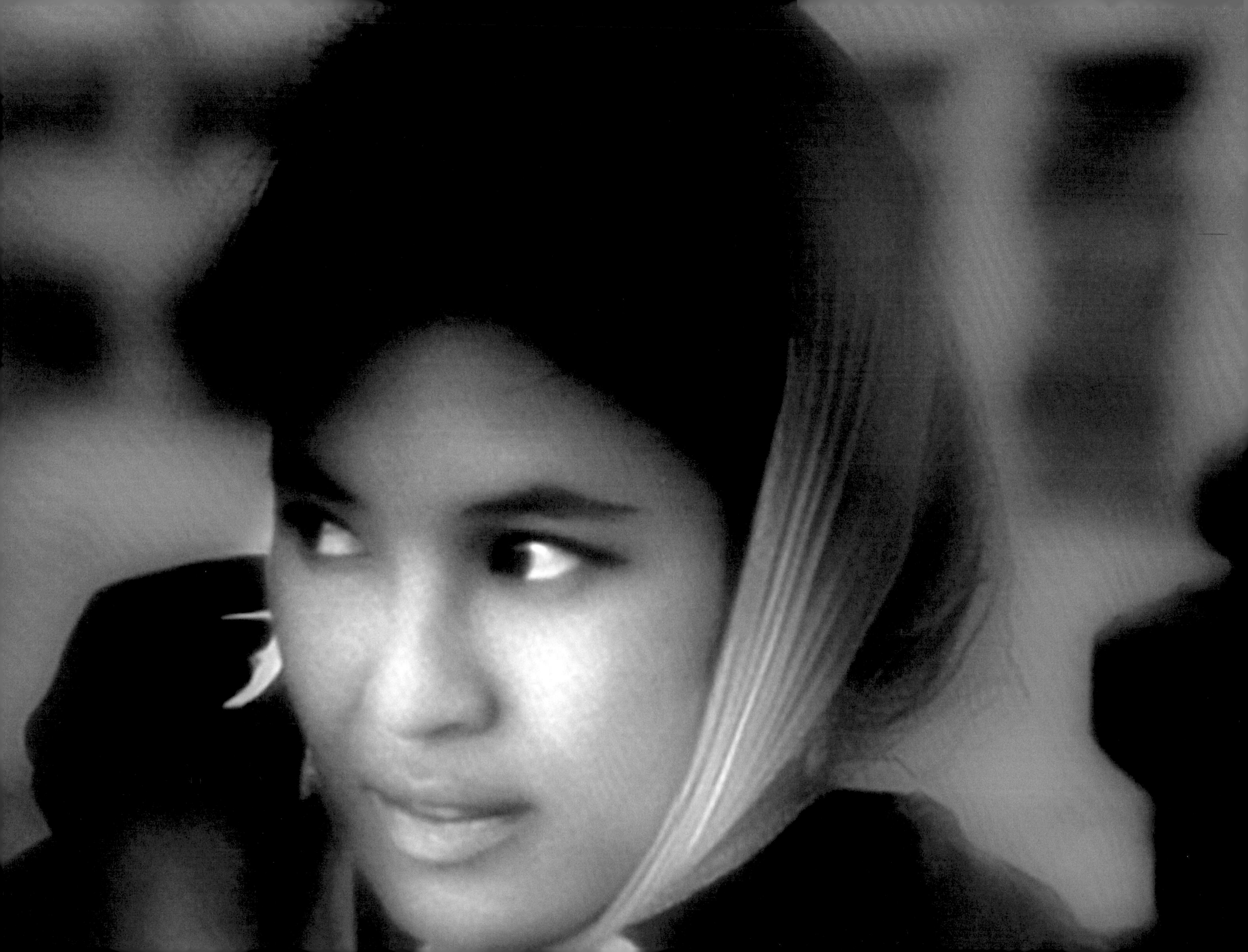

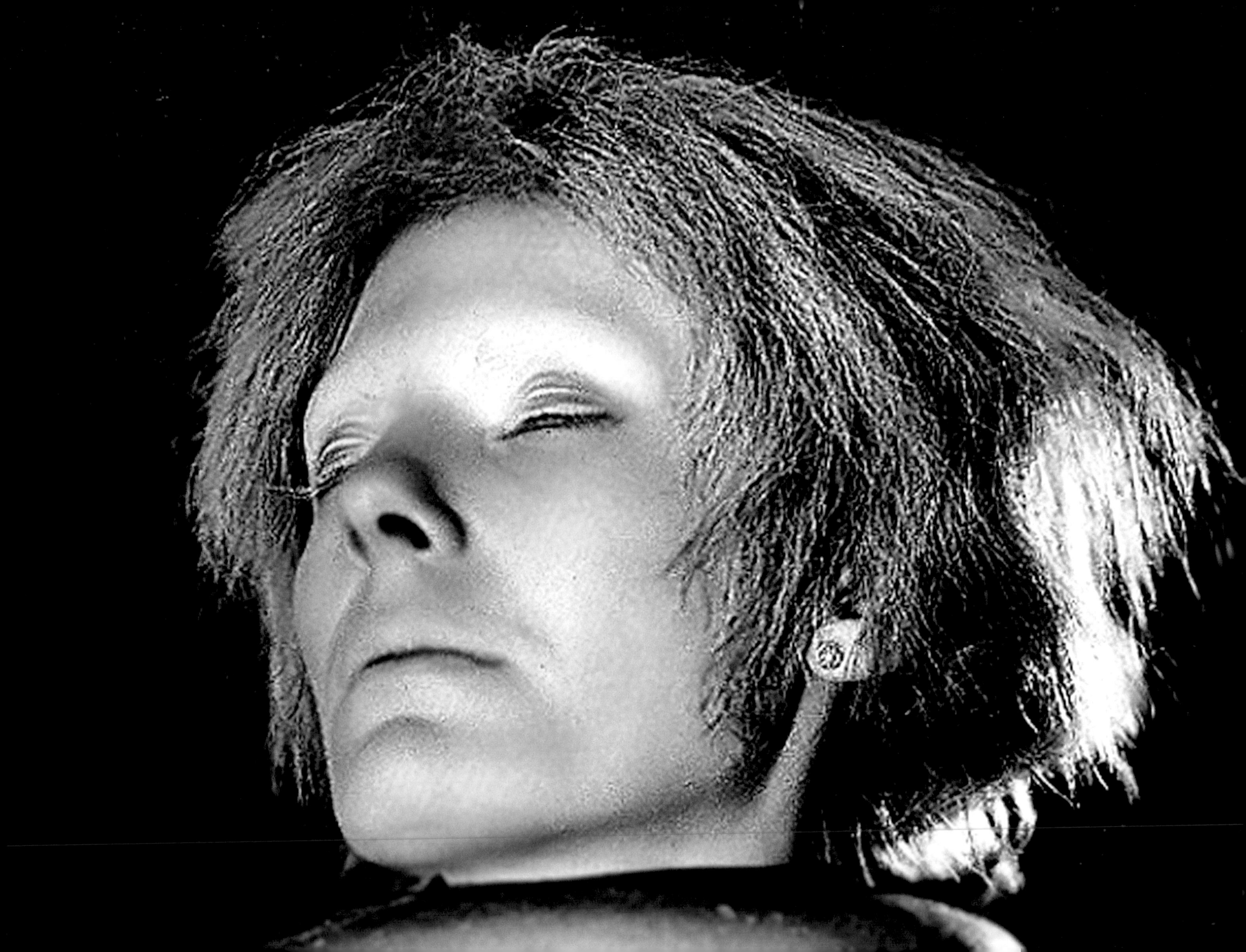

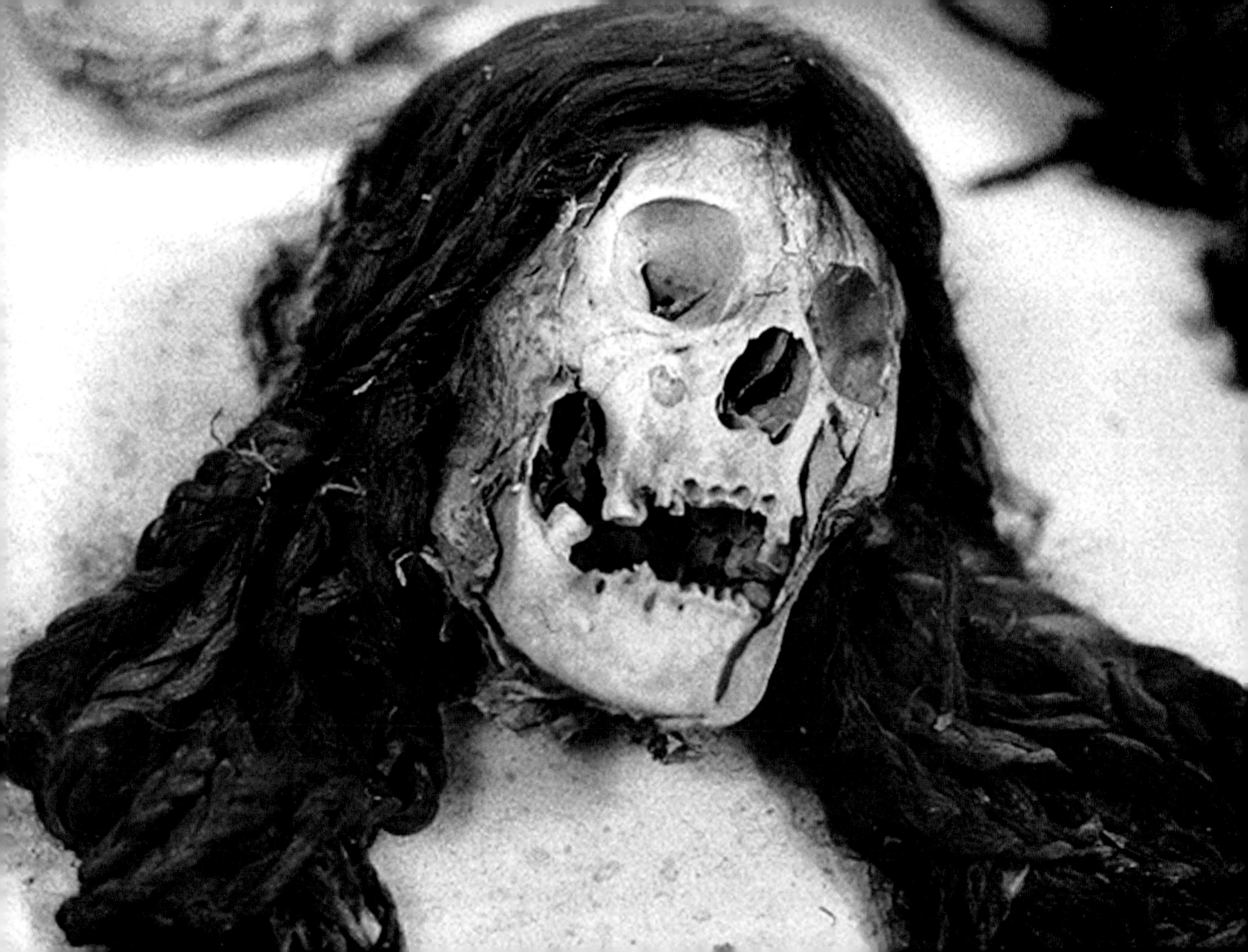

Beast of...

And always the animals

from each trip
you bring back
a gaze
a pose

a gesture
that points
to the truest of humanity
better
than images
of humanity itself

—From *Immemory*

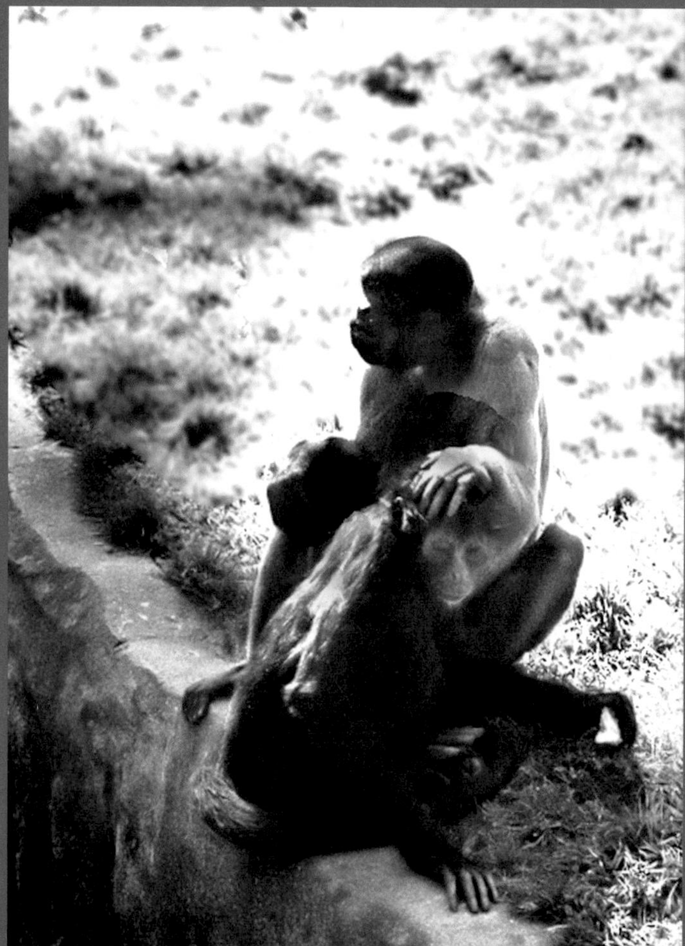

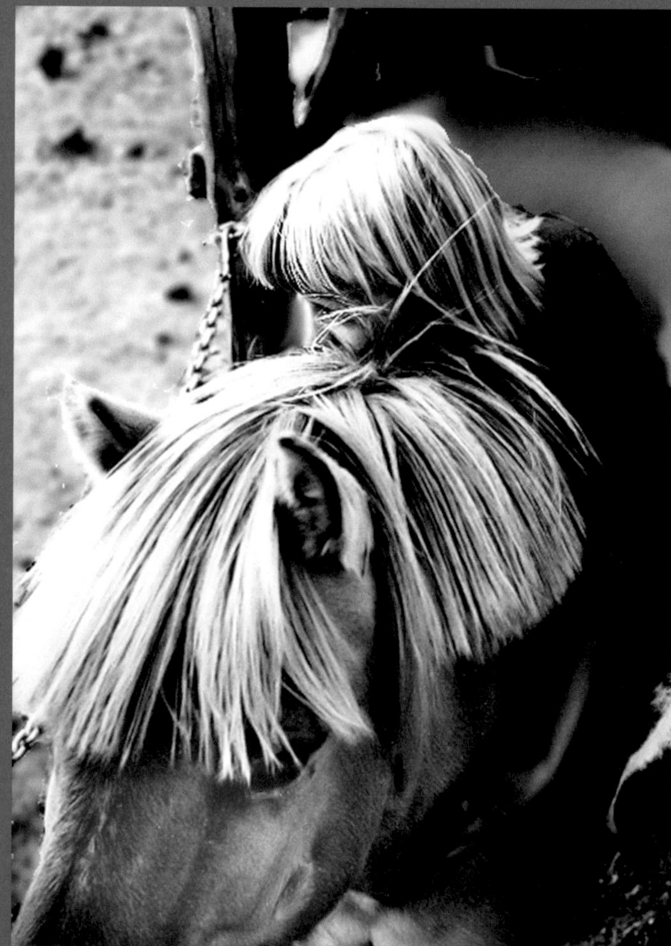

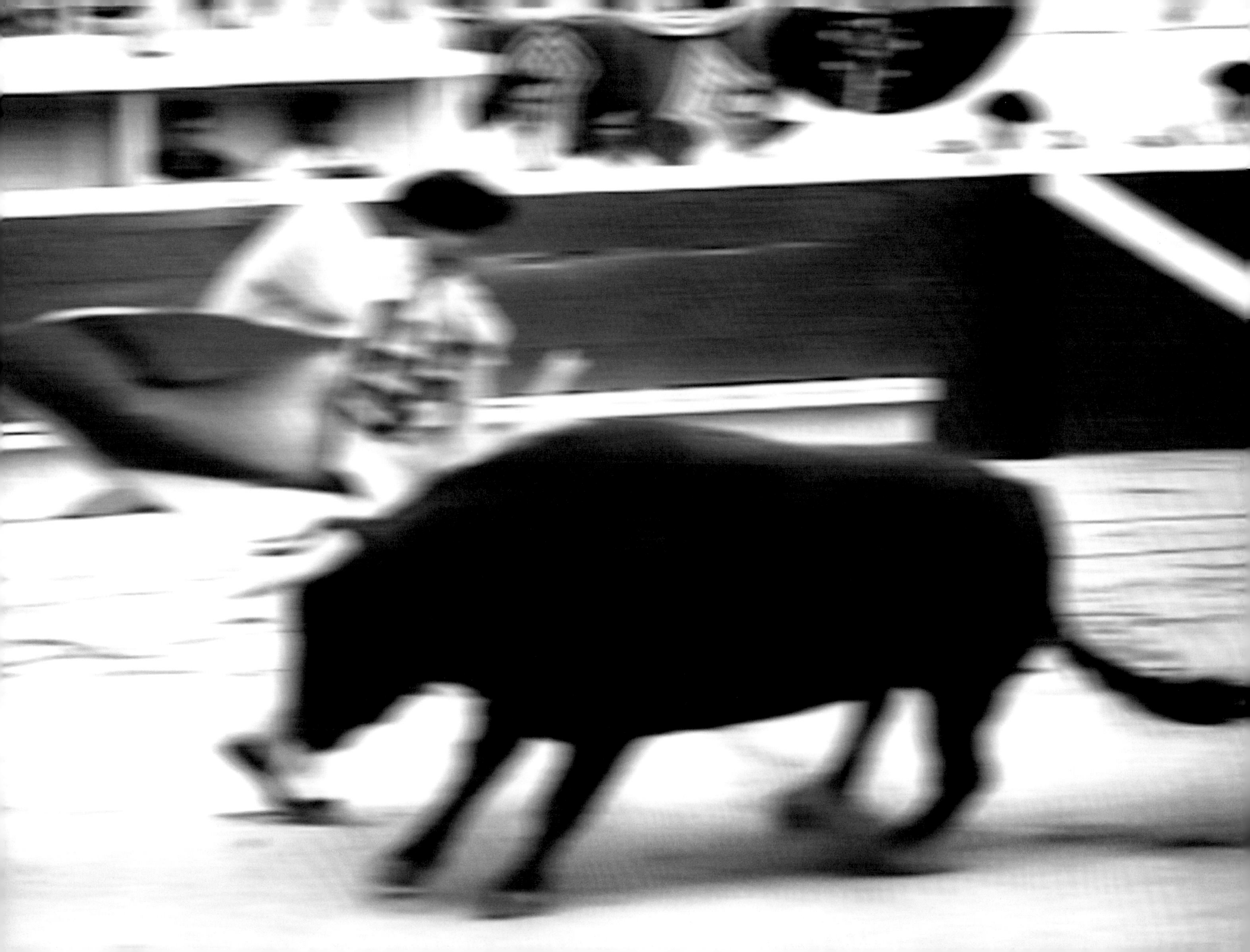

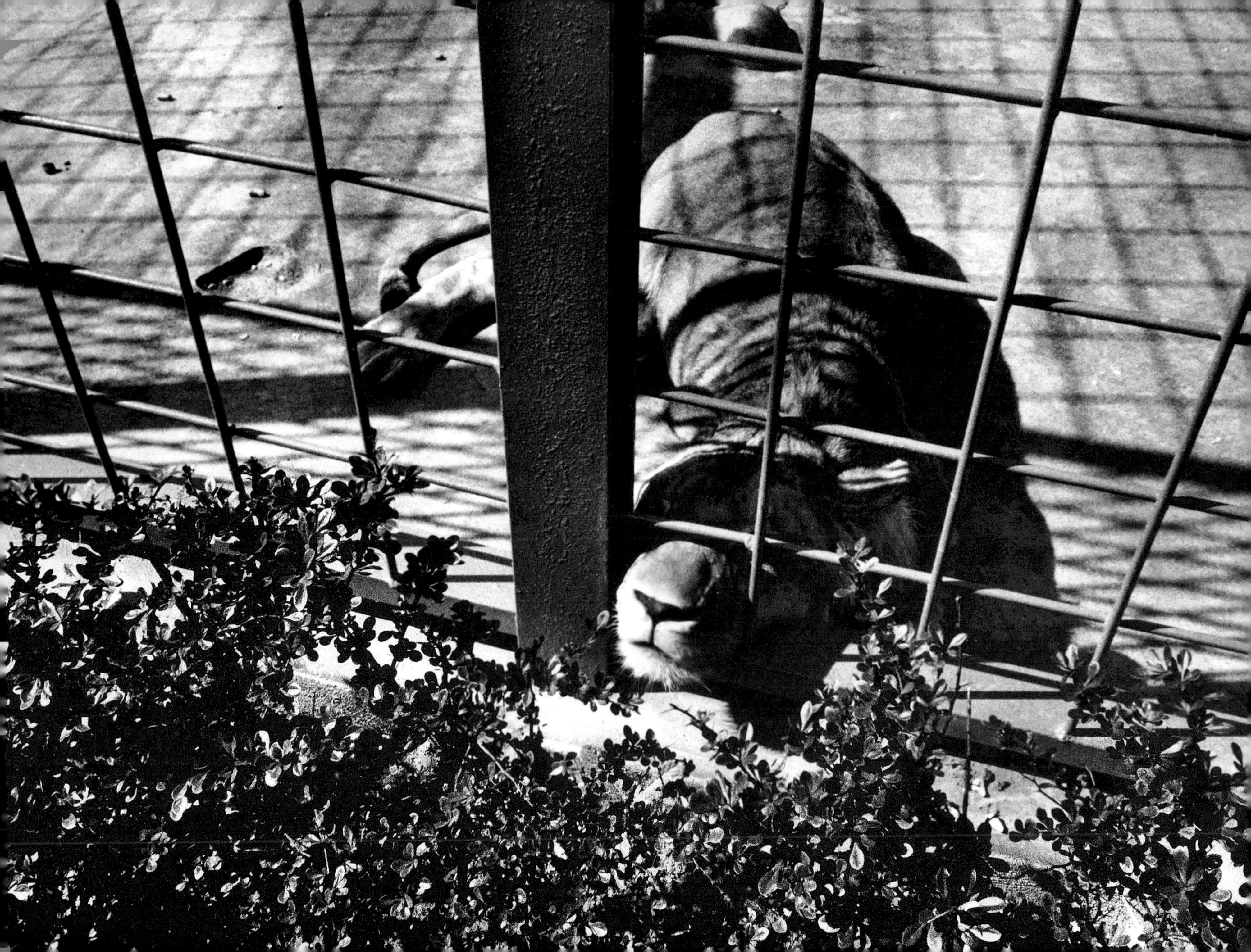

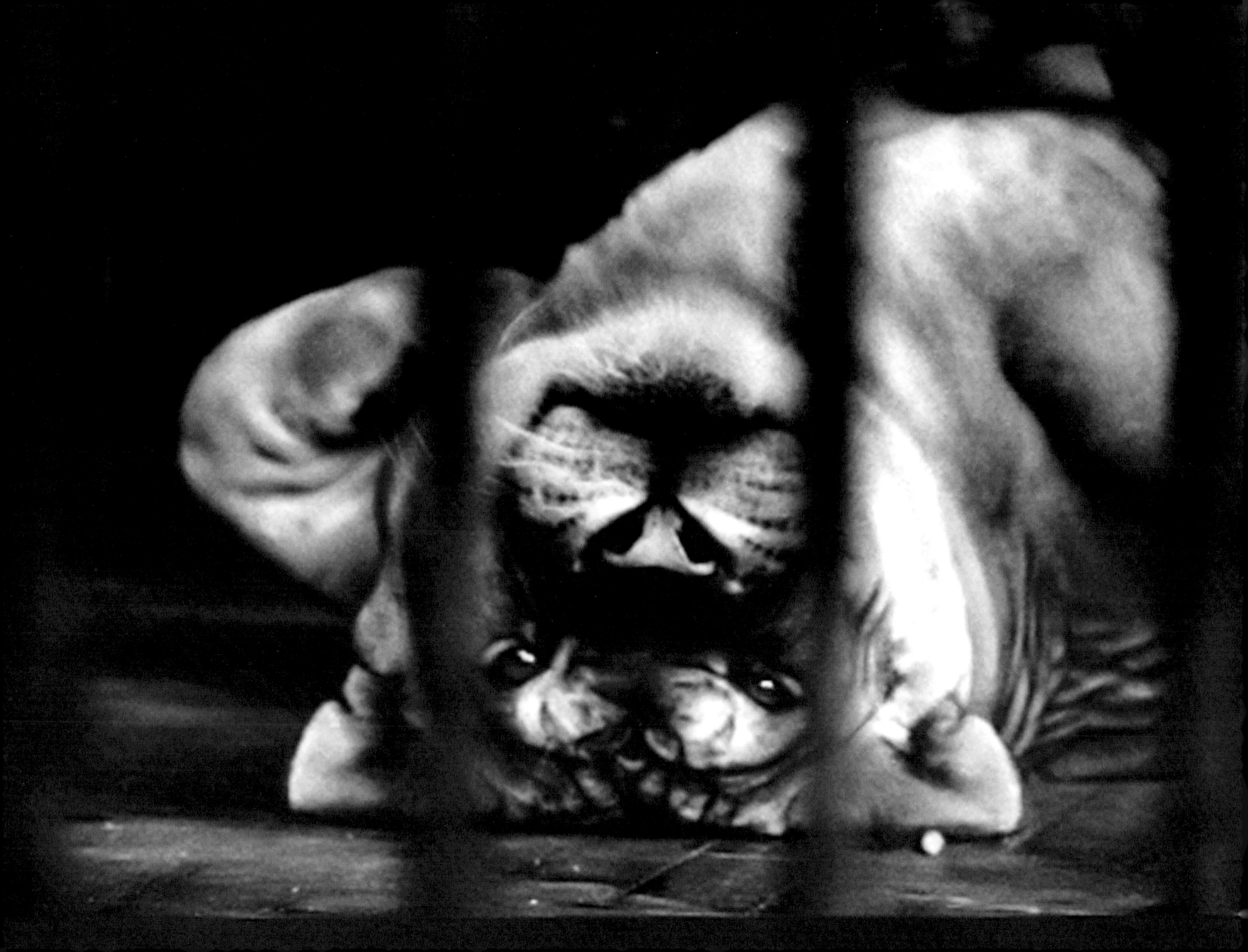

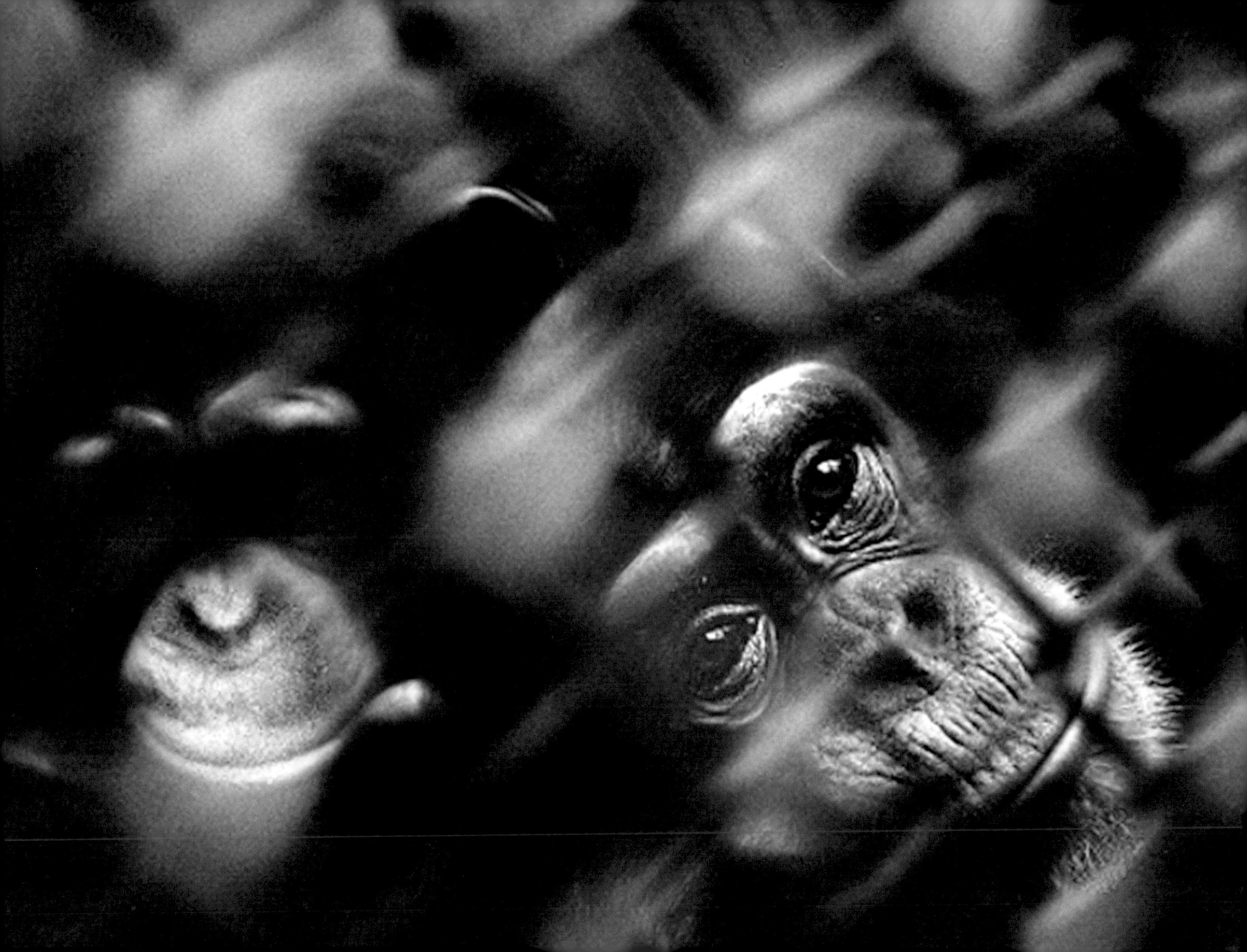

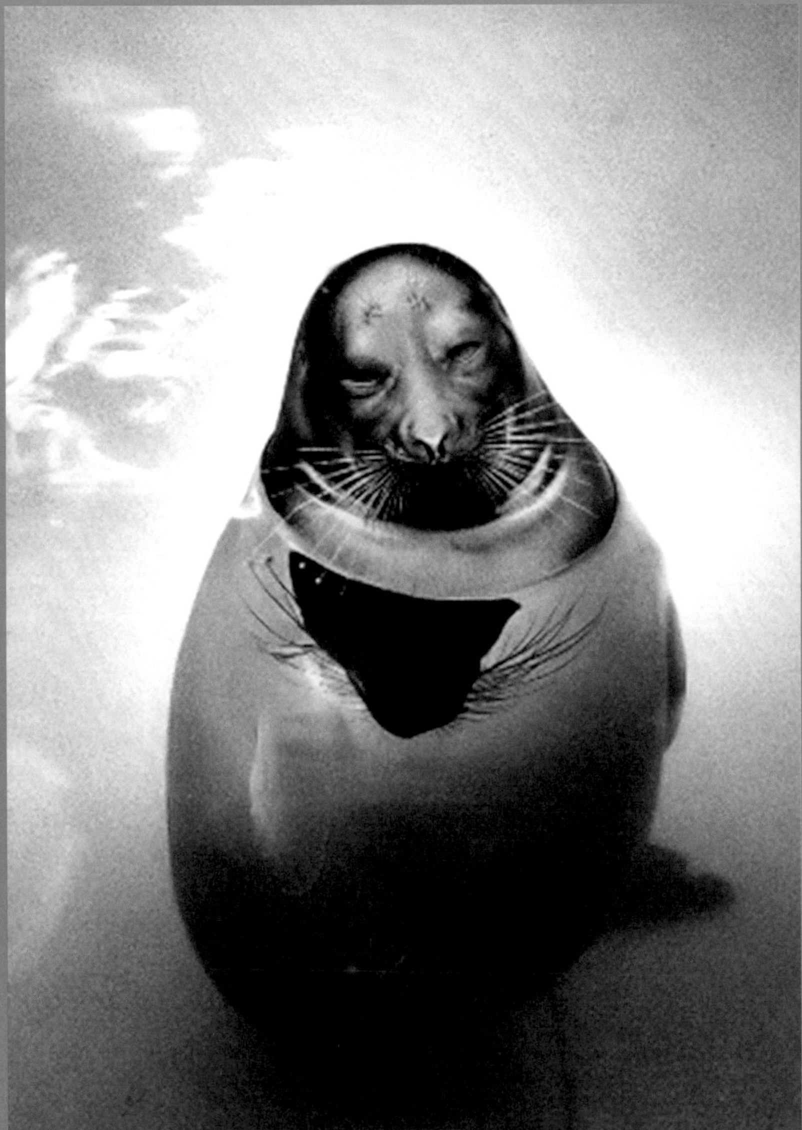

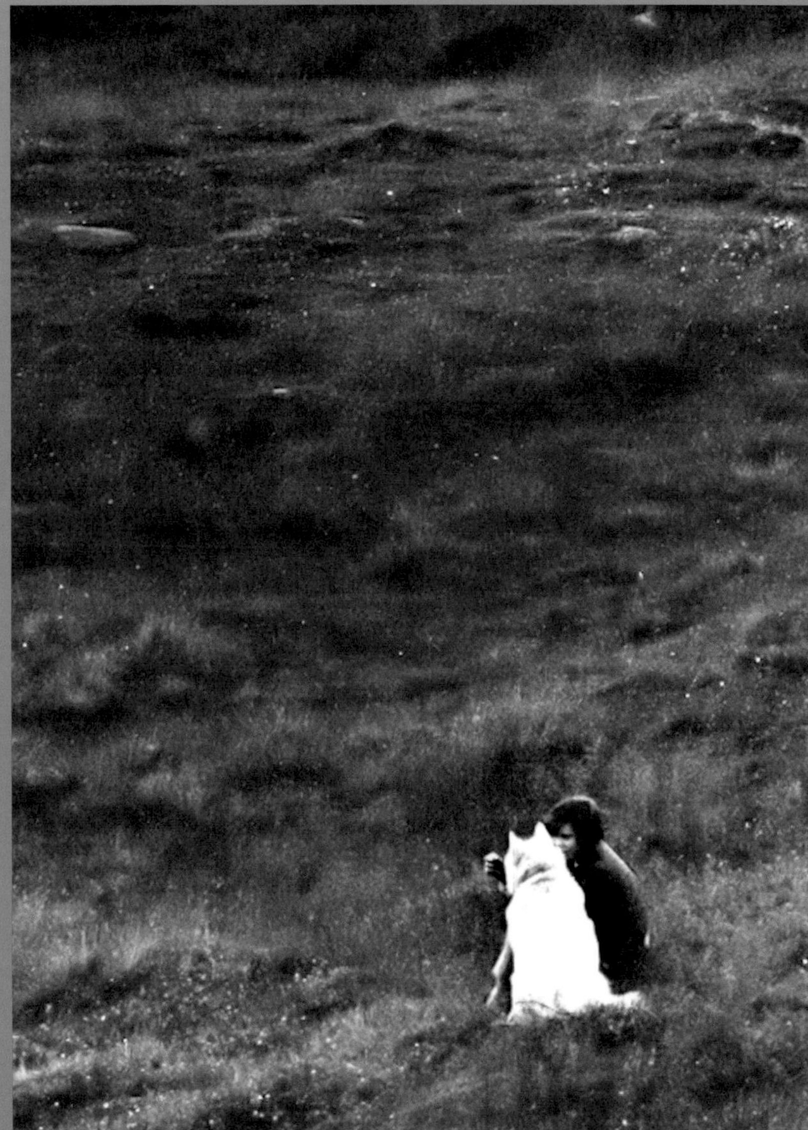

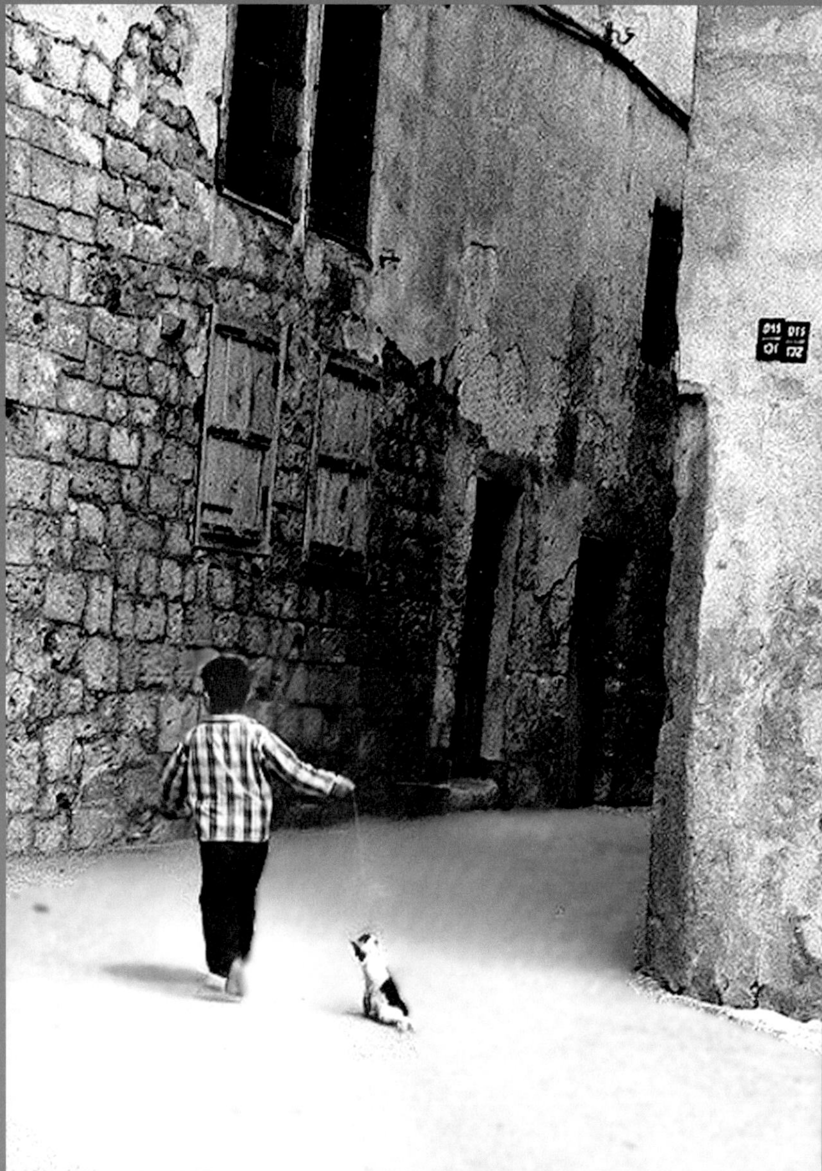

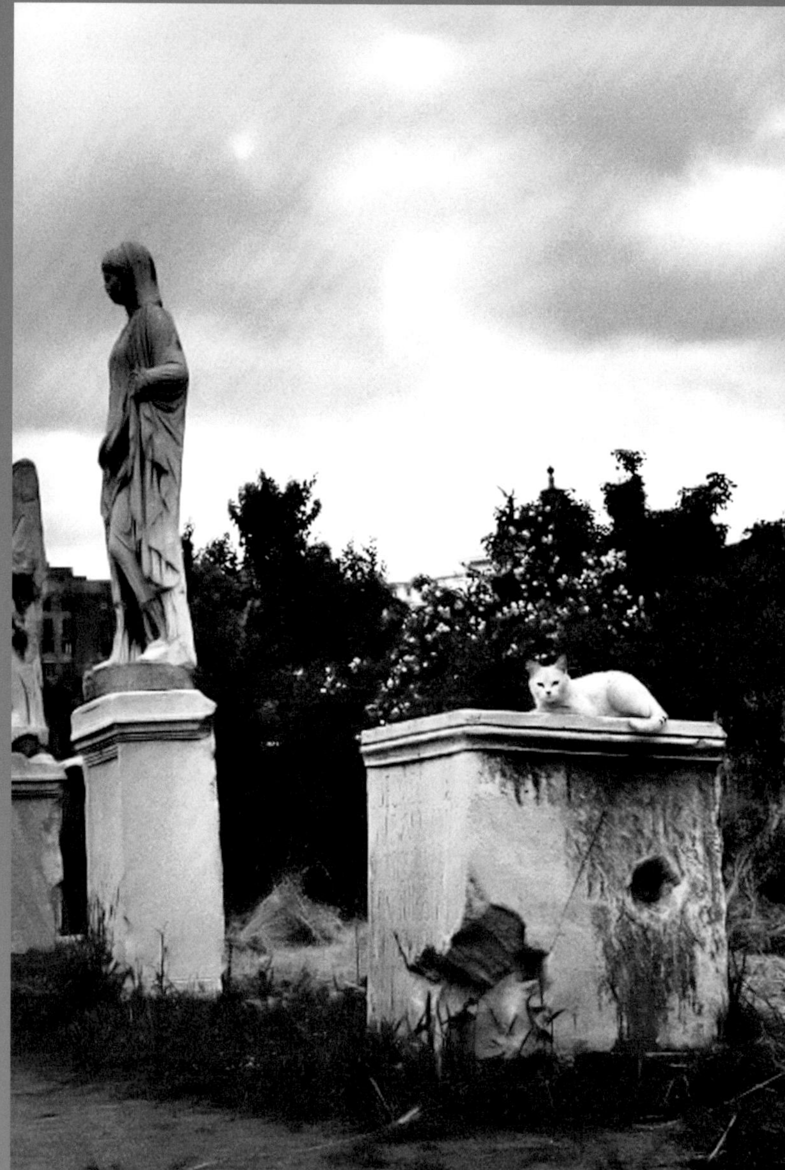

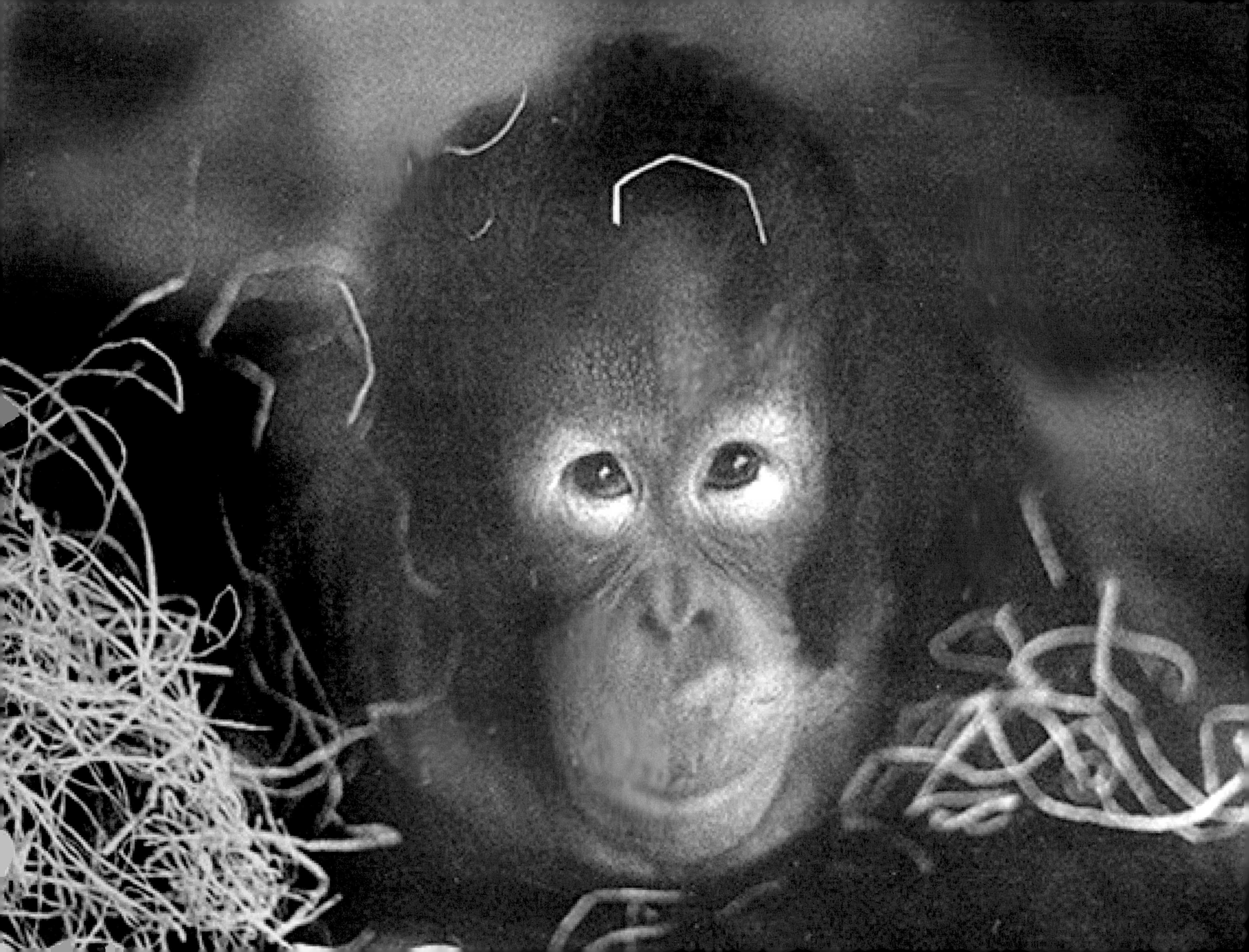

Director's Foreword

Now the moon is almost hidden
The stars begin to hide
The fortunetelling lady
Has even taken things inside
All except for Cain and Abel
And the hunchback of Notre Dame
Everybody is making love
Or else expecting rain
And the Good Samaritan, he's dressing
He's getting ready for the show
He's going to the carnival tonight
On Desolation Row

—Bob Dylan

When Bill Horrigan shared with me the first few images of faces in the crowd that Chris Marker had taken amidst the street demonstrations that coursed through France in 2006, I was stunned by the power of even these low-resolution copies to conjure both the universal and the specific. But what surprised me more was their near instantaneous trigger of another work of art that I couldn't possibly have seen or thought about in more than twenty years, yet its imagery took immediate shape in my mind's eye: James Ensor's astounding canvas, *Christ's Entry into Brussels in 1889* (1888). Filled with a swirling, delirious crowd of masked and hooded faces, this epic painting was born of an extraordinary moment of artistic and political ferment in Ensor's native Belgium. Somehow, across more than a century, Marker had captured that same crush of individual and collectively *unmasked* humanity in a series of modest yet momentous photographs—poignant, haunting, and fiercely political.

Having spent decades resisting the idea of exhibiting still photos taken from his film footage, Marker's astonishing overture to submit these works for our consideration was anything but sudden or capricious. It was rather a gesture of supreme generosity and consummate trust toward a curator with whom he had developed a remarkable rapport over a very long time. In 1995 the Wexner Center had provided Marker with an artist's residency, under the auspices of media arts director Bill Horrigan. The "public" fruits of that collaboration were widely seen internationally as the video installation *Silent Movie* circumnavigated the globe, along with a modest, though highly coveted, publication. But I would argue that the "private" and perhaps more precious consequence of the companionship between Marker and Horrigan was and continues to be the ongoing and exquisite exchange between two force fields of unusual moral and intellectual depth.

We at the Wexner Center are enormously gratified that the sustained relationships we forge with artists allow unlikely opportunities to emerge. Surely *Staring Back* is exemplary of that, but it also underscores what we believe our mission to be: encouraging and enabling the creation, presentation, and multivalent interpretation of the art of our time.

And speaking of multivalency, as I scanned the Web to refresh my memory of Ensor's massive canvas, I came across a rather astounding book, published by the Getty Museum (which owns the painting), pairing Ensor's masterpiece with Bob Dylan's song "Desolation Row," from *Highway 61 Revisited,* his classic 1965 album. Titled *The Superhuman Crew*, this audacious little volume promises a "riveting visual and verbal experience" that somehow links these two radical works of art. Circuitous as it may be, something about the perceived kinship between Ensor and Dylan convinced me that the Marker/Ensor allusion might actually have purchase beyond the idiosyncrasies of my own associative peregrinations. All of which is simply to acknowledge the potency of creative genius to capture the warp and weft of an era.

It is a great honor for the Wexner Center to debut this remarkable body of photographs, and a pleasure to document the occasion with this catalogue, beautifully designed by our Director of Design, Chris Jones, and edited with finesse by Ann Bremner. I would also like to thank art historian Molly Nesbit for gracing its pages with her always illuminating meditations on the phenomenon of Chris Marker. I am also grateful to Exhibitions Manager Jill Davis and Will Fugman, lead installation preparator on this project, for their meticulous attention to realizing the artist's ambitions.

To Bill Horrigan, affectionately known in these parts as *Guillaume*, in a playful nod to Marker's Silent Movie Cat, I am deeply moved by the evident respect, trust—even love—that this exhibition and catalogue represent. Not unlike such legendary partnerships between artist and dealer, writer and editor, actor and director that have shaped our cultural and intellectual history, I daresay the connection between Marker and Horrigan remains one of incalculable dimension for both, and for the ultimate appreciation and understanding of Marker's work and legacy.

As to Chris Marker, I am reminded as I revisit our publication for *Silent Movie* that, at some point along the way, he claims to have chosen cinema because he "would never be, say Robert Frank." And yet, with *Staring Back* there is no denying the affinity between these two masters of photographic imagery. Marker has infused his still portrayals with the same profound humanity and palpable compassion that propel his films. The exquisite empathy embedded in *Staring Back* bespeaks a singular capacity for observation and for finding in a sometimes brutal world a kind of fierce beauty.

—Sherri Geldin

Some Other Time

Bill Horrigan

We are all voyagers, lost between the waves and the clouds; we are eager for sweet water, fresh fruits, firm ground and those others, unknown and like us, who are to be found at the end of every journey. Those fixed points at which one takes breath, and which sailors used to call landfalls, are not the same for everyone and yet are common to all.

—Dominique Aury

Staring Back brings together about two hundred black-and-white photo portraits produced by Chris Marker from 1952 to 2006. It arose unforeseen (but what route better, given how we believe we've come to know him?) from an exchange of letters.

On March 30, 2006, Marker responded to an e-mail I'd sent him about something else altogether, by attaching four photos (see p. 139) he'd just taken of the anti-CPE demonstrations then coursing through Paris and through France generally. Triggered by a remarkably misjudged piece of federal legislation, fronted by Dominique de Villepin and widely taken to diminish further the job security of young people in the first stage of their careers, these demonstrations against the *contrat première embauche* (CPE) had begun in February and continued for over two months, until the legislation was withdrawn in April. Marker intermittently took to the streets to observe these gatherings, and in his e-mail of March 30, he observed, "We're far from the joyful mood of *Chats Perchés*."

The reference is to his then-most-recent film, a documentary for ARTE (the French-German television company), which debuted with considerable fanfare in December 2004. Structured around Marker's investigation of the sudden appearance throughout Paris of a grinning graffiti cat—"M. Chat"—*Chats Perchés* (*The Case of the Grinning Cat*) is a deceptively casual interrogation of the national mood of France from shortly after September 11, 2001, through the quickly ensuing run-up to the United States' war in Iraq, and into 2004.[1] It settles on a series of events causing citizens to take to the streets in demonstrations of protest or solidarity, "political" events in the expansive rather than the narrow sense of the term, with politics seen as a species of human affairs. As a participant-witness, Marker moved through these events discreetly armed with a video camera, taking wry measure of the shifting stakes involved, but invariably delighted to see how the figure of M. Chat himself had begun to appear as a Cheshire-like

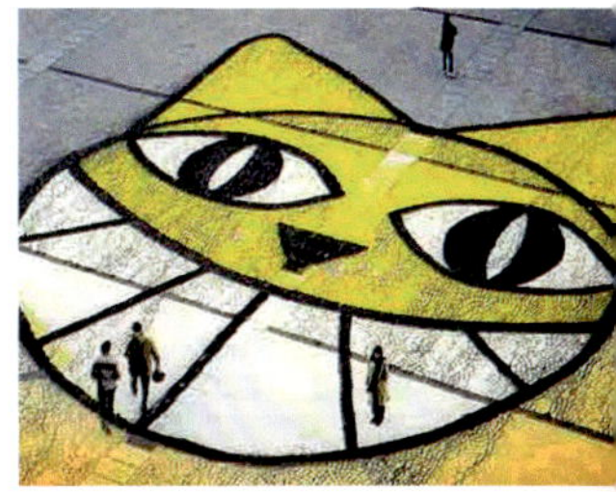

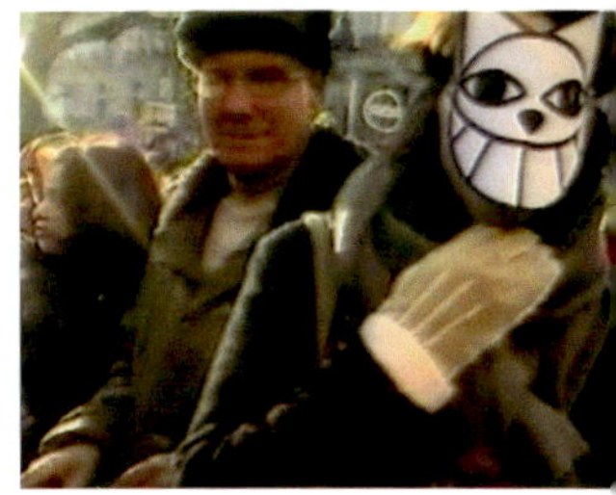

M. Chat drawing for the premiere of *Chats Perchés* (*The Case of the Grinning Cat*) at the Centre Pompidou in Paris, 2004, and M. Chat fan wearing the image on a mask

apparition in the passing parade, drawn on placards, worn as a mask, even popping up on television coverage of the presidential election.

Those who love Marker's work know that in his cosmology, cats and owls are the presiding deities,[2] vaunted above mere humans, hence the labors of the self-effacing begetter of M. Chat would have found no fan more ardent. Marker's pleasure over M. Chat could have been matched only by that of his alter ego, Guillaume-en-Egypte, the companion feline who starred in the artist's 1985 video *Chat écoutant la musique* (*Cat Listening to Music*) and whose cartooned image Marker continues to invoke as the bearer of wisecracking commentary on events of the day, dispatched to the artist's lucky correspondents in frequent e-mail installments. But *Chats Perchés* offers up considerably more than a salute to the unexpected joy of seeing M. Chat peering down from the roofs of Paris. The film links the unfolding of public events Marker observes—people gathering in public to voice concern about the burgeoning clout of Jean-Marie Le Pen's right-wing National Front Party, and about George W. Bush's saber-rattling against Saddam Hussein, and about the rights of Muslim women, and about the territorial integrity of Tibet, and about the chronically contested fact of Israel, and about other matters not smaller in urgency to those who profess them—to produce something like a snapshot of a time and place and of its abiding moods: the nation's temperature taken, as the nation defined itself through the people drawn onto the streets of Paris.

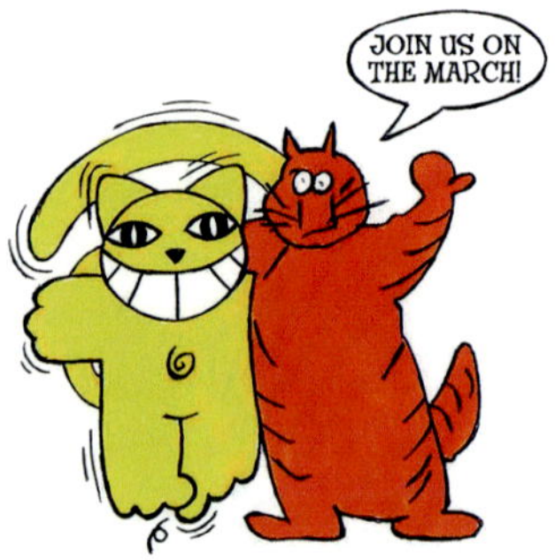

M. Chat and Guillaume-en-Egypte

In that, *Chats Perchés* feels like an epilogue-sequel to *Le Joli Mai*, Marker's dazzling 1962 experiment in direct filmmaking that found him, Pierre Lhomme, and their accomplices dashing around Paris to ask those they encountered their thoughts on politics, work, self-betterment and the meaning of wealth and of poverty, and on France's recent surrender of Algeria and the prolonged trauma of national self-identity that it triggered. Armed with a then-revolutionary lightweight camera and sound-recording equipment, Marker combined the endlessly surprising "performances" of these ordinary citizens with a voice-over commentary (spoken by his friends—and postwar leftist icons—Simone Signoret in the English version and Yves Montand in the French one) that noted early on, "If we dissect this many-faced crowd, we find that it is the sum of solitudes."

As it happens, that's the phrase I recalled when studying the four pictures Marker sent me in March 2006: four images of young people alone in the midst of the multitude, unmindful of his camera's embrace. In response to my admiring reaction to these images, from which depth had been foreshortened in such a way as to rivet the viewer's attention on the passionate faces of the beautiful protesters, burning with *la raison ardente*, Marker offered

> a few words of explanation. These are not bona fide photographs. They're stills from my video footage, somewhat manipulated thru the jujucraft of Photoshop and Painter. It's an experiment I conducted for years, in order to extract meaningful images from the inordinate flow of video and television. I developed the concept of 'superliminal,' which is a sort of counterpoint to Subliminal. Instead of one frame lost in the stream of other, different frames, Superliminal is one frame lost in the stream of almost IDENTICAL frames, or so it seems, for when you take 'em one by one, one happens to be THE real photogram, something nobody then has perceived, not even the guy who shot it (me, in most cases). (April 1, 2006).

In truth I'd gone beyond simply musing over these images, but had proposed that the Wexner Center mount an exhibition of them, in short order, bypassing the normal exhibition schedule typically set years in advance. We would have been able to do a show of Marker's anti-CPE photos within months of the events they were documenting, by using one of the building's spaces outside the domain of the galleries proper, and as they were digital prints, unbudgeted costs could be relatively easily managed. That said, I wasn't entirely confident Marker would agree to our showing his photographs at all;

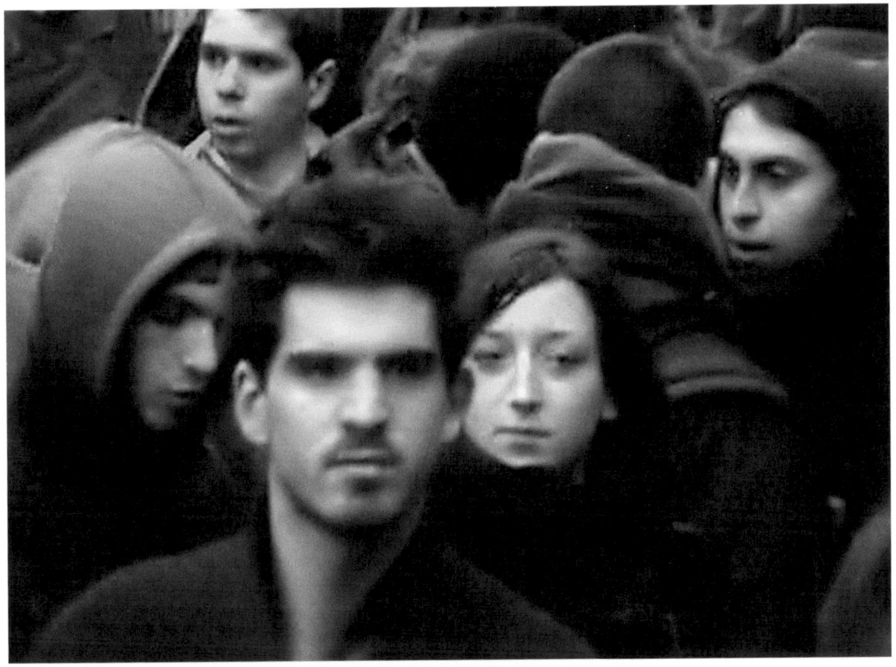

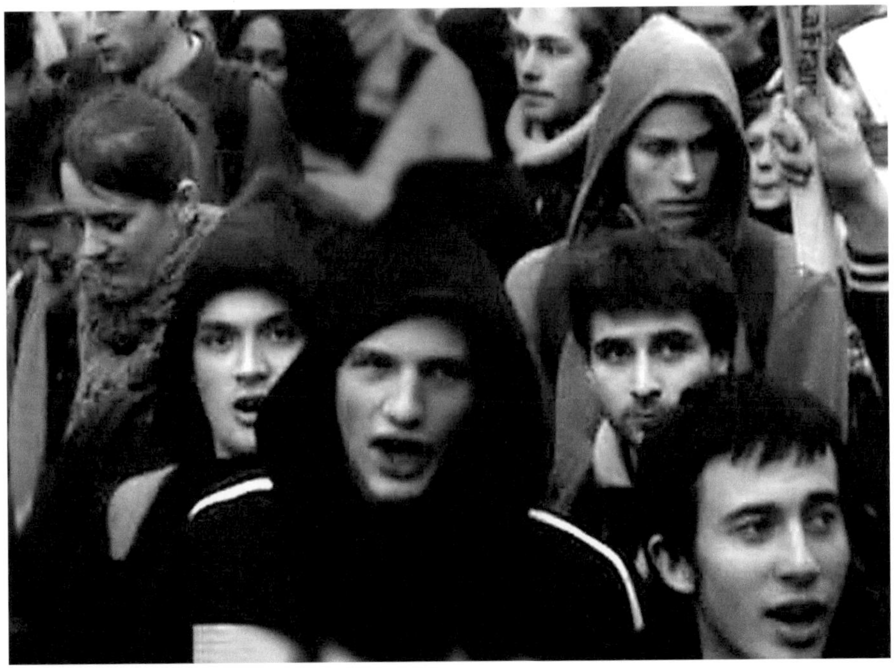

as far as we knew, he'd never consented to a public exhibition of his photographs despite the unflagging interest curators, museums, and galleries here and abroad had shown for decades.[3]

We'd worked with Marker in 1994–95 in commissioning what became *Silent Movie*, a five-monitor video installation, with accompanying digital photographs of its obligingly photogenic "star," Catherine Belkhodja, and comically fictitious movie posters he'd conjured, his hypnotic meditation on his own memories of presound cinema. Delicately elaborated yet dense in its visual, graphic, and musical interconnections (one of the five monitors delivered randomly generated silent film–like intertitles, while an evocative selection of piano solos reverberated throughout the gallery), *Silent Movie* had led a charmed life, leaving Columbus to float to over a dozen other venues around the globe, accompanied by such ancillary merchandise as a T-shirt featuring Guillaume-en-Egypte, bemused at his patron status as "The Silent Movie Cat."

Marker continued to send images as the anti-CPE gatherings accelerated in Paris ("No, it ain't a still from Pudovkin. Just today at the Bastille," ran one e-mail message from April 4), before coming to term in mid-April, as he wrote:

> Back to the demos story: I guess France is the only country on earth where people may battle for two months in order to replace one

Images of the anti-CPE demonstrations, 2006, from "I Stare 1"; these are the four images Marker first e-mailed to Bill Horrigan

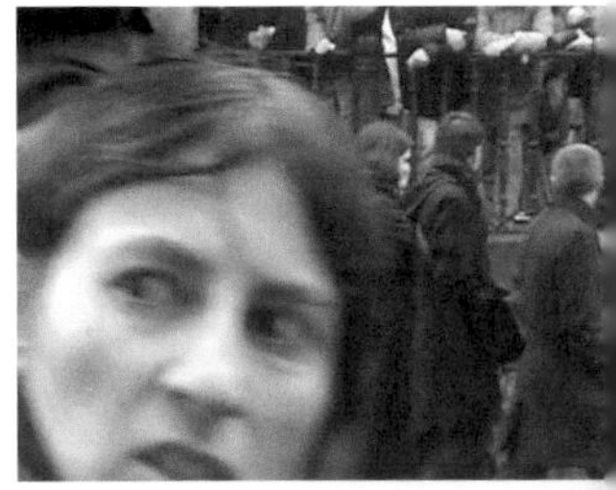

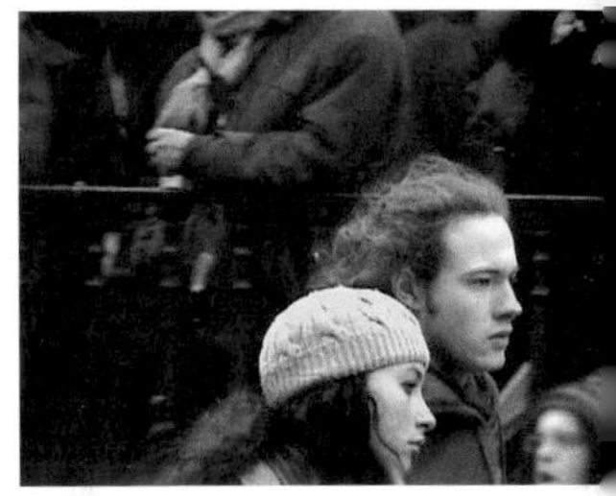

word by another. And it is precisely the word 'replacement' that finally solved the crisis. 'Modification' or 'adaptation' were too soft for the protesters. 'Abrogation' or 'withdrawal' made the government lose face. Someone came up with the great idea of 'replacement' and in a whiff everything went back to order. Perhaps that's an homage to literacy, in a sense. (April 12, 2006)

Meanwhile, we continued to ponder the possibilities for the Wexner Center exhibition, at that point to be presented under his suggested title, *Revenge of the Eye*:

> If subliminal refers to the object the eye doesn't catch, yet the brain does, Superliminal is THE REVENGE OF THE EYE...that on slow-motion catches one image among others apparently identical as being THE image....When one applies this system, as I do here, to his own footage, it may appear just as a refined way of sorting. When applied to alien material, the TV stuff for instance, in pure Duchampesque fashion, the robber becomes the author. Turning to black-and-white and Photoshop manipulations being the last stage of the appropriation. (May 4, 2006)[4]

Marker had already acknowledged the specter of Marcel Duchamp in *Le Souvenir d'un avenir* (*Remembrance of Things to Come*)—the portrait film he and Yannick Bellon had produced in 2001 about her mother, the pathbreaking photojournalist Denise Bellon—in which Duchamp is credited as the artist with "the gaze which in this century has changed ours the most." One of the founding members of the Alliance Photo Agency, Denise Bellon was celebrated for her invaluable photo documentation of early surrealist art exhibitions and the first steps of the Cinémathèque Française, no less than for her visual reporting on many of the remembered and erased political crises from the early 1930s into the Cold War, including sobering assessments of Finland's 1939 prewar mobilization efforts and the legacy of the Nazi concentration camps. Just as *Chats Perchés* uses a succession of public demonstrations over several years to register the mood of France, *Le Souvenir d'un avenir* regards Bellon's photo project as a lens to study the political and artistic landscape of Europe before and after the war. In that respect, despite its ostensible subject, it functions as a resonantly personal commentary from Marker. It's an ordering of an archive—another "refined way of sorting."

As many have pointed out, Marker's passionate engagement with the biases and byways of memory has a physical correlative in the existence of the archive—whether a literal one or in such domesticated forms as the family or vacation photo album or in advanced forms of digital storage and delivery systems. It's by no means reductive to say that Marker's artistic odyssey and vocation, his calling, consists of making and looking at photographed images and of using words to puzzle what they mean, and of showing how their meaning can be made to change. The instantly classic version of this (recognized as such by no less than his postwar mentor André Bazin) comes as early as 1958 in *Lettre de Sibérie* (*Letter from Siberia*), with its triple-repetition of identical footage joined to leftist, rightist, and "balanced" voice-over commentary describing what we're seeing in, roughly, the idioms of *Pravda*, the Voice of America, and UNESCO, respectively. But the passionate curiosity leading him to ponder the evidence of his eyes (it's the essayist in him) and of what the still or film camera has captured is there as early as *Olympia 52* (1952), which charmingly prefigures in film form the entire *Petite Planète* publishing enterprise that produced the now highly coveted series of travel books he edited for Editions du Seuil from 1954 to 1964. In those volumes photos, archival imagery, commentary, and quotation embark on an interchange at once learned and lighthearted—and certainly then-alien to that utilitarian genre. Similarly, his own two volumes of *Commentaires* (1961 and 1967), scripts for films both made and unrealized, deploy photographs not only in the service of the essay-as-scenario but as cross-referencing elements at once illustrative and allusive.[5]

Short works like *Si j'avais quatre dromadaires* (*If I Had Four Camels*) (1966)

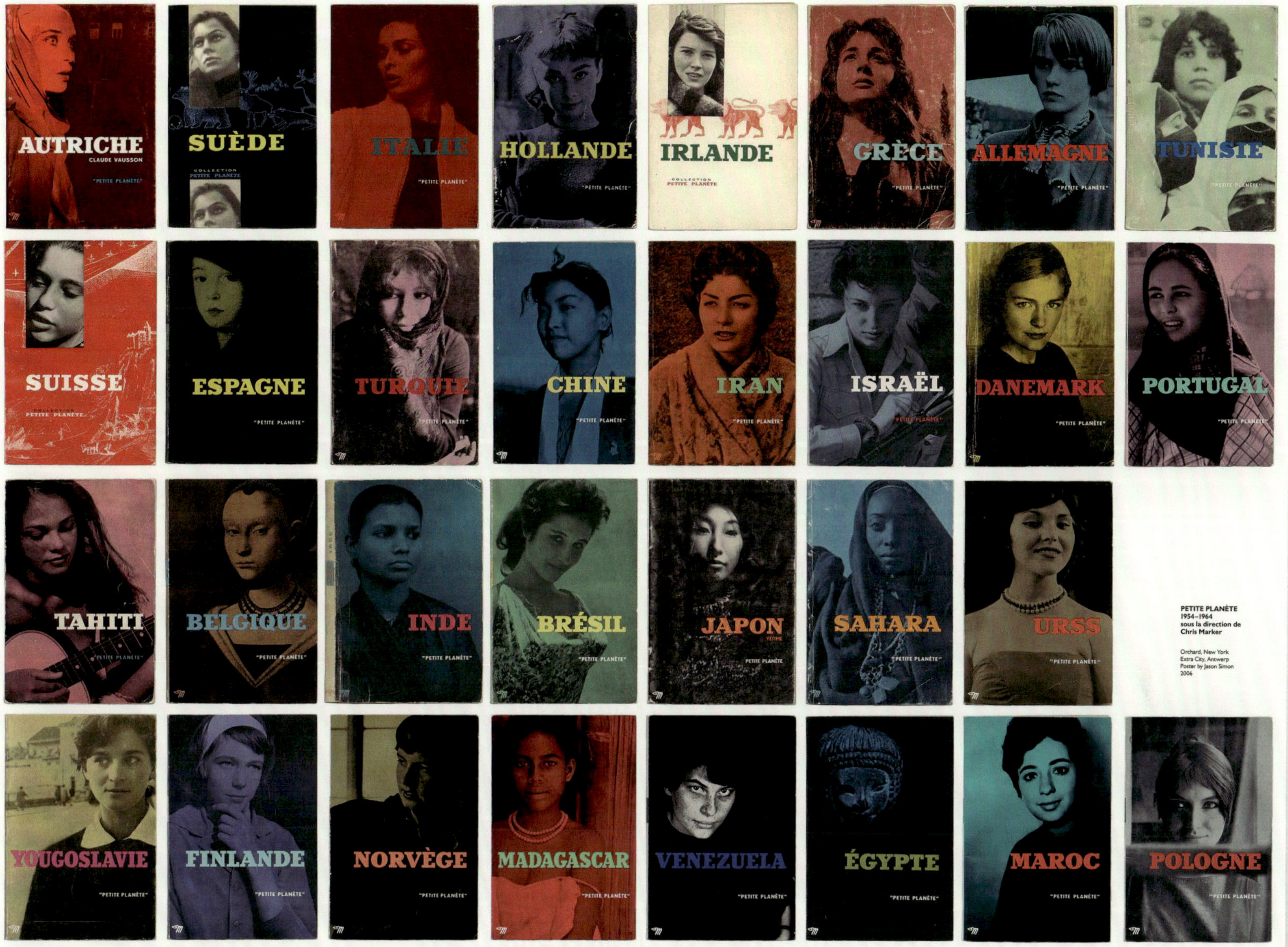

Petite Planète travel books poster, 2006

May 1968 photographs by Chris Marker as reproduced in François Maspero's journal, *Partisans* 42, May–June 1968 (left) and Patrick Seale and Maureen McConville's *French Revolution 1968*, 1968 (right); the image from *Partisans* appears in "I Stare 1"

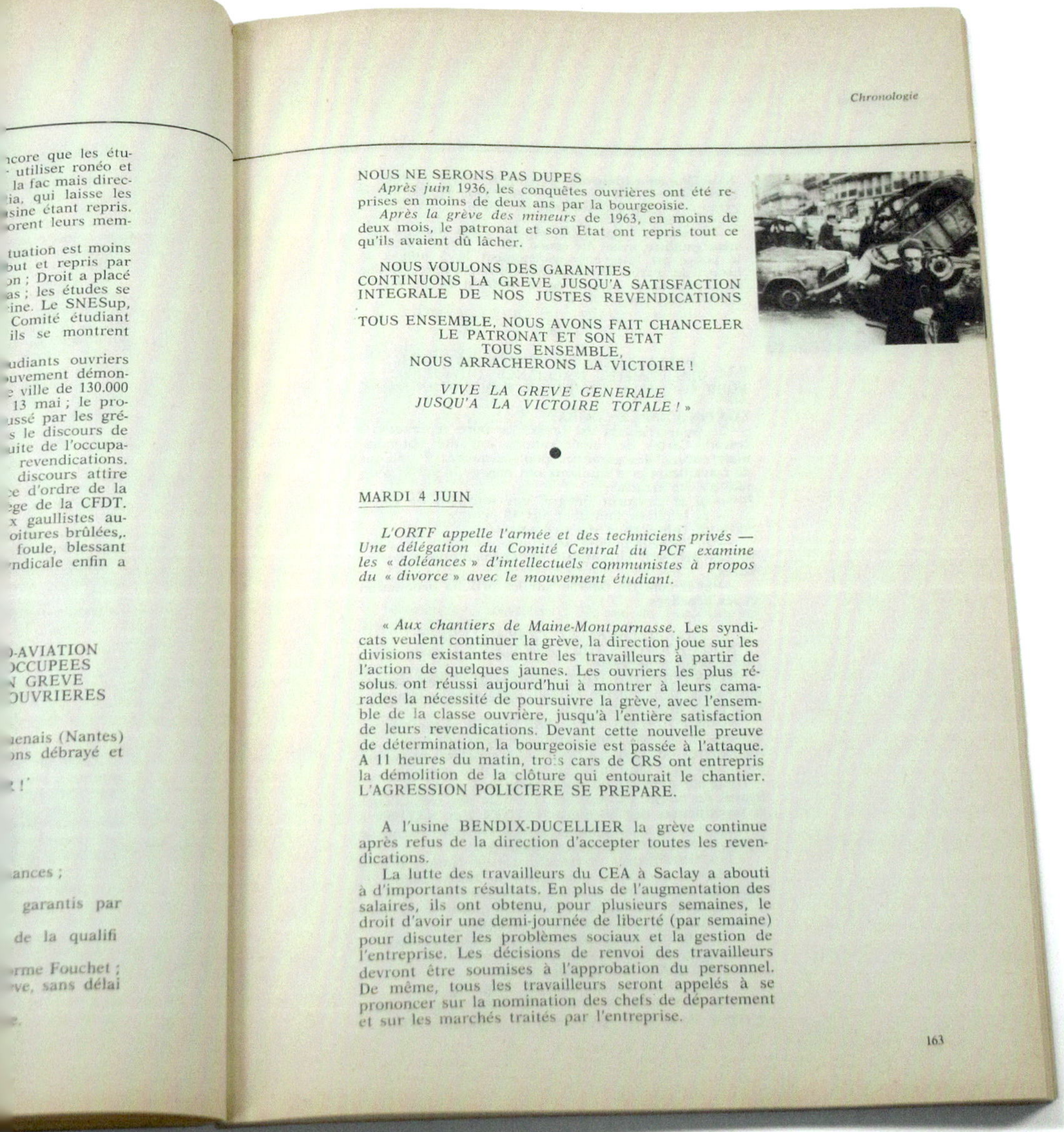

Chronologie

NOUS NE SERONS PAS DUPES
Après juin 1936, les conquêtes ouvrières ont été reprises en moins de deux ans par la bourgeoisie.
Après la grève des mineurs de 1963, en moins de deux mois, le patronat et son Etat ont repris tout ce qu'ils avaient dû lâcher.

NOUS VOULONS DES GARANTIES
CONTINUONS LA GREVE JUSQU'A SATISFACTION INTEGRALE DE NOS JUSTES REVENDICATIONS

TOUS ENSEMBLE, NOUS AVONS FAIT CHANCELER
LE PATRONAT ET SON ETAT
TOUS ENSEMBLE,
NOUS ARRACHERONS LA VICTOIRE !

VIVE LA GREVE GENERALE
JUSQU'A LA VICTOIRE TOTALE ! »

●

MARDI 4 JUIN

L'ORTF appelle l'armée et des techniciens privés — Une délégation du Comité Central du PCF examine les « doléances » d'intellectuels communistes à propos du « divorce » avec le mouvement étudiant.

« *Aux chantiers de Maine-Montparnasse.* Les syndicats veulent continuer la grève, la direction joue sur les divisions existantes entre les travailleurs à partir de l'action de quelques jaunes. Les ouvriers les plus résolus ont réussi aujourd'hui à montrer à leurs camarades la nécessité de poursuivre la grève, avec l'ensemble de la classe ouvrière, jusqu'à l'entière satisfaction de leurs revendications. Devant cette nouvelle preuve de détermination, la bourgeoisie est passée à l'attaque. A 11 heures du matin, trois cars de CRS ont entrepris la démolition de la clôture qui entourait le chantier. L'AGRESSION POLICIERE SE PREPARE.

A l'usine BENDIX-DUCELLIER la grève continue après refus de la direction d'accepter toutes les revendications.

La lutte des travailleurs du CEA à Saclay a abouti à d'importants résultats. En plus de l'augmentation des salaires, ils ont obtenu, pour plusieurs semaines, le droit d'avoir une demi-journée de liberté (par semaine) pour discuter les problèmes sociaux et la gestion de l'entreprise. Les décisions de renvoi des travailleurs devront être soumises à l'approbation du personnel. De même, tous les travailleurs seront appelés à se prononcer sur la nomination des chefs de département et sur les marchés traités par l'entreprise.

163

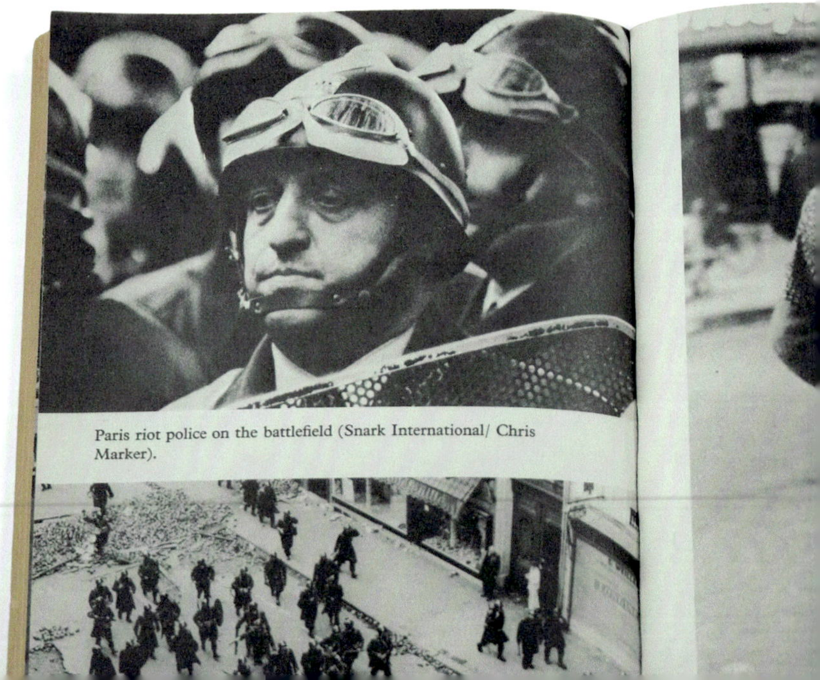

Paris riot police on the battlefield (Snark International/ Chris Marker).

and the *Photo Browse* section of *Zapping Zone*, his 1990 installation, are essentially ordered ransackings of his own photo archives, offering up still images in ever-varied sequences and combinations. For Marker, it is clear that no image is ever lost but simply bides its time while waiting to be called forth to testify. Photos migrate from a lonely self-containment, to the printed page where they converse with text, into the montage factory of film, with each migration bringing additive resonance and keeping the archive alive through the belief that to plunder is to replenish. In *Si j'avais quatre dromadaires*, the proxy photographer and his two friends riff in voice-over to images gathered around the globe (26 countries over a decade), often leavening or disputing the others' interpretations of what they're all seeing. *Photo Browse*, arranged to a wistful Bill Evans tune ("Where has the time all gone to / Haven't done half the things we want to / Oh well, we'll catch up some other time..."), opens with extreme close-ups of contact sheets that Marker's video camera virtually grazes upon. It then pulls back as hundreds of individual prints pass beneath our eyes, mainly randomly sequenced but occasionally organized according to subject (including a set related to his film portrait of Akira Kurosawa, 1985's *A.K.*, and ones from the events of May 1968 in Paris, some of which will reappear in *Staring Back*).

In declaring the still photograph as the central standard, the works harken back inevitably to 1962's *La Jetée*—that film within cinema history having the cut-glass precision of intent and execution one finds in Mozart—and forward to *Le Souvenir d'un avenir*. The entire confrontation with the archive finds its most unfettered rendition in the CD-ROM *Immemory* (1997), whose form accommodates still photos (both as inherited and altered), moving images (his own and others'), and textual commentary (mostly his alone). Poetically conceived as an autobiographical exercise ruled by the solemn mandate of digression, *Immemory* pulverizes linearity. Guillaume-en-Egypte, our on-screen Virgil, constantly encourages detours, skipping ahead and folding back, encouraging associative logic, the logic of the heart, this in the interest of sharing if only briefly, if only lightly, the surface of Marker's memory, the cat's paw loosening the skein. And as we continued to correspond, in spring 2006, about the photo exhibition, the eruption of memory again suggested that we take broader measure of where we'd found ourselves.

In June, Marker wrote,

> Funny you mention *Le Joli Mai*, for I came upon it too, but in a different way. As for the whole thing (*The Revenge*) calls for a sort of archeology of the image, I was wondering if I'd go as far as point what was the real trigger for me: the demo of Feb. 8, 1962, remembered as 'Charonne' by the contemporaries, in relation to the Metro station where 8 people choked to death. It's there that for the first time, in face of senseless police brutality, I decided to use my 16mm camera as a substitute for the gun my primary instincts would have preferred.... That short footage, not too good (the whole thing happened in the dark) was in fact my first step toward a new way to consider filmmaking, and also the origin for *Le Joli Mai*, in which I used it, and everything that followed on the same path until *Chats Perchés*. Hence the idea you may brood about, starting the exhib with a few small prints of these first steps, Charonne and later the Pentagon, as reminders of where I come from, filmwise. Here, some stills. Just an idea, out of the blue, but it's comforting to have a sparring partner. (June 19, 2006)[6]

Whereas I'd been timorous in suggesting a grounding for the 2006 anti-CPE photos anywhere other than in *Le Joli Mai*, Marker clarified in turn the catalyst for *Le Joli Mai* itself, in the so-called Charonne Massacre. The reference is to an event in the waning months of France's war over Algerian independence: the Left had called for a rally to denounce the right-wing *Organisation armée secrète* (which used the methods of terror to oppose France's withdrawal), and the Paris police's brutal response to the gathering had forced demonstrators to flee down the stairs of the Charonne Metro stop, resulting in eight people being killed in the ensuing stampede. Along with

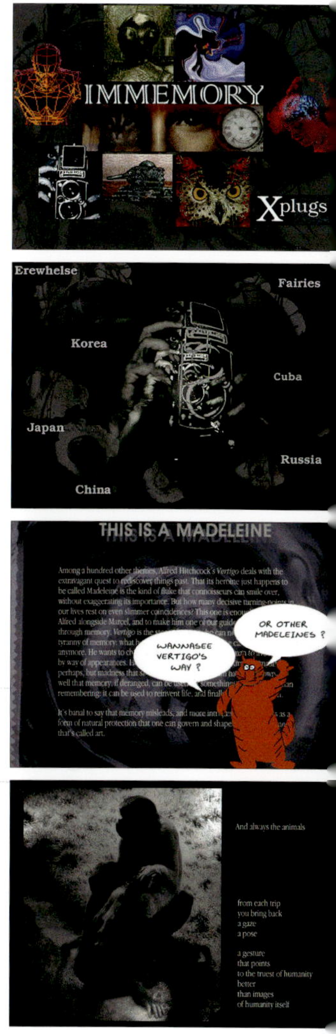

Selected screen images from the *Immemory* CD-ROM; the bottom image appears in "Beast of..."

a still from the Charonne event, Marker attached two from 1967, when he'd participated in an epochal antiwar demonstration at the Pentagon.[7]

My wish from the start had been to shepherd Marker's photos into public light and to offer them as a heretofore cloistered form of communication from an artist who for decades has been sharing the world as he's sought and found it with readers and viewers around the globe—the photos providing, as it were, "another likeness," as I titled the essay I wrote to introduce *Silent Movie*. While he continues to move with virtuosic alacrity among words (in his and others' native tongues), moving images, music, still images, drawings, and digital domains, those who cherish his voice sense that it's all a dazzling, ungraspable work in progress. The contingencies of genre are merely (alas) those that material time and space impose on him, and the essential nature of his achievement can only be begun to be glimpsed when embraced as a perpetually reconstituting web of word-and-image cells, a life-lasting undertaking as time-defiant as Joyce's, yet having in its individual articulations the clarifying directness of the midday sun.

As Marker continued to dispatch photographs, the enveloping pleasure in viewing them grew to feel like gazing through a family photo album, some pictures instantly reminding us of people we had seen before, others drawing tantalizing scenarios, others still simply moving in the face of such improbable beauty. From a photo archive as vast and labyrinthine as Marker's obviously is, when every direction is in truth a detour, the some two hundred images he chose for *Staring Back* became even more provocative as a deliberate gesture; judging, for example, from *Photo Browse* (not to mention his own books and those of others to which he has contributed photos over the years), there could have been hundreds if not thousands more available for inclusion.

The basic binary structure of the exhibition became modified over the next several weeks. Although the full range of photographs included dozens produced from camera negatives, Marker chose to deliver all of them in digital form. He would also periodically indulge my questions about the provenance of specific images within his earlier work, as, for example, when he wrote,

> the bloodied demonstrator was originally in *The Sixth Face* (shot from the steps of the Pentagone, when I gloriously occupied them), then re-used in *Le fond de l'air*. [*Le fond de l'air est rouge—A Grin without a Cat*, 1977/1988/1993] The cellist was in an orchestra pit in Stockholm. (July 14, 2006)

Similarly, precise sequencing and pairing began to emerge:

> …the editor's syndrome functioned automatically, and 'pairs' materialized, some graphic, some geographic, some geometric, some thematic (French cop vs. Japanese protester, seated Chinese boy in Canton vs. seated top model in Paris, Greek monk on Mt. Athos vs. Buddhist monk with cat, sad German activist—that was the night of the first free elections in East Berlin, a disaster for the extreme Left—vs. ko'd Thai boxer, etc.). I give that for what it's worth, but sometimes instinct has its merits." (July 23, 2006)

And, as he had compiled what he called "an 'atmospheric' soundtrack" for the *Silent Movie* exhibition (about twenty piano solos in the favored keys of Satie and Mompou to course through the gallery), so Marker has provided for *Staring Back* an extraordinarily varied collection of CDs and music files to play in random rotation, shuffle mode, ranging from Bill Evans and Kurt Weill, to John Cage and Bach, to Moondog and William Walton.

Staring Back ultimately resolved into four sections: "I Stare 1," "They Stare," "I Stare 2," and "Beast of…". The largest section, "I Stare 1," consists of about seventy-five images, ordered chronologically into six subsections corresponding to the succession (presumably edited from a larger set) of political demonstrations in which Marker has intervened, beginning with Charonne in 1962,

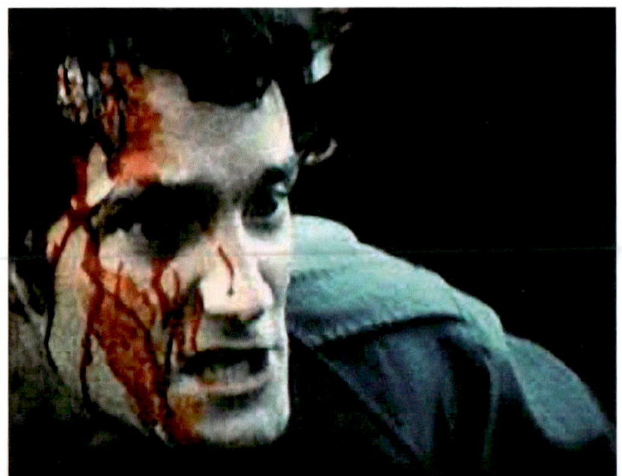

Pentagon image from "I Stare 1" as originally used in the film *La Sixième face du pentagone* (*The Sixth Face of the Pentagon*), 1968

to the Pentagon in 1967, to May 1968 in Paris, to demonstrations in Paris in 2002 (some rendered in *Chats Perchés*), to miscellaneous Parisian demonstrations, and concluding with the anti-CPE pictures of 2006. In an exceedingly rare exception to the rule against his own representation being placed on view, Marker himself figures in an image from the Pentagon series, captured in medium shot as the bare-headed man flanked by two uniformed MPs escorting him into custody. The entire "I Stare 1" section is suspended between two further images: "Once more, a small memory cell. Same location, place de la République, where all major demos start or finish. Same camera angle. And same tree, 40 years older." (July 16, 2006)

"They Stare" is the exploded counter-shot to "I Stare," the two sequences facing each other on opposing walls. Marker has sequenced this series not in chronological fashion but in couples joined vertically, about fifty of them. These are the faces of people who looked upon Marker as he took their measure through his lens: the faces that have seen his face, and taken it with them as he has taken theirs with him. A broad register of gazes meet his, from a passing glimpse to what must have been longer exchanges, from the fortuitous interaction to the studio-like portrait, from fellow passengers

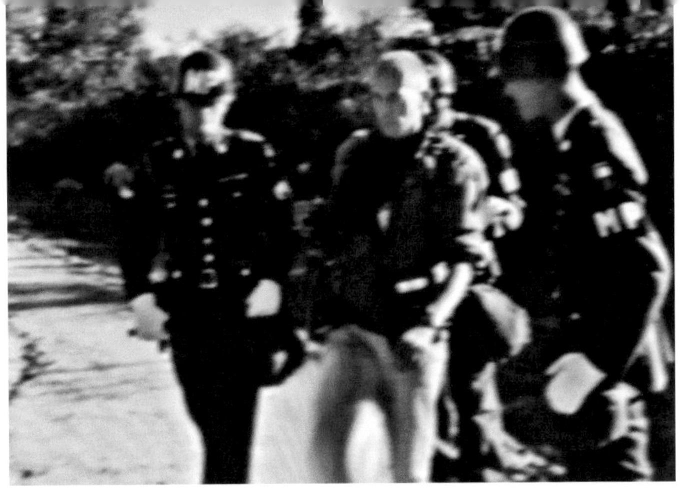

Chris Marker (center) at the Pentagon in 1967, as seen in "I Stare 1"

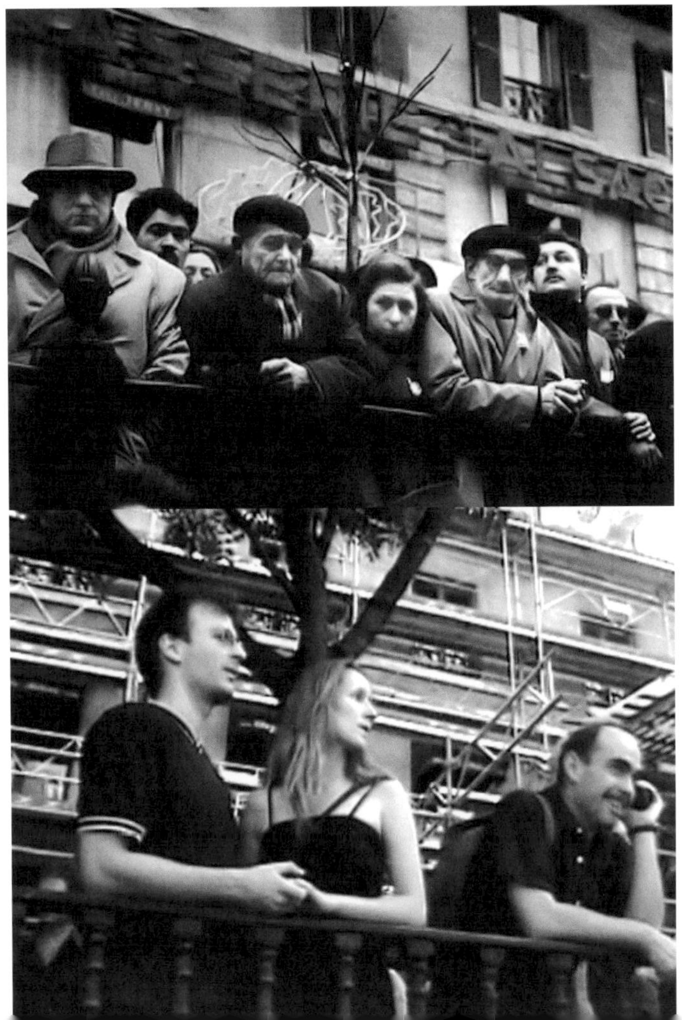

Demonstrators at the place de la République, 1962 and 2002, as seen in "I Stare 1"

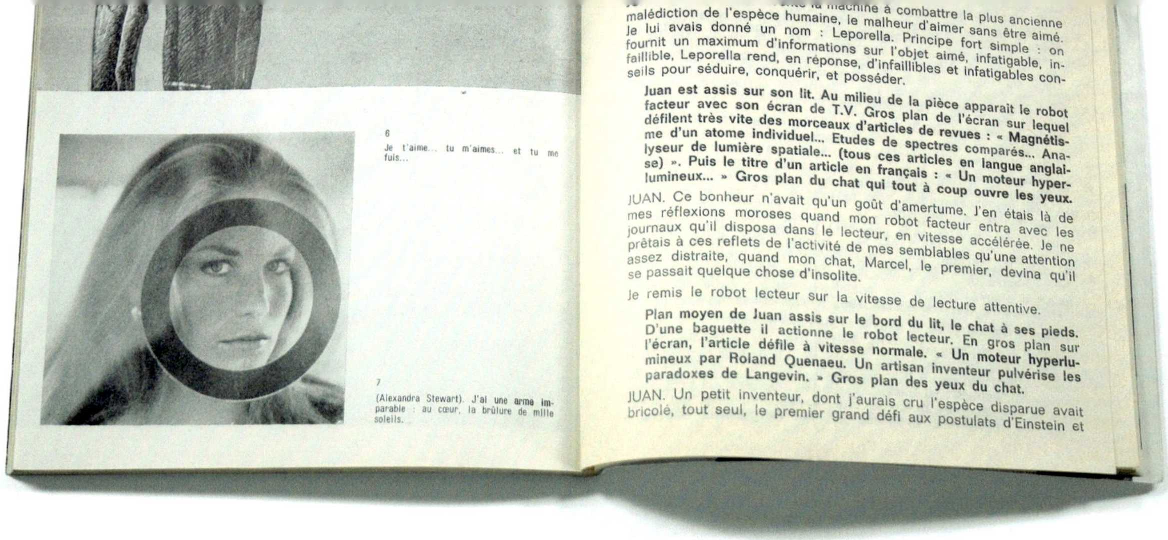

6

Je t'aime... tu m'aimes... et tu me fuis...

7

(Alexandra Stewart). J'ai une arme imparable : au cœur, la brûlure de mille soleils.

machine à combattre la plus ancienne malédiction de l'espèce humaine, le malheur d'aimer sans être aimé. Je lui avais donné un nom : Leporella. Principe fort simple : on fournit un maximum d'informations sur l'objet aimé, infatigable, infaillible, Leporella rend, en réponse, d'infaillibles et infatigables conseils pour séduire, conquérir, et posséder.

Juan est assis sur son lit. Au milieu de la pièce apparait le robot facteur avec son écran de T.V. Gros plan de l'écran sur lequel défilent très vite des morceaux d'articles de revues : « Magnétisme d'un atome individuel... Etudes de spectres comparés... Analyseur de lumière spatiale... (tous ces articles en langue anglaise) ». Puis le titre d'un article en français : « Un moteur hyperlumineux... » Gros plan du chat qui tout à coup ouvre les yeux.

JUAN. Ce bonheur n'avait qu'un goût d'amertume. J'en étais là de mes réflexions moroses quand mon robot facteur entra avec les journaux qu'il disposa dans le lecteur, en vitesse accélérée. Je ne prêtais à ces reflets de l'activité de mes semblables qu'une attention assez distraite, quand mon chat, Marcel, le premier, devina qu'il se passait quelque chose d'insolite.

Je remis le robot lecteur sur la vitesse de lecture attentive.

Plan moyen de Juan assis sur le bord du lit, le chat à ses pieds. D'une baguette il actionne le robot lecteur. En gros plan sur l'écran, l'article défile à vitesse normale. « Un moteur hyperlumineux par Roland Quenaeu. Un artisan inventeur pulvérise les paradoxes de Langevin. » Gros plan des yeux du chat.

JUAN. Un petit inventeur, dont j'aurais cru l'espèce disparue avait bricolé, tout seul, le premier grand défi aux postulats d'Einstein et

Alexandra Stewart, as reproduced in *"La brûlure de mille soleils" L'Avant-Scène Cinema* 89, February 1969 (the article is the shooting script of a short film by Pierre Kast on which Marker worked); the image also appears in "They Stare"

on the Metro to such longtime accomplices as the actress Alexandra Stewart (peering through a porthole) and film editor Christine Aya (caught gamine-like, cigarette in hand).

For a man whose legend includes a prohibition on having his own photo rendered, the "They Stare" pictures are a profoundly poignant relaxation of that embargo, as moving in its way as the moment in *La Jetée* when the protagonist points to the cross section of the sequoia tree and tells his companion, "This is where I come from." Each of the "They Stare" images captures a face turned in curious, pleased recognition to the face of the man at that second beholding them, proof (if photos must be importuned to prove) not simply of the anecdotal coordinates of his global wanderings but of his will, which is his fate, to remember, and to have it remembered, that these are some of the humans with whom he shared a moment of the twentieth and twenty-first centuries. They are the residents of Zone Marker, friends over time alongside beauties glimpsed perhaps a single time, but all intent on meeting the photographer's gaze with mutual and varying intimations of empathy, forbearance, and love in its variegated descents.

As *Sans Soleil*'s narrator remarks about a bar he finds in Tokyo, "It's the kind of place that allows people to stare at each other with equality...the threshold below which any man is as good as any other, and knows it." For those who've not had the fortune ever to meet the artist or who've seen him only in the samizdat-like photos of him surfacing now and again, the portraits of "They Stare" coalesce into a reflected, refracted image of the man: bemused, direct, more than a mild aesthete, and passionately driven to human engagement; a man who, in his first encounter with you, wants to hear the news from the corner of the world you call home. And here we meet the woman first seen, and then to be remembered, in the Praia market in Cape Verde, assuming status as an icon of late twentieth-century global wandering; she who, in *Sans Soleil*, with a turn of her head could stop a motion camera in its tracks, the forward march of film surrendering to the power of the quietly directed gaze.

The "I Stare 2" section, produced in the gallery as oversized contact sheets, contains *Staring Back*'s earliest photos, including that of the Czech triple gold medalist Emil Zátopek triumphing in the Helsinki Olympics, from *Olympia 52*. It's also the section enlivened by portraits of public figures and fellow-travelling artists whose company Marker shared: Simone Signoret, his childhood friend from Neuilly-sur-Seine, and the Russian directors Alexander Medvedkin and Andrei Tarkovsky (all of whom he's also portrayed on film: in 1986's *Mémoires pour Simone*, 1993's *Le Tombeau d'Alexandre* [*The Last Bolshevik*], and 1999's *Une Journée d'Andrei Arsenevich* [*One Day*

Still from *La Jetée*, 1962

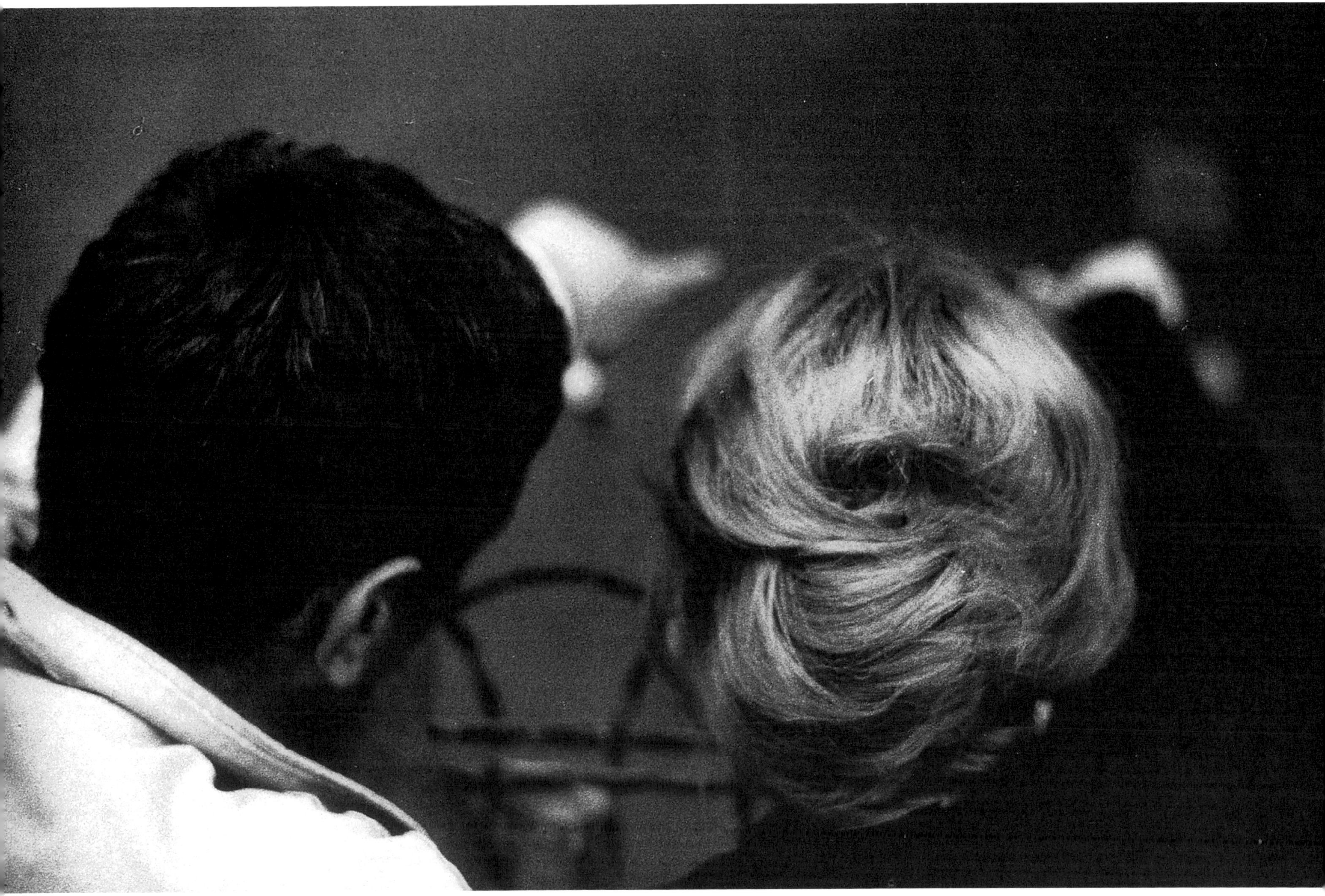

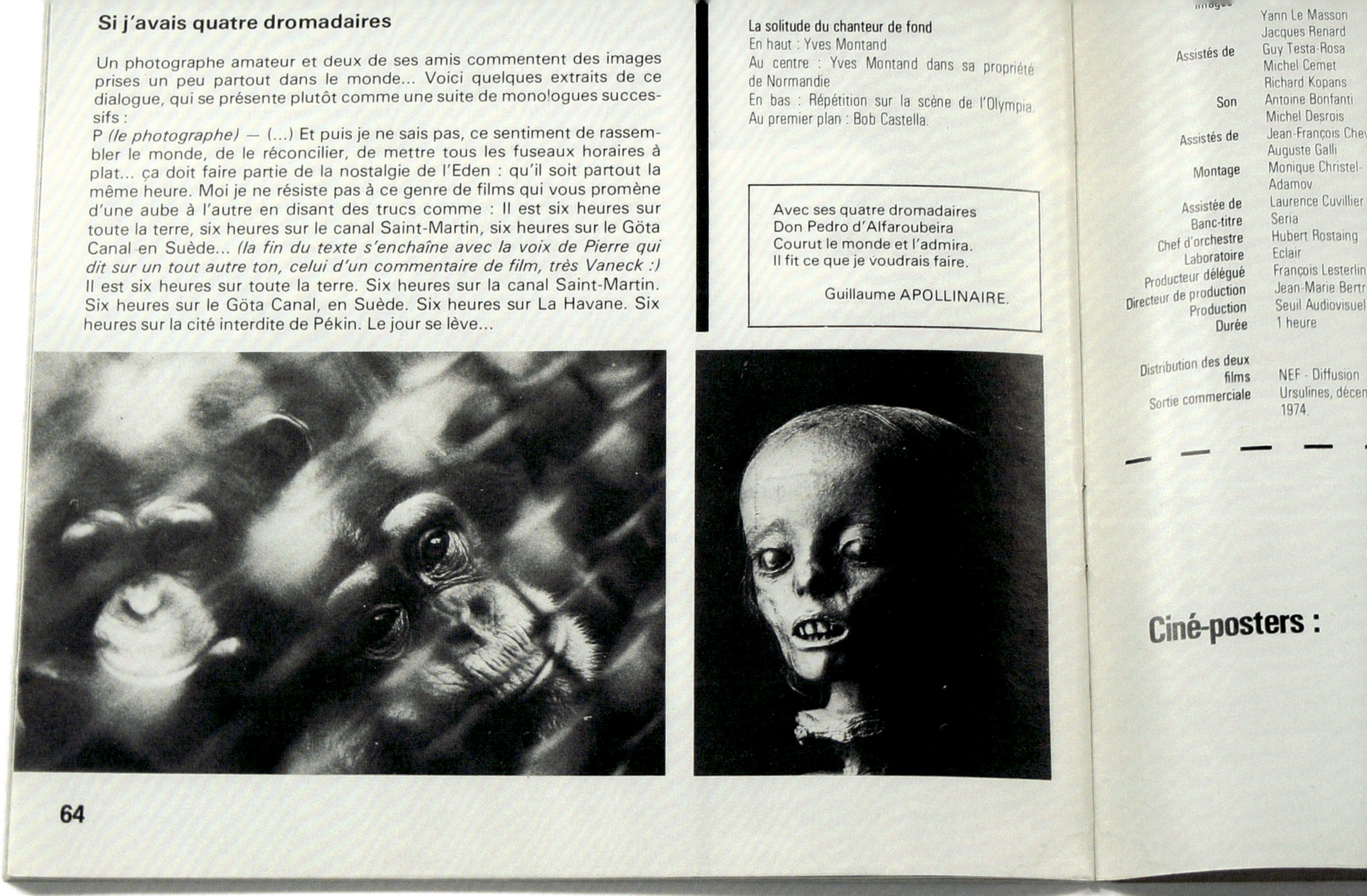

Si j'avais quatre dromadaires

Un photographe amateur et deux de ses amis commentent des images prises un peu partout dans le monde... Voici quelques extraits de ce dialogue, qui se présente plutôt comme une suite de monologues successifs :
P *(le photographe)* — (...) Et puis je ne sais pas, ce sentiment de rassembler le monde, de le réconcilier, de mettre tous les fuseaux horaires à plat... ça doit faire partie de la nostalgie de l'Eden : qu'il soit partout la même heure. Moi je ne résiste pas à ce genre de films qui vous promène d'une aube à l'autre en disant des trucs comme : Il est six heures sur toute la terre, six heures sur le canal Saint-Martin, six heures sur le Göta Canal en Suède... *(la fin du texte s'enchaîne avec la voix de Pierre qui dit sur un tout autre ton, celui d'un commentaire de film, très Vaneck :)* Il est six heures sur toute la terre. Six heures sur la canal Saint-Martin. Six heures sur le Göta Canal, en Suède. Six heures sur La Havane. Six heures sur la cité interdite de Pékin. Le jour se lève...

La solitude du chanteur de fond
En haut : Yves Montand
Au centre : Yves Montand dans sa propriété de Normandie
En bas : Répétition sur la scène de l'Olympia. Au premier plan : Bob Castella.

Avec ses quatre dromadaires
Don Pedro d'Alfaroubeira
Courut le monde et l'admira.
Il fit ce que je voudrais faire.

Guillaume APOLLINAIRE.

64

	Yann Le Masson
	Jacques Renard
Assistés de	Guy Testa-Rosa
	Michel Cemet
	Richard Kopans
Son	Antoine Bonfanti
	Michel Desrois
Assistés de	Jean-François Chev
	Auguste Galli
Montage	Monique Christel-Adamov
Assistée de	Laurence Cuvillier
Banc-titre	Seria
Chef d'orchestre	Hubert Rostaing
Laboratoire	Eclair
Producteur délégué	François Lesterlin
Directeur de production	Jean-Marie Bertra
Production	Seuil Audiovisuel
Durée	1 heure
Distribution des deux films	NEF - Diffusion
Sortie commerciale	Ursulines, décem 1974.

Ciné-posters :

Images from *Si j'avais quatre dromadaires* (*If I Had Four Camels*), 1966, as reproduced in *"Si j'avais quatre dromadaires, La solitude du chanteur de fond*: Deux filme de Chris Marker," *L'Avant-Scène Cinema* 156, March 1975; they are also seen in "Beast of..." (left) and "They Stare" (right) *in the Life of Andrei Arsenevich*], respectively); the cosmopolitan Dutch filmmaker Joris Ivens (whose 1962 *A Valparaiso* he wrote); composer Michel Legrand (collaborator on *Le Joli Mai*); the axiomatic Salvador Dali; Fidel Castro in full action mode (from 1961's *Cuba si*); and actress Delphine Seyrig, here in maquillage to perform in Samuel Beckett's 1964 film, *Comédie*.

Staring Back's concluding section, its valedictory gesture, consists of eleven portraits of animals granting us a berth among them, some zoo-enclosed and some freely ranging. Realizing that animals were "conspicuously absent from the 'Stare' walls," (July 28, 2006), Marker suggested we give them pride of place within the installation by being placed at the very end, the animals pondering God-only-knows-what as they indulge the curious photographer standing in deference before them, a gesture of envoi concluding the photo journey: "Cat, wherever you are, peace be with you."[8]

Like all of Marker's film work prior to *Le Joli Mai* in 1962, *Olympia 52* is rarely seen, especially outside France, and dozens of short and collaborative works subsequent to it remain virtually impossible to view. This is partly through Marker's own disinterest in remaining attached, on some level, to what for him are things of the past (Marker, in 2003: "Twenty years separate *La Jetée* from *Sans Soleil*. And another 20 years separate *Sans Soleil* from the present. Under the circumstances, if I were to speak in the name of the person who made these movies, it wouldn't be journalism, rather spiritism."), and partly through the probably more deciding vagaries of international film/video distribution (involving ownership, rights holders, etc.).[9] Fragments from some of those fugitive works surface in "I Stare 2," including the lovely, swan-like Israeli woman posed at the easel from *Description d'un combat* (*Description of a Struggle*, 1960) and the bespectacled sun-gazers from *Eclipse* (1999), not to mention images from *Chats Perchés* and *La Jetée* (the photographer William Klein and his wife, Janine, posing as messengers from the evolved wreckage beyond World War III), and the glamorous, vamping Catherine Belkhodja from *Silent Movie*.

As I've noted, punctuating the entirety of *Staring Back* are images one recalls from Marker's film, video, and book projects, and from *Immemory*, here regrouped by their creator for this occasion: an elegant reshuffle of the deck, portraits reclaimed from the printed page, from the trove of moving images, from the ever-morphing digital vault. *Staring Back* is, at that, an image archipelago, dispersed over continents horizontally and demolishing time vertically; the owners of its faces are souls encountered perhaps once, or embraced for years by members of the clans who claim as an intimate the man who in stabilizing them as memories now offers them to us—Marker as both confrère and begetter, the sender and the suitor.

For this gathering of those clans, it feels like coming home, not for the first time, but again. As Judy says to Scottie, in Marker's most cherished *Vertigo*, "It's our place."

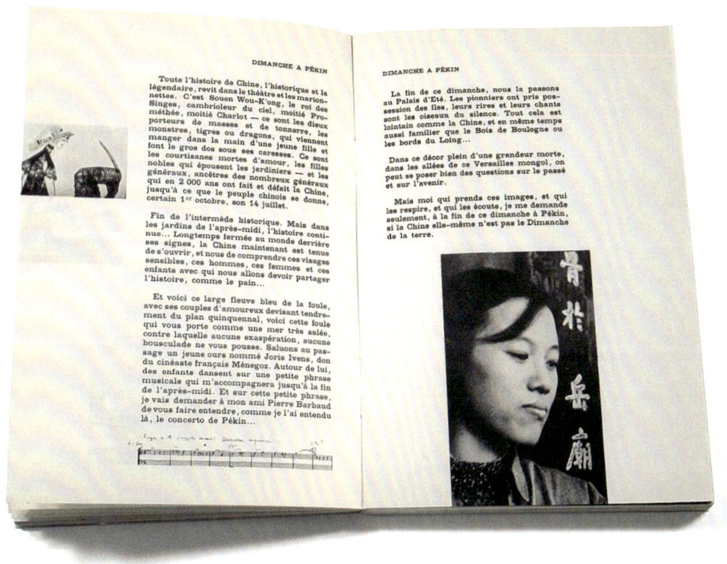
DIMANCHE A PÉKIN

Toute l'histoire de Chine, l'historique et la légendaire, revit dans le théâtre et les marionnettes. C'est Souen Wou-K'ong, le roi des Singes, cambrioleur du ciel, moitié Prométhée, moitié Charlot — ce sont les dieux porteurs de masses et de tonnerre, les monstres, tigres ou dragons, qui viennent manger dans la main d'une jeune fille et font le gros dos sous ses caresses. Ce sont les courtisanes mortes d'amour, les filles nobles qui épousent les jardiniers — et les généraux, ancêtres des nombreux généraux qui en 2 000 ans ont fait et défait la Chine, jusqu'à ce que le peuple chinois se donne, certain 1er octobre, son 14 juillet.

Fin de l'intermède historique. Mais dans les jardins de l'après-midi, l'histoire continue... Longtemps fermée au monde derrière ses signes, la Chine maintenant est tenue de s'ouvrir, et nous de comprendre ces visages sensibles, ces hommes, ces femmes et ces enfants avec qui nous allons devoir partager l'histoire, comme le pain...

Et voici ce large fleuve bleu de la foule, avec ses couples d'amoureux devisant tendrement du plan quinquennal, voici cette foule qui vous porte comme une mer très salée, contre laquelle aucune exaspération, aucune bousculade ne vous pousse. Saluons au passage un jeune ours nommé Joris Ivens, don du cinéaste français Ménegoz. Autour de lui, des enfants dansent sur une petite phrase musicale qui m'accompagnera jusqu'à la fin de l'après-midi. Et sur cette petite phrase, je vais demander à mon ami Pierre Barbaud de vous faire entendre, comme je l'ai entendu là, le concerto de Pékin...

DIMANCHE A PÉKIN

La fin de ce dimanche, nous la passons au Palais d'Eté. Les pionniers ont pris possession des îles, leurs rires et leurs chants sont les oiseaux du silence. Tout cela est lointain comme la Chine, et en même temps aussi familier que le Bois de Boulogne ou les bords du Loing...

Dans ce décor plein d'une grandeur morte, dans les allées de ce Versailles mongol, on peut se poser bien des questions sur le passé et sur l'avenir.

Mais moi qui prends ces images, et qui les respire, et qui les écoute, je me demande seulement, à la fin de ce dimanche à Pékin, si la Chine elle-même n'est pas le Dimanche de la terre.

Image from *Dimanche à Pékin* (*Sunday in Peking*), as reproduced in *Commentaires*, 1961; the same image is seen in "I Stare 2"

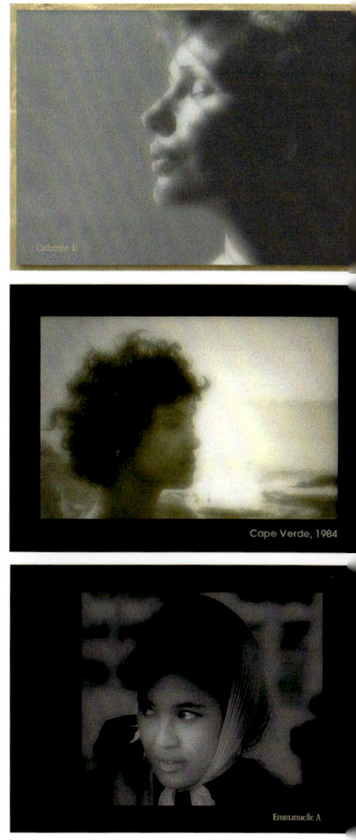

Selected screen images from the *Immemory* CD-ROM; the top image is Catherine Belkhodja in *Silent Movie*; the same figures or images all appear in "I Stare 2"

Notes

1. M. Chat's fame was such that by the time *Chats Perchés* premiered in December 2004, the Centre Pompidou, which hosted multiple screenings of the film, also authorized its creators to produce an enormous drawing of him, measuring over 80 by 160 feet, on the building's plaza. The left-leaning daily, *Libération*, produced a special supplement (December 4–5, 2004) acknowledging the joint phenomenon of M. Chat and Marker's commentary on it, with every page of the issue graphically marked by M. Chat's image, and including a conversation between Marker and M. Chat's primary begetter, Thomas Vuille. (M. Chat is joined on the cover by Guillaume-en-Egypte, above the headline "Chris Marker and M. Chat put their paw on Libé.") Credited to the collective known as CHAT (La Communauté Harmonieuse des Artistes Taciturnes), M. Chat, frequently accompanied by screenings of *Chats Perchés*, has since migrated to such other locales as Sarajevo (where he adorned tramcars), Hong Kong, and New York (where the American debut of *Chats Perchés* in 2006 included a gathering of fans wearing M. Chat masks).

2. *Owls at Noon* is the overarching title Marker has given to an ongoing summary project "to extract a subjective journey through the 20th century." Its first installment, *Owls at Noon Prelude: The Hollow Men*, is a two-channel, eight-screen rumination on the traumas of World War I, echoing T. S. Eliot and set to a Toru Takemitsu composition for piano, which debuted at New York's Museum of Modern Art in 2005. As for the supremacy of cats and owls as essential guides in navigating within Marker's firmament, it's as we're reminded in *Level Five*: "Computer at night, barn-owl's delight; computer in the morning, tom-cat's warning."

3. Going back several decades, Marker's films have periodically been included in, or shown as adjunct screenings to, visual arts exhibitions, but his presence in that arena has dramatically increased through his multimedia installations destined expressly (unlike his films) for a gallery context. Among the few exhibitions to include his still photography are *Hard Light* (P.S. 1 Contemporary Art Center, Long Island City, curated by Klaus Biesenbach and Doug Aitken, 2004), a group show in which storyboard and photo material from *La Jetée* was on view, and *The Unhomely: Phantom Scenes in Global Society* (2nd International Biennial of Contemporary Art, Seville, curated by Okwui Enzewor, 2006), which included a group of Marker's anti-CPE images. A notable recent example of Marker's work "inspiring" visual artists is *Anachronism* (Argos, Brussels, curated by Elena Filipovic, 2007), a group show installed against the exhibition's backdrop of a continuous screening of *La Jetée*. In 2006, Peter Blum Gallery in New York produced *Owls at Noon Prelude: The Hollow Men* as a limited edition, as well as editioning selected digital photo prints by Marker.

4. I wrote a brief text to accompany "The Revenge of the Eye: A Portfolio by Chris Marker," a portfolio of the images that appeared in the summer 2006 issue of *Artforum*, 313–317.

5. The full inventory of Marker's photos as reproduced in books and journals remains to be taken, particularly those appearing outside his own authored works (see the bibliography at the back of this volume for a list) and those in the *Petite Planète* volumes both during and after his editorial stewardship. Photos he took during the events of May 1968 in Paris were reproduced in various French- and English-language books and journals (e.g., Patrick Seale and Maureen McConville's *Red Flag/Black Flag*, New York: Ballantine, 1968, and the very similar British edition, *French Revolution 1968*, published by Penguin Books in association with William Heinemann Ltd, and in François Maspero's journal, *Partisans* 42, May–June 1968), both under his own name and as credited to Snark International, the loosely organized photo agency formed around that time. As for the *Petite Planète* series itself, an "authorized" poster consisting of cover images selected by Marker was produced by the artist Jason Simon, for New York's Orchard Gallery, in 2006. In providing Simon mild guidance on this endeavor, Marker located the cover for the spoof *Petite Planète* guide to Mars, which is glimpsed several times as it wends its way through the Bibliothèque Nationale en route to being catalogued in *Toute la mémoire du monde*, Alain Resnais' 1956 film on which Marker assisted.

6. The Charonne massacre in 1962 was itself a deathly epilogue to the roundup in October in 1961 of hundreds of Algerians in Paris, spearheaded by the Vichy-tainted chief of police, Maurice Papon, resulting in as many as an estimated 200 among the disappeared. Both the atrocities and their subsequent erasure from popular memory over the next several decades are analyzed in the 1992 documentary *Drowning by Bullets* (directed by Philip Brooks and Alan Hayling), which includes footage from *Le Joli Mai*. As it happens, I was writing this note on the day Papon's death was announced (February 18, 2007). Peace be to his victims, and then to him.

7. Marker elaborated on his Pentagon experience, in an e-mail from August 10, 2006: "As you remember, there was something fishy in the whole affair. How came that an unbreakable line of armed soldiers was precisely interrupted at the outset of the small path that leads to the main entrance by a single rope guarded by a few marshals? During the night I spent on the steps of this illustrious building in the company of my colleagues from the press corps, I heard them exchanging their own puzzlement. 'There's something weird here,' I remember one of them saying aloud. I chose not to enter that debate in *The Sixth Face*. Having held the ground for a whole night could symbolically be taken as a point for the Movement, that was enough (see how you can enter the field of propaganda against your will?). Perhaps on the other side it appeared useful to exaggerate the danger of the protesters ('these irresponsible kids come to threaten our most sacred places')—hence the surprising facility of our breakthrough. So everybody was manipulating everybody as usual. A new detail came recently by an unexpected twist: it happens that the man in charge for the Pentagon security was none other than Donald Rumsfeld.…And in an interview where he heavily described his glorious life, he mentioned that in order to avoid any regrettable accident, the weapons of the soldiers were not loaded!"

8. *Immemory* contains within its dizzying multitudes a series of charming monologues, "Beast Wishes," by zoo animals (Albert of Okinawa, Sophie of Copenhagen, Marfa of Moscow, Molly of London, and Ty Lai of Paris) flaunting their connoisseurship as they ponder masterpieces by the likes of Modigliani and Botticelli.

9. An appalling casualty of the politics of "international coproduction," Marker's thirteen-part *L'Heritage de la chouette* (*The Owl's Legacy*, 1989), about the foundational residue of Greek antiquity within the developed world, remains inaccessible following its "withdrawal" by the Onassis Foundation, its primary funder. As Marker recently remarked, "If ARTE hadn't kept, fortunately, a Beta master of the editing, the whole film would have sunk to the bottom of the Aegean Sea." (February 6, 2007).

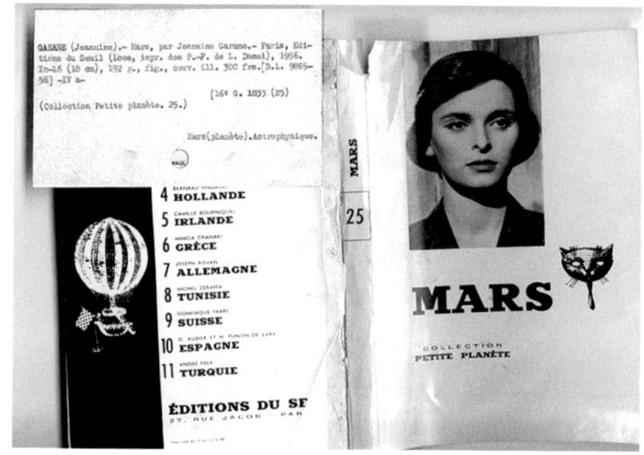

Spoof *Petite Planète* guide to Mars

In Hindsight

Molly Nesbit

There is no end to the staring.

Nothing the matter there. Lately when the man called Chris Marker draws a project to a close, the end has been difficult to find. It is not like the films we have prized, where the ends involve inversions: a man sees the moment of his own death at the end of *La Jetée*; in *Sans Soleil* another man leaves us with an equal and opposite moment when poetry will be made by everyone and there will be emus in the Zone; at the close of *The Last Bolshevik,* Tolchan believes in nothing anymore, except music. And yet these same films are the ones where a fellow traveller, always the best of friends even when the news gets worse, recounts his observations, writes letters, and looks out for both beauty and beast. Therefore he does not let Tolchan have the last word. Music, the traveller remarks, was "his version of the black hole, a whole era condensed into one life, a whole life condensed into few notes. Yes, I know the word that will come to many to describe men like you, Tolchan, Vertov—dinosaurs. But look what happened to dinosaurs—kids love 'em."

We have come to prize him. The fellow traveller tells us tales about faraway places, about people so like and unlike ourselves that the us and them, the I and They, blur strangely, but never will naively combine and go gray. Black and white remain, not a catchphrase, not a clarity, just shadow and light and hole.

Under his direction these scenes multiplied. We may be forgiven for mixing up the ends and beginnings. So many come to mind. Thirty years ago *A Grin without a Cat* ended with a helicopter chase. A camera in the helicopter watched as two wolves ran, whipped by the chopper's wind, cringing. They were being gunned down. But this film had begun elsewhere. Marker's script had a preface that wondered what would happen to the images of the latest revolutions, to his own outtakes and to the other aftereffects of TV documentary; he hazarded a guess about the existence of a collective immemory, which is to say a memory more ancient than memory, a memory immemorial. The film he proposed would make a montage of the outtakes he'd repressed and the collective immemory. There would be no resolution in 1977. It would end instead with the wolves.

The idea of an immemory would not leave him. It led him, twenty years later, to make the CD-ROM *Immemory,* itself now becoming the montage. This immemory of 1997 was a field stacked with beliefs and facts and images through which one clicked at a private pace, one screen yielding to the next, deeper and deeper down paths full of choices and splits. Here a different way of working was beckoning. It was not the linear edit of rhythm but an edit of small combinations of images and ideas, pairings in a field, an ambient edit punctuated by a cartoon cat offering menus of choice. This immemory was technically finite, but seemingly endless. The fellow traveller, who is also known as the man called Chris Marker, had given up the necessity of ends.

Immemory contains all kinds of records: for example we find there a rare copy of *Coréennes,* the book he put together as a "court métrage," or short film, in 1959. That book had ended with his letter to a cat. To the cat he speaks his heart:

> It is with the face turned toward me that I have true relations. No longer are there Korea or Koreans, singular and plural of the same night, but only these familiar faces (and that is the Golden Fleece).
>
> (I know you have the intelligence—cats understand such things—not to see me playing Humankind against History, all those capital Hs with which one works up a sweat of understanding each morning, barbells for the intellectual. I know that my relations with these faces, with these familiar people, all filter through history, and that to help or to harm them there are other means than pataphysics. But if the Big Issues must be involved in this relation, let that remain between them and me—it is not for the onlookers. At the bottom of this trip is human friendship. The rest is silence.)

The silence would not be absolute, of course. In *Immemory* the letter was given a new postscript. There he speaks of worlds rejected now by history, that history newly demarcated after 1989, that theater again brightly decorated and lit by revised ideologies. He says:

> The end of our century demands something else. What's more, the notion of historical progress, of a powerful "current of history," never mattered to me except in a deliberate play of the word "current": not a directional flow over some chart plotted out by infallible commanders (there again, the ambiguity of the word "leader"), but instead the possibility to grasp the current meanings of the historical present, full of sound and fury, told, and so on. If I ever had a passion in the field of politics, it's a passion for understanding. Understanding how people manage to live on a planet like ours. Understanding how they seek, how they try, how they make mistakes, how they get over them, how they learn, how they lose their way. That immediately put me on the side of the people who seek and make mistakes, as opposed to those who seek nothing, except to conserve, defend themselves, and deny all the rest.

Immemory brought the man called Chris Marker to the twenty-first century where he continues to make films, but fewer. He still hopes for ground comparable to the now-devalued CD-ROM technology, something to give him anew the field that can be both honeycombed and mined. Meantime there are projects like this one with the staring where we see the people again. It began as an outtake of *The Case of the Grinning Cat*, a diary film begun in 2000 and finished in 2004. He ended it with an echo—the cry of the lone wolf:

> Legend has it that duke Gediminas, the founder of Vilnius, had a dream in which a wolf howled on a hill. A priest deciphered the dream: the duke must build a city whose name would be heard throughout the world, like the howling of the wolf.

From this, another wave, this time not a film, but photographs, a field of faces drawn from the pictures of a lifetime. Many of these photographs show people who have taken to the streets to demonstrate against history or to try to make it turn. The tides of time being strong, they meet resistance; they need to be able to run like Olympians. He stares at them. Others stare at him. It is the staring of a lifetime. Will it become an immemory? They share one trait: Marker has set the entire effort of the field into black and white. We will see their faces. Black and white will bind them?

When the color of the world, or a color photograph, is translated into the register of black and white, shadow increases and light quickens; the photograph acquires a different, deeper space. The stare acquires the properties of night vision. We find ourselves in a world better seen by cats and owls. You should know that outside this book, this room, there is another project waiting in the wings, unfinished, that Marker is calling *Owls at Noon*. So far, it too, is being done in black and white. Owls of Minerva, the owls at noon must be roused from their sleep. What wakes them? What will they see? At noon the sun goes vertical, Apollo rides high and the world is, for a minute, shadow-less. Outside the staring, is a world becoming white? Whatever position we have been given here, it is provisional. But then, the fellow traveller has been telling us for years to expect this. All positions are provisional. All time flies.

We sit on fences. For those of you reading this and who will know the project about staring only as a book, remember that this line of pages contains the reflection of a field that has been designed for a wedge-shaped room where "They Stare" and "I Stare" occupy facing walls. Marker has orchestrated some of the pairs and sequences, but he has left the rest open. We are meant to sit on our fences between facing fields. He has added a field of sympathetic animals. All around us the friends and strangers and fellow travellers en route in life's nighttimes are caught staring and dreaming. But mindfully. These stares have stored up memories of their own. They give the eyes their depth.

When would a person's memory yield to the field of immemory? Is the immemory impersonal? There's the rub—inevitably minds always hold not only one's own memories but the memories of others as well. The memories of others, what they call their ideas, are what is commonly called knowledge. In short, minds are largely filled by matter not their own. But what is a mind of one's own? Or a stare of one's own? This is a problem for a poet.

> *A god can do it. But will you tell me how*
> *a man can enter through the lyre's strings?*
> *Our mind is split. And at the shadowed crossing*
> *of heart-roads, there is no temple for Apollo.*
>
> *Song, as you have taught it, is not desire,*
> *not wooing any grace that can be achieved;*
> *song is reality. Simple, for a god.*
> *But when can we be real? When does he pour*
> *The earth, the stars, into us? Young man,*
> *it is not your loving, even if your mouth*
> *was forced wide open by your own voice—learn*
>
> *to forget that passionate music. It will end.*
> *True singing is a different breath, about*
> *nothing. A gust inside the god. A wind.*

It is Rainer Maria Rilke's answer in the "Third Sonnet to Orpheus."[1] It could accompany the staring, Chris Marker being, when all is said and done, a dangerous poet himself. He has given us history as current, history as wind. We are blown around. We are holes gusting inside. We are caught between stares. And yet, like him, we are mindful. When he was very young, just before the Second World War, the man later called Chris Marker headed up a literary magazine called *Le trait d'union*. He was in high school. At that time he had the good fortune to have Jean-Paul Sartre, who was also very young, as his philosophy teacher. Sartre taught them an expanded idea of philosophy. He gave them an essay on John Dos Passos for their magazine. He introduced them to the new American literature—Hemingway, Steinbeck, Faulkner. It was a literature marked, Sartre liked to say then, by a different temporality, complete with holes in memories and holes in its time.[2] The man who saw the instant of his death in *La Jetée* had come there through a memory that opened a hole in time. A hole in time can be held forever in a photograph.

These are the depths of these photographs. We stare, remembering Sartre and Faulkner, who was in turn remembering his Shakespeare with *The Sound and the Fury*. And *Light in August*? What of the memory that swept through chapter 6? Is it not part of the immemory now, something that shines in the eyes that are staring? Something endless?

> Memory believes before knowing remembers. Believes longer than recollects, longer than knowing even wonders. Knows remembers believes a corridor in a big long garbled cold echoing building of dark red brick sootbleakened by more chimneys than its own, set in a grassless cinderstrewnpacked compound surrounded by smoking factory purlieus and enclosed by a ten foot steel-and-wire fence like penitentiary or a zoo, where in random erratic surges, with sparrowlike childtrebling, orphans in identical and uniform blue denim in and out of remembering but in knowing constant as the bleak walls, the bleak windows where in rain soot from the yearly adjacenting chimneys streaked like black tears.[3]

Or black cats.

Notes

1. Rainer Maria Rilke, "Third Sonnet to Orpheus," in *Ahead of All Parting: the Selected Poetry and Prose of Rainer Maria Rilke*, ed. and trans. Stephen Mitchell (New York: Modern Library), 415.

2. See Sartre's essays on Dos Passos and Faulkner which, after the war, were collected in *Situations I* (Paris: Gallimard, 1947). Both Simone Signoret and Anatole Dauman have recounted the story of Sartre at the Lycée Pasteur in their memoirs: *La Nostalgie n'est plus ce qu'elle était* (Paris: Seuil, 1976), 32; and *Anatole Dauman. Argos Films. Souvenir-Ecran* (Paris: Centre Georges Pompidou, 1989), 14–15, respectively.

3. William Faulkner, *Light in August* (New York: Random House, 1932), 88.

Filmography and Bibliography

Filmography

The filmography and bibliographical information below was assembled from multiple sources. For more complete information on the numerous articles, stories, commentaries, and scenarios by Chris Marker, as well as his film collaborations, please consult the following sources (all listed in the bibliography): Catherine Lupton, *Chris Marker: Memories of the Future*; Birgit Kämper and Thomas Tode, eds., "Chris Marker: Filmessayist," *CICIM*, 45–47; Laurent Roth and Raymond Bellour, *A propos du CD-ROM Immemory de Chris Marker*; and "The Travels of Chris Marker," *Film Comment* (May–June and July–August 2003), two special sections of the journal containing an abundance of critical commentary on all aspects of Marker's career.

Films

Les statues meurent aussi (*Statues Also Die*) (codirected with Alain Resnais, 1950, 30 mins.)

Olympia 52 (1952, 82 mins.)

Dimanche à Pékin (*Sunday in Peking*) (1956, 22 mins.)

Lettre de Sibérie (*Letter from Siberia*) (1958, 62 mins.)

Les Astronautes (codirected with Walerian Borowczyk, 1959, 14 mins.)

Description d'un combat (*Description of a Struggle*) (1960, 60 mins.)

Cuba si (1961, 52 mins.)

La Jetée (1962, 28 mins.)

Le Joli Mai (1962, 165 mins.; English-language version, 118 mins.)

Le Mystère Koumiko (*The Koumiko Mystery*) (1965, 54 mins.)

Si j'avais quatre dromadaires (*If I Had Four Camels*) (1966, 49 mins.)

Loin du Viêt-nam (*Far from Vietnam*) (collective film edited and with commentary by Chris Marker, 1967, 115 mins.)

A Bientôt, j'espère (codirected with Mario Marret, 1968, 44 mins.)

La Sixième face du pentagone (*The Sixth Face of the Pentagon*) (codirected with François Reichenbach, 1968, 28 mins.)

Classe de Lutte (collectively produced by the Medvedkine Group of Besancon, 1969, 40 mins.)

On vous parle de Brésil: Tortures (1969, 20 mins.)

On vous parle de Prague: le deuxième process d'Artur London (1969, 28 mins.)

Jour de tournage (1969, 11 mins.)

On vous parle de Brésil: Carlos Marighela (1970, 20 mins.)

On vous parle de Paris: Maspero, les mots ont un sens (1970, 20 mins.)

La Bataille des dix millions (*The Battle of the Ten Million*) (1970, 58 mins.)

Sochaux 11 Juin 68 (collectively produced by the Medvedkine Group of Sochaux; edited by Chris Marker, 1970, 20 mins.)

Le Train en marche (*The Train Rolls On*) (1971, 32 mins.)

Week-End à Sochaux (collectively produced by the Medvedkine Group of Sochaux, 1971–72, 54 mins.)

Vive la baleine (codirected with Mario Ruspoli, 1972, 30 mins.)

On vous parle de Chili: ce que disait Allende (codirected with Miguel Littin, 1973, 16 mins.)

L'ambassade (*Embassy*) (1973, 20 mins.)

Puisqu'on vous dit c'est possible (*Since We Say It's Possible*) (collective film edited by Chris Marker, 1974, app. 60 mins.)

La solitude du chanteur de fond (*The Loneliness of the Long Distance Singer*) (1974, 60 mins.)

La Spirale (*Spiral*) (collaborative film organized by Chris Marker, 1975, 155 mins.)

Le fond de l'air est rouge (*A Grin without a Cat*) (1977, 240 mins.; English-language version, 1993, 180 mins.)

Junkopia (1981, 6 mins.)

Sans Soleil (*Sunless*) (1982, 100 mins.)

2084 (1984, 10 mins.)

A.K. (1985, 71 mins.)

Mémoires pour Simone (1986, 61 mins.)

L'Héritage de la chouette (*The Owl's Legacy*) (1989, 13 episodes, each 26 mins.)

Berliner Ballade (1990, 20 mins.)

Getting Away with It (1990, 4 mins.)

Le Tombeau d'Alexandre (*The Last Bolshevik*) (1993, 116 mins.)

Le 20 heures dans les camps (*Prime Time in the Camps*) (1993, 28 mins.)

Video Haikus (*Petite ceinture, Tchaika, Owl Gets in Your Eyes*) (1994, app. 3 mins.)

Casque bleu (*Blue Helmet*) (1995, 26 mins.)

Level Five (1996, 106 mins.)

Une Journée d'Andrei Arsenevich (*One Day in the Life of Andrei Arsenevich*) (1999, 95 mins.)

Un Maire au Kosovo (2000, 27 mins.)

Le Souvenir d'un avenir (*Remembrance of Things to Come*) (codirected with Yannick Bellon, 2001, 42 mins.)

Chats Perchés (*The Case of the Grinning Cat*) (2004, 59 mins.)

Multimedia

Quand le siècle a pris formes (*Guerre et Revolution*) (*When the Century Took Shape [War and Revolution]*) (1978). Produced for the Centre Georges Pompidou's exhibition *Paris–Berlin, 1900–1930*, and then entered into its permanent collection. *Quand le siècle a pris formes* is a single-channel, double-screen loop, set to a Hanns Eisler musical accompaniment (16 mins., dimensions variable). It was included in *Romancing the Wreck/Looking Away*, a group show curated by Bruce Jenkins and Linda Norden at Harvard University Art Museums' Sert Gallery (2003).

Zapping Zone (*Proposals for an Imaginary Television*) (1990). Produced for the Centre Georges Pompidou's *Passages de l'image* exhibition in 1990 (which subsequently travelled to Barcelona, Columbus, San Francisco, and Toronto, 1991–92), and then entered into its permanent collection. *Zapping Zone* originally consisted of 14 monitors and 7 computer screens, along with numerous photos, slides, and photomontages, arranged in a concentrated gallery space. Its original iteration included the following single-channel titles: *Matta '85* (1985, 14 mins.), *Christo '85* (1985, 24 mins.), *Bestiare: Chat écoutant la musique; An Owl is an Owl is an Owl; Zoo Piece* (1985, 9 mins.), *Tokyo Days* (1988, 24 mins.), *Berlin '90* (1990, 20 mins.), *Photo Browse* (1990, 17 mins.), *Détour Ceausescu* (1990, 8 mins.), *Théorie des ensembles* (1991, 11 mins.). At various points in the 1990s, additional pieces were added, including *Azulmoon* (1992, loop), *Coin fenêtre* (1992, 10 mins.), *Slon Tango* (1993, 4 mins.), *Bullfight/Okinawa* (1994, 4 mins.), *E-clip-se* (1999, 8 mins.), as well as edited clips of Marker's own work.

Silent Movie (1995). Commissioned by the Wexner Center for the Arts. *Silent Movie* is a five-monitor, five-channel video installation, with a computer interface producing random variations within each channel; along with eighteen black-and-white video stills; ten computer-generated film posters; and eighteen piano solos that play in random rotation. It was subsequently seen in the exhibition *Hall of Mirrors: Art and Film since 1945*, organized by the Museum of Contemporary Art, Los Angeles, and in over a dozen other venues internationally from 1995 to 2004.

Immemory One (1997). Commissioned by the Centre Georges Pompidou. *Immemory One* is a

CD-ROM–based installation, with one computer monitor, and two video projectors (dimensions variable). It was subsequently seen in *Documenta X* (1997) and at the Wexner Center for the Arts in *Body Mécanique* (1998).

Immemory (1997). Produced by Centre Georges Pompidou, with the participation of the Centre pour l'image contemporain, St-Gervais, Geneva, and Films de l'Astrophore: commercial CD-ROM edition. English-language edition produced by Exact Change, 2003.

Roseware (1998–99). Developed by Laurence Rassel (of Constant, Brussels, in association with the Atelier des Jeunes Cinéastes), with Marker's endorsement. A temporary multimedia installation seen in Graz, Austria (Steirische Herbst, 1998), and at the Fundació Antoni Tàpies in Barcelona (1999), *Roseware* extended one of the premises of *Immemory*: "there will be enough familiar codes here (the photo of the trip, the family album, the favorite animal) for readers to be able to subconsciously substitute their own images for mine, their memories for mine, for my *Immemory* to serve as a springboard for their own pilgrimage in Time rediscovered." Visitors brought their own images and documents to the installation, where they were assisted in rendering them (via scanners, computers, and cameras) into digital chapters of a collective memory including those of other users, and of Marker's *Immemory*.

Owls at Noon Prelude: The Hollow Men (2005). Commissioned by the Museum of Modern Art, New York, and curated by Colin McCabe. *Owls at Noon Prelude: The Hollow Men* is a two-channel, eight-screen loop, set to *Corona* by Toru Takemitsu, played by Roger Woodward (19 mins., dimensions variable). Subsequently seen at Prefix Institute of Contemporary Art, Toronto (2006), and Institute of Modern Art, Brisbane (2007).

Bibliography

Books by Chris Marker

Le Coeur net. Paris: Éditions du Seuil, 1949. English translation: *The Forthright Spirit*, trans. Robert Kee and Terence Kilmartin. London: Allan Wingate, 1951.

L'homme et sa liberté: jeu dramatique pour la Veillée. Paris: Éditions du Seuil, 1949.

Giradoux par lui-même. Paris: Éditions du Seuil, 1952.

Regards sur le mouvement ouvrier (with Benigno Cacares). Paris: Éditions du Seuil, 1952.

Regards neufs sur la chanson (with Pierre Barlatier). Paris: Éditions du Seuil, 1954.

Collection Petite Planète, ed. Chris Marker. Paris: Éditions du Seuil, 1954–1964.

Coréennes. Paris: Éditions du Seuil, 1959.

Commentaires. Paris: Éditions du Seuil, 1961. Reprinted as *Commentaires I*. Paris: Éditions du Seuil, 1967. Includes the texts of *Les statues meurent aussi, Dimanche à Pékin, Lettre de Sibérie, l'Amérique rêve, Description d'un combat*, and *Cuba si*.

Commentaires II. Paris: Éditions du Seuil, 1967. Includes the texts of *Le Mystère Koumiko*, *Soy Mexico*, and *Si j'avais quatre dromadaires.*

Le fond de l'air est rouge: Scènes de la troisième guerre mondiale, 1967–1977. Paris: François Maspero, 1978.

La Renfermée: la Corse (photos by Chris Marker; text by Marie Susini). Paris: Éditions du Seuil, 1981.

Le Dépays. Paris: Herscher, 1982.

La Jetée. New York: Zone Books, 1992.

Selected Texts and Commentaries by Chris Marker

"Cuba si." *L'Avant-Scène Cinéma* 15 (July 1961): 45–52.

"Les Hommes de la baleine." *L'Avant-Scène Cinéma* 24 (March 1963): 46–51.

"La jetée." *L'Avant-Scène Cinéma* 38 (June 1964): 28–35.

"Le mystère de l'atelier quinze." *L'Avant-Scène Cinéma* 61–2 (July–September 1966): 73–78.

"Le Mer et les jours." *L'Avant-Scène Cinéma* 68 (March 1967): 61–66.

"A Valparaiso." *L'Avant-Scène Cinéma* 76 (December 1967): 50–57.

"Le train en marche." *L'Avant-Scène Cinéma* 120 (December 1971): 11–14.

"Le fond de l'air est rouge: le commentaire." *Jeune Cinéma* 107 (January 1978): 3–9.

"Sunless." *Semiotexte* 4, no. 3 (1984): 33–40.

"A.K." *L'Avant-Scène Cinéma* 403–4 (June–July 1991): 124–41.

"Le Tombeau d'Alexandre." *Positif* 391 (September 1993): 49–54.

"Effets et gestes" (photos by Chris Marker; text by Jean-Claude Carrière). *Vogue* (Paris) 752 (December 1994): 208–211, 263.

"A free replay (notes on *Vertigo*)," in *Projections 4½*, ed. John Boorman and Walter Donohue (London: Faber and Faber, 1995), pp. 123–130. Translated from *Positif*, June 1994.

"The Rest Is Silent." In *Chris Marker: Silent Movie* (exhibition catalogue), 57–62. Columbus: Wexner Center for the Arts, The Ohio State University, 1995. French translation as "The Rest Is Silent," with new introduction. *Trafic* 46 (2003): 57–62.

"Click in the Space (A New Concept in Mouse-Clicking)" (1992). In *Do It* (exhibiton catalogue), 56–58. New York: Independent Curators Incorporated, 1997.

"Marker Mémoire" (introduction to film retrospective). Cinémathèque Française program guide, January–February 1998, 4–8.

"Dial M for Memory" (image portfolio). *Grand Street* 64 (Spring 1998): 184–89.

"Filmic Memories." *Film Quarterly* 52, no. 1 (Fall 1998): 66.

"The last word (for now)" (afterword). In *Always Subject to Change: The Wexner Center at Ten*, 102. Columbus: Wexner Center for the Arts, The Ohio State University, 1999.

"Immemory." *Immemory* (CD-ROM liner notes). Cambridge, MA: Exact Change, in association with the Centre Georges Pompidou and Les Films de l'Astrophore, 2002.

"Nouvelles du Doppelwelt." *Positif* 500 (October 2002): 3, 6–7.

"Essai filmé sur l'art du photographe à partir des archives de Denise Bellon" (with Yannick Bellon). Production notes from Les films de l'équinoxe on *Le Souvenir d'un avenir*, January 2003.

"Marker Direct" (interview with Chris Marker by Samuel Douhaire and Annick Rivoiere). *Film Comment* (May–June 2003): 38–41. Translated from *Libération*, March 5, 2003.

"Avertissement," *Chats Perchés* (DVD booklet), 16. Paris: ARTE–Les Films du Jeudi copublication, 2004.

"Chats discutent" (conversation between Chris Marker and the creator of "M. Chat"). *Libération*, December 4, 2004. Translated excerpt as "A Cat Conversation" in press materials for *The Case of the Grinning Cat*, First Run/Icarus Films, *www.frif.com*, 2006.

"Pour Mario." *Les Groupes Medvedkine: Le film est une arme*. (DVD booklet), 11–19. Paris: Iskra-Editions Montparnasse copublication, 2006.

Selected Books and Articles on Chris Marker

Aaland, Mikkel. "Chris Marker and the Frontiers of Memory." *Digital Creativity* (March 1996): 27–32.

Abrantes, Eduardo. "The Principle of Revelation." *Film-Philosophy* 10, no. 1 (2006): 1–14.

Alter, Nora M. *Chris Marker*. Urbana: University of Illinois Press, 2006.

Bellour, Raymond. "Trois gestes (Jonas Mekas, Rinko Kawauchi, Chris Marker)." *Trafic* 60 (Winter 2006): 13–27.

Benoliel, Bernard. "Groupes Medvedkine." *L'image, le monde* 3 (Autumn 2002): 24–59.

Chris Marker: Silent Movie (exhibition catalogue). Columbus: Wexner Center for the Arts, The Ohio State University, 1995.

Cooper, Sarah. *Selfless Cinema?: Ethics and French Documentary*. London: Legenda, 2006.

Cortés, José Miguel G. "Places of Memory." In *Lugares de la Memoria* (exhibition catalogue). Castelló: Espai d'Art Contemporani de Castelló, 2001, 278–302.

Darke, Chris. "Musique concrète." *Film Comment* (March–April 2005): 14.

Dilorio, Sam. "Everyday Optics: Representations of the French Quotidian, 1945–2000." Ph.D. diss., University of Pennsylvania, 2003.

Dubois, Philippe, ed. "Recherches sur Chris Marker" (dossier). *Théorème* 6 (2002).

Durand, Régis. "Sans commune mesure?" In *Sans commune mesure* (exhibition catalogue), 20–63. Paris: Centre national de la photographie, 2002.

Eisenchitz, Bernard, ed. "Chris Marker." Rome: Pesaro Film Festival Catalogue (dossier), 1993. Reprinted in *Trafic* 19 (1996).

Enwezor, Okwui, ed. *The Unhomely: Phantoms Scenes in Global Society* (exhibition catalogue). Seville: 2nd International Biennial of Contemporary Art, 2006.

Evers, Lucas and Peter van Hoof, eds. *Re: Mark: Marker* (exhibition catalogue). Amsterdam: Cinema de Balie and Montevideo/Time Based Arts, 1999.

Gauthier, Guy. *Chris Marker, écrivain multimédia ou voyage à travers les médias*. Paris: Harmattan, 2001.

Gerber, Jacques. *Anatole Dauman: Pictures of a Producer*, trans. Paul Willemen. London: British Film Institute, 1992.

Horak, Jan-Christopher. "Chris Marker's Reality Bytes." *Aperture* 149 (Fall, 1996): 60–65.

Horrigan, Bill. "The Revenge of the Eye." *Artforum* 44, no. 10 (Summer 2006): 312–317.

Jacob, Gilles. "Chris Marker and the Mutants." *Sight and Sound* 35 (Autumn 1966): 165–68.

Kämper, Birgit and Thomas Tode, eds. "Chris Marker: Filmessayist." *CICIM* 45–47 (1997).

Klawans, Stuart. "The Days of May." *The Nation*, May 13, 2002.

London, Barbara. *Video Spaces*. New York: Museum of Modern Art, 1995.

Lupton, Catherine. *Chris Marker: Memories of the Future*. London: Reaktion Books, 2005.

Lupton, Catherine. "Chris Marker: The Art of Memory." *Film Studies* 6 (Summer 2005): 46–48.

Mayo, Nuria Enguita, ed. *Chris Marker* (exhibition catalogue). Barcelona: Fundació Antoni Tàpies, 1998.

Murphy, Jay. "More of what it is: catching up with Chris Marker." *Afterimage* 33, no. 2 (September–October 2005): 31–36.

Nesbit, Molly. "Chris Marker." *Artforum* 34, no. 8 (April 1996): 96–97, 126.

Orlow, Uriel. "Chris Marker: The Archival Power of the Image." In *Lost in the Archives*, ed. Rebecca Comay. Toronto: Alphabet City, 2002.

Picard, Andrea. "Prelude as Postscript." *Cinema Scope* (Spring 2006): 59–61.

Pourvali, Bamchade. *Chris Marker*. Paris: Cahiers du Cinéma, 2003.

Quandt, James. "Grin without a Cat." Toronto: Cinematheque Ontario Programme Guide, Fall 1993, 4–7.

__________. "The Gesture of Memory." Toronto: Cinematheque Ontario Programme Guide, Spring 1997, 8–11.

Rafferty, Terrence. "Chris Marker." In *The Thing Happens*. New York: Grove Press, 1993, 63–74.

Rancière, Jacques, in conversation with Fulvia Carnevale and John Kelsey. "Art of the Possible." *Artforum* 45, no. 7 (March 2007): 256–259, 261–264, 266–267, 269.

Roth, Laurent and Raymond Bellour. *A propos du CD-ROM Immemory de Chris Marker*, ed. Yves Gevaert. Paris: Centre Georges Pompidou, 1997.

Sanborn, Keith. "Shades without Colour." *Artforum* 43 (Summer 2005): 79.

Siegel, Joshua. *Chris Marker Video Premieres* (program notes). New York: Museum of Modern Art, January 1994.

Slater, Ben. "Reclaimed: The Tokyo Mystery." *Vertigo* 3, no. 4 (Winter 2007): 30–31.

Smith, Gavin, ed. "The Travels of Chris Marker: Part 1" (dossier). *Film Comment* 39, no. 3 (May–June 2003).

__________. "The Travels of Chris Marker: Part 2" (dossier). *Film Comment* 39, no. 4 (July–August 2003).

Swenson, Ingrid, ed. *Chris Marker: Silent Movie and selected screenings* (exhibition catalogue). London: Pier and Beaconsfield, 1999.

Thomson, David. "Chris Marker." In *The New Biographical Dictionary of Film*, 563–565. New York: Alfred A. Knopf, 2002.

Tode, Thomas. "Film—That Was Last Century!" *Film Studies* 6 (Summer 2005): 81–88.

Van Assche, Christine, Catherine David, and Raymond Bellour. *Passages de l'image* (exhibition catalogue). Paris: Centre Georges Pompidou, 1990.

Van Wert, William. "Chris Marker: The SLON Films." *Film Quarterly* 32, no. 3 (Spring 1979): 38–46.

Wollen, Peter. "Fire and Ice." In *Other than Itself: Writing Photography*, ed. John X. Berger and Olivier Richon. Manchester: Cornerhouse Publications, 1989.

Wood, Michael. "Immemory Lane." *Artforum* 41, no. 6 (February 2003): 33.

Acknowledgments

I want first to thank Wexner Center Director Sherri Geldin for her immediate support of this project; without that, neither this book nor its accompanying exhibition would have come into being. Thanks also to former Chief Curator of Exhibitions Helen Molesworth for her early encouragement and advice. In addition, I'd like to single out Designer Chris Jones and Editor Ann Bremner for envisioning a book worthy to stand as the companion to the *Chris Marker: Silent Movie* catalogue they conjured in 1995, and Exhibitions Manager Jill Davis for shepherding all aspects of this project with a steady hand, aided by Preparator Will Fugman, Curatorial Assistant Molly Reinhoudt, and Head Registrar Megan Cavanaugh. It's also my pleasure to thank my colleagues in the media arts department for their daily shows of forbearance and support: Dave Filipi, Jennifer Lange, Paul Hill, Mike Olenick, and Chris Stults.

Molly Nesbit, whose graceful essay closes this volume, Jason Simon, and Bruce Jenkins all provided stirring companionship and insight as this project evolved. Gratitude as well to the gallerist Rachel Lehmann, whose generosity informed a series of meetings in New York in 2000 and 2001, attended by a loose group of scholars, critics, and artists enamored of Chris Marker's work; and to Peter Blum Gallery.

Thanks finally, in the end as in the beginning, to Chris Marker for entrusting us with these vestiges of what he has seen.

—Bill Horrigan

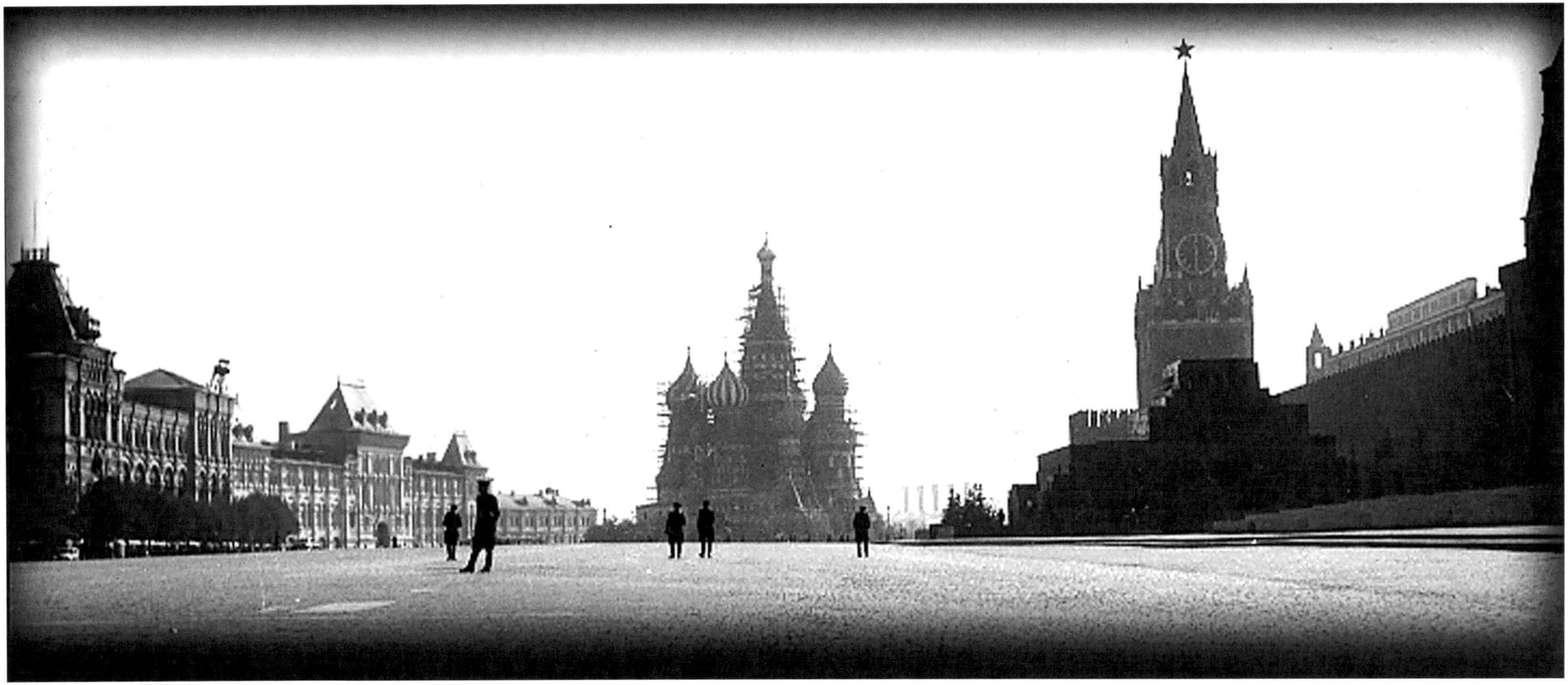